1998

ARCHAEOLOGICAL FIELDWORK OPPORTUNITIES BULLETIN

Compiled and edited by
SUSANNA BURNS

Published by the

ARCHAEOLOGICAL INSTITUTE OF AMERICA
Boston and New York 1998

KENDALL/HUNT PUBLISHING COMPANY
4050 Westmark Drive   Dubuque, Iowa 52002

Cover photograph is reproduced courtesy of Richard A. Boisvert, Coordinator, New Hampshire State Conservation and Rescue Archaeology Program (SCRAP). Volunteers pictured are excavating at the Israel River Complex, a Paleoindian site in Coos County, New Hampshire.

Copyright © 1998 by Archaeological Institute of America

ISBN 0-7872-4535-6

Printed in the United States of America
10 9 8 7 6 5 4 3 2 1

TABLE OF CONTENTS

ARCHAEOLOGICAL INSTITUTE OF AMERICA

The Archaeological Institute of America (AIA) has been serving both the public and the scholarly community for over one hundred years. It is dedicated to the encouragement and support of archaeological research and publication, to informing the public about archaeology, and to the protection of the world's cultural heritage. The AIA and its members invite you to share in and support the innovations and developments in the world of archaeology.

Founded in 1879, the AIA is a nonprofit, scientific and educational organization chartered through the Smithsonian Institution by the United States Congress. It is the oldest archaeological organization in North America with some 11,000 members in its 96 Local Societies in the United States and AIA-Canada. Since its inception, the AIA has been a leading proponent worldwide of professional archaeology. Its mission is accomplished through a variety of programs and activities designed to meet the needs and interests of its members and the public.

Members of the AIA may belong to a Local Society in the United States or Canada and enjoy lectures, field trips, films, museum visits and membership on local committees. (See list of AIA Local Societies in this publication for their locations and contacts.)

PROGRAMS AND ACTIVITIES OF THE AIA

Publications:

Archaeology: In print since 1948, *Archaeology* is a richly illustrated magazine with a circulation of 160,000. Articles, written by professionals for both the public and the scholar, provide accounts of the latest discoveries in archaeology worldwide. *Archaeology* regularly publishes book and film reviews, listings of museum exhibits, and archaeological news. A travel guide of international excavations open to visitors is published annually. A special listing is devoted to the nationally sponsored lectures sent from the Institute to its affiliated Local Societies.

American Journal of Archaeology: Published quarterly, the *AJA*, with close to 4,000 subscribers, is one of the most widely distributed scholarly journals devoted to archaeology in the world. The *AJA* has earned its high reputation by publishing for over 100 years important research by some of the world's most distinguished scholars. The *AJA* devotes its issues to the study of the art and archaeology of ancient Europe and the Mediterranean world, including the Near East and Egypt, from prehistoric to Late Antique times.

Both publications are available as a benefit of membership in the AIA or by subscription. For information on other AIA publications, which include *Archaeology on Film*, *Archaeology in the Classroom: A Resource Guide for Teachers and Parents*, and numbers from our *Monographs New Series* and *Colloquia and Conference Papers*, contact the AIA.

Other Activities:

The Lecture Program: The AIA annually provides over 270 lectures by noted archaeologists and scholars to its 96 Local Societies in the United States and AIA-Canada. Each year, more than 19,000 people attend these lectures that cover the broad range of archaeological discovery today.

Tours: For travelers, the AIA sponsors rewarding and exciting tours for members to many parts of the world. Each tour is led by a prominent scholar whose expertise in the field brings to life the civilizations of the past. The intineraries include visits to see archaeological sites, current excavations, monuments and architecture, and museums.

Fellowships: For students and aspiring archaeological professionals, the AIA awards several fellowships for archaeological research. The Olivia James Travelling Fellowship, the Harriet and Leon Pomerance Fellowship, the Anna C. and Oliver C. Colburn Fellowship, and the Woodruff Traveling Fellowship provide funds for travel and study in Greece, the Aegean Islands, Sicily, Italy, Turkey, and other parts of the world. The Kenan T. Erim Award sponsors scholarly work related to Aphrodisias, and the Helen M. Woodruff Fellowship supports research at the American Academy in Rome.

Regional Symposia: The AIA annually awards grants to two Local Societies to assist in funding Regional Symposia on subjects of special interest to Society members.

Annual Meeting: The AIA holds an Annual Meeting with the American Philological Association, at which professionals present the latest results of their archaeological fieldwork and research around the world.

Placement Service: In conjunction with the American Philological Association, the AIA provides a Placement Service for archaeologists and scholars in related fields.

For information on becoming a member of the AIA, contact:

ARCHAEOLOGICAL INSTITUTE OF AMERICA
Located at Boston University
656 Beacon Street
Boston, Massachusetts 02215-2010
(617) 353-9361, FAX: (617) 353-6550, E-Mail: aia@bu.edu
WWW: http://csa.brynmawr.edu/aia.html

ARCHAEOLOGICAL FIELDWORK OPPORTUNITIES BULLETIN

INTRODUCTION

The *Archaeological Fieldwork Opportunities Bulletin (AFOB)* is an annual publication of the AIA that is designed to introduce both the student and the amateur archaeologist to the experience of actual excavation or survey. While not everyone interested in archaeology will want to go out into the field, for those who do, the *AFOB* aims to provide a comprehensive list of fieldwork and educational opportunities in the field.

The entries listed here come from a variety of sources. Many are ongoing projects which appeared in last year's *AFOB*, while others have been supplied by professional archaeologists, institutions, and related organizations. We regret the omission of entries submitted too late for publication in this edition and hope that we will hear from the directors in time for next year's *AFOB*. **The firm deadline for the 1999 AFOB is October 15, 1998.** Unless otherwise noted, the AIA does not sponsor or endorse any of the excavations, fieldwork, or programs which are listed in the *AFOB*; it also attempts to include only programs supervised by professional archaeologists.

The 1998 edition of the *AFOB* is divided, as in the past, into major geographical regions. Each entry attempts to provide essential facts about the excavation or program. Applicants should, however, seek further information before making a decision. Keep in mind age requirements, responsibilities at the site, working and living conditions, etc. A self-addressed, stamped envelope will facilitate a quick response to your inquiry (International Postal Reply Coupons are available from your local post office when writing to overseas organizations). If you have missed a deadline, you should not give up on an excavation which you find particularly interesting. Write immediately to the contact person expressing your enthusiasm. The opportunity may be available for the following season, and there is always the chance that the volunteer or staffing needs have not yet been met.

If you have applied and have been accepted as a volunteer or as a student in a field school, it is very important to let the project director know if you have changed your mind about going or find it impossible to join the program. Directors depend on a certain number of participants, and if there are "no shows," the director finds himself shorthanded.

The *AFOB* is the first step in identifying the best fieldwork opportunity for you. Your persistence and creativity can lead to work which is not listed herein. Meet professional archaeologists through attending lectures sponsored by your AIA Local Society (see listing in this *AFOB*) or at the AIA's Annual Meeting. Subscribe to *Archaeology* Magazine and other archaeological publications to keep abreast of current work in the field. If the work at a particular site intrigues you, do not hesitate to express your interest and willingness to work to the lecturer, excavation director, or author of the article.

In producing the *AFOB*, the AIA aims to bring together the amateur and professional archaeologist in the most vital area of activity—at work in the field. Many of the projects listed in the *AFOB* will accept newcomers with no prior experience in the field. There are also numerous opportunities for those who have excavated or surveyed before. Whatever program you decide upon, the benefits derived from it will be twofold; not only will you learn a great deal about a specific site and its history, but you will also be educated in sound practices and techniques applicable to all archaeology.

Funds from the sale of the *AFOB* are used to defray the cost of AIA programs and administration.

SUPPLEMENTAL INFORMATION

Before you leave—Many countries require permission and clearance for foreign workers through antiquities services and government agencies. Unless the option is clearly stated, appearing at a site unannounced would be personally irresponsible and might place the expedition in an uncomfortable situation. Once advance contact has been established with a representative of the expedition team, find out what equipment is necessary, what clothes are the most sensible for work and leisure time, what will be the general schedule of operations, and what amount of sight-seeing will be available.

Read about the local culture and climate, and plan your packing accordingly. Pack as lightly as possible, since space is often limited and transportation may be less than efficient. As with most travel, you must be able to carry your own luggage, and a good test is to limit yourself to what you can comfortably carry for a quarter-mile trot.

Check into necessary vaccinations and have thorough physical and dental examinations. Identify your need for health and travel insurance. Some expeditions provide the former, and you should know what facilities will be available in the unlikely event that you require treatment.

Bring a small medicine kit with the usual bandages, disinfectants, and ointment. Additional items which are on the worker/traveler's list are an alarm clock, a good flashlight with extra batteries and light bulbs, sunglasses, scarf or work hat (readily available in many local markets), sunscreen, regional guide book, reading material (a good, long book can be traded around for fresh material after you have finished it), notebook, pens and pencils, measuring tape marked in inches and centimeters, a canteen, and a good pocketknife. This is merely a suggested checklist; check with the director for a list for his/her particular program.

At the site—The success of an archaeological expedition depends, to a great extent, on the excavation team. Organization is a key factor in the smooth management of the work schedule, and the field director must be able to depend on a responsive and responsible staff. If you have never worked on an excavation before, do some homework and keep a flexible and cooperative attitude. The former will ensure that you will have some familiarity with professional archaeology, the material which is under investigation, the local culture, and climate.

The latter will certainly make you a better worker and a more pleasant person to live with under what can be less than ideal conditions. You, personally, will find the experience a great deal richer for your efforts.

The director and supervisors will appreciate your questions and your attention to detail and procedure, and there are a number of "dig-life" lessons to learn by word of mouth from others who have had experience. If you find that you have time on your hands and wish to make the most of the season, staff are usually more than willing to give informal instruction in the different skills required by an expedition (drafting, recording, etc.)

Try to set up a personal schedule outside of work hours. You will have a better chance of maintaining a comfortable working/sleeping/leisure schedule and a stock of clean clothes. Take the opportunity to keep a daily journal, describing the work you are doing, camp life, the weather, etc. Months or years later, you will be able to recall the sense of the excavation.

In closing—Archaeological fieldwork is not the romantic treasure-hunt of Hollywood movies. On the contrary, archaeology is a blend of scientific disciplines and requires, therefore, methodical attention to procedure and detail. The processes of archaeological investigation change constantly and most expeditions are staffed by individuals with a variety of specialized skills over an extended period of time. You can learn a great deal from the experienced excavators and specialists. As part of an expedition you will have an opportunity to contribute personally to the preservation of our past.

AIA CODE OF ETHICS

The Archaeological Institute of America is dedicated to the greater understanding of archaeology, to the protection and preservation of the world's archaeological resources and the information they contain, and to the encouragement and support of archaeological research and publication. In accordance with these principles, members of the AIA should:

1) Seek to ensure that the exploration of archaeological sites be conducted according to the highest standards under the direct supervision of qualified personnel, and that the results of such research be made public;

2) Refuse to participate in the illegal trade in antiquities derived from excavation in any country after December 30, 1970, when the AIA Council endorsed the UNESCO Convention on Cultural Property, and refrain from activities that enhance the commercial value of such objects;

3) Inform appropriate authorities of threats to, or plunder of archaeological sites, and illegal import or export of archaeological material.

BIBLIOGRAPHY

This bibliography is compiled by the Archaeological Institute of America and is provided as an introduction to archaeology in general as well as to the archaeology in various geographical areas. The list is not complete, but further specialized bibliographies will be found under individual fieldwork descriptions.

GENERAL:

Aitken, Martin J. *Science-Based Dating in Archaeology.* New York: Longman, 1990.

Barber, Russell J. *Doing Historical Archaeology: Exercises Using Documentary, Oral, and Material Evidence.* Englewood Cliffs, NJ: Prentice Hall, 1994.

Barker, Philip. *Techniques of Archaeological Excavation.* 3rd ed., London: B.T. Batsford, 1993.

Bass, George F. *Archaeology Beneath the Seas: A Personal Account.* New York: Walker, 1975.

Bell, James A. *Reconstructing Prehistory: Scientific Method in Archaeology.* Philadelphia: Temple University Press, 1994.

Branigan, Keith. *Archaeology Explained.* London: Duckworth, 1988.

Bray, W., and D. Trump. *The Penguin Dictionary of Archaeology.* 2nd ed., New York: Viking, 1982.

Carpenter, Rhys. *The Humanistic Value of Archaeology.* Westport, CT: Greenwood Press, 1971.

Ceram, C.W. (Kurt W. Marek). *Gods, Graves, and Scholars: The Story of Archaeology.* 2nd ed., London: V. Gollancz, 1974.

Dancey, William S. *Archaeological Field Methods: An Introduction.* Minneapolis: Burgess, 1981.

Daniel, Glyn. *A Short History of Archaeology.* New York: Thames and Hudson, 1981.

Daniels, Steve, and Nicholas David. *The Archaeology Workbook.* Philadelphia: University of Pennsylvania Press, 1982.

De Camp, L. Sprague, and Catherine C. de Camp. *Ancient Ruins and Archaeology.* Garden City, NJ: Doubleday, 1964.

Deetz, James. *Invitation to Archaeology.* Garden City, NJ: Natural History Press, 1967.

Dillon, Brian D., ed. *The Student's Guide to Archaeological Illustrating.* 2nd ed., Los Angeles: Institute of Archaeology, University of California at Los Angeles, 1985.

Ehrenberg, Margaret. *Women in Prehistory.* Oklahoma Series in Classical Culture 4, Norman: University of Oklahoma Press, 1989.

Fagan, Brian M. *Archaeology: A Brief Introduction.* New York: Harper Collins, 1992.

Fagan, Brian M. *In the Beginning: An Introduction to Archaeology.* 8th ed., Boston: Little, Brown & Co., 1994.

Fagan, Brian M. *Quest for the Past: Great Discoveries in Archaeology.* 2nd ed., Prospect Heights, IL: Waveland Press, 1994

Fagan, Brian M. *Time Detectives: How Archaeologists Use Technology to Recapture the Past.* New York: Simon & Schuster, 1995.

Fagan, Brian M. *Snapshots of the Past.* Walnut Creek, CA: Altamira Press, 1995.

Falk, Lisa, ed. *Historical Archaeology in Global Perspective.* Washington, DC: Smithsonian Institution Press, 1991.

Feder, Kenneth L. *Frauds, Myths, and Mysteries. Science and Pseudoscience in Archaeology.* Mountain View, CA: Mayfield, 1990.

Green, Ernestine L. *Ethics and Values in Archaeology.* New York: Free Press, 1984.

Greene, Kevin G. *Archaeology: An Introduction.* 3rd ed., Philadelphia: University of Pennsylvania Press, 1995.

Hayden, Brian. *Archaeology: The Science of Once and Future Things.* New York: W.H. Freeman, 1993.

Hodder, Ian. *Theory and Practice in Archaeology*. New York: Routledge, 1995.

Joukowsky, Martha S. *A Complete Manual of Field Archaeology*. Englewood Cliffs, NJ: Prentice-Hall, 1980.

Kerber, Jordan E. *Coastal and Maritime Archaeology: A Bibliography*. Metuchen, NJ: Scarecrow Press, 1991.

Macaulay, Rose. *Pleasure of Ruins*. New York: Thames and Hudson, 1984.

McIntosh, Jane. *The Practical Archaeologist: How We Know What We Know about the Past*. New York: Facts on File, 1986.

Oliver, Adrian. *Safety in Archaeological Fieldwork*. Practical Handbooks in Archaeology 6, London: Council for British Archaeology, 1989.

Orser, Charles E., Jr., and Brian M. Fagan. *Historical Archaeology: A Brief Introduction*. New York: Harper Collins, 1995.

Patterson, Thomas C. *The Theory and Practice of Archaeology: A Workbook*. Englewood Cliffs, NJ: Prentice Hall, 1994.

Rathje, William L., and Michael B. Schiffer. *Archaeology*. New York: Harcourt Brace Jovanovich, 1982.

Renfrew, Colin, and Paul Bahn. *Archaeology: Theories, Methods, and Practice*. New York: Thames and Hudson, 1991.

Scott, Elizabeth M., ed. *Those of Little Note: Gender, Race, and Class in Historical Archaeology*. Tucson: University of Arizona Press, 1994.

Sharer, Robert J., and Wendy Ashmore. *Archaeology: Discovering Our Past*. 2nd ed., Mountain View, CA: Mayfield, 1993.

Sherratt, Andrew, ed. *Cambridge Encyclopedia of Archaeology*. New York: Crown Publications and Cambridge University Press, 1980.

Stiebing, William H., Jr. *Uncovering the Past. A History of Archaeology*. New York: Oxford University Press, 1994.

Thomas, David H. *Archaeology: Down to Earth*. New York: Harcourt Brace Jovanovich, 1991.

Throckmorton, Peter, ed. *History from the Seas: Shipwrecks and Archaeology from Homer's Odyssey to the Titanic*. London: Mitchell Beazley, 1987.

Webster, David L., Susan T. Evans, and William T. Sanders. *Out of the Past: An Introduction to Archaeology*. Mountain View, CA: Mayfield, 1993.

Facts on File Publications, New York, publishes an excellent series of reference books on the ancient world, written by noted authorities for particular regions and cultures. Titles include: *Atlas of Ancient America*, *Atlas of Ancient Egypt*, *Atlas of the Greek World*, *Atlas of the Roman World*, *Dictionary of Archaeology*, and *Encyclopedia of the Ancient Greek World*.

Time-Life Books, Alexandria, VA, publishes two well-written and illustrated series of special interest. Titles in the Emergence of Man Series include: *The First Cities*, *The First Farmers*, and *The Monument Builders*. Titles in the Lost Civilizations Series include: *China's Buried Kingdoms*, *Inca: Lords of Gold and Glory*, and *Wondrous Realms of the Aegean*.

Archaeological Guidebooks, Blue Guides is an excellent series of guide books published by Ernest Benn Limited, London and Tornbridge. Individual volumes cover countries of Western Europe, the Mediterranean region, and Turkey.

NORTH AMERICA:

Anderson, Frank G. *Southwestern Archaeology: A Bibliography*. New York: Garland, 1982.

Bass, George, ed. *Ships and Shipwrecks of the Americas: A History Based on Underwater Archaeology*. New York: Thames and Hudson, 1988.

Cordell, Linda S. *Ancient Pueblo Peoples*. Washington, DC: Smithsonian Institution Press, 1994.

Deetz, James. *In Small Things Forgotten: The Archaeology of Early American Life*. New York: Doubleday, 1996.

Fagan, Brian M. *Ancient North America: The Archaeology of a Continent*. New York: Thames and Hudson, 1995.

Ferguson, Leland. *Uncommon Ground: Archaeology and Early African America, 1650–1800*. Washington, DC: Smithsonian Institution Press, 1992.

Folsom, Franklin, and Mary Elting Folsom. *America's Ancient Treasures: A Guide to Archaeological Sites and Museums in the United States and Canada*. 4th ed., Albuquerque: University of New Mexico Press, 1993.

Geier, C., and S. Winter, eds. *Look to the Earth: Historical Archaeology and the American Civil War*. Knoxville: University of Tennessee Press, 1994.

Jennings, Jesse D. *Prehistory of North America*. Mountain View, CA: Mayfield, 1989.

Kennedy, Roger. *Hidden Cities: The Discovery and Loss of Ancient North American Civilization*. New York: Free Press, 1994.

Lekson, Stephen H., and Rina Swentzell. *Ancient Land, Ancestral Places*. Santa Fe: Museum of New Mexico Press, 1993.

Mason, Ronald J. *Great Lakes Archaeology*. New York: Academic Press, 1981.

Matson, R.G., and Gary Coupland. *The Prehistory of the Northwest Coast*. San Diego: Academic Press, 1994.

Noel Hume, Ivor. *Martin's Hundred: The Discovery of a Lost Colonial Virginia Settlement*. New York: Knopf, 1982.

Schlesier, Karl H., ed. *Plains Indiana, A.D. 500–1500: The Archaeological Past of Historic Groups*. Norman: University of Oklahoma Press, 1995.

Schobinger, Juan. *The First Americans*. Grand Rapids, MI: Eerdmans, 1994.

Snow, Dean R. *Archaeology of New England*. New York: Academic Press, 1980.

Willey, Gordon R., and Jeremy A. Sabloff. *A History of American Archaeology*. 3rd ed., New York: W.H. Freeman, 1993.

Williams, Stephen. *Fantastic Archaeology: The Wild Side of North American Prehistory*. Philadelphia: University of Pennsylvania Press, 1991.

CENTRAL AND SOUTH AMERICA:

Adams, Richard E.W. *Prehistoric Mesoamerica*. Revised ed., Norman: University of Oklahoma Press, 1991.

Burger, Richard L. *Chavin: The Origins of Andean Civilization*. New York: Thames and Hudson, 1995.

Coe, Michael D. *The Maya*. 5th ed., New York: Thames and Hudson, 1994.

Conrad, Geoffrey W. *Religion and Empire: The Dynamics of Aztec and Inca Expansionism*. New York: Cambridge University Press, 1984.

Davies, Nigel. *The Ancient Kingdoms of Mexico*. New York: Penguin Books, 1983.

Davies, Nigel. *The Incas*. Niwot, Colorado: University of Colorado Press, 1995.

Fagan, Brian M. *Kingdoms of Gold, Kingdoms of Jade: The Americas before Columbus*. New York: Thames and Hudson, 1991.

Gillespie, Susan D. *The Aztec Kings: The Construction of Rulership in Mexican History*. Tucson, AZ: University of Arizona Press, 1989.

Hammond, Norman. *Ancient Maya Civilization*. New Brunswick, NJ: Rutgers University Press, 1994.

Henderson, John S. *The World of the Ancient Maya*. Ithaca, NY: Cornell University Press, 1981.

Jennings, Jesse D., ed. *Ancient South Americans*. New York: W.H. Freeman, 1983.

Lange, Frederick W., and Doris Z. Stone, eds. *The Archaeology of Lower Central America*. Albuquerque: University of New Mexico Press, 1984.

Morris, Craig, and Adriana von Hagen. *The Inka Empire and Its Andean Origins*. New York: American Museum of Natural History and Abbeville Press, 1993.

Moseley, Michael E. *The Incas and Their Ancestors. The Archaeology of Peru*. New York: Thames and Hudson, 1992.

Schele, Linda, and David Freidel. *Forest of Kings: The Untold Story of the Ancient Maya*. New York: William Morrow, 1990.

Sharer, Robert. *The Ancient Maya*. 5th ed., Stanford, CA: Stanford University Press, 1994.

GREAT BRITAIN, IRELAND, EUROPE (excluding Greece and Italy):

Arnold, C.J. *Roman Britain to Saxon England.* Indiana University Press, 1984.

Barrett, John C. *Fragments from Antiquity: An Archaeology of Social Life in Britain, 2900–200 B.C.* Oxford: Blackwell, 1994.

Bewley, Robert. *The English Heritage Book of Prehistoric Settlements.* North Pomfret, VT: B.T. Batsford, 1995.

Burl, Aubrey. *A Guide to the Stone Circles of Britain, Ireland, and Brittany.* New Haven, CT: Yale University Press, 1995.

Castleden, Rodney. *The Stonehenge People: An Exploration of Life in Neolithic Britain 4700–2000 B.C.* London: Routledge, 1990.

Champion, Timothy. *Prehistoric Europe.* Orlando, FL: Academic Press, 1984.

Chippindale, Christopher. *Stonehenge Complete.* Revised ed., New York: Thames and Hudson, 1994.

Cohat, Yves. *The Vikings: Lords of the Sea.* Translated by Ruth Daniell. New York: H.N. Abrams, 1992.

Daniel, Glyn, and Paul Bahn. *Ancient Places: The Preshistoric and Celtic Sites of Britain.* London: Constable, 1987.

Dyer, James. *Ancient Britain.* North Pomfret, VT: B.T. Batsford, 1990.

Ellis, Peter B. *The Druids.* Grand Rapids, MI: Eerdmans, 1995.

Gamble, Clive. *The Palaeolithic Settlement of Europe.* New York: Cambridge University Press, 1986.

Harbison, Peter. *Irish High Crosses.* Syracuse: Syracuse University Press, 1995.

Hodder, Ian. *The Domestication of Europe.* Oxford: Basil Blackwell, 1990.

Jackson, Gordon. *The History and Archaeology of Ports.* North Pomfret, VT: David & Charles, 1984.

Jones, Barri, and David Mattingly. *An Atlas of Roman Britain.* Oxford: Basil Blackwell, 1990.

Lloyd, David. *The Making of English Towns.* North Pomfret, VT: David & Charles, 1984.

Potter, T.W., and Catherine Johns. *Roman Britain.* Berkeley: University of California Press, 1992.

Schick, Kathy D., and Nicholas Toth. *Making Silent Stones Speak: Human Evolution and the Dawn of Technology.* New York: Simon & Schuster, 1993.

Spindler, Konrad. *The Man in the Ice: The Discovery of a 5000-Year-Old Body Reveals the Secrets of the Stone Age.* New York: Harmony Books, 1994.

Welch, Martin. *Discovering Anglo-Saxon England.* University Park, PA: Pennsylvania State University Press, 1992.

Wells, Peter S. *Farms, Villages, and Cities.* Ithaca, NY: Cornell University Press, 1984.

Whittle, Alasdair. *Neolithic Europe: A Survey.* Cambridge: Cambridge University Press, 1985.

Wood, Michael. *In Search of the Dark Ages.* New York: Facts on File, 1987.

GREECE:

Barber, R.L.N. *The Cyclades in the Bronze Age.* London: Duckworth, 1987.

Biers, William R. *The Archaeology of Greece: An Introduction.* 2nd ed., Ithaca, NY: Cornell University Press, 1987.

Biers, William R. *Art, Artifact, and Chronology in Classical Archaeology.* New York: Routledge, 1992.

Carter, Jane B. *The Ages of Homer.* Austin: University of Texas Press, 1995.

Castleden, Rodney. *Minoans: Life in Bronze Age Crete.* London: Routledge, 1990.

Chadwick, John. *The Mycenaean World.* Cambridge University Press, 1976.

Coldstream, J.N. *Geometric Greece.* New York: St. Martin's, 1977.

Constantine, D. *Early Greek Travellers and the Hellenic Ideal.* Cambridge: Cambridge University Press, 1984.

Coulson, William D.E., and Patricia N. Freiert. *Greek and Roman Art, Architecture, and Archaeology: An Annotated Bibliography.* 2nd ed., New York: Garland, 1987.

Dickinson, Oliver. *The Aegean Bronze Age.* Cambridge University Press, 1994.

Grant, Michael. *The Visible Past: Recent Archaeological Discoveries of Greek and Roman History.* New York: Charles Scribner's Sons, 1990.

Green, Richard, and Eric Handley. *Images of the Greek Theatre.* Austin: University of Texas Press, 1995.

Healy, John F. *Mining and Metallurgy in the Greek and Roman World.* London: Thames and Hudson, 1978.

Hurwit, Jeffrey M. *The Art and Culture of Early Greece, 1100480 B.C.* Ithaca, NY: Cornell University Press, 1985.

Leontis, Artemis. *Topographies of Hellenism: Mapping the Homeland.* Ithaca: Cornell University Press, 1995.

MacKendrick, Paul L. *The Greek Stones Speak: The Story of Archaeology in Greek Lands.* New York: Norton, 1981.

MacDonald, William A., and Carol G. Thomas. *Progress into the Past: The Rediscovery of Mycenaean Civilization.* 2nd ed., Bloomington: Indiana University Press, 1990.

Morris, Ian. *Burial and Ancient Society: The Rise of the Greek City-State.* Cambridge: Cambridge University Press, 1987.

Morris, Ian, ed. *Classical Greece: Ancient Histories and Modern Archaeologies.* Cambridge: Cambridge University Press, 1994.

Murray, Oswyn, and Simon Price, eds. *The Greek City: From Homer to Alexander.* Oxford: Clarendon Press, 1990.

Osborne, Robin. *Classical Landscape with Figures: The Ancient Greek City and Its Countryside.* Dobbs Ferry, NY: Sheridan House, 1987.

Owens, E.J. *The City in the Greek and Roman World.* London: Routledge, 1991.

Pollitt, J.J. *The Art of Ancient Greece: Sources and Documents.* Revised ed., Cambridge: Cambridge University Press, 1990.

Rich, John, and Andrew Wallace-Hadrill, eds. *City and Country in the Ancient World.* New York: Routledge, 1991.

Robertson, D.S. *Greek and Roman Architecture.* Cambridge: Cambridge University Press, 1971.

Snodgrass, Anthony. *Archaic Greece: The Age of Experiment.* Berkeley: University of California Press, 1980.

Starr, Chester G. *The Ancient Greeks.* New York: Oxford University Press, 1971.

Taylour, William. *The Mycenaeans.* Revised ed., London: Thames and Hudson, 1983.

Tomlinson, Richard A. *Greek and Roman Architecture.* London: British Museum Press, 1995.

Van Andel, Tjeerd H., and Curtis Runnels. *Beyond the Acropolis: A Rural Greek Past.* Stanford: Stanford University Press, 1987.

Warren, Peter. *The Aegean Civilizations.* 2nd ed., New York: Peter Bedrick Books, 1989.

Wood, Michael. *In Search of the Trojan War.* New York: Facts on File, 1985.

ITALY AND NORTH AFRICA:

Bradley, Keith R. *Slavery and Rebellion in the Roman World.* Bloomington: Indiana University Press, 1990.

De Puma, Richard Daniel, and Jocelyn Penny Small, eds. *Murlo and the Etruscans: Art and Society in Ancient Etruria.* Madison: University of Wisconsin Press, 1994.

Greene, Kevin. *The Archaeology of the Roman Economy.* Berkeley: University of California Press, 1986.

Holloway, R. Ross. *The Archaeology of Ancient Sicily.* New York: Routledge, 1991.

Holloway, R. Ross. *The Archaeology of Early Rome and Latium.* New York: Routledge, 1994.

Lance, Serge. *Carthage: A History.* Translated by Antonia Nevill, Cambridge, MA: Blackwell, 1995.

MacKendrick, Paul L. *The Mute Stones Speak: The Story of Archaeology in Italy.* 2nd ed., New York: Norton, 1983.

MacNamara, Ellen. *The Etruscans*. Cambridge, MA: Harvard University Press, 1991.

Mattingly, David J. *Tripolitania*. Ann Arbor: University of Michigan Press, 1995.

Richardson, Emeline Hill. *The Etruscans: Their Art and Civilization*. 2nd ed., Chicago: University of Chicago Press, 1976.

Ridley, Ronald T. *The Eagle and the Spade: Archaeology in Rome during the Napoleonic Era*. New York: Cambridge University Press, 1992.

Scarre, Chris. *Chronicle of the Roman Emperors: The Reign-by-Reign Record of the Rulers of Imperial Rome*. New York: Thames and Hudson, 1995.

Wallace-Hadrill, Andrew. *Houses and Society in Pompeii and Herculaneum*. Princeton: Princeton University Press, 1994.

Wheeler, Mortimer. *Roman Art and Architecture*. New York: Thames and Hudson, 1985.

Wiedemann, Thomas. *Adults and Children in the Roman Empire*. New York: Routledge, 1989.

NEAR EAST AND TURKEY:

Akurgal, Ekrem. *Ancient Civilizations and Ruins of Turkey: From Prehistoric Times until the End of the Roman Empire*. Istanbul: Haset Kitabevi, 1985.

Bean, George E. *Turkey Beyond the Maeander: An Archaeological Guide*. 2nd ed., London: Murray, 1989.

Bean, George E. *Lycian Turkey: An Archaeological Guide*. 2nd ed., London: Murray, 1989.

Bean, George E. *Aegean Turkey: An Archaeological Guide*. 2nd ed., London: Murray, 1989.

Ben-Tor, Amnon. *The Archaeology of Ancient Israel*. Translated by R. Greenberg, New Haven, CT: Yale University Press, 1992.

Cook, J.M. *The Troad: An Archaeological and Topographical Study*. Oxford: Clarendon Press, 1973.

Curtis, John, ed. *Later Mesopotamia and Iran: Tribes and Empires 1600–539 B.C.* London: British Museum Press, 1995.

Freely, John. *Classical Turkey*. New York: Viking Penguin, 1990.

Kennedy, Hugh. *Crusader Castles*. New York: Cambridge University Press, 1994.

Levy, Thomas E., ed. *The Archaeology of Society in the Holy Land*. New York: Facts on File, 1995.

Lloyd, Seton. *The Archaeology of Mesopotamia: From the Old Stone Age to the Persian Conquest*. New York: Thames and Hudson, 1984.

Lloyd, Seton. *Ancient Turkey: A Traveller's History of Anatolia*. Berkeley: University of California Press, 1989.

Maisels, Charles Keith. *The Emergence of Civilization: From Hunting and Gathering to Agriculture, Cities, and the State in the Near East*. London: Routledge, 1993.

Mitchell, Stephen. *Anatolia: Land, Men, and Gods in Asia Minor I: The Celts in Anatolia and the Impact of Roman Rule*. Oxford: Clarendon Press, 1993.

Postgate, J.N. *Early Mesopotamia: Society and Economy at the Dawn of History*. New York: Routledge, 1992.

Ruby, Robert. *Jericho: Dreams, Ruins, Phantoms*. New York: Henry Holt, 1995.

Saggs, H.W.F. *Babylonians*. Norman: University of Oklahoma Press, 1995.

Shanks, Hershel, ed. *Ancient Israel: A Short History from Abraham to the Roman Destruction of the Temple*. Englewood Cliffs, NJ: Prentice-Hall, 1988.

Slatter, Enid. *Xanthus: Travels of Discovery in Turkey*. London: Rubicon Press, 1994.

EGYPT:

Aldred, Cyril. *The Egyptians*. New York: Thames and Hudson, 1987.

David, Rosalie. *Discovering Ancient Egypt*. New York: Facts on File, 1994.

El Mahdy, Christine. *Mummies, Myth, and Magic in Ancient Egypt*. New York: Thames and Hudson, 1989.

Ford, Barbara. *Howard Carter: Searching for King Tut*. New York: W.H. Freeman, 1995.

Kemp, Barry. *Ancient Egypt: The Anatomy of a Civilization*. New York: Routledge, 1991.

Knapp, Bernard. *The History and Culture of Ancient Western Asia and Egypt*. Chicago: Dorsey, 1988.

Murnane, William J. *Penguin Guide to Ancient Egypt*. New York: Penguin Books, 1983.

Reeves, Nicholas. *The Complete Tutankhamun*. New York: Thames and Hudson, 1990.

Spencer, A. Jeffrey. *Early Egypt: The Rise of Civilization in the Nile Valley*. Norman: University of Oklahoma Press, 1995.

Trigger, Bruce G. *Early Civilizations: Ancient Egypt in Context*. Cairo: The American University in Cairo Press, 1993.

Wilson, Hillary. *Understanding Hieroglyphs: A Complete Introductory Guide*. Lincolnwood, IL: Passport Books, 1995.

SUB-SAHARA AFRICA AND ASIA:

Agrawal, D.P. *The Archaeology of India*. London: Curzon Press, 1982.

Chakrabarti, Dilip K. *Ancient Bangladesh: A Study of the Archaeological Sources*. Delhi: Oxford University Press, 1992.

Chang, Kwang-chih. *The Archaeology of Ancient China*. 4th ed., New Haven, CT: Yale University Press, 1986.

Clark, J. Desmond, and Steven A. Brandt, eds. *From Hunters to Farmers: The Causes and Consequences of Food Production in Africa*. Berkeley: University of California Press, 1984.

Fagan, Brian M. *The Journey from Eden: The Peopling of Our World*. New York: Thames and Hudson, 1990.

Fagan, Brian M. *People of the Earth: An Introduction to World Prehistory*. 8th ed., New York: Harper Collins, 1995.

Fairservis, Walter Ashlin. *The Roots of Ancient India: The Archaeology of Early Indian Civilization*. New York, Macmillan, 1971.

Johanson, Donald, and James Shreeve. *Lucy's Child: The Discovery of a Human Ancestor*. New York: Avon, 1989.

Kennedy, Kenneth A.R., and Gregory L. Possehl, eds. *Studies in the Archaeology and Palaeoanthropology of South Asia*. Atlantic Highlands, NJ: Humanities Press, 1984.

Kirch, Patrick V. *The Evolution of the Polynesian Chiefdoms*. New York: Cambridge University Press, 1984.

Leakey, Richard, and Roger Lewin. *Origins Reconsidered: In Search of What Makes Us Human*. New York: Doubleday, 1992.

Lewin, Roger. *Bones of Contention: Controversies in the Search for Human Origins*. New York: Simon & Schuster, 1987.

Lewin, Roger. *In the Age of Mankind: A Smithsonian Book of Human Evolution*. Washington, DC: Smithsonian Institution Press, 1988.

O'Connor, David. *Ancient Nubia: Egypt's Rival in Africa*. Philadelphia: The University Museum of Archaeology and Anthropology, University of Pennsylvania, 1993.

Parpola, Asko. *Deciphering the Indus Script*. New York: Cambridge University Press, 1994.

Rawson, Jessica. *Ancient China: Art and Archaeology*. New York: Harper and Row, 1980.

Sampson, C.G. *The Stone Age Archaeology of Southern Africa*. New York: Academic Press, 1980.

Stringer, Christopher, and Clive Gamble. *In Search of the Neanderthals: Solving the Puzzle of Human Origins*. New York: Thames and Hudson, 1994.

Trinkaus, Erik, and Pat Shipman. *The Neandertals. Of Skeletons, Scientists, and Scandal*. New York: Vintage Books, 1994.

Wenke, Robert J. *Patterns in Prehistory: Humankind's First Three Million Years*. Oxford: Oxford University Press, 1990.

WORLDWIDE OPPORTUNITIES

ARCHAEOLOGICAL FIELDWORK SERVER

WWW: http://www.cincpac.com/afs/testpit.html

This regularly updated World Wide Web site posts openings for volunteers, paid workers, field schools, and contract jobs.

ARCHAEOLOGY ABROAD

31-34 Gordon Square
London WC1H OPY, United Kingdom
(44) 171 387-7050, ext. 4750
FAX: (44) 171 383-2572
E-mail: arch.abroad@ucl.ac.uk
WWW: http://britac3.britac.ac.uk/cba/archabroad.html

Archaeology Abroad provides information about opportunities for archaeological fieldwork and excavation outside the United Kingdom. Three bulletins are issued annually—in March, May, and October—and are available by subscription. The March bulletin contains information on excavations that are taking place in the summer and early autumn of that year. The May bulletin contains information received since March together with repeat details of excavations for which application deadlines have not yet passed. The October bulletin advertises a few excavations that either take place early in the following year or for which longer preparations are necessary. *Archaeology Abroad* has recently started to produce a new series of Fact Sheets, providing information about opportunities for volunteers in countries from which few advertisements are received. These can be obtained by sending a large self-addressed envelope to the Archaeology Abroad office. The first in the series is Southeast Asia, covering the countries of Southern and Eastern Asia.

EARTHWATCH

680 Mt. Auburn Street, Box 403
Watertown, MA 02272
(800) 776-0188 or (617) 926-8200
FAX: (617) 926-8532
E-mail: info@earthwatch.org
WWW: http://www.earthwatch.org

Earthwatch, a non-profit organization founded in 1972, supports scientific field research worldwide. Volunteers join research expeditions and work side by side with professors and researchers from around the world. In 1998, EarthCorps members can choose from over 150 research expeditions. In addition, Earthwatch now provides college credit through an accredited program with Drexel University. Numerous Earthwatch expeditions are listed in the AFOB. Contact Earthwatch for complete details on all 1998 expeditions.

General information about the program:
Dates needed: All year; each session lasts approximately 2 weeks.
Application deadline: Usually 90 days prior to departure.
Minimum age: 16.
Experience required: None.
Academic credit: Inquire.
Cost: Tax-deductible contributions range from ca. $500–$3000 and will vary with each project.

UNIVERSITY RESEARCH EXPEDITIONS PROGRAM

University of California
Berkeley, CA 94720-7050
(510) 642-6586
FAX: (510) 642-6791
E-mail: urep@uclink.berkeley.edu
WWW: http://shanana.berkeley.edu/urep/

The University Research Expeditions Program (UREP) of the University of California (UC) brings together the general public and UC researchers to participate in archaeology projects worldwide. Volunteers will join UC researchers in 1998 on a wide range of projects, which last year included excavations and/or surveys in medieval monasteries on Aran Island in Ireland; pre-Inca village settlements on Lake Titicaca, Peru; Maya farming communities in the Yucatan; a Moche ceremonial center in coastal Peru; Mesolithic sites in Germany; and early nomadic settlements in California. Four UREP expeditions are listed in the AFOB. Contact UREP for complete details on all 1998 expeditions.

General information about the program:
Dates needed: All year; each session lasts approximately 2–3 weeks.
Application deadline: None.
Minimum age: 16.
Experience required: None, but curiosity, adaptability, and team spirit.
Academic credit: Inquire.
Cost: Tax-deductible contributions range from ca. $800–$2000 and will vary with each project.

US/ICOMOS (The United States Committee, International Council on Monuments and Sites)

Ellen Delage, Program Director
401 F Street NW, Room 331
Washington, DC 20001-2728
(202) 842-1862
FAX: (202) 842-1861
WWW: http://www.icomos.org/usicomos

ICOMOS is an international non-governmental organization composed of 90 national committees which form a world alliance for the preservation and protection of historic buildings, districts, and sites. Founded in 1965, it maintains a secretariat in Paris that serves as a central point for exchange of information. ICOMOS is one of two official advisors to the World Heritage Convention, an international treaty designed to protect the world's great environmental and cultural sites.

US/ICOMOS is seeking US-citizen graduate students or young professionals for paid internships in Australia, Chile, Croatia, France, Ghana, Great Britain, India, Lithuania, Poland, Romania, Russia, the Slovak Republic, Spain, Transylvania, Turkey, and other countries during the summer of 1998. Participants work for public and private nonprofit historic preservation organizations and state agencies, under the direction of professionals. Internships in the past have required training in architecture, architectural history, landscape architecture, materials conservation, history, archaeology, site interpretation, museum studies, and cultural tourism. For more information, contact Ellen Delage, Program Director, at the above address.

General information about the internship:
Dates needed: Three months in summer of 1998.
Application deadline: March 9.
Requirements: Applicants must be graduate students or young professionals, 22–35 years of age, with at minimum a bachelor's degree. The program is intended for those with a career commitment in the field, and applicants should be able to demonstrate their qualifications through a combination of academic and work experience. Speaking ability in the national language is desirable. Attendance at the orientation and final debriefing programs is obligatory.
Cost: In some countries with convertible currency, interns will be paid a stipend equivalent to $4000 for the 12-week internship. In other cases, the stipend is based on local wages. Exchanges offer partial or full travel grants.

UNITED STATES

USA
Location: Nationwide
Site: National Forests throughout the US
Period: Various

Volunteers:

Minimum age: Age and experience requirements vary by project. Minimum age for most projects is 18. On occasion volunteers as young as 12 are allowed to participate if accompanied by a responsible adult.
Dates needed: Year-round. Projects vary in length from a weekend to one month. Application deadlines vary by project.
Cost: Costs vary by project, but there is no registration or participation fee. Facilities vary depending on the activity and location. Many projects involve back-country camping where volunteers are responsible for their own food and gear. Others offer meals prepared by a "camp cook" for a small fee. Still others provide hook-ups for RVs, or volunteers may stay at local hotels and travel to the site each day.

Sponsor: USDA Forest Service
Contact: Passport in Time Clearinghouse (PIT)
Attn: Carol Ellick
PO Box 31315
Tucson, AZ 85751-1315
(800) 281-9176; (520) 722-2716
FAX: (520) 298-7044
E-mail: SRIArc@aol.com

Passport in Time (PIT) is a volunteer program which provides opportunities for individuals and families to work with professional archaeologists and historians on historic preservation projects. The projects are varied, including archaeological excavation, historic structure restoration, field survey, taking oral histories, and laboratory work. The *PIT Traveler*, a newsletter containing information on current projects, is published twice a year, in March and September. Programs from the Winter/Spring *PIT Traveler* are listed in this edition of the AFOB; all deadlines are February 15. Additional programs will be listed in the Summer/Fall *PIT Traveler*. To receive the newsletter and an application form, contact PIT at the address listed above.

USA
Location: Nationwide
Site: National Forests throughout the US
Period: Paleoindian–Historic

Volunteers:

Dates needed: April–November. Length of stay varies, but usually ranges from a minimum of 4 weeks to 4 months (or longer).
Application deadline: March 30.
Minimum age: 18.
Experience required: None.
Cost: Program provides lodging in government barracks, a per diem of approximately $60–$90 per week, and insurance (worker's compensation). Travel to forest not included.

Director: Gerry Gates, Forest Archaeologist
Sponsor: USDA Forest Service
Contact: Modoc National Forest
800 W. 12th Street
Alturas, CA 96101-3132
(916) 233-5811

The Heritage Resource Management (HRM) Volunteer Program provides the opportunity for college students and other interested individuals to learn while participating in "on-the-job" situations in Heritage Resource Management. The National Forests of the United States cover the length and breadth of the nation geographically, and cover its cultural and archaeological/historical background as well. Volunteers will work with forest archaeologists and historians to conduct a wide range of historic preservation activities, including archaeological surveys, excavations, artifact processing and cataloging, archival research, oral histories, etc. The experience gained will help qualify volunteers for paid positions in the following field seasons.

USA
Location: Nationwide
Site: Various sites throughout the US, primarily in the southwest
Period: Prehistoric and historic

Dates of programs: 12–16 weeks sessions throughout the year. Some longer term positions (6 months–1 year) are also available.
Application deadlines: Throughout the year. Contact SCA for details.
Minimum age: 18.
Experience required: Some college-level course work in archaeology and anthropology.
Academic credit: Per individual's institution if desired.
Cost: Participants receive a grant for round-trip transportation to their program area, a weekly stipend to offset living expenses, free housing, insurance (though personal insurance coverage is recommended), and a uniform allowance, if required.

Director: Wallace Elton, Resource Assistant Program
Sponsor and
Contact: Mel Tuck, Assistant Director
Student Conservation Association (SCA)
PO Box 550
Charlestown, NH 03603
(603) 543-1700
FAX: (603) 543-1828
WWW: http://www.sca-inc.org

The Student Conservation Association (SCA), the nation's oldest and largest provider of volunteers for full-time conservation work, has been recruiting and fielding high school and college students, and interested adults, for public service projects since 1957. This year the SCA is offering approximately 1100 expense-paid volunteer positions, nationwide. Participants selected for SCA programs contribute their time and skills toward the protection and management of natural and cultural resources within national parks, forests, wildlife refuges, and other sites. Possible upcoming projects include work at the Tusayan Museum in Arizona; cataloging archaeological materials at Mesa Verde National Park in Colorado; and monitoring cultural resources, including rock art and other archaeological sites, at Lava Beds National Monument in California.

ALABAMA
Location: Montgomery
Site: Jere Shine (and others)
Period: Mississippian (AD 1000–1500)

Field School:
Dates: June 1–July 27
Application deadline: May 1
Academic credit: 8 semester hours from University of Oklahoma

Cost: Tuition: $477 (Oklahoma resident), $1406 (non-resident). Program provides lodging and local commute. Travel to Oklahoma, meals, and insurance not included.

Volunteers:
Dates needed: May 25–July 31
Application deadline: May 1
Minimum age: 18
Experience required: None
Cost: Program provides lodging and local commute. Travel to Oklahoma, meals, and insurance not included.

Bibliography: Anderson, David G., "Stability and Change in Chiefdom-Level Societies: An Examination of Mississippian Political Evolution on the South Atlantic Slope" in *Lamar Archaeology*, M. Williams and G. Shapiro (eds.), Tuscaloosa: University of Alabama Press, 1990, pp. 187–213. Blitz, John H., *Ancient Chiefdoms of the Tombigbee*, Tuscaloosa: University of Alabama Press, 1993. Knight, Vernon J., Jr., "The Formation of the Creeks" in *The Forgotten Centuries*, C. Hudson and C.C. Tesser (eds.), 1994, pp. 373–392. Sheldon, Craig T., *The Mississippian-Historic Transition in Central Alabama*, Ph.D. dissertation, Department of Anthropology, University of Oregon, Eugene, University Microfilms, Ann Arbor, 1974.

Director, Sponsor, and
Contact: Dr. Cameron B. Wesson
                 Oklahoma University
                 Department of Anthropology
                 521 Dale Hall Tower
                 Norman, Oklahoma 73019
                 (405) 325-4458
                 FAX: (405)325-7386
                 E-mail: Cameron.Wesson-1@ou.edu
                 WWW: http://faculty-staff.ou.edu/w/cameron.wesson-1/home.html

The project will investigate the rise of political complexity during the Mississippian period in the Tallapoosa River Valley of central Alabama. Research centers on the poorly defined Shine chiefdom in an attempt to refine our understanding of Mississippian social, political, and economic developments in the region. This research represents the first comprehensive effort to address the Mississippian occupation of this portion of Alabama and will provide data critical to refining our understanding of social and political developments in the area. The primary research goals are to improve our knowledge of the local chronology, reconstruct regional settlement systems, define the spatial limits of Shine and its surrounding polities, and examine the relationship between Shine peoples and the larger Mississippian world.

The field school will integrate students in all stages of research. Students will be introduced to the principles of field archaeology and laboratory analysis, and will participate in mapping, survey, excavation, analysis, and curation of recovered materials. Individuals with defined research interests will be accommodated, and will be allowed to pursue advanced research with these collections.

ALASKA
Location: Central Tanana Valley
Site: Broken Mammoth Site
Period: Paleoindian–Late Prehistoric (10,000–500 BC)

Field School:
Dates: June 1–June 26
Application deadline: April 15

Experience required: Good physical condition and an introductory course in archaeology are preferred.
Academic credit: 3 credits (400 level anthropology course) from University of Alaska Anchorage.
Cost: $300 tuition and $975 fee for 2 days lodging in Anchorage, on-site meals, travel between Anchorage and project, and field excavation equipment. Travel to Alaska, off-site meals, insurance (mandatory), books, laundry, and showers additional. Students are encouraged to bring their own camping equipment.

Bibliography: West, F.H., (ed.), *American Beginnings*, University of Chicago Press, 1996.

Director, Sponsor, and
Contact: David R. Yesner
                 Department of Anthropology
                 University of Alaska Anchorage
                 3211 Providence Drive
                 Anchorage, AK 99508
                 (907) 786-6845 or (907) 786-6840
                 FAX: (907) 786-6850
                 E-mail: AFDRY@uaa.alaska.edu

The Broken Mammoth site and field camp are located off the Richardson Highway and sit atop a 70-foot-high ridge overlooking the Tanana River. A multicomponent site with at least four cultural horizons, Broken Mammoth was a lookout, hunting camp, butchering station, lithic workshop, and dwelling site used repeatedly from the Late Pleistocene up to late prehistoric times. Radiocarbon dates from its lowest component range back almost 11,800 years, making it one of the oldest reliably dated sites in North America, pre-dating the Clovis occupation to the south. The site is notable for the collections of mammoth tusk fragments. Well-preserved animal bones, including bison and elk, are found in its lowest cultural levels.

Topics covered by the field school will include Late Pleistocene human occupation and paleoenvironment of the region; faunal analysis; archaeological survey; lab, photographic, and floatation techniques; site formation processes; stratigraphy; and prehistoric subsistence technologies, with a focus on giving students practical, hands-on experience.

ALASKA
Location: Kodiak archipelago, Afognak Island
Site: Settlement Point and Igvak
Period: ca. AD 1400 (Igvak); 18th century AD (Settlement Point)

Position(s): Archaeologists, Assistants
Dates needed: May 15–September 15
Application deadline: End of January.
Experience required: Fieldwork and knowledge of Alaskan peoples.
Salary: Inquire.
Cost: Program provides lodging, meals, insurance, local commute, and travel to Afognak. Personal travel and expenses not included.

Volunteers/Field School:
Dates: ca. June 1–August 31
Application deadline: None
Minimum age: Inquire
Academic credit: 2 credits for one-week session from University of Alaska, Anchorage
Experience required: None
Cost: Tuition if participating for credit (to be determined) and program fee (ca. $1720 per six-day session) for lodging, meals, local commute, and insurance. Travel to Alaska not included.

Bibliography: Reading material and bibliography supplied upon application.

Director:	Mary Patterson
Sponsor:	Afognak Native Corporation; Alutiiq Culture Center
Contact:	Afognak Native Corporation
	215 Mission Road, #212
	Kodiak, AK 99615-6327
	(800) 770-6014 or (907) 486-6014
	FAX: (907) 486-2514
	E-mail: dig@afognak.com
	WWW: http://www.afognak.com

"Dig Afognak," a participatory program with opportunities for both the amateur archaeologist and the student, is part of a long-term research effort aimed at reconstructing the prehistoric lifeways of the Alutiiq people. Professional archaeologists, amateurs, and students work together with the Native Alaskan landowners, the Koniag Alutiiq, who are also sponsors of the program.

Two sites, located at the abandoned village of Katenai, are currently being excavated. The Igvak site, an early Russian artel or combination fort/trading post, is providing new information on the early Russian/Native contact period of Alaska. The site has already yielded the largest trade bead collection in North America. The Settlement Point site is a pre-contact transitional site from the Little Ice Age, dated to ca. AD 1400. It is hoped that the excavation will provide insight into how the Little Ice Age affected the maritime-based cultures of the Kodiak Archipelago. The Katenai village area provides a unique opportunity to study a pre-contact and post-contact site simultaneously, allowing teams to share information from both sites as it is discovered. Participants will work in all phases of the project. When not helping to excavate or survey, they work at the on-site lab, learning to clean and preserve the artifacts they have helped to excavate.

ALASKA

Location: Kodiak Archipelago
Site: Tanginak Spring Site (KOD 481)
Period: Ocean Bay I (ca. 7000 BP)

Field School: Enrollment limited to 15
Dates: June 22–August 10
Application deadline: April 15
Academic credit: 12 undergraduate or 5 graduate credits from the University of Washington
Experience required: None, but must be outdoor-oriented and enthusiastic about camping in a remote Alaskan location.
Cost: Tuition: ca. $1125 (undergraduate), $1260 (graduate), and $500 for lodging (in large "dormitory" tents), meals, and local commute. Travel to Old Harbor, Alaska, lodging and meals in Old Harbor (ca. 3–5 days), personal camping gear (sleeping bags, etc.), and insurance not included.

Bibliography: Clark, Donald W., "Pacific Eskimo: historical ethnography" (pp. 185–197) and "Prehistory of the Pacific Eskimo region" (pp. 136–148) in *Handbook of American Indians*, Vol. 5:Arctic, David Damas (ed.), Washington, DC: Smithsonian Institution, 1984. Crowell, Aron C., "Prehistory of Alaska's Pacific Coast" in *Crossroads of Continents: Cultures of Siberia and Alaska*, William W. Fitzhugh and Aron C. Crowell (eds.), Washington, DC: Smithsonian Institution Press, 1988 pp. 130–140. Aigner, Jean S., and Terry Del Bene, "Early Holocene maritime adaptation in the Aleutian Islands' in *Peopling of the New World*, Jonathan E. Ericson, R.E. Taylor, and Rainer Berger (eds.), Los Altos, CA: Ballena Press, 1982.

Director, Sponsor, and	
Contact:	Dr. Ben Fitzhugh
	University of Washington
	Department of Anthropology
	Box 353100
	Seattle, WA 98195-3100
	(206) 543-5240
	FAX: (206) 543-3285
	E-mail: fitzhugh@u.washington.edu

The 1998 University of Washington Field School will be conducted at the Tanginak Spring Site, on the southeast side of the majestic Kodiak Archipelago in the Gulf of Alaska. The site is located on a beautiful beach-rimmed cove that has been the home for maritime hunter-fisher-gatherers throughout the past 7000 years. The importance of the Tanginak Spring Site derives from its antiquity (7000–7500 years old), large artifact assemblage, and stratification (several "floors" one on top of each other). This excavation at one of the oldest known sites on the Kodiak Archipelago will generate important information about early human colonization of this region and aspects of the lifestyles of its early inhabitants.

During the field school, student-instructor teams will rotate fieldwork and lab/cook duty. Instruction will include morning classes on archaeological method and theory, the goals of this particular project, and its relation to the archaeology of Kodiak and southern Alaska. Field instruction will involve standards in archaeological surveying, map-making, excavation, note-taking, and photography. Lab instruction will include cleaning, cataloging, artifact analysis, and elementary computer mapping. Field trips (for survey and sight-seeing) will also be made to other archaeological sites and landmarks within hiking distance from the camp.

ALASKA

Location: Sitka, Tongass National Forest
Period: Various

Volunteers: 2 volunteers will be accepted at a time.
Dates needed: April 1–30. Must commit to at least 10 days.
Minimum age: 18
Experience required: Patience and a willingness to piece puzzles together required; interest in historical research desirable.
Cost for participant: Free forest service housing available. Contact PIT for further details.

Sponsor:	USDA Forest Service
Contact:	Passport in Time Clearinghouse (PIT)
	See page 8 for contact information.

In 1928–1929 the U.S. Navy undertook a thorough aerial reconnaissance of southeast Alaska and took hundreds of aerial photographs. These photographs hold a tremendous amount of information about existing land use and occupation during this specific period of time. The "1929 U.S. Navy Aerial Photo Indexing Project" will involve plotting flight lines on a set of topographic maps and indicating where each photo was taken. These photos identify old smokehouses, fox farms, canneries, potentially old Native village sites, associated fishing-industry activities, etc., and this set of maps will be extremely useful for planning future heritage projects. In addition, there is a large collection of file cards detailing special uses permitted on the forest back to 1906. These cards identify past activities and provide historical information. The volunteer will need to become familiar with the geography of the forest in order to sort through this file, identifying locations of activities described on each of the cards. Data from the cards will be entered into a data table.

ARIZONA
Location: Coconino National Forest
Site: Anderson Pass
Period: Archaic–Sinaguan

Rock Art Recording Field School
Dates: June 13–21
Application deadline: Until filled.
Experience required: None, but all participants must be in very good physical condition for hiking and rock scrambling.
Academic credit: Inquire.
Cost: $20 for membership in Arizona Archaeological Society and $80 field school program and training. Participant must bring own camping equipment and food.

Bibliography: A reading list will be provided prior to attendance.

Sponsors: Arizona Archaeological Society,
              Coconino National Forest
Director and
Contact: Jane Kolber
              PO Box 1844
              Bisbee, AZ 85603
              Tel/FAX: (520) 432-3402
                 (no long distance calls returned)
              E-mail: jkolber@theriver.com

The program involves intensive training in various methods of detailed non-intrusive rock art recording and on-site recording of prehistoric petroglyphs located in a pinyon-juniper forest. There will also be lectures on conservation, interpretation, regional pre-history, world rock art, dating, and other subjects.

ARIZONA
Location: Coconino County
Site: Cohonina "fort" sites and pithouse
Period: Pueblo I–III (ca. AD 850–1300)

Field School: Enrollment limited to 16.
Dates: June 1–July 24
Application deadline: March 15
Academic credit: 9 units of graduate credit from Northern Arizona University
Prerequisites: All applicants must be either graduate students or advanced degree students. Applicants will be accepted based on academic performance, letters of recommendation, a letter of interest, and other materials.
Cost: Tuition (to be announced) and all other expenses, including lab fees, lodging, meals, insurance, local commute, and travel to Arizona. Program will provide meals for field trips.

Directors: Dr. David R. Wilcox, Museum of Northern Arizona;
Dr. Christian E. Downum, Northern Arizona University
Sponsor and
Contact: Dr. Christian E. Downum
              1998 NAU Field School
              Northern Arizona University
              Department of Anthropology
              PO Box 15200
              Flagstaff, AZ 86011-5200
              (520) 523-3180
              FAX: (520) 523-9135
              E-mail: Chris.Downum@NAU.edu

The joint NAU/MNA field school places equal emphasis on archaeological survey and excavation. Survey will take place at an elevation of about 7000 feet in a pine forest environment and will be focused in the area surrounding Cohonina "fort" sites built and occupied during the late 11th–12th century AD. Excavations will focus on an earlier (11th century AD) Cohonina pithouse site located in a ponderosa pine forest at an elevation of 7200 feet. It was part of a large, dispersed community centered on a walled plaza site believed to have been an important regional center. The research goals are to explore the evolution of Cohonina culture from its appearance early in the Pueblo I Period of pueblo prehistory to its disappearance or merging with the western Pueblo culture in the 13th century AD.

Students will receive introductory and advanced training in principles of archaeological survey, excavation, mapping, site recording, and artifact analysis, as well as the interpretation of living surfaces and architectural units. There will be heavy emphasis on archaeological typology, and the essential categories of prehistoric material on the Colorado Plateau will explored, including ceramics, ground stone, shell, and chipped stone. In addition to fieldwork, there will be several field trips to important sites and regions in the Southwest, including Chaco Canyon, Mesa Verde, Chavez Pass, the Verde Valley, the Flagstaff Area, and the Phoenix Basin.

ARIZONA
Location: Coronado National Forest, near Sierra Vista
Site: Historic Mines in the Huachuca Mountains
Period: Late 19th–Early 20th centuries AD

Volunteers: 10 openings.
Dates needed: May 11–15. Must commit to full session.
Application deadline: February 15
Minimum age: 18
Experience required: Volunteers should have an interest in mining and historical archaeology, and be able to hike moderate distances over rough mountainous terrain.
Cost: Contact PIT for details.

Sponsor: USDA Forest Service
Contact: Passport in Time Clearinghouse (PIT)
              See page 8 for contact information.

Miners have searched the "Sierra de Huachuca" for precious metals since Spanish Colonial times. Stories of hidden treasure waiting to be discovered still abound. Efforts to find the elusive deposits of gold, silver, copper, and tungsten peaked in the late 19th and early 20th centuries. The remnants of small mining camps, mines, and processing mills dot the mountains, many of them within the limits of the Miller Peak Wilderness Area. PIT volunteers will locate, map, and record these historical-period mining features and related artifacts.

ARIZONA
Location: Coronado National Forest, near Sonoita
Site: Kentucky Camp
Period: 20th century AD

Volunteers: 15 openings.
Dates needed: April 20–24. Must be able to stay for at least 3 days.
Application deadline: February 15
Minimum age: 12; under 18 must be accompanied by adult.
Experience required: Adobe stabilization work is not difficult, but can be physically challenging; volunteers with interest or skills in adobe construction, carpentry, or archaeological survey and mapping are welcome.

Cost: Contact PIT for details.

Sponsor: USDA Forest Service
Contact: Passport in Time Clearinghouse (PIT)
See page 8 for contact information.

At the turn of the century, Kentucky Camp was the headquarters for the Santa Rita Water and Mining Company. Now it is one of the most well-preserved "ghost towns" in southern Arizona. As adobe buildings require ongoing maintenance and stabilization, the 1998 project will focus on patching, mudding, and replacing adobe bricks, and repointing foundations. Time will also be spent recording historic mining features and related sites, using a global positioning system (GPS) and other survey tools.

ARIZONA
Location: Coronado National Forest, near Sonoita
Site: Kentucky Camp
Period: 20th century AD

Volunteers:
Dates needed: December–June. Must commit to one week; longer stays encouraged.
Application deadline: Open
Minimum age: 21
Experience required: Independence and self-reliance, interest in history, and willingness to communicate with the public required; general handyperson skills desirable.
Cost: Contact PIT for details.

Sponsor: USDA Forest Service
Contact: Passport in Time Clearinghouse (PIT)
See page 8 for contact information.

The Forest Service is seeking friendly but independent caretakers for Kentucky Camp, once headquarters for a turn-of-the-century hydraulic-mining operation. Four of five adobe buildings are in initial stages of restoration and interpretation, and the caretaker would be responsible for greeting the public, answering questions, and interpreting the history of the site. Caretakers may also do some restoration and maintenance on the property.

ARIZONA
Location: Dragoon, AZ

Museum Internships:
Dates: Year-round.
Application deadline: Four months before desired start date.
Cost: Intern responsible for all expenses except lodging.

Director: Dr. Anne I. Woosley
Sponsor and
Contact: The Amerind Foundation, Inc.
2100 N. Amerind Road
PO Box 400
Dragoon, AZ 85609
(520) 586-3666
FAX: (520) 586-4679
E-mail: amerind@theriver.com

The Amerind Foundation is a private, nonprofit archaeological research facility and museum focusing on Native American cultures. The Foundation offers internships related to archaeological research or museum programs.

ARIZONA
Location: Flagstaff
Site: Elden Pueblo
Period: AD 1150–1275

Programs at Elden Pueblo: Elden Pueblo serves as an educational site for the public on the nature and practice of archaeological research. Most archaeological programs involve practice with some aspect of archaeological survey, mapping, excavation, artifact processing, and prehistoric technology. A variety of programs are conducted at Elden Pueblo every year.

General Information about all programs:
Dates: Programs take place from May 16–October 1, except for laboratory days (see below).
Application deadline: Open
Minimum age: 18, if not with a family group.
Experience required: None.
Cost: Varies by program, but fees are usually ca. $70–100 per week and cover training and field trips. A primitive camping area is available at no charge. Lodging, meals, and travel are the responsibility of the participant.

Public Days: 10:00 am–4:00 pm
Dates: May 16, June 27, July 11, August 1, September 19
Minimum age: Children under 16 must be accompanied by an adult.
Cost: Free
Students of all ages are welcome to come for the day, see the site, and learn about archaeology through hands-on experience. Bring water, sunscreen, a jacket, and lunch. No reservations required.

Laboratory Days: 10:00 am–4:00 pm
Dates: January 31, February 21, March 7
Minimum age: 10
Cost: Free
Students participate in the processing and analysis of artifacts from Elden Pueblo, learning how to interpret Sinagua artifacts and piece together the history of Elden Pueblo. No reservations required.

Archaeological Camp for Children:
Dates: June 29–July 3, 9:00 am–12:00 pm
Age range: 9–12
Cost: $50 fee
During this archaeological camp, children excavate, wash artifacts, make maps, and document their work as they learn how archaeology reveals the history of Elden Pueblo and the first residents of Flagstaff, the prehistoric Sinagua.

Arizona Archaeological Society Advanced Field School:
Dates: July 20–July 31
Experience required: Must be a member of the Arizona Archaeological Society to participate.
Cost: $75 fee. AAS membership is additional. Inquire for details.
This field school for members of the AAS will cover advanced excavation and recording methods. The work this summer will focus on completing and synthesizing the last several seasons of fieldwork.

Programs for Teachers: Maximum of 30 students per session.
Dates: Per arrangement
Cost: $300 per 4-hour session.
Any educational group is eligible to participate in the programs at Elden Pueblo for a program fee. Educators workshops are routinely offered to supply teachers with curricular materials. Specialized programs meeting your curricular and educational needs can also be designed.

Volunteers:
Dates: Inquire.
Minimum age: 18
Experience required: None, but must have own transportation.

Volunteers are welcome to participate in the Elden Pueblo Project operations. Those interested should send letter of interest to: Peter Pilles, Coconino National Forest, 2323 E. Greenlaw Lane, Flagstaff, AZ 86004.

Bibliography: Kelly, Roger E., "Elden Pueblo: An Archaeological Account," *Plateau*, 42(3), 1970, pp. 79–91. Hohmann, John W., "Sinagua Social Differentiation: Inferences Based on Prehistoric Mortuary Practices," *The Arizona Archaeologist*, 17, Phoenix: Arizona Archaeological Society, 1982. Fewkes, Jesse W., "Archaeological Field-Work in Arizona: Field Season of 1926," *Smithsonian Miscellaneous Collections*, 78(7), 1927, pp. 207–232. Pilles, Peter J., Jr., "The Sinagua: Ancient People of the Flagstaff Region," *Wupatki and Walnut Canyon: New Perspectives on History, Prehistory, and Rock Art*," Santa Fe: School of American Research, 1987. Phagan, Carl J., and Peter J. Pilles, Jr., "Public Participation Archaeology at Elden Pueblo," *Fighting Indiana Jones in Arizona*, A.E. Rogge (ed.), Proceedings of the American Society for Conservation Archaeology, 1988.

Sponsors: Coconino National Forest, Arizona Natural History Association, Arizona Archaeological Society
Director and
Contact: Joelle Clark
Elden Pueblo Program Manager
Arizona Natural History Association
Coconino National Forest
PO Box 3496
Flagstaff, AZ 86003-3496
(520) 527-3450
E-mail: Joelle.Clark@nau.edu

Elden Pueblo is a 65-room pueblo with trash mounds, smaller pueblos, kivas, a large community room, and numerous pit houses that both pre-date and are contemporaneous with the main pueblo. It is the type site for the Elden Phase of the Northern Sinagua tradition (AD 1150–1250), although earlier components are also present. While much of the site was excavated in 1926 by Jesse Walter Fewkes and John P. Harrington of the Smithsonian Institution, new excavations are being undertaken to confirm data, collect new information, and stabilize the pueblo as a public archaeology project. Recent excavations have revealed much about the construction sequence of the site, late Sinagua social organization, subsistence, and the role of the site as a major trade center for the area. Evidence verifying a long-term eruptive sequence for Sunset Crater volcano is helping to confirm new geological as well as archaeological interpretations for the region.

ARIZONA
Location: Homol'ovi Ruins State Park
Site: Homol'ovi I
Period: Hopi, 13th century AD

Volunteers:
Dates: 12 sessions, June–August. Contact Earthwatch for details.
Application deadline: 90 days prior to departure. (Applications will be accepted after that time if space is available.)
Minimum age: 16
Experience required: None, but volunteers must be physically capable of performing some strenuous work at high altitudes under an intense sun.

Cost: $695 for one week, $1195 for two weeks, $1495 for three weeks covers all expenses except travel to staging area (Winslow, AZ) and insurance.

Bibliography: Adams, E. Charles, *The Origin and Development of the Pueblo Katsina Cult*, Tucson: University of Arizona Press, 1991. Adams, F. Charles, et.al., "The Homol'ovi Research Program," *Kiva* 54(3) (various articles pertaining to research conducted by the Arizona State Museum), 1989. Adams, E. Charles, et. al., *River of Change: Prehistory of the Middle Little Colorado River Valley, Arizona*, Arizona State Museum Archaeological Series No. 185, University of Arizona, Tucson (various articles by Homolovi Research Program staff and others), 1996.

Directors: Charles Adams and Richard Lange, Arizona State Museum, University of Arizona
Sponsor and
Contact: Earthwatch
See page 7 for contact information.

In 1998, excavation will continue at Homol'ovi I, one of seven major pueblos along the middle Little Colorado River in northeastern Arizona. This 500-room pueblo was occupied during a period of critical changes in the political, religious, and economic orientation of the region, and teams will work to discover who settled the complex, when it was settled, and whether it grew gradually or expanded as the result of a mass migration.

Volunteers will spend most days in the field, with some days in the lab. Fieldwork involves excavating and photographing buried artifacts, mapping artifact location, and completing forms. Lab work involves washing, cataloging, sorting, and analyzing artifacts. Past volunteers have discovered more than 200,000 artifacts, including ceramics, stone work, animal bone, and bone and shell tools.

ARIZONA
Location: Near Springerville
Site: Casa Malpais Pueblo
Period: AD 200–1500

Volunteers:
Dates: Team I: October 4–17, Team II: October 25–November 7, Team III: July 3–14, 1999, Team IV: July 17–28, 1999.
Application deadline: 90 days prior to departure. (Applications will be accepted after that time if space is available.)
Minimum age: 16
Experience required: None.
Cost: $1395 covers all expenses except travel to staging area (Casa Malpais Museum, Springerville, Arizona) and insurance.

Director: Miles Gilbert, Casa Malpais Archaeological Program
Sponsor and
Contact: Earthwatch
See page 7 for contact information.

Casa Malpais Pueblo was built high on an extinct volcano by the Mogollon, an Indian people who lived in southeastern Arizona and southwestern New Mexico between AD 200–1500. The site includes petroglyphs, a Great Kiva (a massive rectangular structure thought to have been the pueblo's ceremonial center), formal stairways, a large plaza, natural catacombs (fissures in the basalt, some extending 15 meters down, in which the Mogollon buried their dead), and petroglyphs. Research indicates that the placement of certain structures and petroglyphs have astronomical significance relating to the summer and winter solstices. Work at this National Historic Landmark will attempt to determine when the pueblo was abandoned, if it served as a local ceremonial center or was regional, and whether artifacts indicate the presence of both Anasazi (ancestral Hopi) and Mogollon (ancestral Zuni) cultures here. Both modern Hopi and Zuni Indians claim direct cultural ties with Casa Malpais.

The site is composed of basalt cobbles, used to build pueblo walls, which have collapsed both inside and outside room blocks. Volunteers will excavate and screen soil within pueblo rooms using trowels, whisk brooms, and other hand tools; collect, record, draw, and photograph artifacts and bones; and stabilize walls by making and applying mud mortar and replacing wall stones. In the museum's lab, work will include washing finds, identifying animal bones, and reassembling pots of green-on-white "proto-Zuni glazeware" and other ceramic types.

ARIZONA
Location: Tucson
Site: Sabino Canyon Ruin
Period: AD 1000–1350

Field School:
Dates: Year-round
Application deadline: 10 days prior to requested start date.
Academic credit: Options are available for college internship credit and Arizona Archaeological Society certification.
Cost: Program fee ($69 per day, $130 for two days, $189 for 3–12 days) and all other expenses. Discounts for group enrollment.

Bibliography: Cordell, Linda S., *Prehistory of the Southwest*, Orlando, Florida: Academic Press, 1984. Gregonis, Linda M., and Karl J. Reinhard, *Hohokam Indians of the Tucson Basin*, Tucson: University of Arizona Press, 1979. Haury, Emil W., *The Hohokam: Desert Farmers and Craftsmen. Excavations at Snaketown, 1964–1965*, Tucson: University of Arizona Press, 1976 Kelly, Isabel T., *The Hodges Ruin: A Hohokam Community in the Tucson Basin*, Anthropological Papers No. 30, Tucson: University of Arizona Press, 1978. Dart, Allen, and Marc B. Severson, *Purposes and Plan for the Archaeological Program at the Sabino Canyon Ruin*, Archaeology Report No. 95–4, Tucson: Old Pueblo Archaeology Center, 1995.

Director: Allen Dart
Sponsor and
Contact: Old Pueblo Archaeology Center
PO Box 40577
Tucson, AZ 85717-0577
(520) 798-1201

The Sabino Canyon Ruin excavation is conducted by the Old Pueblo Archaeology Center in cooperation with the Fenster School of Southern Arizona, which owns the ruins property. The Sabino Canyon Ruin, a Hohokam Indian settlement, contains visible remains of several adobe housing compounds and less obvious indications of pit houses. Excavations have so far revealed remnants of adobe walls, pithouses, a dog burial, canals, and hundreds of painted and undecorated pottery sherds and other materials, including ground and carved stone, projectile points and other flaked stone, carved seashell jewelry, animal bones, and botanical specimens that include burned corn.

The Sabino Canyon Ruin field school is being offered to the public as a means of funding continuing archaeological research at the ruin and publication of results. Participants receive a basic introduction to Southwestern archaeology and learn excavation techniques and methods of recording, sketching, and mapping archaeological features. All artifacts recovered during the program will ultimately be housed at the Arizona State Museum.

ARIZONA
Location: Greater Tucson area
Site: To be determined
Period: To be determined

Field School:
Dates: Fall/Winter
Application deadline: Inquire.
Academic credit: 3 credits from Pima Community College
Cost: ca. $87 in-state, $147 out-of-state tuition and all other expenses.

Director, Sponsor, and
Contact: David Stephen
Pima County Community College District
West Campus
2202 W. Anklam Road
Tucson, Arizona 85709-0165
(520) 206-6022

The Pima Community College Center for Archaeological Field Training provides high-quality undergraduate education and training in archaeology and anthropology with an emphasis on extensive field training. Due to Tucson's mild winter climate, field classes are taught throughout the winter months. They are conducted on actual archaeological sites and include training in excavation techniques, methods of archaeological surveying, site mapping, and the recording of archaeological data. Students have the opportunity to use traditional equipment as well as field computers and electronic surveying and geophysical instruments. Materials and information collected in the field are further studied in the context of laboratory courses allowing students to gain proficiency in the techniques and methods of artifact processing, identification, classification, and analysis.

ARIZONA
Location: Q Ranch, (working cattle ranch) near Young
Site: Q Ranch Pueblo
Period: AD 1150–1350

Field school:
Dates: July 12–25
Application deadline: July 5
Academic credit: Arizona Archaeological Society Certification (optional). Two classes are offered which may be taken for certification: Ceramics of the Q Ranch and Surrounding Area, and Southwestern Prehistory: Western Pueblo.
Cost for participant: $65 per week registration fee. Campground, with latrine and primitive shower, is available for a nominal fee, or for an additional fee, there is lodging in the ranch house, which includes three meals per day.

Bibliography: Cordell, Linda S., *Prehistory of the Southwest*, New York: Academic Press, 1984. Cordell, Linda S., and George Gummerman, *Dynamics of Southwestern Prehistory*. Reid, Jefferson, and Stephanie Whittlesey, *The Archaeology of Ancient Arizona*.

Director: John W. Hohmann, Ph.D.
Sponsor: Arizona Archaeological Society
Contact: Joyce Eyman
5319 N. 26th Street
Phoenix, AZ 85016
(602) 955-2885

Q Ranch Pueblo is a masonry ruin of the Western Pueblo Culture Group that dates to AD 1265. It was abandoned around AD 1380 after much of the pueblo burned in a catastrophic fire. Many artifacts were left behind, providing an wide array of materials left for archaeological interpretation. The pueblo is located on a working cattle ranch, with juniper and pine trees, deer and elk, and many types of birds in the area. Training is offered for both the beginning and advanced student and includes excavation, ruin stabilization, mapping, historic archaeology, prehistoric ceramic technologies, and archaeological laboratory techniques.

ARIZONA
Location: Winslow on the Homol'ovi Ruins State Park
Sites: A pithouse village (AZJ:14:36) and a pueblo (AZJ:14:282)
Period: 12th and 13th century AD

Field School:
Dates: June 6–July 18
Application deadline: March 16
Academic credit: 6 undergraduate or graduate credits from the University of Arizona
Cost: ca. $650 tuition plus $700 fee for lodging, meals, travel to project area from Tucson, and local commute. Travel to Tucson, insurance, and incidentals not included

Bibliography: Hays, Kelley Ann, E. Charles Adams, and Richard C. Lange, "Regional Prehistory and Research" in *Homol'ovi II: Archaeology of an Ancestral Hopi Village, Arizona*, E. Charles Adams and Kelley Ann Hays (eds.), Tucson: The University of Arizona Press, 1991, pp. 1–9. Young, Lisa C., "Mobility and Sedentism: Changes in Storage during the Pit House to Pueblo Transition" in *River of Change: Prehistory of the Middle Little Colorado River Valley, Arizona*, E. Charles Adams (ed.), Arizona State Museum Archaeological Series 185, Tucson: Arizona State Museum and The University of Arizona, pp. 37–52. Cordell, Linda S., *Prehistory of the Southwest*, New York: Academic Press, 1984, pp. 214–243.

Director: Dr. Lisa C. Young
Sponsors: University of Arizona, Archaeological Field School; Homol'ovi Research Program, Arizona State Museum
Contact: University of Arizona
   Department of Anthropology
   Emil W. Haury Building
   Tucson, AZ 85721-0030
   (520) 621-2585
   FAX: (520) 621-2088
   E-mail: lcyoung@ccit.arizona.edu

The primary objective of the University of Arizona field school is to provide advanced training in the field techniques of archaeology, including mapping, excavation, survey, care of specimens, identification, analysis, and interpretation. This year, excavations will focus on a pithouse village and a nearby pueblo in the Homol'ovi Ruins State Park; research will compare the prehistoric economy and social organization used at the two sites. Fieldwork is augmented with an intensive teaching program of lectures, discussion, and computerized laboratory analysis.

ARKANSAS
Location: Arkansas County
Site: Menard-Hodges, Lake Dumond
Period: Prehistoric–Historic

Training Program for Amateur Archaeologists:
Dates: June 5–21
Application deadline: May 8

Minimum age: 16. Younger volunteers accepted if accompanied by an adult.
Experience required: None
Academic credit: Arkansas Archeological Society certification
Cost: $20 for membership in the Arkansas Archeological Society, registration fee (depends upon number of days attending, but runs from $30–$40), $12.50 for certification program (optional), and all other expenses. The Society arranges for camping and facilities at a minimal daily fee.

Bibliography: Ford, James A., *Menard Site: The Quapaw Village of Osotouy on the Arkansas River*, Anthropological Papers of the American Museum of Natural History, Vol. 48, Part 1, 1961. Arnold, Morris A., *Colonial Arkansas, 1686–1804: A Social and Cultural History*, University of Arkansas Press, 1991.

Director: Dr. John House, Arkansas Archeological Survey
Sponsors: Arkansas Archeological Survey; Arkansas Archeological Society
Contact: Hester Davis
   Arkansas Archeological Society
   PO Box 1222
   Fayetteville, AR 72702-1222

The Annual Training Program for Amateur Archaeologists will be held at the Menard-Hodges National Historic Landmark site, and at the nearby Lake Dumond site. Menard-Hodges is considered to be the Quapaw village of Osotouy, where Henri de Tonti founded the first Arkansas Post in 1686. The exact location of this Post has not been identified, but is thought to be at Lake Dumond. Previous excavations have revealed 17–18th century material at Lake Dumond and prehistoric and protohistoric material at Menard-Hodges.

The Arkansas Archeological Training program is designed to accommodate anyone who wishes to learn about field archaeology, but all participants must be members of the Arkansas Archeological Society. The program includes an orientation, seminars, and supervised excavation and laboratory experience. All participants must attend the orientation and those enrolling in the certification program must fulfill certain requirements. Otherwise, volunteers may register for as many (or as few) days as they like. Full details are available in early March and appear along with registration forms in the March/April issue of the Society's newsletter, *Field Notes*.

ARKANSAS
Location: Parkin Archeological State Park, NE Arkansas, 35 miles west of Memphis, TN
Site: Parkin
Period: Mississippian/Protohistoric (AD 1000–1600)

Field School:
Dates: June 30-August 8
Application deadline: May 31
Academic credit: 6 undergraduate or graduate credits from the University of Arkansas
Cost: $456 undergraduate or $750 graduate tuition, $15 ($25 for graduate students) application fee for students not enrolled at the University of Arkansas, $63.80 for lodging, $200 for food (cook provided).

Volunteers:
Dates needed: September–June
Application deadline: None
Minimum age: 17
Experience required: None

Cost: Program provides lodging (camping at nearby state park). Volunteer responsible for all other expenses.

Bibliography: Davis, Hester A., "An Introduction to Parkin Prehistory," *The Arkansas Archeologist*, 7(1–2), 1966, pp. 1–40. Klinger, Timothy C., "Parkin Archeology: A Report on the 1966 Field School Test Excavations at the Parkin Site," *The Arkansas Archeologist*, 16–18, 1977, pp. 45–80. Morse, Dan F., and Phyllis A. Morse, *Archeology of the Central Mississippi Valley*, New York: Academic Press, 1983, pp. 290–295. Morse, Phyllis A., *Parkin: The 1978–1979 Archeological Investigations of a Cross County, Arkansas Site*, Research Series No. 13, Fayetteville: Arkansas Archeological Survey, 1981. Morse, Phyllis A., "The Parkin Site and the Parkin Phase," *Towns and Temples Along the Mississippi*, David H. Dye and Cheryl Anne Cox (eds.), Tuscaloosa: University of Alabama Press, 1990, pp. 118–134. Mitchem, Jeffrey M., "Investigations of the Possible Remains of de Soto's Cross at Parkin," *The Arkansas Archeologist* 35, 1996, pp. 87–95. Mitchem, Jeffrey M., "Mississippian Research at Parkin Archeological State Park," *Proceedings of the 14th Annual Mid-South Archaeological Conference*, Special Publication No. 1, Memphis: Panamerican Consultants, 1996, pp. 25–39.

Director, Sponsor, and
Contact: Dr. Jeffrey M. Mitchem
Parkin Archeological State Park
Arkansas Archeological Survey
PO Box 241
Parkin, AR 72373-0241
(870) 755-2119
E-mail: jeffmitchem@juno.com

Parkin is a fortified Mississippian village site with deposits over a meter deep in some areas. The site covers 17 acres and is surrounded by a defensive moat. The location of the site, along with Spanish artifacts found there, suggest that it is the town of Casqui, visited by the Hernando de Soto expedition in 1541. It is the type site for the Parkin phase and is the largest and best-preserved Parkin phase site. Current research is focused on recovering information about domestic structures and subsistence. The remains of house floors are abundant in the village area, and both botanical and faunal remains are well preserved and common on the floors.

Most excavation is by trowels and small hand tools, and excavated soil is water-screened on site. Flotation of soil samples is also carried out on-site to recover charred plant remains. A Visitor Information Center adjacent to the site houses an archaeological laboratory and curation facility. Field school students will learn basic techniques of excavation, transit use, mapping, record keeping, laboratory methods, and flotation. Archaeological method and theory and local prehistory will also be addressed.

CALIFORNIA
Location: Angeles National Forest, 12 miles from Palmdale
Site: Mt. Gleason Historic Mining District Survey
Period: 19th century AD

Volunteers: 6–8 openings.
Dates needed: April 20–24. Must commit to full session.
Application deadline: February 15
Minimum age: 18
Experience required: Archaeological experience desirable.
Cost: Contact PIT for details.
Sponsor: USDA Forest Service
Contact: Passport in Time Clearinghouse (PIT)
See page 8 for contact information.

At the turn of the century, Mt. Gleason was the location of a mining boom. Mines for gold and copper sprouted up throughout the mountainside, and a "modern" wagon road was built to access the mines. PIT volunteers and archaeologists will record the road and the mines, some of which still have standing structures. A portion of the area is covered by dense brush, so arduous hiking can be expected.

CALIFORNIA
Location: Jolon, Monterey County
Site: Mission San Antonio de Padua
Period: AD 1771–1834

Field School:
Dates: June 21–July 31
Application deadline: May 30
Academic credit: 6 quarter credits from California Polytechnic State University
Cost: $1103 covers tuition, lodging, and weekday meals. Travel to site and weekend meals not included.

Bibliography: Englehardt, Zephyrin, *San Antonio de Padua, The Mission in the Sierras*, Santa Barbara: Mission Santa Barbara, 1929 (recently reprinted in paperback). Hoover, Robert L., and Julia G. Costello, *Excavations at Mission San Antonio, 1976–1978*, Monograph 26, Institute of Archaeology, University of California, Los Angeles, 1985.

Director, Sponsor, and
Contact: Dr. Robert L. Hoover
Social Sciences Department
California Polytechnic State University
San Luis Obispo, CA 93407
(805) 544-0176
FAX: (805) 544-2528

In its 21st year of operation, the field school is an intensive combination of lectures, excavation, and laboratory analyses of historical archaeological materials from Mission San Antonio. The mission was founded in 1771, the third of 21 Franciscan religious establishments in Spanish California. Attention will be focused on the methods of historic archaeology. Students should expect warm, dry weather and be in good physical condition, have tetanus shots, and bring sleeping bags and pillowcases. Accommodations are in single furnished dormitory rooms with two sets of hot communal showers and electricity. Housekeeping chores are cooperative. Meals are provided communally as guests of the Franciscans in the mission refectory.

CALIFORNIA
Location: Joshua Tree National Park
Site: Keys Desert Queen Ranch and vicinity
Period: Prehistoric and historic (19th and early 20th centuries)

Field School:
Dates: June 29–July 31
Application deadline: June 1
Academic credit: 6 semester credits from University of Nevada, Las Vegas. 2 credit and non-credit options also available.
Cost: $420 for six credits, $140 for two credits, ca. $135 fee for non-credit option, plus ca. $20 per day for lodging, meals, and local commute, and ca. $35 for field kit. Accommodations are in communities near the park.

Sponsors: University of Nevada, Las Vegas; Quaternary Studies Center, Desert Research Institute; Joshua Tree National Park

Directors and
Contacts: Dr. Claude N. Warren, Professor Emeritus
Department of Anthropology and Ethnic Studies
University of Nevada, Las Vegas
Las Vegas, NV 89154
(702) 895-3590 or (702) 895-3986
E-mail: WARRENC@nevada.edu
or
Dr. Joan S. Schneider
Department of Anthropology
University of California, Riverside
Riverside, CA 92521
(909) 787-3986
FAX: (909) 787-5409
E-mail: JSCHNEID@citrus.ucr.edu

Research during the field school will focus on Keys Desert Queen Ranch, a National Register of Historic Places site, and the adjacent Wonderland of Rocks in the north-central part of Joshua Tree National Park at about an elevation of about 4300 feet. This area is surrounded by spectacular rock formations and lies within the high desert pinyon-juniper zone. Students will learn skills required to accomplish a broad range of tasks during archaeological survey and excavation at historical and prehistoric sites. There will also be instruction in geomorphology and paleoclimatology. Students take field notes, keep daily journals, do field maps, illustrations, and field photography, prepare computerized artifact catalogs, and do limited artifact analyses. The Mojave Desert has high mid-day and afternoon temperatures, so survey and excavation will be conduced in the early morning hours on most days. Afternoons will be devoted to laboratory work and writing.

CALIFORNIA
Location: San Diego, Presidio Park
Site: San Diego Presidio
Period: AD 1769–1835

Dates of excavation and field school: All year
Application deadline: None

Position(s): Crew chiefs, lab technicians
Experience required: Excavation experience preferred.
Salary: Variable, ranging from small stipend to regular wages as member of staff.
Cost: All expenses.

Field School and Public Archaeology Programs:
Academic credit: 2 classes (4 weeks each), 3 quarter units each, from University of California at San Diego Extension. It is anticipated that credit will only be made available during the summer months.
Cost: $295 tuition and all expenses.

Volunteers:
Minimum age: 13 (younger with permission of Principal Investigator).
Experience required: None
Cost: All expenses.

Bibliography: Farnsworth, Paul, and Jack S. Williams (eds.), "The Archaeology of the Spanish Colonial and Mexican Republic Periods," *Historical Archaeology*, 26(1), 1992. Deagan, Kathleen, *Artifacts of the Spanish Colonies of Florida and the Caribbean 1500–1800*, Washington, DC: Smithsonian Institution Press, 1987. Pourade, Richard F., *The History of San Diego—The Explorers*, San Diego: Union Tribune Publishing Company, 1960; *The History of San Diego—The Time of the Bells*, San Diego: Union Tribune Publishing Company, 1961; *The History of San Diego—The Silver Dons*, San Diego: Union Tribune Publishing Company, 1963.

Director, Sponsor, and
Contact: Jack S. Williams, Principal Investigator
Center for Spanish Colonial Archaeology
San Diego Presidio Archaeology Project
4060 Morena Boulevard, Suite G, 250
San Diego, CA 92117
(619) 483-4589 or (619) 910-2851

The presidio of San Diego is the oldest European settlement in California, and is the birthplace of the state. A combined mission/presidio settlement was founded at San Diego in 1769. Five years later the mission was moved to a new location, and the original site was taken over by the military. During the later 18th century, the settlement evolved into a large adobe citadel that included rooms for the garrison, workshops, storehouses, and homes of civilian settlers. Between 1830 and 1840, the military colony was slowly abandoned. Since the middle 19th century, most of the remains have escaped disturbance. After 1920, the site was transformed into a public park. The 1998 season will focus on the ruins of the north wing, a 50-room complex made up of colonial residences and fortifications. Approximately 40 rooms were exposed during the last three years.

CALIFORNIA
Locations: Survey in Santa Cruz and Monterey Bay Counties and excavation in San Francisco
Sites: Various prehistoric and historic sites and Spanish Colonial Chapel in Presidio
Period: Prehistoric–WWII and AD 1776–1834

Field School:
Dates: June 15–July. (Survey: June 15–July 2, Excavation: July 6–24)
Application deadline: March 20
Academic credit: 6 credits (3 for survey, 3 for excavation) from Cabrillo College, transferable to University of California system.
Prerequisites: An introductory course in archaeology.
Cost: $658 covers California resident tuition (non-residents add $112 per credit), instructional materials, field equipment, most meals and lodging during the excavation session, and course-related travel. Detailed information supplied upon application.

Directors: Rob Edwards, Charr Simpson-Smith; Leo Barker
Sponsors: Cabrillo College; US Forest Service, Los Padres Forest; National Park Service, San Francisco Presidio
Contact: Cabrillo College
Archaeological Technology Program
6500 Soquel Drive
Aptos, CA 95003
(408) 479-6294
FAX: (408) 479-6425
E-mail: redwards@cabrillo.cc.ca.us

The Archaeology Technology Program's 1998 field school will focus on survey and excavation. The survey instruction covers advanced field training in various site survey techniques, mapping, and sampling, as well as discussion of archival record preparation. Survey takes place at selected prehistoric and historic sites on the central coast of California. Excavation training takes place at the Spanish and Mexican Period Presidio (fort) of San Francisco and includes professional archaeological field techniques, note taking, collecting soil samples, field processing of artifacts, wet screening, data entry including the Harris Matrix for stratigraphic control, theodolite transit use for mapping, and interpretation to the public. The program prepares students for entry level work in archaeology and cultural resource management activities.

COLORADO
Location: Cortez
Site: Mitchell Springs
Period: AD 700–1250

Field School:
Dates: Session 1: May 17–28, Session 2: May 31–June 11, Session 3: June 14–25. Enrollment limited to 24 students per session.
Application deadline: Continuous enrollment until filled.
Academic credit: 4 credit hours from Glendale Community College
Cost: $333 ($233 for residents of Maricopa County) for tuition and fees. Student responsible for all other expenses. There are many local motels and campgrounds in all price ranges. Carpools will be arranged when appropriate.

Bibliography: Any basic reading on Anasazi/Pueblo cultural history and archaeological techniques.

Directors: Linda W. Smith, PhD, and Don Dove, MA
Sponsor and
Contact: Field School Admissions
Admissions and Records
Glendale Community College
6000 W. Olive Avenue
Glendale, AZ 85302
(602) 435-3307

During the previous seven seasons, Glendale Community College students have dug test trenches at Mitchell Springs which have indicated the presence of continuous Anasazi occupation from Late Basketmaker–Pueblo III phases. This summer, a new area of the 90-acre parcel, which contains a number of sites, will be tested, using 1 x 3 meter trenches. The introductory field school will include lectures on basic archaeological field techniques and Anasazi culture, field-work at the Mitchell Springs site, and visits to Mesa Verde and the Anasazi Heritage Center. It is an intensive twelve-day, ten-hour-per-day experience, which is exhausting but very rewarding.

COLORADO
Location: Crow Canyon Archaeological Center, Cortez
Site: Shields Pueblo
Period: AD 1150–1300

Educational Programs/Volunteers:
Dates: February–November. Week-long Adult Excavation Programs; Month-long Field School for High School Students; Week-long Cultural Explorations Study Tours (domestic and international).
Application deadline: Until filled.
Experience required: None
Minimum age: 14 for High School Field School; 16 for other programs.
Academic Credit: Optional. Credit available from Colorado State University; number of credits vary by program.
Cost: Varies by program. Basic fee for a week-long excavation program is $850 for adults; $825 for seniors, 55 and over; $750 for alumni. Tuition for month-long High School Field School is $3450. Fees cover lodging, meals, entry fees, and local transportation. Insurance and travel to Colorado not included.

Bibliography: Ambler, Richard J, *The Anasazi*, Arizona: Museum of Northern Arizona, 1977. Jones, DeWitt and Linda S. Cordell, *Anasazi World*, Graphic Arts Publishing Company, 1985. Lipe, William D. (ed.), *The Sand Canyon Archaeological Project, A Progress Report*, Crow Canyon Archaeological Center, 1992. Thompson, Ian. "The Search for Sediments on the Great Sage Plain," *Archaeology*, September/October 1995, pp. 58–63. Naranjo, Tito, "Reflections on the Bluewater People," *Archaeology*, September/October 1995, p. 62.

Director: Bruce Grimes
Sponsor and
Contact: Shannon Gallagher
Crow Canyon Archaeological Center
23390 County Road K
Cortez, CO 81321
(800) 422-8975 or (970) 565-8975
FAX: (970) 565-4859
E-mail: sgallagher@crowcanyon.org
WWW: http://www.crowcanyon.org

Students and volunteers are sought to assist veteran archaeologists at Shields Pueblo and in the research laboratory. Crow Canyon is completing a new five-year research design which will guide its research into the 21st century. The theme, "Communities Through Time: Migration, Cooperation, and Conflict," focuses on the ancient Pueblo Indian communities of the vast Mesa Verde archaeological region in southwestern Colorado and southeastern Utah. Participants make a significant contribution to Crow Canyon's research.

Crow Canyon Cultural Explorations seminars visit significant natural and cultural places in the American Southwest and beyond. In 1998, Crow Canyon will sponsor excavation in Fiji on the island of Waya, and in Alaska through the Dig Afognak! program. Cultural Exploration programs based at the Crow Canyon campus provide instruction in aspects of Native American culture, including pottery making and silversmithing.

COLORADO
Location: Near Cortez
Site: Near Lowry Ruin
Period: Pueblo II/Pueblo III

Field School:
Dates: May 18–July 3
Application deadline: April 1
Academic credit: 8 hours from Fort Lewis College
Cost: $68 per credit resident tuition, $260 per credit non-resident tuition, plus lodging (camping), meals, and travel to program. Program provides insurance and local commute.

Bibliography: Available on request.

Director: Dr. W. James Judge
Sponsor and
Contact: Department of Archaeology
Fort Lewis College
Durango, CO 81301
(970) 247-7409
E-mail: Judge_j@fortlewis.edu
WWW: http://www.fortlewis.edu/arts-sci/anthro/anthro.html

The field school is an integral part of a ten-year research project on an important Pueblo-II/Pueblo-III site, located adjacent to the Lowry Ruin about 25 miles northwest of Cortez, Colorado. The Lowry Ruin is an excavated and stabilized Chacoan outlier. Seven weeks of intensive field training in survey, testing, and excavation of architectural structures comprise the field school. Training includes field methods, experimental archaeology, and interpretation of research results to the visiting public.

COLORADO
Location: Dolores
Site: Anasazi Heritage Center
Period: AD 600–1300

Internships:
Dates needed: Inquire; interns should plan to stay for eight weeks.
Application deadline: April 1
Minimum age: College
Experience required: Inquire.
Cost: Inquire.
Academic credit: Available as arranged with intern's institution.

Bibliography: Cordell, Linda S., *Prehistory of the Southwest*, Academic Press Inc., 1984. *Handbook of the North American Indian,* Vol. 9. *River of Sorrows—History of the Lower Dolores River Valley.*

Sponsors: Bureau of Land Management; Anasazi Heritage Center
Director and
Contact: LouAnn Jacobson
Anasazi Heritage Center
27501 Highway 184
Dolores, CO 81323
(970) 882-4811

Applications will be accepted for up to six intern positions: one in site survey and monitoring, four in collections management, and one in exhibit development. The Anasazi Heritage Center is a state-of-the-art museum committed to the preservation and interpretation of the Northern San Juan Anasazi. Applications should include a current resume and statement regarding applicant's career goals. Contact the Director for more information and details on specific job descriptions.

COLORADO
Location: Near Gunnison
Site: Tenderfoot
Period: Paleoindian–Archaic

Field School:
Dates: June and July
Application deadline: May 15
Academic credit: 4 credits from Western State College, Gunnison
Cost: Tuition (ca. $350 resident or $1200 non-resident). Student responsible for all other expenses.

Volunteers: Contact the Director for details.

Director, Sponsor:
Contact: Dr. Mark Stiger
Department of Anthropology
Western State College of Colorado
Gunnison, Colorado 81231
E-mail: mstiger@western.edu

The Western State College of Colorado field school at the open-air Paleoindian–Archaic site of Tenderfoot will stress proper field excavation techniques such as mapping, recording, note-taking, sketching, photographing, and interpreting stratigraphy. Students will continue work on extensive horizontal excavations uncovering firepits, structures, and stone tools to learn about changes in hunting and gathering lifeways.

CONNECTICUT
Location: Bridgewater
Site: Cipola
Period: Archaic–Woodland

Field School:
Dates: June 1-July 2
Application deadline: June 1
Academic credit: 6 credits from Western Connecticut State University. There may be a 3-credit option. Inquire.
Cost: ca $187 per credit tuition. Program provides field kit and transportation to site. Students bring own water and lunch each day.

Bibliography: Weinstein, Laurie (ed.), *Enduring Traditions: The Native Peoples of New England*, Westport CT: Bergin and Garvey, 1994, in particular chapter by Trudi Lamb Richmond. Articles by Russ Handsman, published in *Artifacts*, the former publication of the American Indian Archaeological Institute (now Institute for American Indian Studies) in Washington, CT. His articles deal with the "Fort Hill" district which includes Bridgewater.

Director, Sponsor, and
Contact: Dr. Laurie Weinstein
Western Connecticut State University
E-mail: Weinstein@wcsu.ctstateu.edu
(203) 837-8453

The project will consist of surveying and testing a new site which is adjacent to a site with known Archaic–Woodland components. The site is also near Lover's Leap, a well-known historic Indian area. However, due to extensive pot hunting, much of the significant information about that site has been lost. Students will work in the field three days a week and do lab work on the fourth day. Students may also be asked to support their archaeological work with documentary research about the Bridgewater-New Milford area. There may be a limited excavation of the site during the field season. Field days usually start at 8:00 am and end back at school by 4:00 pm. The class is usually informal and fun.

CONNECTICUT
Location: Florence Griswold Museum, Old Lyme
Site: Griswold Museum grounds
Period: 18th and early 19th century

Dates of excavation and field school: June and July. Exact dates to be announced.
Application deadline: June 15

Field School:
Academic credit: 4 or 8 credits from Connecticut College
Cost: $610 or $1220 tuition, plus all other expenses.

Volunteers:
Minimum age: 16
Experience required: None
Cost: Volunteer responsible for all expenses.

Bibliography: Deetz, James, *In Small Things Forgotten: The Archaeology of Early American Life*, Doubleday, 1995. Orser, C., and B. Fagan, *Historical Archaeology*, Mayfield Publishing Co., 1995.

Directors: Dr. Harold Juli, Dr. Stuart Reeve
Sponsors: Connecticut College; Florence Griswold Museum
Contact: Dr. Harold Juli
Connecticut College
Box 5492
New London, CT 06320
(860) 439-2228
E-mail: hdjul@conncoll.edu

This will be the first season of a project designed to reconstruct the landscape history of the 19th-century houses on the grounds of the Florence Griswold Museum. This field school in historical archaeology provides instruction in excavation, mapping, relationship of archaeology to history, architectural reconstruction, and environmental analysis.

CONNECTICUT

Location: Uncasville
Site: Original Mohegan Reservation (established 1663)
Period: Pre- and Post-Contact Mohegan Sites

Field School:
Dates: May 26–July 2
Application deadline: May 15
Academic credit: 6 credits from Indiana University-Purdue University Indianapolis or Eastern Connecticut State University
Cost: Indiana residents: $636 undergraduate tuition, $864 graduate tuition for Indiana residents. All others: $894 undergraduate tuition, $990 graduate tuition. Lodging is by arrangement with Eastern Connecticut State University.

Sponsors: The Mohegan Nation; Eastern Connecticut State University, School of Continuing Education; Indiana University-Purdue University, Indianapolis, Department of Anthropology
Director and
Contact: Dr. Jeffrey C. M. Bendremer
Mohegan Tribal Archaeologist
Department of Anthropology and Sociology
Indiana University-Purdue University, Indianapolis
425 University Boulevard, 413E Cavanaugh Hall
Indianapolis, IN 46202
(317) 274-9847
FAX: (317) 274-2347
E-mail: jbendrem@iupui.edu

The Mohegan Nation, a federal recognized tribe, is reclaiming a large portion of their original reservation in Uncasville. As a part of this process of restoring former tribal lands, this field school will catalog and investigate cultural resources and archaeological sites in the Mohegan Homeland. These resources include at least two fortified village sites, three tribal burial grounds, numerous Mohegan homesteads, and the Mohegan Church, as well as many areas with high archaeological potential for both pre- and post-contact sites. The field school will work under direct supervision of the Cultural Resources Department of the Mohegan Tribe Planning Department and Tribal Council. Students will engage in subsurface systematic testing as well as intensive excavation when deemed appropriate by the tribal government. Non-intrusive techniques, such as surface reconnaissance, mapping, photography, and remote sensing will also be emphasized. In addition, students will participate in an exploration of the relationship between archaeologists and Native Peoples of North America, both past and present, through speakers, lectures, and the daily experience of working on the Mohegan Reservation.

FLORIDA

Location: Florida Keys National Marine Sanctuary, Islamorada
Site: Survey of Spanish galleons, English frigates, and American schooners
Period: 18th and 19th centuries AD

Field School:
Dates: July 13–22
Application deadline: June 30
Academic credit: Optional. May be arranged though students own institution.
Cost: Divers: $699/four days, $899/seven days, $1099/ten days; Non-Divers: $499/four days, $799/seven days, $899/ten days covers training, boating and diving expenses, equipment (tanks, air, and weights), research and survey materials, teaching packet, and museum entrance fees. Lodging, food, rental gear, insurance, and incidentals are not included.

Bibliography: Bass, George F. (ed.), *Ships and Shipwrecks of the Americas: A History Based on Underwater Archaeology*, London: Thames and Hudson, 1988. Mathewson, R. Duncan III (ed.), *Seafarers Journal of Maritime Heritage*, Vol. 1, Key West, FL and Woodstock, VT: Seafarers Heritage Library Ltd., 1987. Meylach, M., *Diving to a Flash of Gold*, Garden City, NY: Doubleday, 1971.

Director, Sponsor, and
Contact: R. Duncan Mathewson III, PhD
National Center for Shipwreck Research Ltd.
PO Box 1123
Islamorada, FL 33036
(305) 852-1690
FAX: (305) 852-8617
E-mail: reddog1690@aol.com

The 9th annual "Dive into History" Marine Archaeology Summer Field School in the Florida Keys is an archaeological survey of the lost 1733 Spanish treasure fleet and other shipwrecks. The field school is an integral part of an on-going effort to inventory and assess shipwreck sites as submerged cultural resources along the Florida Keys. The results of the project will help to establish site-specific criteria to develop a coherent management plan for the preservation and protection of hundreds of fragile historic shipwrecks throughout the Florida Keys National Marine Sanctuary. All work is conducted under an "Archaeological Research and Recovery" permit from NOAA, US Department of Commerce.

All participants will have an opportunity to gain practical experience in a variety of archaeological techniques, including underwater mapping, *in situ* artifact recording, excavation, hull structure interpretation, artifact registration, small finds photography, numismatics, ceramic analysis, and archival research. Bad weather days will be spent processing artifacts and conducting lab work at the Maritime Museum of the Florida Keys. Field trips in Key West will include visits to local diver's haunts, shipwreck museums, and historical sites.

HAWAII

Location: Hawaii Volcanoes National Park
Site: Various
Period: AD 400–present

Volunteers:
Dates needed: Year-round, must be able to stay for 4–6 months. The next field season is expected to begin in January 1998.
Application deadline: None
Minimum age: 21

Experience required: Degree in anthropology/archaeology or related field. Survey and site recording skills. Knowledge of GPS and ArcView highly desired. Ability to work well with others and independently without supervision. Field conditions in the park are very harsh and applicants are expected to be in excellent physical condition. Individuals with asthma may be particularly vulnerable to the sulfuric fumes emanating from Kilauea volcano.

Cost: Program provides lodging, on-site insurance, and $7 stipend for each day worked.

Bibliography: Kirch, Patrick V., *Feathered Gods and Fishhooks*, Honolulu: University of Hawaii Press, 1985. Ladefoged, Thegn, Gary F. Somers, and Melia Lane-Hamasaki, *A Settlement Pattern Analysis of a Portion of Hawaii Volcanoes National Park*, Western Archaeological and Conservation Center, Publications in Anthropology, No. 44, 1987. Handy, E.S. Craighill, and Mary Kawena Pukui, *The Polynesian Family System in Ka'u, Hawai'i*, Charles E. Tuttle Company, 1972.

Director, Sponsor, and
Contact: Catherine Glidden
      Hawaii Volcanoes National Park
      PO Box 52
      Hawaii National Park, HI 96718
      (808) 967-8226

The Hawaii Volcanoes National Park Cultural Resources Program requires ongoing volunteer help. The next field season will be conducted within the Puna-Ka'u Historic District. This 13,000-acre area is on the National Register of Historic Places and includes thousands of archaeological sites. One of the goals of the ongoing archaeological survey project is to increase our understanding of prehistoric subsistence practice specifically within upland areas of this large district. Previous archaeological investigations have been concentrated in coastal regions of the park, leaving a gap in our understanding of human activities in mid and upper elevation zones. Several villages have been identified in preliminary surveys, including the village of Holei. This ancient hamlet, located along the edge of a precipitous cliff with a distant view of the ocean, includes over 50 archaeological features such as habitation terraces, petroglyphs, caves, and trails.

HAWAII
Location: Kona Coast State Park, island of Hawaii
Site: S.S. *Maui*, 25' depth
Period: 20th century shipwreck

Field School: Enrollment limited to 15 students.
Dates: June 15–July 17 (tentative)
Application deadline: April 15
Academic credit: 6 graduate credits from University of Hawaii at Manoa. The course is graduate level but undergraduates are encouraged to apply and are accepted with the consent of the Instructor.
Experience required: University of Hawaii Scientific Diver authorization is required to participate in the diving aspects of the course.
Cost: Tuition ($131 per credit for Hawaii residents, $158 per credit for non-residents) and $800 fee for lodging and meals in the field (3 weeks) and project-related travel. Lodging and meals while not in field (2 weeks) and medical insurance (mandatory) not included.

Instructor: Hans Van Tilburg, Nautical Archaeology and Maritime History, East Carolina University

Sponsor and
Contact: Steve H. Russell
      University of Hawaii, Summer Session
      UH Marine Option Program
      1000 Pope Road, #229
      Honolulu, HI 96822
      (808) 956-8433
      FAX: (808) 956-2417
      E-mail: mop@hawaii.edu
      WWW: http://www2.hawaii.edu/mop/

Fieldwork during the 1998 Maritime Archaeology Techniques Course will take place on an early 20th-century steamship shipwreck, the S.S. *Maui*. The remains of the shipwreck are located on the leeward coast of the island of Hawaii in approximately 25 feet of water. The site will be documented with underwater photography/videography and mapping, using standard underwater archaeological techniques. Students will get hands-on experience with remote sensing instruments. Steamships were critical to inter-island trade in early 20th-century Hawaii, and the S.S. *Maui* is one of only two steamship wreck sites in Hawaii. The course will commence on Oahu for one week, move to the island of Hawaii for three weeks in the field, then return to Oahu for report writing and project wrap-up.

HAWAII
Location: Maui
Site: Slopes of Haleakal
Period: AD 1000–1900

Field School: Enrollment limited to 15 students.
Dates: May 25–July 3
Application deadline: April 3
Academic credit: 6 upper division or graduate credits from Northern Illinois University
Prerequisites: No fieldwork experience is necessary, but previous course work in anthropology/archaeology is desirable.
Cost for participant: $2300 covers tuition, lodging, insurance, and local commute. Travel to Maui and meals not included.

Bibliography: Kirch, Patrick V., *Feathered Gods and Fishhooks*, Honolulu: University of Hawaii Press, 1985. Kolb, Michael J., "Monumentality and the Rise of Religious Authority in Precontact Hawai'i, *Current Anthropology*, 35(5), 1994, pp. 521–547; "Ritual activity and chiefly economy at·an upland religious site on Maui, Hawai'i, *Journal of Field Archaeology*, 21(3), 1994, pp. 417–436.

Director: Dr. Michael J. Kolb, E-mail: aloha@niu.edu
Sponsors: Northern Illinois University; Department of Hawaiian Homelands; State Historic Preservation Division
Contact: Arlene B. Neher
      Northern Illinois University
      Liberal Arts and Sciences External Programming
      DeKalb, IL 60115-2895
      (815) 753-5200
      FAX: (815) 753-5202
      E-mail: aneher@niu.edu
      WWW: http://aloha.anthro.niu.edu/Fldsch.htm

The Northern Illinois University Archaeological Field School will take place on the slopes of Haleakal volcano on the island of Maui. The upcountry region of Maui is rich with well-preserved habitation sites integrated within an extensive dryland agricultural field system and a network of ritual sites. This area represents a community within an outlying political district in the Maui chiefdom. Students will excavate sites to help reconstruct traditional habitation and subsistence practices related to temple construction, upcountry settlement, and dryland forest exploitation. They will also spend time locating and mapping additional sites to help articulate past settlement patterns and their relationship within the community. State-of-the-art mapping equipment and traditional excavation techniques will be used to record information about pre-European contact settlement and habitation activities.

ILLINOIS
Location: Kampsville
Site: Center for American Archaeology (CAA)
Period: Late Woodland

Five-Week High School Program:
Dates: June 22–July 31. Enrollment is offered on the flexible schedule. Students may enroll for one or more weeks.
Application deadline: Two weeks before start of program.
Academic credit: Contact CAA for details.
Cost: $450 per week covers tuition, lodging, and weekday meals. Travel to project, insurance, weekend meals, and other personal expenses not included.

High school juniors and seniors and professional archaeologists will conduct excavations at a Middle Woodland habitation site. The Five-Week Program provides training in many aspects of archaeology, including excavation, artifact analysis, geomorphology, botany, zoology, and experimental archaeology. Students conduct independent research under the guidance of an archaeologist as a mentor in order to further their archaeological experience. The research conducted by these students can provide an advantage in seeking careers in the sciences and related academic fields.

Teacher Workshop Field Schools
Dates: August 3–7, August 10–14
Application deadline: Two weeks before start of program.
Academic credit: Participants often earn credit in education of anthropology through their local universities or colleges. Chicago Public School teachers can earn credit through Lane Promotional Credit Courses.
Cost: $300

Teachers will learn how to develop units which incorporate archaeology with the sciences, mathematics, and social sciences. Hands-on activities, in the field and classroom, are an integral part of the program. Day activities include an introduction to field excavation techniques, lab analysis, and replicating artifacts using prehistoric technologies. Evenings are devoted to enrichment activities and sessions with resident and visiting scholars.

Field Schools for Adults:
Dates: May 25-29, June 1–5, June 15–19
Application deadline: Two weeks before start of program.
Academic credit: Adults may use training in partial fulfillment of the excavation requirement for the Illinois Association for the Advancement of Archaeology Avocational Certification program.
Cost: $300

Participants will excavate a Middle Woodland habitation site, under the direction of Dr. Jodie O'Gorman, using current field techniques and methodologies. Contact the CAA for complete details.

Flintknapping Specialty Field School
Dates: June 15–19
Application deadline: Two weeks before start of program
Academic credit: Contact CAA for details.
Cost: $325

Stone tools and the remains of stone tool production are the most conspicuous prehistoric artifacts used to interpret the past. Understanding stone tool manufacture is critical to interpreting the role of lithic technologies in prehistoric societies. During the special five-day Flintknapping Field School, students will create their own lithic reproductions using prehistoric flintknapping tools and techniques. The identification and treatment of chert, the raw material used in stone tool production, is central to the course.

Ceramic Technology Field School
Dates: June 9–13
Application deadline: Two weeks before start of program.
Academic credit: Contact CAA for details.
Cost: $325

Clay artifacts hold many clues to the past. To decipher these clues one must be familiar with ceramic technology and the role pottery has as a living craft tradition. Field school participants will go on field trips, learn to distinguish various natural clay sources, collect clay that is best suited for the class, and learn to process the clay. The instructor will provide a cultural background and oral history to accompany the production of ceramics as a living craft tradition.

Sponsor and
Contact: Center for American Archaeology (CAA)
Education Programs
Department 1, PO Box 366
Attn: Brenda Nord
Kampsville, IL 62053-0366
(618) 653-4316
FAX (618) 653-4232

ILLINOIS
Location: Near East St. Louis
Site: Cahokia
Period: ca. AD 800–1400

Field School:
Dates: June 22–August 14
Application deadline: April 30
Academic credit: 2 credits from Northwestern University for full session. 1 and 3 credit options are also available.
Cost: $1596 for one credit or $3192 for two credits for Northwestern University undergraduates; $1596 or $2793 for visiting students; $810 or $1620 for high school teachers covers tuition, lodging and local commute. Meals and travel to Illinois not included.

Bibliography: Fowler, Melvin L., *The Cahokia Atlas: A Historical Atlas of Cahokia Archaeology*, Studies in Illinois Archaeology No. 6, Springfield: Illinois Historical Preservation Agency, 1989. Iseminger, William R., "Mighty Cahokia." *Archaeology* 49:3, May/June, 1996, pp. 30–37. Pauketat, Timothy R., and Thomas E. Emerson (eds.), *Cahokia: Domination and Ideology in the Mississippi World*, Lincoln: University of Nebraska Press.

Director: Dr. Mary Beth Trubitt
Sponsor and
Contact: Archaeological Field School
Northwestern University
Department of Anthropology
1810 Hinman Avenue
Evanston, IL 60208-1310
(847) 491-3968
FAX: (847) 467-1778
E-mail: mtrubitt@nwu.edu

The 1998 Northwestern University Archaeological Field School will take place at the Cahokia site, a late prehistoric mound center. During the Mississippian period (AD 1050–1350), Cahokia was the center of a chiefdom in the American Bottom region of the Mississippi River Valley. Cahokia is a complex site with over 100 mounds (including the largest prehistoric earthen mound in North America), a wooden stockade, and extensive residential areas.

The University's West Cahokia Project focuses on household craft production at Cahokia. Prestige goods and utilitarian objects of stone, ceramic, and marine shell were produced by Mississippian period craftworkers, and research indicates that craft activities typically took place within residential areas. Participants will investigate craft production while excavating domestic features that provide clues to the social, economic, and political activities of Mississippian households. Students receive training in aspects of archaeological fieldwork including site survey and mapping with transit, excavation and recording techniques, artifact identification, and preliminary artifact processing in the field laboratory.

ILLINOIS
Location: Will County, Near Wilmington
Site: Custer Park Site
Period: Middle Woodland

Dates of excavation and field school: Session I: June 1–12, Session II: June 15–26, Session III: July 6–17
Application deadline: May 16. Registration is March 16–May 16.

Field School:
Academic credit: 1 credit per session from Governors State University, University Park, Illinois
Cost: Tuition ($87 per credit for Illinois residents, $261 per credit for non-residents) plus $35 equipment fee. Student responsible for all other expenses.

Volunteers:
Minimum age: 18
Experience required: None
Cost: Volunteer responsible for all expenses.

Program for Junior High and High School Students:
Minimum age: A special Junior High and High School section run by the local Grand Prairie Archaeological Society will be held concurrently with the excavation. Contact the Director for details.
Experience required: None
Cost: Volunteer responsible for all expenses.

Bibliography: On request, copies of local newspaper feature articles from the past three years of excavation at this site will be sent.

Director   Robert Gergen, 362 S. Main St., Kankakee, IL 60901, (815) 932-0146
Sponsors: Governors State University; Grand Prairie Archaeological Society; South Suburban Archaeological Society
Contact: Dr. A. Bourgeois
(708) 534-4012 or
FAX: (708) 534-7895
E-mail: a-bourge@govst.edu

This field school in archaeological methods and materials with investigate a 2000-year-old Havanna-Hopewell habitation site. Instruction will include surveying techniques, surface collection, excavation techniques, feature excavation, mapping, artifact identification, artifact analysis, laboratory processing, and cataloging directed

by professionally trained archaeologists. Sessions meet Monday through Friday from 8:00 am–12:00 noon. Excellent camping facilities are available through nearby Kankakee State Park.

INDIANA
Location: St. Joseph County, NW Indiana
Site: Bennac Village site (Roman Catholic settlement) and Goodall site (prehistoric habitation)
Period: Historic Pioneer (ca. AD 1840) and Middle Woodland (200 BC–AD 400)

Field School:
Dates: May 20–June 26
Application deadline: May 20 (Early enrollment encouraged.)
Academic credit: 6 semester hours (undergraduate or graduate) from University of Notre Dame
Cost: $1308 tuition and fees and all expenses except major equipment and supplies.

Director, Sponsor, and
Contact: Dr. Mark R. Schurr
Department of Anthropology
University of Notre Dame
Notre Dame, IN 46556
(219) 631-7638
FAX: (219) 631-4209
E-mail: Mark.R.Schurr.l@nd.edu
WWW: http://www.nd.edu/~mschurr

The field school is conducted as part of an ongoing study of the relations between agricultural intensification and social complexity in a temperate forest ecosystem over the last three millennia. This year's excavations will investigate the Goodall site, a Middle Woodland hamlet, and the Bennac Village site, an historic period "metis" (mixed Native American and French Roman Catholic) cabin site.

The Notre Dame archaeology field school teaches geophysical remote sensing techniques for site investigation and traditional field methods. The curriculum includes introductions to the use of a total station (laser transit) and equipment for magnetic and resistivity surveys. Student teams will learn how to operate the geophysical survey instruments, use the instruments to conduct geomagnetic and soil resistivity surveys, and produce maps of geophysical survey data. In addition to geophysical techniques, students will learn how to use surveying equipment to make an accurate site map, how to discover and record archaeological sites, how to conduct archaeological excavations, and how to process and analyze archaeological finds.

INDIANA
Location: Greene County
Site: Heaton Farm
Period: Late Prehistoric

Field School:
Dates: May 12–June 18
Application deadline: March 13
Academic credit: 6 undergraduate of graduate credits from Indiana University
Cost: Tuition varies depending on student status. Inquire for details. Program provides commute to/from site and major field equipment. Lodging, meals, insurance, and personal equipment not included.

Bibliography: Kellar, James H., *An Introduction to the Prehistory of Indiana*, Indianapolis: Indiana Historical Society, 1983. Redmond, Brian G., and Robert G. McCullough, "The Late Woodland to Late

Prehistoric occupations of central Indiana," ms. of paper presented at the Urbana Late Woodland Conference, March 1, 1997, University of Illinois, Urbana-Champaign.

Director: Christopher S. Peebles
Sponsor and
Contact: Glenn A. Black Laboratory of Archaeology
423 North Fess Street
Indiana University
Bloomington, IN 47405
(812) 855-9544
FAX: (812) 855-1864
E-mail: lbush@indiana.edu

This field school is an important part of the research program of the Glenn A. Black Laboratory of Archaeology at Indiana University. The site chosen for excavation is Heaton Farm, a multi-component habitation site in south central Indiana. Much of the 1998 field season will be devoted to completing excavation of two Late Prehistoric structures encountered in 1996 and 1997. The program emphasizes practical field experience and will cover archaeological survey, excavation techniques, and the preparation of field documents. A laboratory course emphasizing cataloging and analysis is offered in the eight weeks immediately following the field school.

KANSAS
Location: Meade County
Site: 14MD306 (tentative)
Period: Prehistoric, Middle Ceramic (AD 1000–1500)

Field School:
Dates: June 6–13 (tentative). A detailed announcement and application form will be included in the January/February issue of the *Kansas Preservation* newsletter. To be added to the mailing list, write to the Historic Preservation Office at the address listed below.
Application deadline: May 8 (tentative)
Academic credit: 1 credit from Emporia State University (optional)
Minimum age: 10. Children between the ages of 10–14 must work with a parent or sponsoring adult at all times; all those under 18 must be accompanied on the project by a legally responsible adult.
Cost: ca. $15 registration fee and all expenses.

Directors: Virginia A. Wulfkuhle, Martin Stein, Barry Williams
Sponsors: Kansas State Historical Society; Kansas Anthropological Association
Contact: Virginia A. Wulfkuhle
Kansas State Historical Society
Archaeology Office
6425 SW 6th Avenue
Topeka, KS 66615-1099
(913) 272-8681, ext. 268
FAX: (913) 272-8682
E-mail: vwulf@hspo.wpo.state.ks.us

The Kansas Archeology Training Program (KATP) is a cooperative effort of the Kansas State Historical Society (KSHS) and the Kansas Anthropological Association (KAA). The KATP offers participants an opportunity to learn archeological concepts and methods through hands-on experience and classroom instruction under the supervision of professional archaeologists from the KSHS. The 1998 program will investigate one or more prehistoric sites in southwest Kansas and will include block excavations, an artifact processing laboratory, formal classes, and an possibly archaeological site survey.

KENTUCKY
Location: Central Kentucky
Site: Various
Period: Paleoindian, Mississippian, Historic 19th century AD

Field School:
Dates: June 12–August 7
Application deadline: May 1
Academic credit: 3 or 6 credits from University of Kentucky
Cost: Tuition (varies) and all expenses except local commute. Write for details.

Bibliography: Brewer, Priscilla J., *Shaker Communities, Shaker Lives,* Hanover: University Press of New England, 1986. Stein, Stephen J., *The Shaker Experience in America,* New Haven: Yale University Press, 1992. Smith, Bruce, *Mississippian Emergence,* Washington, DC: Smithsonian Institution Press, 1990.

Directors: Richard Jefferies, Kim A. McBride, Leon Lane
Sponsor, and
Contact: University of Kentucky
Department of Anthropology
211 Lafferty Hall
Lexington, KY 40506-0024
(606) 257-2860

The University of Kentucky will conduct an eight-week summer archaeological field school at prehistoric and historic sites in central and southeastern Kentucky. The specific sites to be investigated have not been selected yet, but probably will include a restored Shaker village, a Mississippian village, and several rock shelters containing Archaic and Woodland components. Training in survey, mapping, archaeological testing, and full-scale excavation will be part of the program. Students will also learn preliminary artifact identification, cataloging, and analysis. Special projects may provide a introduction to the analysis of documentary records. Lectures and at least one field trip will round out the experience.

KENTUCKY
Location: Mammoth Caves National Park
Site: "Main Cave"
Period: Prehistoric–Historic

Volunteers:
Dates: Team I: July 12–21, Team II: July 22–31
Application deadline: 90 days prior to departure. (Applications will be accepted after that time if space is available.)
Minimum age: 16, however the Directors do not encourage teenagers to participate unless they are accompanied by an adult.
Experience required: None, but physical agility is important and those with a tendency towards claustrophobia should not participate. Volunteers should be prepared to walk with heavy loads and be able to spend up to eight hours at a time in underground passages. Previous spelunking experience is helpful. Individuals who enjoy attention to detail and precision, and who have secretarial, artistic, engineering, photography, and surveying skills welcome.
Cost: $695 covers all expenses except travel to staging area (Nashville, Tennessee) and insurance.

Director: George Crothers, Washington University; Robert Ward, US National Park Service
Sponsor and
Contact: Earthwatch
See page 7 for contact information.

More than 100 years of archaeological investigations demonstrate that people have been using Mammoth Cave for varied purposes for almost 4000 years. Historic structures, prehistoric features, "in situ" artifacts, and possibly human burials are located along tour trails and viewed by over 500,000 visitors annually. This project will document the location and condition of the cultural resources within the toured portions of Mammoth Cave and on the surface area in the vicinity of the cave entrance.

MAINE
Location: Cushing
Site: St. George River Historic Archaeological Survey
Period: Early 17th century–early 18th century

Volunteers/Field School: The 1998 field season will permit only a very few volunteers, but a larger work force is anticipated for 1999.
Dates: June 15–July 24
Application deadline: March 31
Minimum age: 17
Experience required: Some familiarity with archaeological field techniques desired; training in historical archaeology preferred.
Academic credit: Optional 3–6 undergraduate or graduate credits from the University of Maine.
Cost: Program provides lodging, week-day meals, and local commute. Travel to Maine, weekend meals, and insurance not included. For those desiring credit, the following tentative fee schedule applies: $30 registration fee; $119 per credit (undergraduate) or $179 per credit (graduate) for Maine residents; $337 per credit (undergraduate) or $506 per credit (graduate) for non-residents.

Bibliography: Deetz, James, *In Small things Forgotten*. Faulkner, Alaric, *The French at Pentagoet*. Hume, Ivor Noel, *Artifacts of Colonial America*.

Director, Sponsor, and
Contact: Alaric Faulkner
           Department of Anthropology
           University of Maine
           South Stevens 5773
           Orono, ME 04469-5773
           E-mail: faulkner@maine.maine.edu

The 1998 St. George River Historic Archaeological Survey will concentrate testing efforts on two important 17th-century locations on the frontier between New England and Acadia. The settlement of Saquid on Pleasant Point is believed to have been homesteaded by an English family by the name of Foxwell in the early 1630s and subsequently taken over by French entrepreneur Charles D'Aulnay in 1635. Also to be tested is a huge, unidentified storage cellar. This secluded cellar, apparently a company storehouse for wintering over, was first noted as being in ruins as early as 1735 and remains essentially as it was last described in 1873.

MARYLAND
Location: Annapolis
Site: Various
Period: 17th century–present

Field School:
Dates: June 1–July 10
Application deadline: May 1
Academic credit: 6 undergraduate or graduate credits from the University of Maryland
Cost: Tuition: $1176 (undergraduate) or $1778.50 (graduate) for Maryland residents, $2730 (undergraduate) or $2546.50 (graduate) for non-residents; ca. $85 fee; and all other expenses.

Volunteers:
Dates needed: June 10–July 11
Application deadline: Open
Minimum age: 13
Experience required: None
Cost: Volunteer responsible for all expenses.

Bibliography: Leone, Potter, and Shackel, "Toward a Critical Archaeology," *Current Anthropology*. 28:3, pp. 283–302. Shackel, Paul A., and Barbara J. Little (eds.), *Historical Archaeology of the Chesapeake*, Washington, DC: Smithsonian Institution Press, 1994. Shackel, Paul A., *Personal Discipline and Material Culture: An Archaeology of Annapolis, Maryland 1695-1870*, Tennessee: University of Tennessee Press, 1993.

Director: Dr. Mark P. Leone
Sponsors: University of Maryland, College Park; Historic Annapolis Foundation
Contacts:
For more information:
           Dr. Mark P. Leone, Jessica Neuwirth, or Eric Larsen
           University of Maryland
           Department of Anthropology
           1111 Woods Hall
           College Park, MD 20742
           (301) 405-1423
For registration forms:
           University of Maryland
           Office of Continuing Education
           Summer and Special Programs
           Reckord Armory
           College Park, MD 20742
           800-711-UMCP or (301) 405-1423

1998 marks the University of Maryland's 17th season of excavation in historic, urban Annapolis. In continuing its emphasis on the role of archaeology in contemporary society, the 1998 field school will carry on with the long-term investigation of the city's African-American past. Excavations will focus on one or more distinct households within the historic district to explore the variety of African-American life within the city and to examine the development of neighborhoods over the 19th and 20th centuries.

The field school is an intensive six-week program, devoting eight hours daily to archaeological field and laboratory work. Participants will be introduced to techniques commonly used in historical archaeology, including surveying with a transit, laying out excavation units, excavation with shovels and trowels, mapping, drawing, field photography, and note taking. At the project's laboratory students will be instructed in artifact identification and processing (with emphasis on ceramics and glass) and basic data entry procedures. In addition to fieldwork, students will engage in discussions through weekly readings and lectures as well as site tours around Annapolis.

MARYLAND
Location: Dorchester County
Site: Chicone Indian Town
Period: 17th–18th centuries AD

Field School:
Dates: May 27–June 30
Application deadline: March 15

Academic credit: 4 credits from Washington College. Credit is transferable to other institutions.

Prerequisites: Prior coursework in Anthropology or American colonial history is preferred, but not mandatory. The ability to carry out sustained physical activity is mandatory.

Cost: $900 for tuition. On-site lodging is ca. $100. Meals (cooking facilities on-site) and transportation not included.

Director, Sponsor, and
Contact: Virginia Busby
        Washington College
        Department of Sociology and Anthropology
        300 Washington Ave.
        Chestertown, MD 21620
        (804) 977-8533 (in Virginia)
        E-mail: vrb5q@virginia.edu
            or
        Jeanette Sherbondy
        same address as above
        (410) 778-7761
        E-mail: jeanette.sherbondy@washcoll.edu

Chicone Indian Town is a 17th and 18th century Nanticoke Indian village site located along the Nanticoke River on Maryland's eastern shore. Chicone Indian Town was mapped by John Smith during his 1609 explorations of the Chesapeake Bay. The town served as the principal village of Nanticoke Indians and contained the palisaded residence of their "emperor" or chief during most of the Colonial period. Research is aimed at understanding transformations in the organization of the Nanticoke community and the village settlement pattern within the context of European contact and colonization. This summer's excavations will focus on two outlying house sites dating to the 17th century within the larger village landscape.

The course is designed to provide students with an introduction to theoretical concerns of anthropological archaeology and an in-depth understanding of field methods. The focus of the course will be on issues of Contact-period archaeology, and it will consist of lectures, readings, writing assignments, and archaeological survey, and excavation. Laboratory experience will also be provided, with students spending time each week processing and learning to identify artifacts. Field trips to other archaeological sites in the Chesapeake region as well as guest lecturers will complement the course content.

MARYLAND
Location: St. Leonard
Site: Jefferson Patterson Park and Museum
Period: Colonial

Volunteers:
Dates needed: Summer, Wednesday–Sunday
Application deadline: None, but pre-registration required.
Minimum age: 15 unless accompanied by an adult
Experience required: None, but must be willing to work outdoors.
Cost: Volunteer responsible for all expenses.

Bibliography: Pogue, Dennis, *King's Reach*. Available from JPPM Gift Shop, (410) 586-8501.

Director, Sponsor, and
Contact: Kirsti Uunila
        Jefferson Patterson Park and Museum
        10515 Mackall Road
        St. Leonard, MD 20685
        (410) 586-8555

Participants in the Jefferson Patterson Park and Museum Volunteer Archaeology Program will surface collect the untested portion of a field previously found to contain prehistoric and historic sites, and will conduct excavations on a colonial site. This site was probably associated with King's Reach, a plantation house occupied between ca. 1690–1715 that is located just a short distance away. Extensive excavations at the King's Reach site in the 1980s revealed the house of a well-to-do planter. The program will help answer research questions about the site and assist the museum in its development plans, but its primary focus is to train members of the public in the techniques of archaeology. Volunteers will learn how archaeologists find sites, and how they investigate and analyze the sites that are discovered. Participants will also get to work in the laboratory, cleaning and cataloguing artifacts.

MARYLAND
Location: Southern Maryland
Site: Historic St. Mary's City
Period: 1634–Present

Field School:
Dates: June 10–August 16
Application deadline: May 1
Academic credit: 8 credits from St. Mary's College of Maryland.
Prerequisites: Prior coursework is preferred but not required. The ability to engage in active physical labor is essential.
Cost: ca. $900 for tuition. Student responsible for all other expenses; housing is available at a reduced cost through St. Mary's College.

Director, Sponsor, and
Contact: Timothy B. Riordan
        Historic St. Mary's City
        P.O. Box 39
        St. Mary's City, MD 20686

Historic St. Mary's City is a state-supported, outdoor museum located at the site of Maryland's first capital. This year's excavations will be conducted at a multicomponent site known as the Nuthead Press Site (18 ST 1-14). The site includes one and possible two 17th-century structures. Testing in this area in 1992 revealed a pit filled with oyster shell which yielded over 20 lead printing types. This may be the location of William Nuthead's printing press established ca. 1686. The site also includes the remains of two 19th-century slave cabins.

The program is an intensive experience in colonial archaeology. The first week of the class is devoted to lectures on history, archaeological methods, and material culture studies. Students will learn artifact identification by working with one of the best archaeological collections of colonial material in the country. During the following nine weeks, students participate in excavation, recording, and analysis on site in an internationally famous archaeological district. Field trips to nearby archaeological sites are also planned.

MARYLAND
Location: Southern Maryland coastal plain
Site: Mount Calvert
Period: Multi-component prehistoric and historic

Position(s): Laboratory/Field Assistant
Dates needed: mid May–mid July
Application deadline: April 15
Experience required: BA in anthropology or related field. Work with volunteers and the public. Oral and written communication skills.
Salary: $4500
Cost: Program provides lodging, meals, and local transportation.

Volunteers:
Dates needed: 10 days in late May
Application deadline: May 1
Minimum age: 16
Experience required: None
Cost: Registration fee ($15 for Archaeological Society of Maryland members; $30 for non-members) and all expenses.

Bibliography: Dent, Richard J., *Chesapeake Prehistory: Old Traditions, New Directions*, New York: Plenum Publishing, 1995. Shackel, Paul A., and Barbara J. Little (eds.), *Historical Archaeology of the Chesapeake*, Washington, DC: Smithsonian Institution Press, 1994.

Director: Donald K. Creveling
Sponsors: Archaeological Society of Maryland; Maryland National Capital Park & Planning Commission; Maryland Historical Trust
Contact: Tyler Bastian
                  Maryland Historical Trust
                  100 Community Place
                  Crownsville, MD 21032
                  (410) 514-7661

The Field Session in Maryland Archaeology is an annual event sponsored by the Archaeological Society of Maryland under the guidance of the staff of the State Office of Archaeology and other professional archaeologists. The purpose of the field session is to train lay persons in archaeological methods through hands-on involvement while making meaningful contributions to the study of Maryland archaeology. The 28th Annual Field Season will be held at Mount Calvert on the Patuxent River. A tobacco plantation and farm since the 1720s, Mount Calvert is the site of an earlier Colonial port and government center as well as multiple prehistoric Native American occupations. Volunteers will participate in surface collection, shovel test pitting, unit excavation, processing and identification of artifacts, workshops in artifact identification, and attend lectures on the history and prehistory of the Patuxent River drainage. Volunteers may also have opportunities to participate in a nearby underwater archaeology project scheduled for the same time as the Field Session.

MASSACHUSETTS
Location: Ashburnham
Site: Shaker Farm and other 19th century sites
Period: Historical

Field School: In addition to the field school described below, there are special programs for children and families. Contact the Director for details.
Dates: One- and two-week sessions, June–August
Application deadline: May 15
Academic credit: 3 undergraduate or graduate credits from Fitchburg State College and others by arrangement.
Cost: $320 tuition, $585 for lodging and meals (participants are housed locally with families associated with the dig or the Museum), and $118 for optional weekend excursions to other New England archaeological and historic sites.

Sponsors: New England School of Archaeology; Fitchburg Art Museum; Ashburnham Historical Society
Director and
Contact: Dr. Peter Timms, Director
                  Fitchburg Art Museum
                  185 Elm Street
                  Fitchburg, MA 01420
                  (508) 345-4207

Located in a woodland setting, this early 19th-century site was used by the Harvard Community of Shakers to provide summer pasture for livestock and bark for tanning. Foundations and cellar holes of the barn, and residence and out-buildings are well preserved and rich in artifacts. Daily lectures on method, theory, and interpretation enrich practical field experience. Special topics include instrument survey, photography, and drafting. In the dig house, excavators process and preserve archaeological materials. Now in its sixth season, the Shaker Farm site is the first of four sites (others are a school, a mill, and a tavern) to be excavated in a planned long-term research project investigating 19th-century Ashburnham.

MICHIGAN
Location: Battle Creek
Site: Shepard Site (20CA104)
Period: 1830s–present

Field School:
Dates: May 4–June 24
Application deadline: March 15
Academic credit: 6 credits from Western Michigan University
Cost: Tuition varies according to student status. Inquire for details. Program provides local commute. Student responsible for all other expenses.

Volunteers:
Dates needed: May 4–June 24
Application deadline: April 15
Minimum age: 16
Experience required: None
Cost: Volunteer responsible for all expenses.

Bibliography: Nassaney, M.S., et al, *Archaeological and Historical Investigations in Battle Creek, Michigan: The 1996 Season at the Warren B. Shepard Site (20CA104)*, Archaeological Report No. 20, Department of Anthropology, Western Michigan University, Kalamazoo, 1997 (in press). Rotman, D.L., and M.S. Nassaney, "Class, Gender, and the Built Environment: Deriving Social Relations from Cultural Landscapes in Southwest Michigan," *Historical Archaeology* 31(7), 1997 (in press).

Director, Sponsor, and
Contact: Dr. Michael Nassaney
                  Department of Anthropology
                  124 Moore Hall
                  Western Michigan University
                  Kalamazoo, MI 49003-5032
                  (616) 387-3969
                  FAX: (616) 387-3999
                  E-mail: nassaney@wmich.edu

The 1998 Western Michigan University archaeological field school will continue excavations begun in 1996 at the Shepard site in Battle Creek. The site is associated with a brick Greek Revival House built in the early 1850s and occupied by Battle Creek's first school teacher, Warren B. Shepard. Previous investigations employed background research, geophysical survey, and subsurface testing to identify a range of 19th and early 20th century features and artifact deposits. Work proposed for 1998 will consist of more intensive work adjacent to the house and further efforts to locate and identify outbuildings that were associated with the farmstead.

Students will receive instructions in research design and the political economy of cultural landscapes in historical southwest Michigan. Training will focus on standard techniques of historical site excavation, as well as the processing, cataloging, and preliminary analysis of artifacts and feature data. Further geophysical survey may be conducted at nearby sites in conjunction with the southwest Michigan Historical Landscape Project which seeks to examine changes in the built environment and variations at the regional scale over the past 170 years of Euroamerican settlement.

MICHIGAN
Location: Mackinaw City
Site: Michilimackinac
Period: AD 1715–1781

Position(s): Crew
Dates needed: June 7–August 29
Application deadline: March 15
Experience required: Previous field experience
Salary: $6.45 per hour; 40 hours per week
Cost: Program provides discounted lodging. Employee responsible for all other expenses.

Volunteers:
Dates needed: June 21–August 22
Application deadline: March 15
Minimum age: 18 (14 if with parent)
Experience required: Duties will match previous experience. Volunteers are needed to interpret to park visitors, and public speaking skills are welcome. Those with no archaeological experience will be trained to assist the professional staff in water-screening deposit. Only those with previous excavation experience will be considered for volunteer excavator positions.
Cost: Volunteer responsible for all expenses except lodging.

Bibliography: Stone, Lyle M., "Fort Michilimackinac, 1715–1781: An Archaeological Perspective on the Revolutionary Frontier," *Anthropological Series*, Vol. 2, Michigan State University, E. Lansing, 1974. Heldman, Donald P., and Roger T. Grange, Jr., "Excavations at Fort Michilimackinac 1978–79: The Rue de la Babillarde," *Archaeological Completion Report Series*, No. 3., MISPC, Mackinac Island, Michigan, 1981. Halchin, Jill Y., "Excavations at Fort Michilimackinac, 1983–1985: House C of the Southeast Rowhouse, The Solomon-Levy-Parant House," *Archaeological Completion Report Series*, No. 11, MISPC, Mackinac, Island, Michigan, 1985.

Director, Sponsor, and
Contact: Dr. Lynn L.M. Evans
Mackinac State Historic Parks
PO Box 873
Mackinaw City, MI 49701
(616) 436-4225

The Mackinac Island State Park Commission has had an on-going archaeological program at Michilimackinac since 1959. The excavation takes place within the walls of reconstructed Colonial Michilimackinac, a state historic park with museum exhibits and costumed interpreters. The 1998 season will be the first at the South Southwest Row House since 1968. Returning to complete investigation of this house will allow the project to tie together data from two eras of excavation. The house was built in the 1730s and demolished when the garrison moved to Mackinac Island in 1781.

MICHIGAN
Location: Western Upper Peninsula
Site: Carp River Forge, or Fayette, or Fort Wilkins
Period: AD 1840s–1890s

Field School:
Dates: June 9–July 16
Application deadline: June 1
Academic credit: Variable; up to 9 undergraduate or graduate credits from Michigan Technological University
Cost: ca. $110 per credit in-state, $220 per credit out-of-state tuition, and nominal lab fees. Program provides local commute and lodging is subsidized. Meals not included.

Volunteers:
Dates needed: June 11-July 16. Minimum stay of one week.
Application deadline: May 1
Minimum age: 18
Experience required: None
Cost: Volunteer responsible for all expenses except local commute and partial lodging (subsidized by program).

Director, Sponsor, and
Contact: Dr. Patrick Martin
Social Sciences
Michigan Technological University
Houghton, MI 49931
(906) 487-2070
FAX: (906) 487-2468
E-mail: pem-194@mtu.edu
WWW: http://www.ss.mtu.edu/IA/iahm.html

The 1998 season marks the fifth year of a cooperative venture between the Industrial Archaeology Program at Michigan Tech and the Michigan Historical Center. This cooperative project provides research support for interpretation, preservation, and public education in the state, while offering opportunities for training participants in the methods and techniques of historical and industrial archaeology. Possible sites to be studied in the 1998 season include: Carp River Forge, the first iron-producing facility on Lake Superior, located in Negaunee; Fort Wilkins, the 1844 US Army post at Copper Harbor, on the tip of the Keweenaw Peninsula; and Fayette, an iron-smelting company town on Lake Michigan's Garden Peninsula, near Escanaba.

MINNESOTA
Location: Headwaters of the Mississippi
Site: Felknor
Period: 500–2000 BC (Ojibwe/Anishinabe)

Field School:
Dates: June 21–August 14
Application deadline: April 1
Academic credit: 6 credits from Hamline University
Cost: Tuition (to be determined) and $375 for lodging and most meals.

The program combines field training in archaeology with an introduction to Ojibwe (Anishinabe) culture and lifestyles. The archaeological component consists of training in survey, excavation, mapping, field recording, fine-scale recovery, and taking laboratory samples. The cultural component includes experimentation with flint knapping, digging clay and constructing clay vessels, basket making, hide tanning, collecting herbs and wild foods, and the construction and decoration of articles with porcupine quills and beads. Field trips to geological, archaeological, and cultural destinations emphasize the connection of sites and cultures to the landscape.

Teacher Workshop: Enrollment limited to 15. The target audience for this program are teachers of grades 3–12, especially in social studies, history, and cultural studies.

Dates: July 26–19
Application deadline: May 1
Academic credit: 3 credits from Hamline University
Cost: $471 covers tuition, and lodging and meals for five days at Hamline University's field camp.

"Immersion Archaeology for Teachers" will be conducted at Felknor site and provide teachers with hands-on experience at an excavation plus an introduction to traditional Anishinabe cultural practices through the study of ethnoarchaeology and practice of experimental archaeology. Teachers will explore the role of archaeology in the classroom and how to incorporate it into teaching plans.

Instructors: Field School: Dr. Christy Hohman Caine and Grant Goltz, Hamline University, and Sharon McKenna, Anishinabe teacher. Teacher Workshop: Phyllis C. Messenger, James Myster

Sponsor and
Contact: Hamline University
Anthropology Department
1536 Hewitt Avenue
Minneapolis, MN 55415
(612) 641-2247/2253
WWW: http://www.hamline.edu/depts/anthropology

The field school and teacher workshop take place as part of a long-term excavation at the Felknor site, an Ojibwe (Anishinabe) site occupied since ca. 2000 BC. Both programs consist of archaeological and anthropological components.

MINNESOTA
Location: To be determined
Site: To be determined
Period: To be determined

Position(s): Field supervisors and Field technicians
Dates needed: July–Fall
Application deadline: None
Experience required: Field supervisors: MA in anthropology, archaeology, history, or related field. Minimum of five years field experience, supervisory experience preferred. **Field technicians:** BA in anthropology, archaeology, history, or related field. Field school or commensurate experience. **Both:** Must have demonstrated ability and enjoyment dealing with people in general, school children, adult volunteers, and teachers. Experience in public archaeology is a definite asset.
Salary: Field supervisors: from $12 per hour and up, based on experience. **Field technicians:** $9–$12 per hour based on experience.
Cost: Employee responsible for all expenses.

Field School:
Dates: July and August
Application deadline: Inquire
Academic credit: 4–5 credits from University of Minnesota, Hamline University, Carleton College, or University of Wisconsin-River Falls
Cost: Tuition (to be determined) and all expenses.

Volunteers:
Dates needed: July and August
Application deadline: None
Minimum age: 10
Experience required: None
Cost: Volunteer responsible for all expenses.

Project Coordinator: Beth Nodland

Sponsor and
Contact: Institute for Minnesota Archaeology (IMA)
3300 University Avenue, SE
Suite 204
Minneapolis, MN 55415
(612) 627-0315
(612) 623-0177

The Institute for Minnesota Archaeology Public Archaeology Programs provides state-of-the-art field training in excavation techniques, site interpretation, artifact identifications, and public archaeology in both historic and prehistoric research areas. Contact the IMA for specific site and research information.

MISSISSIPPI
Location: De Soto National Forest
Site: Camp Danzler
Period: Late 19th–Early 20th century AD

Volunteers:
Dates needed: April 27–May 1, May 4–8. Must be able to stay for at least one full session.
Application deadline: February 15
Minimum age: 12, under 18 must be accompanied by adult.
Experience required: Ability to move dirt with shovels and trowels required, photography and mapping skills desirable.
Cost: Contact PIT for details.

Sponsor: USDA Forest Service
Contact: Passport in Time Clearinghouse (PIT)
See page 8 for contact information.

At the turn of the century, nearly 60 percent of all Mississippians worked in the timber business, either directly or indirectly. Scattered along the Illinois Central Gulf Railroad were dozens of logging mill towns. Camp Danzler was one of the early logging mill towns. Preliminary survey and excavation have revealed the possible locations of the mill, the turpentine-processing station, and the town where the loggers lived. In 1997, excavation in the African-American section of the town uncovered numerous artifacts, including toys, bottle glass, ceramics, and an old shoe. Excavation in this area will continue in 1998.

MISSISSIPPI
Location: Walls
Site: Woodlyn (22DS517)
Period: Woodland, Mississippian, Historic (19th and 20th centuries)

Dates of excavation and field school: May 11–July 3
Application deadline: April 15

Field School:
Academic credit: 6 undergraduate or graduate credits from The University of Memphis
Cost: Tuition: $554 (undergraduate), $876 (graduate) for Tennessee residents; $1860 (undergraduate), $2082 (graduate) for non-residents, and all other expenses.

Volunteers:
Minimum age: 18
Experience required: None
Cost: Volunteer responsible for all expenses

Bibliography: Dye, D.H., and C.A. Cox, *Towns and Temples Along*

the Mississippi, Tuscaloosa: University of Alabama Press, 1990. Morse. D.F., and P.A. Morse, *Archaeology of the Central Mississippi Valley*, San Diego: Academic Press, 1983. McNutt, C.H., *Prehistory of the Central Mississippi Valley*, Tuscaloosa: University of Alabama Press, 1996.

Director, Sponsor, and
Contact: Dr. David H. Dye
The University of Memphis
Department of Anthropology
Memphis, TN 38152-6671
(901) 678-3330
FAX: (901) 678-2069
E-mail: daviddye@cc.memphis.edu

For the second season, the University of Memphis field school returns to Woodlyn (22DS517), a multi-component site occupied during the Woodland and Mississippian Periods. The 1998 field school will focus on a late Mississippian house discovered during the first field season. Students receive instruction and experience in field excavation techniques, surface collecting, mapping, photography, and laboratory techniques. In addition, additional education is provided in the skills necessary to the field of contract archaeology. Students learn how to conduct Phase I surveys, respond to Requests for Proposals, and survey sites.

MISSOURI
Location: St. Louis County
Site: Fort Bellefontaine
Period: AD 1805–1826

Field School:
Dates: June 1–July 10
Application deadline: May 15
Academic credit: 6 undergraduate or graduate credits from the University of Missouri, St. Louis. Teachers may earn graduate credit in anthropology in two related courses: "Archaeology of Missouri for Teachers" and "Cultural Diversity for Teachers."
Requirements: Must be able to engage in strenuous activity in the heat; a doctor's statement must be included with application.
Cost: Tuition: $748.80 undergraduate, $947.40 graduate, $595 non-credit and all other expenses.

Director: Van Reidhead
Sponsor, and
Contact: Lynn Davis
Department of Anthropology
University of Missouri, St. Louis
8001 Natural Bridge
St. Louis, MO 63121-4499
(314) 553-6020

Built in 1805, Fort Bellefontaine was the first American fort west of the Mississippi. Commissioned early in Thomas Jefferson's presidency, it was his first garrisoned outpost in the newly purchased Louisiana Territory. The fort featured prominently in the country's westward expansion. Lewis and Clark, among others, left from the fort on their expedition up the Missouri River. The fort was moved to Jefferson Barracks in 1826, after which the site was occupied by farmers. In 1909, it was sold to the City of St. Louis for the construction of the Missouri Hills Home for boys and has been maintained in that capacity ever since. The goals of the investigation are to corroborate the archival documentation of the fort, to establish a chronology of the various historic occupations, and to assemble a cultural history

of the interaction between the fort and Missouri farmsteads in the early 1900s.

The focus of the last five field seasons has been to locate the perimeter of the fort and any remaining foundations. An intact cellar has been uncovered, along with indications of associated building foundations that appear to be part of the fort. In 1997, a large multi-room structure was partially excavated. In 1998, excavations will focus on the areas near the cellar and the continued excavation of the multi-room structure. Participants will gain experience in basic excavation techniques, mapping, recording, photography, laboratory techniques, and the analysis and identification of early 19th century cultural materials. A field trip to another fort site is planned.

NEBRASKA
Location: Bellevue, greater Omaha area
Site: Fontenelle Forest
Period: AD 1000–1400

Field School:
Dates: June 1–July 24
Application deadline: April 1
Academic credit: 9 credits from the University of Nebraska-Lincoln
Cost: Contact the University of Nebraska for information on registering for credit hours and current tuition. Program provides lodging, meals, and local commute. Students must provide their own camping gear and personal excavation equipment. Details provided upon application.

Volunteers:
Dates needed: June 1–July 24. Minimum stay of 2 weeks.
Application deadline: April 15
Minimum age: Inquire
Experience required: None
Cost: Program provides lodging at a local campground (volunteers must provide their own camping equipment), meals, and local commute. Travel to Nebraska and insurance not included.

Bibliography: *Nebraska History Magazine* 75(1), 1994, chapters 10 and 11. Blakeslee, Donald J., "A Model for the Nebraska Phase," *Central Plains Archaeology* 2(1), 1990, pp. 29–56. Gradwohl, David M., *Prehistoric Villages in Eastern Nebraska*, Nebraska State Historical Society Publications in Anthropology No. 4, Nebraska State Historical Society, Lincoln, 1969.

Sponsor: University of Nebraska-Lincoln; Fontenelle Forest
Director and Volunteer
Contact: Eric Kaldahl
Department of Anthropology
University of Arizona
Tucson, AZ 85721
(520)-318-0638
FAX: (520)-621-2088
E-mail: ekaldahl@u.arizona.edu

Field School
Contact: University of Nebraska
Department of Anthropology
Lincoln, NE 68588
(420)-472-2411
FAX: (420) 472-9642

The Fontenelle Forest Research project involves the excavation of five earthlodges associated with the Nebraska phase. The Nebraska phase consists of small-scale farming villages which occupied the wooded river valleys of eastern Nebraska, western Iowa, and northeastern Kansas from AD 1000–1400. The project seeks to understand the development of earthlodge clusters and to pursue questions of household and social changes which developed throughout the life history of site occupations.

NEVADA
Location: Huntington Valley
Site: Jacobs Well Pony Express
Period: AD 1860s–1880s

Field School: Limited to 15 students.
Dates: July 13–August 13
Application deadline: June 1
Academic credit: 6 credits from the University of Nevada, Reno
Cost: $900 covers tuition, lodging at field camp, and meals during days in the field. Travel to Reno not included.

Director, Sponsor, and
Contact:　　Dr. Donald L. Hardesty
　　　　　　　University of Nevada, Reno
　　　　　　　Department of Anthropology
　　　　　　　Mail Stop 096, 1664 N. Virginia Street
　　　　　　　Reno, NV 89557-0006
　　　　　　　(702) 784-6704
　　　　　　　E-mail: hardesty@scs.unr.edu

The University of Nevada, Reno, field school in historical archaeology will continue the excavation of the Jacobs Well pony express and overland stage station in eastern Nevada's Huntington Valley. Excavations at the site in 1995, 1996, and 1997 located the remains of several buildings, a blacksmithing facility, a well, and a charcoal making facility. Students will be taught the practice and theory of fieldwork in historical archaeology, including site survey, mapping, excavation, recording, and field laboratory processing.

NEVADA (and California and Oregon)
Location: Northwestern Great Basin including portions of Nevada, Oregon, and California
Site: Various
Period: 6500–11,000 BP

Field School: Enrollment limited to 12 advanced undergraduate students, graduate students, or professionals with previous archaeology or geology experience.
Dates: May 25–June 30
Application deadline: May 1
Academic credit: 6 undergraduate or graduate credits from the University of Nevada, Reno.
Cost: $1550 covers tuition, fees, and meals. Travel to Reno not included.

Director, Sponsor, and
Contact:　　Don D. Fowler
　　　　　　　University of Nevada
　　　　　　　Department of Anthropology
　　　　　　　Mail Stop 096, 1664 N. Virginia Street
　　　　　　　Reno, NV 89557-0006
　　　　　　　(702) 784-6969
　　　　　　　E-mail: sundance@scs.unr.edu

The program will emphasize the application of basic principles of geology and geomorphology to archaeological problems and, where possible, will be integrated with on-going archaeological investiga-

tions. Instruction involves problem-oriented, in-field examination of specific localities, supplemented by lectures. Topics of instruction include: process geomorphology; recognition and analysis of large- and small-scale land forms; depositional environments and associated sediments; paleoenvironments; stratigraphic relationships; formational and transformational processes unique to specific depositional and geomorphic settings; artifact modification; criteria for distinction between natural and cultural features; in-field development of geologic/geomorphic histories of archaeological sites; criteria for evaluation of archaeological site integrity; geoarchaeological interpretations; and the use of geomorphic and paleoenvironmental data for interpretation and evaluation of site location criteria. Students will be required to maintain field notebooks and prepare reports on individual projects.

NEW HAMPSHIRE
Location: Coos County
Site: Israel River Complex
Period: Paleoindian

Dates of excavation and field school: June 22–July 31 (three 2-week sessions). Individuals may participate for the full six weeks of the field school, however, a minimum two-week commitment is required.
Application deadline: May 29

Field School:
Academic credit: 2–6 undergraduate or graduate credits from Plymouth State College
Cost: $175–$205 per credit tuition (depending on residency and student status) and all expenses except local commute. Local accommodations will be made available at an economical rate.

Volunteers:
Minimum age: 16
Experience required: None, but familiarity with stone tools and manufacturing debris, land survey and mapping skills, and graphic arts experience welcome.
Cost: Volunteer is responsible for all expenses except local commute. Local accommodations will be made available at an economical rate.

Bibliography: Carty, Frederick, and Arthur Spiess, "The Neponset Paleoindian Site in Massachusetts, *Archaeology of Eastern North America*," Vol. 20, 1992, pp. 19–37. Curran, Mary Lou, "New Hampshire Paleo-Indian Research and the Whipple Site," *The New Hampshire Archeologist*, Vol. 33/34, 1994, pp. 29–52. Gramly, R. Michael, "The Vail Site: A Paleo-Indian Encampment in Maine," *Bulletin of the Buffalo Society of Natural Sciences*, Vol. 30, 1982. Spiess, Arthur, and Deborah Brush Wilson, *Michaud: A Paleo-Indian Site in the New England-Maritimes Region*, Occasional Publications in Maine Archaeology 6, 1987.

Sponsors:　　NH Division of Historical Resources; Institute for NH Studies, Office of Continuing Education, Plymouth State College
Director and
Contact:　　Dr. Richard A. Boisvert
　　　　　　　NH. Division of Historical Resources
　　　　　　　PO Box 2043
　　　　　　　Concord, NH 03302-2043
　　　　　　　(603) 271-6433

The New Hampshire State Conservation and Rescue Archaeology Program (SCRAP) is dedicated to the education and involvement of avocational archeologists in the archaeology of New Hampshire and is designed for both neophytes and experienced volunteers. The

SCRAP Summer Field School is run in conjunction with the Plymouth State College Summer Field School and provides for interaction between avocational volunteers and academic students. All participants receive instruction on proper field and laboratory methods. Academic students also attend seminar discussions and do projects relevant to the field school objectives and drawn from their own skills and interests; past projects have included analytical papers, photo essays, lesson plans, and museum exhibits.

The 1998 field school will focus on a group of Paleoindian sites identified as the Israel River Complex. The complex is significant because of its potential to provide data on the earliest peopling of this region and to expand the understanding of inter-regional interaction through analysis of the patterns of raw material utilization and stylistic/technological variation of the lithic assemblage. To date three sites have been recorded and additional sites are anticipated as reconnaissance continues. Rescue efforts will be conducted as needed on portions of other Paleoindian sites in the complex.

NEW HAMPSHIRE
Location: On Great Bay in Newmarket
Site: Gray (NH40-25)
Period: Late Archaic–Late Woodland

Dates of excavation and field school: July 1–30
Application deadline: June 19

Field School:
Academic credit: 4 credits from Franklin Pierce College
Cost: $195 per credit tuition, $100 equipment fee, and all other expenses except local commute and insurance.

Volunteers:
Minimum age: 17
Experience required: None, but note-taking and general writing skills preferred.
Cost: Volunteer responsible for all expenses except local commute.

Bibliography: Hecker, Howard M., "Jasper Flakes and Jack's Reef Points at Adams Point: Speculations on Interregional Exchange in Late Middle Woodland Times in Coastal New Hampshire," *The New Hampshire Archaeologist*, Vol. 35, No. 1, 1995, pp. 61–83; in preparation: *A Preliminary Report on the 1997 Excavation Season at Gray's Point (NH40-25) in Newmarket, NH*. Snow, Dean R., *The Archaeology of New England*, New York: Academic Press, 1980.

Director, Sponsor, and
Contact: Howard M. Hecker, PhD
             Anthropology Department
             Franklin Pierce College
             College Road, PO Box 60
             Rindge, NH 03461-0060
             (603) 899-4260
             After May 17: (603) 659-3221

Since 1992, the Great Bay Archaeological Field School Project of Franklin Pierce College has been engaged in the survey and excavation of three prehistoric Woodland-age sites on Adams Point on the western side of Great Bay. These sites are located in an estuarine environment and consist of concentrations of lithic and ceramic artifacts in addition to the midden remains from the exploitation of shellfish (oyster and clam) and terrestrial mammals (deer, beaver, raccoon, etc.). However, because of the absence of an Archaic and early Woodland age presence on Adams Point, a survey was conducted in 1997 to locate sites dating to these periods. One promising

site was identified (the Gray Site) and a small excavation was initiated. The site appears to be a complex multi-component site, and artifactual remains so far recovered show that the prehistoric occupants were heavily engaged in the reduction of milky quartz since this raw material represents well over 90% of the debitage recovered. The plans for the 1998 season are to delimit the extent of the Archaic component, to define the main Woodland-age habitation area(s), and to collect more information on subsistence activities.

Students will receive instruction in archaeological field methods including survey techniques, mapping, laying out a site grid, and formal excavation. In the laboratory, students will begin the preliminary processing of recovered artifacts, which involves materials analysis, measurement taking, artifact drawing, and photography.

NEW JERSEY
Location: Little Silver, Monmouth County
Site: Parker Farm
Period: 17th–19th centuries AD

Dates of excavation and field school: Saturdays, May 16–June 27
Application deadline: May 14

Field School:
Academic credit: 3 credits from Monmouth University
Cost: $1152 tuition and $35 summer session fee. Student responsible for all other expenses.

Volunteers:
Minimum age: 16
Experience required: None
Cost: $50 for training and $10 per day materials fee. Volunteer responsible for all other expenses.

Bibliography: Deetz, James, *In Small Things Forgotten: An Archaeology of Early American Life*, Doubleday, New York, 1996. Noel Hume, Ivor, *A Guide to the Artifacts of Colonial America*, Alfred Knopf, New York, 1970. Wacker, Peter O., and Paul G. Clemens, *Land Use in Early New Jersey: A Historical Geography*, New Jersey Historical Society, Newark, 1995.

Director, Sponsor, and
Contact: Richard Veit
             Monmouth University
             Department of History and Anthropology
             400 Cedar Avenue
             West Long Branch, NJ 07764-1898
             (908) 571-3440, ext. 2099
             E-mail: rveit@mondec.monmouth.edu

This will be Monmouth University's second season of excavations at the Parker Farm. The house purportedly dates to 1667, making it the oldest house in Little Silver, and one of the oldest standing structures in Monmouth County. The farm was established by Joseph and Peter Parker, two Quakers from Portsmouth, Rhode Island. Their descendants would continue to farm the land for the next 328 years. In 1995, Julia Parker left the farm to the Borough of Little Silver, which hopes to develop it into a museum. Excavations carried out in 1998 will focus on two topics: 1) identifying archaeological deposits around the house, and 2) determining the age of the structure. Previous excavations have revealed deposits dating from both the 18th and 19th centuries. In order to understand the house and archaeological deposits in their cultural context, a variety of other local historic sites will be visited. Volunteers are welcome.

NEW JERSEY
Location: Northern New Jersey
Site: Three sites to be determined
Period: Archaic/Woodland, Late Woodland/Contact, Historic

Field School:
Dates: May 26–June 19
Application deadline: April 15
Academic credit: 6 undergraduate or graduate credits from Montclair State University. Non-credit applications by special arrangement.
Cost: ca. $600 undergraduate tuition and $700 field school fee. (Graduate tuition information available upon request.) Lodging available at additional cost. Meals, insurance, and travel expenses are the responsibility of the student.

Director, Sponsor, and
Contact: Dr. Stanley L. Walling
           Montclair State University
           Center for Archaeological Studies
           104 Dickson Hall
           Upper Montclair, NJ 07043
           (973) 655-5164
           E-mail: Walling@saturn.montclair.edu
              or
           Matthew S. Tomaso, Coordinator
           (address same as above)
           973-655-7990
           E-mail: Tomasom@alpha.montclair.edu
           WWW: http://www.shss.montclair.edu/anthro/
              archflds.html

The Montclair State University Center for Archaeological Studies Field School provides intensive training in a wide variety of archaeological field techniques and experiences at diverse research environments, including at least one prehistoric site and at least one historic project per year. Depending on the needs of the projects and the students, training is provided in mapping and surveying, intensive and test excavation, general reconnaissance, controlled surface collection, and archival and documentary research. In 1998, the program will continue its focus on historic and prehistoric mining and quarrying sites, Contact Period economics, and geoarchaeology.

NEW MEXICO
Location: Bernalillo County, near Albuquerque
Site: LA 162 (Paa-ko)
Period: Rio Grande Classic and Historic (AD 1300–1675)

Field School:
Dates: June 21–July 31
Application deadline: April 25
Academic credit: 2 or 3 quarter courses from the University of Chicago
Cost: ca. $1500 per course. Inquire for details.

Bibliography: Lambert, M.F., *Paa-ko: Archaeological Chronicle of an Indian Village in North Central New Mexico*, School of American Research, Monograph No. 19, Santa Fe, 1954. Lycett, M.T., "Spanish Contact and Pueblo Organization: Long Term Implications of European Colonial Expansion in the Rio Grande Valley, New Mexico," *Columbian Consequences, Volume I: Archaeological and Historical Perspectives on the Spanish Borderlands West*, D.H. Thomas (ed.), Washington, DC: Smithsonian Institution Press, 1989, pp. 115–125. Nelson, N.C., "Ancient Cities of New Mexico," *American Museum Journal*, 15, 1915, pp. 389–394.

Director, Sponsor, and
Contact: Mark T. Lycett
           Summer Archaeological Field Studies Program
           Department of Anthropology
           University of Chicago
           1126 East 59th Street
           Chicago, IL 60637

The 1997 University of Chicago archaeological and paleoecological field studies program will take place at LA 162 (Paa-ko), a pueblo site in the Middle Rio Grande Valley. This project centers on the changing relationships between demography, settlement, and economy following European colonization of the Rio Grande. Work will be based at a large pueblo settlement inhabited both before and after the arrival of Spanish colonists and missionaries. Long a subject of archaeological interest, large villages occupied at the time of European contact provide an opportunity to investigate cultural continuity and change through a well-preserved and diverse material record.

Students will receive training in surface documentation, transit mapping, excavation, artifact processing, and preliminary artifact analysis. Through evening seminars, guest lectures, and field trips participants will be given a background in archaeological, historical, and environmental studies in the North American Southwest, and be introduced to current research in southwestern archaeology.

NEW MEXICO
Location: Cibola National Forest
Site: Pit houses and pueblos on the Anasazi-Mogollon frontier
Period: AD 1000–1300

Volunteers:
Dates needed: May 4–8. Must commit to full session
Application deadline: February 15
Minimum age: 18
Experience required: Volunteers must be in good physical condition; mapping and photographic skills desirable.
Cost: Contact PIT for details.

Sponsor: USDA Forest Service
Contact: Passport in Time Clearinghouse (PIT)
           See page 8 for contact information.

One of the poorly understood areas in Southwestern archaeology is the contact zone between the prehistoric Mogollon and Anasazi culture areas. The project area is on the western fringes of the Gallinas mountains that border the San Augustin Plains. This area has traditionally been thought to have been occupied by peoples who exhibited a mixture of Mogollon and Anasazi attributes. Volunteers will assist archaeologists in exploring the foothills to locate prehistoric pueblo and pit-house sites that are believed to date from AD 1000 to 1300. Volunteers will also assist in documenting and mapping.

NEW MEXICO
Location: Jemez Mountains, near Bandelier National Monument,
Site: James Young Ranch
Period: Prehistoric–historic

Field School:
Dates: June 7–July 12
Application deadline: May 1
Academic credit: 6 undergraduate or graduate credits from the University of New Mexico.
Cost: ca. $87 per credit hour for undergraduates, $95 per credit hour for graduates, and $700 for lodging and meals.

Director: W.H. Wills
Sponsor and
Contact: Field School, Attn: Erika Gerety
Anthropology Department, Room 240
University of New Mexico
Albuquerque, NM 87131-1086
(505) 277-4524
E-mail: erika@unm.edu

The James Young Ranch was the location of the Canada de Cochiti land grant (AD 1722–1880) and the field school research program is centered on a long-term investigation of community evolution within the land grant. During the 1998 field session, survey of the James Young Ranch and excavation of 18th-century historic Hispanic land grant sites will continue. Students will be trained in archaeological field methods, including excavation, data recording, and interpretation. The field school places special emphasis on remote sensing techniques, including the use of proton magnetometers, aerial imagery, and Global Positioning Satellite methods for surveying. Day field trips are scheduled to nearby archaeological projects and a weekend field trip is scheduled for Chaco Canyon, New Mexico.

NEW MEXICO
Location: San Miguel County
Site: Tecolote Pueblo
Period: Anasazi, AD 1050–1250

Field School: Enrollment is limited to 10 students.
Dates: May 18–June 6
Application deadline: March
Prerequisites: Anthropology course or equivalent.
Academic credit: 4 semester hours from New Mexico Highlands University
Cost: ca. $70 per credit hour tuition (subject the change) and all expenses. Assistance in locating reasonably priced local housing is available.

Bibliography: Text: Dancey, William S., *Archaeological Field Methods: An Introduction*, Minneapolis: Burgess Publishing Co., 1981. General reading on Pueblo culture and the basic stages of Anasazi cultural rise and decline.

Director: Robert Mishler
Sponsor and
Contact: Robert Mishler or Blaire McPherson
Department of Behavioral Sciences
New Mexico Highlands University
Las Vegas, NM 87701
(505) 454-3283
FAX: (505) 454-3331
E-mail: bobmishler@venus.nmhu.edu

The New Mexico Highlands University 1998 Field School will be held at Tecolote Pueblo, a late Anasazi Pueblo on the Tecolote River, between Santa Fe and Taos. Students will be provided training in field excavation techniques and artifact analysis. Emphasis is on individual instruction and broad skill development. The fourth week of the program includes a camping tour of Anasazi sites in New Mexico and Arizona.

NEW MEXICO
Location: Santa Fe National Forest
Site: Gallina Cultural Site
Period: 11th–13th century AD

Volunteers:
Dates needed: May 18–23. Must commit to full season.
Application deadline: February 15
Minimum age: 18
Experience required: Sense of humor required; mapping, recording, and photography skills desirable. Work entails strenuous hiking and climbing steep slopes.
Cost: Contact PIT for details.

Sponsor: USDA Forest Service
Contact: Passport in Time Clearinghouse (PIT)
See page 8 for contact information.

Volunteers will relocate sites documented by previous survey. The sites are 11th–13th century towers, pit houses, and rough masonry block structures call "unit houses." In 1998 sites will be redocumented and previously recorded information will be updated.

NEW MEXICO
Location: Near Taos
Site: Pot Creek Cultural Site
Period: Ancestral Pueblo site, AD 1050–1250

Field School:
Dates: May 28–July 16 (tentative)
Application deadline: April 15
Academic credit: 6 or 9 credits from Southern Methodist University
Cost: $315 per credit hour tuition and $1813 fee for lodging, meals, and local commute from campus to site.

Bibliography: Adler, Michael, "Why is a Kiva? Archaeological Interpretation of Prehistoric Pit structures in the Taos Region, Northern New Mexico," *Journal of Anthropological Research,* Albuquerque, Winter 1993. Crown, Patricia, "Evaluating the Construction Sequence and Population of Pot Creek Pueblo, Northern New Mexico," *American Antiquity,* 56, 1991, pp. 291–314. Woosley, Anne I., "Puebloan Prehistory of the Northern Rio Grande. Settlement, Population, and Subsistence," *The Kiva,* 51, 1986, pp. 143–164.

Director, Sponsor, and
Contact: Dr. Michael Adler
Southern Methodist University
Department of Anthropology
PO Box 750336
Dallas, TX 75275-0336
(214)-768-2684
E-mail: madler@mail.smu.edu
WWW: http://web.cis.smu.edu/~smutaos/potcreek.htm

Excavations will be conducted at Pot Creek Pueblo, a late prehistoric settlement at Fort Burgwin an interdisciplinary research and teaching facility located at 7500 feet in a mountain valley ten miles south of Taos. Extensive prehistoric ruins recorded to date attest to the early occupation of the area by Native American groups, with later occupations by both Hispanic and Anglo populations. Pot Creek Pueblo is one of the largest known late prehistoric settlements in the northern Rio Grande region and is presently being studied to better understand social and ecological conditions present during the prehistoric occupation of the Taos region. Excavations on the site will investigate prehistoric use of both domestic and sacred space during the process of population aggregation and village formation.

During the SMU Summer Field Program in Archaeology students will participate in research demanding a high level of responsibility in observing, recovering, and analyzing archaeological resources. Each student will receive training in a wide range of field methods, including archaeological survey, site excavation techniques, sampling strategies, data recording (including mapping and photography), laboratory processing and materials analysis, as well as interpretation and report preparation. In addition to excavation and survey experience, there will be evening lectures on Southwestern prehistory and archaeological methods and participants will take field trips to major archaeological areas in the Southwest.

NEW MEXICO

Location: West of Truth or Consequences
Site: Las Animas Village and two Palomas Hamlets
Period: AD 1000–1450

Field School:
Dates: June 8–July 10
Application deadline: March 9
Academic credit: 6 undergraduate or graduate credits from Arizona State University
Cost: ca. $598 tuition and $600 fee for lodging, meals, and local commute. Insurance and some weekend expenses not included. Students must provide their own tents.

Bibliography: Anyon, Roger, and Steven A. LeBlanc, *The Galaz Ruin: A Prehistoric Mimbres Village in Southwestern New Mexico*, Albuquerque: Maxwell Museum of Anthropology and University of New Mexico Press, 1984. Nelson, Margaret C. (ed.), *Ladder Ranch Research Project: A Report on the First Season*, Albuquerque: Technical Series of the Maxwell Museum of Anthropology, No. 1, 1984. Nelson, Margaret C., "Changing Occupational Patterns Among Prehistoric Horticulturalists in Southwest New Mexico," *Journal of Field Archaeology* 20, 1993, pp. 43–57. Nelson, Margaret C., "Classic Mimbres Land Use in the Eastern Mimbres Region, Southwestern New Mexico," *The Kiva* 58, 1993, pp. 264–279.

Directors: Drs. Margaret Nelson and Michelle Hegmon
Sponsor and
Contact: Arizona State University
Department of Anthropology
Tempe, AZ 85287-2402
(602) 965-6213
E-mail: MNelson@anthro.la.asu.edu
WWW: http://www.asu.edu/clas/anthropology

The Eastern Mimbres Archaeological Project (EMAP) is a multi-year research program investigating the Classic Mimbres and Postclassic occupations in southwest New Mexico. The project focuses on understanding processes of social and economic reorganization following the apparent abandonment of Classic Mimbres villages at AD 1150, and on subsequent re-aggregation at around AD 1300. Particular research topics include mobility and land-use strategies, ceramic production and exchange, architectural form, and regional interaction. 1998 fieldwork will include excavation at the site of Las Animas Village, survey along Las Animas Creek, and excavation at two small Classic Mimbres–Postclassic sites on Palomas Creek.

The field school is incorporated into the research project, giving students an opportunity to participate in the research process and to learn about its various aspects, ranging from research design to final publication. Students receive hands-on training in archaeological excavation, survey, artifact recording, and analysis, supplemented by evening lectures and some formal instruction. The project is located in a remote and beautiful setting along the drainages that flow from the Black Range into the Rio Grande; access to amenities is limited, but wildlife is abundant.

NEW YORK

Location: Ashland
Site: Thomas/Luckey
Period: Late Woodland Owasco (AD 1000–1300)

Field School:
Dates: May 26–July 3
Application deadline: None
Academic credit: 6 credits from Binghamton University.
Cost: Tuition (to be determined—1997 rates were $822 for New York residents, $2076 for non-residents) fees, small equipment, books, and all other expenses except commute from University to site and return.

Director, Sponsor, and
Contact: Laurie Miroff
Binghamton University
Department of Anthropology
PO Box 6000
Binghamton, NY 13902
(607) 777-2722
E-mail: be25800@binghamton.edu

The Late Woodland Thomas/Luckey site is an Owasco/Iroquois village, located along the Chemung River. The project represents a phase of a larger project designed to explore Iroquoian history along the "southern door" of Iroquoia. Students participating in the 1997 field school excavated a longhouse measuring 16 meters long and 6.5 meters wide. Associated with the longhouse were 50 features, including roasting pits, fire hearths, and deep storage pits. The 1998 field school will return to the site to further investigate Owasco-period community patterning. Areas around the longhouse will be examined for evidence of additional structures, activity areas, and a palisade wall. Students will receive training in basic field methods, including excavation, field photography, survey, and mapping. Lectures, scheduled for rain days, will provide background on Iroquois culture.

NEW YORK

Location: Bronx campus of Fordham University
Site: Rose Hill Manor
Period: AD 1694–1896

Volunteers:
Dates needed: ca. June–August
Application deadline: None
Minimum age: High school
Experience required: None
Cost: All expenses.

Bibliography: Melick, Harry C.W., *The Manor of Fordham and Its Founder*, New York: Fordham University Press, 1950. Taaffe, Thomas Gaffney, *A History of St. John's College, Fordham, N.Y.*, New York: Catholic Publication Society, 1891. Gannon, Robert I., S.J., *Up To the Present: The Story of Fordham*, Garden City: Doubleday, 1967. Literature on the excavation provided upon request.

Director: Dr. Allan S. Gilbert
Sponsor: Fordham University; Bronx County Historical Society
Contact: Department of Sociology and Anthropology
Fordham University
Bronx, NY 10458
(718) 817-3850

Fordham University occupies an 85-acre campus in New York's borough of the Bronx. When the school opened in 1841 as St. John's

College, the oldest building was reputed to be an old farmhouse with a history extending back into colonial times. The property was among the earliest in the central Bronx to be settled by Europeans. From 1694, it was deeded to a Dutchman, whose family maintained the farm for another two generations. After the Revolution, the last of the colonial owners was forced to flee as a Loyalist, and the new owner, a wealthy New York merchant named Robert Watts, christened the estate Rose Hill after the Watts family's ancestral home in Scotland.

By 1839, the property had been acquired by the New York Diocese with the goal of transforming it into a Catholic college and seminary. Wings had been added to the house by the Watts family, and major renovations were undertaken by the college in 1856 and the early 1880s, but structural problems brought about its demolition in 1896. Excavations since 1985 have uncovered parts of the east wing and center hall foundations, revealing several cisterns, paths, drywells, a coal bin, and a chronological sequence of mortars, stuccoes, restorable window panes, and nails that provide a glimpse of construction techniques in early houses in the New York area.

NEW YORK

Location: West of Cobleskill
Site: Haviland
Period: Early Archaic

Field School:
Dates: June 29–August 7
Application deadline: June 1
Academic credit: 1–4 from SUNY Cobleskill. Credits are based on modules of one credit per week. Non-credit modules are available through the Iroquois Indian Museum.
Cost: Tuition: $128 per credit for New York residents, $209 per credit for non-residents. Program provides insurance and local commute. Student responsible for all other expenses.

Bibliography: "The Haviland Site: The Early Archaic in Schoharie County," *The Bulletin* (Journal of the NYS Archaeological Association, Fall 1995).

Sponsor: Iroquois Indian Museum; Howes Cave
Director: Dr. John P. Ferguson
Social Sciences
SUNY Cobleskill
Cobleskill, NY 12043
(518) 234-5139
(518) 234-2276

Discovered in 1993, the site is a single component bifurcate and biface workshop, dating to 8200–9600 BP. The school will be taught by an anthropologist and an archaeologist, students will receive field experience along with laboratory and classroom work.

NEW YORK

Location: Cortland County
Site: 35 CO 30 and adjacent sites
Period: Late Archaic and Woodland, plus "mystery fish weir"

Dates of excavation and field school: May 21–June 24
Application deadline: Registration by April recommended.

Field School:
Academic credit: 6 semester hours of undergraduate or graduate credit from SUNY College at Cortland
Cost: Tuition (1998 rates to be determined) and all expenses except local commute (travel from campus to site), use of laboratory facilities, and field trips to other sites or museums. Students provide their own drinking water and lunch.

Volunteers: Volunteers will be accepted only if paid enrollments in the field school are able to support the program. Auditing the course for a nominal fee is an option.
Minimum age: 16
Experience required: None, but artistic, photographic, writing/ printing, mapping, computer, or other relevant skills welcome.
Cost: All expenses except local commute.

Bibliography: Articles in the *Bulletin and Journal,* New York State Archaeological Association, *Chesopiean, Man in the Northeast,* and *American Antiquity.* Ritchie, W.A., *Archaeology of New York State.* Funk, R.E., *Aboriginal Settlement Patterns in the Northeast.* Field school reports on 35 CO 30 prepared for the US Army Corps of Engineers by the field school Director (1993, 1996, 1997).

Sponsor: SUNY Cortland Summer School Program
Director and
Contact: Dr. Ellis E. McDowell-Loudan
Sociology/Anthropology Department
Box 2000, SUNY Cortland College
Cortland, NY 13045
(607) 753-2485
FAX (607) 753-5973
E-mail: LOUDANE@snycorva.cortland.edu

35 CO 30 is a multi-component site which does not appear to be stratified. There are several distinct loci where surface indications have revealed use by diverse prehistoric groups at different times— one area yielded soapstone fragments and rhyolite debitage, suggesting a Transitional component; several others yielded chert debitage, blackened soils, and large quantities of fire-altered rock, with small projectile points of Late Archaic types; another area revealed small fragments of prehistoric pottery, stone netsinkers, and chert debitage, and may relate to the Middle or Late Woodland periods. Offshore from the site, in the Otselic River, there is a stone structure, V-shaped, with the point of the V facing downstream. This structure appears to be the remnant of a fish or eel weir or trap. So far, the date for this structure is unknown.

The archaeological field school program contributes to the ongoing study of the prehistoric Archaic and Woodland cultural patterns of the area. Students participate in the Director's research and learn research design, site survey, mapping, recording, and excavation and laboratory techniques. Fundamentals of flotation, soil analysis, and lithic, floral, faunal, and ceramic analysis will be explained and applied to site study. Library and Internet research, as appropriate, will be used to supplement what the field and laboratory work reveal. Museum tours and lectures augment field and lab training.

NEW YORK

Location: Fort Edward
Site: Rogers Island
Period: French and Indian War (1755–1766)

Dates of excavation and field school: June 15–July 24
Application deadline: June 15

Field School:
Academic credit: 3–6 credits from Adirondack Community College, Bay Road, Queensbury, NY 12804, (518) 743-2236
Cost: $76 per credit hour for New York residents and $149 for non-residents, and all expenses except local commute and insurance.

Volunteers:
Minimum age: 18
Experience required: None
Cost: All expenses except local commute and insurance.

Bibliography: Cuneo, John R., *Robert Rogers of the Rangers*, Ticonderoga, NY: Fort Ticonderoga Museum, 1988. Hill, William H., *Old Fort Edward*, Fort Edward, NY: Privately printed, 1929. Starbuck, David R. (ed.), *Archaeology in Fort Edward*, Queensbury, NY: Adirondack Community College, 1995. Starbuck, David, "America's Forgotten War, *Archaeology* 50(1), January/February 1997, pp. 60–63.

Sponsor: Adirondack Community College; Town of Fort Edward
Director and
Contact: David R. Starbuck
              PO Box 147
              Fort Edward, NY 12828
              (518) 747-2926

Fort Edward and Rogers Island were used as a main base of encampment by the British throughout the French and Indian War. The Fort's construction began in 1755, at which time it was one of the first well-made British forts in North America. By the late 1750s it was the centerpiece of a complex of huts, barracks, and hospitals occupied by 16,000 British and Provincial soldiers. The 1998 field school will focus on huts and barracks sites on Rogers Island in the Hudson River. A full-time laboratory will be run in conjunction with the fieldwork.

NEW YORK
Location: Geneva
Site: Townley-Read/New Ganechstage
Period: AD 1710–1750 (Seneca Iroquois)

Field School:
Dates: July 13–August 21
Application deadline: Inquire
Academic credit: 4 credits from Columbia University
Cost: ca $2600 tuition and application fee, and ca. $300 for lodging and meals. Student must have medical insurance. Program provides local commute.

Director and
Sponsor: Dr. Nan Rothschild, Columbia University
Contact: Kurt Jordan
              (607) 387-5082
              E-mail: kj23@columbia.edu

This archaeological field school will be the first season of excavation at the Townley-Read /New Ganechstage site, a Seneca Iroquois village occupied from ca. AD 1710–1750. The field school will concentrate on the excavation and mapping of residential features in order to obtain information on the house forms and productive and consumptive activities practiced by Seneca households at the site. Very little residential archaeological data has been collected from 18th-century Iroquois sites, and the site presents an exciting opportunity to revisit Seneca community life during this period. The field school will incorporate a cultural program run by the descendants of the Senecas who lived at Townley-Read/New Ganechstage and involve the interpretation of geophysical data in addition to unit and feature excavation, surface collection, mapping, artifact processing, and preliminary analysis of archaeological remains.

NEW YORK
Location: Ithaca vicinity
Site: Carman Site and others
Period: ca. AD 1575

Field School:
Dates: June 8–July 20
Application deadline: May 5
Academic credit: 6 credits from the University of Pittsburgh
Cost: ca. $2000 covers tuition, lodging, meals, and local commute.

Bibliography: Trigger, Bruce, *Natives and Newcomers*, Montreal: McGill-Queen's University Press, 1985. Snow, Dean, *The Iroquois*, Cambridge, MA: Blackwell Publishers Inc., 1994. Bradley, James, *Evolution of the Onondaga Iroquois*, Syracuse, NY: Syracuse University Press, 1987.

Director, Sponsor, and
Contact: Dr. Kathleen M. Allen
              University of Pittsburgh
              Department of Anthropology
              3B13 Forbes Quad
              Pittsburgh, PA 15260
              (412) 648-7511

The Carman site is one of several late prehistoric/early contact period Iroquois village sites located west of Lake Cayuga. Shortly after this site was occupied, the population apparently relocated to the eastern side. Investigations at the Carman site have focused on identifying settlement patterns at this site and relating the occupation here to earlier and later ones in the area. The 1998 field school will focus on exposing additional longhouse structures on this site. In addition, other village sites in the region will be identified and tested for regional settlement pattern studies. Students will gain experience in surface collection, basic excavation techniques, site survey, on-site recording, and the identification, processing, and preliminary analysis of late prehistoric and early contact period cultural material.

NEW YORK
Location: Lake George
Site: Fort William Henry
Period: AD 1755–1757

Dates of excavation and field school: July 20–August 28
Application deadline: July 20

Field School:
Academic credit: 3–6 credits from Adirondack Community College, Bay Road, Queensbury, NY 12804, (518) 743-2236.
Cost: $76 per credit hour for New York residents and $149 for non-residents, and all other expenses except local commute and insurance.

Volunteers:
Minimum age: 18
Experience required: None
Cost: All expenses except local commute and insurance.

Bibliography: Cooper, James Fenimore, *The Last of the Mohicans*, New York: Penguin Books, 1850. Steele, Ian K., *Betrayals: Fort William Henry and the "Massacre,"* New York: Oxford University Press, 1990. Starbuck, David R., "Anatomy of a Massacre," *Archaeology*, Nov/Dec 1993, pp. 42–46. Starbuck, David R. "A Retrospective on Archaeology at Fort William Henry, 1952–1993," *Northeast Historical Archaeology*, Vol. 20, 1991, pp. 8-26.

Sponsors: Adirondack Community College; The Fort William Henry Corporation
Director and
Contact: David R. Starbuck
PO Box 147
Fort Edward, NY 12828
(518) 747-2926

Fort William Henry is best known as the site of the massacre in James Fenimore Cooper's novel, *The Last of the Mohicans*. However, it was an important frontier fort on the front line of British expansion into the interior of New York. Constructed in 1755, it was occupied by British soldiers and provincials until August of 1757, at which time it came under siege from an overwhelming force of French and Indians under the command of the Marquis de Montcalm. After a six-day bombardment, the 2300 British soldiers surrendered, and many were subsequently killed or taken prisoner by Native Americans once their column left the fort. The fort was then burned down and never rebuilt.

In the 1950s a group of businessmen bought the site, sponsored an archaeological excavation, and they reconstructed the fort on its original site. However, records have not survived that document exactly what was exposed or where. This is the second season of new excavations intended to locate areas that were not seriously disturbed during the 1950s excavation. The 1998 season will focus on part of the parade ground and dumps outside the east wall of the fort. Artifact processing will be conducted in a field laboratory at the fort.

NEW YORK
Location: Wayne County, North Rose
Site: Joel N. Lee Farmstead
Period: ca. AD 1827–1945

Field School:
Dates: 6 weeks in July–August
Application deadline: 2 weeks prior to start of program.
Academic credit: 3–6 credits from St. John Fisher College
Cost: Tuition (inquire for details) and all other expenses except on-site insurance.

Volunteers:
Dates needed: 6 weeks in July–August
Application deadline: None
Minimum age: 12 (6th grade)
Experience required: None, but interest in local history, patience, and a sense of humor helpful.
Cost: Volunteer responsible for all expenses except on-site insurance.

Bibliography: Morton, Ann, "J.N. Lee Farm Site, North Rose, Wayne Co., NY, Interim Report, 1995 Field Season," *Iroquoian*, 1997. Hubka, Thomas C., *Big House, Little House, Back House, Barn*, Hanover: University Press of New England, 1984.

Sponsors: St. John Fisher College;
Wayne County Historical Society
Director and
Contact: Dr. Ann Morton
Department of Anthropology
St. John Fisher College
3690 East Avenue
Rochester, NY 14618
(716) 385-8211
E-mail: morton@sjfc.edu

The Joel N. Lee farmstead is a very typical 19th-century rural

settlement site, and the work of the past seven field seasons have revealed significant information about the rural history of America. The 1998 season will again incorporate a full field school program with a public archaeology "camp" with students working together with interested volunteers, aged 12–80. Excavations will focus on the original well and possible associated buildings of the Lee farmhouse, on the barn/shelter occupied after the farmhouse fire of 1880, and on the "new" farmhouse. Participants will learn basic excavating techniques, soil analysis, site survey, on-site recording, and processing, identification, and preliminary analysis of material.

NORTH CAROLINA
Location/Site/Period: To be announced in January. There are several possibilities, including continued work on the Chesapeake Bay Flotilla dating to the War of 1812 and sunk in the Patuxent River in Maryland, a survey to find late 18th-century shipwrecks on the coast of Belize, and work on wrecks in North Carolina.

Field School in Maritime History and Nautical Archaeology
Dates: June 25–July 31
Application deadline: April 30
Academic credit: 2 semester hours from East Carolina University.
Prerequisites: All participants who plan to dive must have SCUBA certification and must complete the University's scientific dive training class, offered during the First Summer Session (May 19–June 22). There is an additional fee for this class. Inquire for details.
Cost: Tuition is to be determined (rates for 1997 were $256 for North Carolina residents and $1151 for non-residents). Lodging is provided in the field. There is a group meal plan while in the field for ca. $150. Lodging and meals in Greenville (including time spent for dive training) are the student's responsibility. Proof of health insurance is required.

Director, Sponsor, and
Contact: Dr. Lawrence Babits
Program in Maritime History & Nautical Archaeology
East Carolina University
Greenville, NC 27858
(919) 328-6097

Founded in 1981, the Program in Maritime History and Nautical Archaeology has a distinguished international reputation in the field. Faculty and students have pursued many premier projects around the world, including investigations of the USS *Monitor*, CSS *Alabama*, 16th-century sites in Bermuda, and the Yorktown Shipwreck Archaeological Project. The Program offers students a multidisciplinary curriculum, with hands-on experience to provide the broad background of expertise needed in this field.

The summer field school provides qualified students with a basic introduction to maritime history and the scientific methods and techniques employed in nautical archaeological research. Following the completion of scientific diver training, where students will be introduced to principles of nautical archaeological technique, participants will move to the field location. Students will participate in classroom lectures, workshops, and seminars. On-site activities provide practical experience in site-excavation techniques, underwater mapping, and documentation procedures. Non-diving students gain experience in historical research and artifact analysis.

NORTH DAKOTA (or South Dakota)
Location: Along the Missouri Trench
Site: Various
Period: Various

Position(s): 1 Lab Director, 2–3 Field Supervisors
Dates needed: July 31–August 10
Application deadline: July 22
Experience required: Field experience required. Ability to work well with others highly desirable.
Salary: Depends on experience.
Cost: Employee responsible for all expenses.

Volunteers:
Dates needed: August 1–9. Volunteers are expected to contribute a minimum of 8 hours but may elect to stay for the entire field session.
Application deadline: July 22
Minimum age: 16. 10–15 if with adult.
Experience required: None, but interest in archaeology.
Cost: Volunteer responsible for all expenses. Some free camping will be available.

Director, Sponsor, and
Contact: Ed Brodnicki
                US Army Corps of Engineers
                215 N. 17th Street
                Omaha, NE 68102
                (402) 221-4888

The Omaha District, Corps of Engineers, has held a volunteer archaeological program for the past 15 years. The goal of the program is to teach volunteers proper excavation and cataloging techniques while conducting needed work at an important site which is being damaged by erosion. Care is taken to select a site with good access and safe conditions. Field trips and other evening activities are also planned. Volunteers can participate in trips to museums, pow-wows, and tours of historic districts, and prehistoric or paleontological sites.

OHIO
Location: Northeast Ohio
Site: White Fort
Period: Woodland-Late Prehistoric (ca. AD 200-1600)

Field School:
Dates: Session I: June 15–July 3, Session II: July 7–24
Application deadline: Inquire.
Minimum age: 18
Academic credit: Optional. Credit available from Cleveland State University, College of Education; and Hiram College.
Cost: Museum membership ($25–$45), $250 tuition for each three-week session, and all other expenses. Cost of college credit is additional. Inquire for details.

Director, Sponsor and
Contact: Dr. Brian G. Redmond
                Dept. of Archaeology
                The Cleveland Museum of Natural History
                1 Wade Oval Drive, University Circle
                Cleveland, Ohio 44106-1767
                (216) 231-4600 x301
                FAX: (216) 231-5919
                E-mail: fieldschool@cmnh.org

The Cleveland Museum of Natural History's 1998 Field School in Archaeology will conduct survey and test excavations at a prehistoric Native American habitation site located in northeast Ohio. This site contains well-preserved remains of Woodland-period campsites and a possible late prehistoric village component that are thought to span the time interval between AD 200 and 1600. Students will receive training in archaeological field survey and excavation techniques as well as methods of data recording and artifact identification.

OKLAHOMA
Location: Western OK, near Elk City
Site: Certain (34BK46)
Period: Late Archaic ca. 2000 BP

Field School:
Dates: June 8–July 17
Application deadline: May 15
Academic credit: 1–6 credits from the University of Oklahoma
Cost: Tuition: $63.15 per credit for Oklahoma residents, $193.65 per credit for non-residents. Student responsible for all other expenses. Lodging is at a campsite and students must bring their own tents.

Bibliography: Bement, L.C., and K.J. Buehler, "Preliminary Results from the Certain Site: A Late Archaic Bison Kill in Western Oklahoma," *Plains Anthropologist* 39, 1994, pp. 173–183. Buehler, K.J., "Where's the Cliff?: Late Archaic Bison Kills in the southern Plains" in "Southern Plains Bison Procurement and Utilization from Paleoindian to Historic," L. Bement and K. Buehler (eds.) *Plains Anthropologist Memoir* 29(42), 1997, pp. 135–143.

Directors: Dr. Leland C. Bement and Kent J. Buehler
Sponsor: University of Oklahoma
Contact: Oklahoma Archeological Survey
                111 E. Chesapeake
                Norman, OK 73019
                (405) 325-7211
                E-mail: Lbement@ou.edu or kbuehler@ou.edu

The University of Oklahoma's 1998 archaeology field school will be held at the Certain site (34BK46) a late Archaic bison kill site containing multiple kill episodes. This will be the fourth season at the Certain site, and previous work has identified seven kill episodes and multiple processing areas. Main objectives of the project include identifying the number of kills at the site, the nature of these kills, processing techniques used, and identifying the culture or cultures responsible for the kills. The lithic assemblage includes projectile points, resharpening flakes, choppers, hammerstones, and bifacial knives. In addition to learning excavation techniques, each student will learn the use of mapping equipment including alidade, transit, and total mapping station; photography; lab techniques; and survey.

OREGON
Location: Fort Rock Basin, central Oregon
Site: Carlon Village
Period: Late Holocene (500–2500 BP)

Field School:
Dates: June 22–July 31
Application deadline: June 1 (Early application advised.)
Prerequisites: A serious interest in archaeology and the physical ability to work in the summer heat. Completion of a junior or senior level university course in geomorphology or soils with a grade of 'B' or better for the geoarchaeology course.
Academic credit: 8 credit hours from the University of Oregon
Cost: ca. $1750 covers tuition, lodging, meals, and local commute from University of Oregon to site. Travel to Oregon and insurance not included.

Directors: Dr. C. Melvin Aikens (Anthropology); Dr. Dennis L. Jenkins (Anthropology); Dr. Patricia McDowell (Geography)

Sponsor and:
Contact: Department of Anthropology
1218-University of Oregon
Eugene, OR 97403-1218
(541) 346-3026

The field school will continue research conducted by the Fort Rock Basin Prehistory Project since 1989. Excavations in 1998 will investigate the circumstances leading to the construction of eight large boulder-ringed houses located on a hilltop on the shore of a currently dry lake. Dating the structures, understanding the subsistence patterns associated with their occupation, and figuring out how the builders moved the large boulders, many of them weighing more than a ton, will be a major portion of the research effort. Vandalism has seriously disturbed most of these buildings, and returning them to their former shapes while attempting to stabilize and preserve them for future generations will complete the research effort.

A concurrent program in geoarchaeology is offered through the Department of Geography under the direction of Dr. McDowell. This course focuses on geomorphology and soils of semiarid landscapes, environmental change, description of cultural and non-cultural soil profiles, geomorphic stratigraphy, geomorphic mapping, and archaeological site-environment relationships. Students in this program also have the opportunity to learn basic techniques of archaeological excavation and survey.

OREGON
Location: Malheur National Forest
Site: John Day
Period: 19th–20th century

Volunteers:
Dates needed: April 1–May 31. Must commit to 5 days (weekends excluded).
Application deadline: February 15
Minimum age: 15. Under 18 must be with a responsible adult or have written consent.
Experience required: Computer skills desirable.
Cost: Contact PIT for details.

Sponsor: USDA Forest Service
Contact: Passport in Time Clearinghouse (PIT)
See page 8 for contact information.

Volunteers help to compile an inventory, index subjects, and start a computer database of the Malheur National Forest photo collection, which dates from the turn of the century to the present.

OREGON
Location: Siuslaw National Forest, near Hebo
Site: CCC Camp Nestucca
Period: AD 1930s

Volunteers:
Dates needed: April 20–24. Must commit to full session.
Application deadline: February 15
Minimum age: 18
Experience required: Surveying, mapping, photography skills desirable.
Cost: Contact PIT for details.

Sponsor: USDA Forest Service
Contact: Passport in Time Clearinghouse (PIT)
See page 8 for contact information.

The Civilian Conservation Corps (CCC) Camp Nestucca housed over 200 men during the 1930s. Volunteers will join the Hebo Ranger District Heritage Team to clear away the forest debris so that the site can be mapped, photographed, and evaluated. This is the third CCC-PIT project offered by the Siuslaw National Forest to honor the men and their contributions to preserving the coastal environment.

OREGON
Location: Umatilla National Forest
Site: Historic Records Curation in Pendleton
Period: early 20th century–WWII

Volunteers:
Dates needed: April 1–May 31. Must commit to 3 days (weekends excluded).
Application deadline: February 15
Minimum age: 18
Experience required: General familiarity with computers and willingness to work with old, dusty records desirable.
Cost: Contact PIT for details.

Sponsor: USDA Forest Service
Contact: Passport in Time Clearinghouse (PIT)
See page 8 for contact information.

The Umatilla National Forest files contain historical documents dating back 100 years. These records including photos, timber-sale contracts, grazing-permit correspondence, and other documents from the early part of the century up to World War II. Volunteers will document these records in a computer catalog system to allow the Forest Service and other researchers to easily access the information.

OREGON
Location: Umatilla National Forest, Pendleton
Site: Drift Fence Campground
Period: 4500 BP

Volunteers:
Dates needed: April 1–May 31. Must commit to 5 days (weekends excluded).
Application deadline: February 15
Minimum age: 13
Experience required: General familiarity with computers and measuring instruments desirable.
Cost: Contact PIT for details.

Sponsor: USDA Forest Service
Contact: Passport in Time Clearinghouse (PIT)
See page 8 for contact information.

The Drift Fence Campground is a rich prehistoric campsite that was occupied as long ago as 4500 years. PIT volunteers will help with the analysis of artifacts recovered from this site. Work will include washing and numbering artifacts and filling out forms with basic information on each artifact.

PENNSYLVANIA
Location: Allegheny National Forest, near Warren
Site: Various
Period: Middle Archaic-Late Prehistoric

Field School:
Dates: June 1–July 10
Application deadline: May 23

Academic credit: 3 or 6 credits from Mercyhurst College. Undergraduate, graduate, and qualified high school juniors and seniors are welcome to apply.

Cost: $25 registration fee and $627–$2286 (depending on grade level and number of credits) for tuition. Program provides lodging (camping), local commute, and on-site insurance. Meals not included.

Bibliography: 1995 Adovasio, J.M., and A.J. Quinn, "Test Excavations at 36WA132, Allegheny National Forest," 1995 (report prepared by Mercyhurst Archaeological Institute, Mercyhurst College, for the United States Forest Service). Adovasio, J.M., A.J. Quinn, and J.E. Thomas, "Archaeological Investigations at the Buckaloons (36WA132), Allegheny National Forest, Pennsylvania," paper prepared for the 61st Annual Meeting of the Society for American Archaeology, New Orleans, Louisiana, April 10–14, 1996.

Director: J.M. Adovasio
Sponsor and
Contact: Sue Prescott
Department of Archaeology and Anthropology
Mercyhurst College
Erie, PA 16546
(814) 824-2581

The 1998 Mercyhurst Archaeological Institute Field Training Program will involve survey and excavation in several sections of the Allegheny National Forest. The project will include a systematic Phase I survey of a ca. 10–12 acre portion of the forest which includes numerous sites spanning virtually the entire Holocene. The survey will feature piece-plotted data of literally all historic and prehistoric artifacts encountered by means of a Leitz Set II b2 infrared theodolite with integrated data logger. The project will also involve continued intensive excavation of a stratified Middle Woodland residential locus with Ohio Hopewell affinities and the continued testing of a series of stratified rockshelter sites whose occupation minimally spans the Middle Archaic through Late Prehistoric periods.

Students will be exposed to the latest methodologies in archaeology, geoarchaeology, excavation techniques, field and laboratory photography, mapping, laboratory procedures, artifact analysis, human osteology, computer applications, and many other techniques employed in contemporary archaeological and geoarchaeological excavations.

PENNSYLVANIA
Location: Bucks County, near Center Bridge
Site: Hendrick Island, in the Delaware River
Period: 3000 BC–European contact (possibility of earlier deposits)

Dates of excavation and field school: May 18-June 30
Application deadline: May 17

Field School:
Academic credit: 3 or 6 credits from Temple University
Cost: $196–$400 per credit tuition, depending on student status. Student responsible for all additional expenses, except field equipment. Travel arrangements and car pools will be arranged during initial class meetings on campus. There are a number of full-service campgrounds nearby.

Volunteers: Minimum stay of 3 days.
Minimum age: High school senior
Experience required: None, but must be willing to work outdoors.
Cost: Volunteer responsible for all expenses.

Bibliography: Course texts: Hester, Thomas, Harry Shafer, and Kenneth Feder, *Field Methods in Archaeology*, Mountain View, California: Mayfield Publishing Company, 1997. Sutton, Mark, and Brooke Arkush, *Archaeological Laboratory Methods: An Introduction*, Dubuque, Iowa: Kendall Hunt Publishing, 1996.

Director, Sponsor, and
Contact: Dr. Michael Stewart
Department of Anthropology
Temple University
Philadelphia, PA 19122
(215) 204-6188
E-mail: schurch@ushwy1.com

During investigations on Hendrick Island, students and volunteers will contribute to the study of Native American prehistory as they are trained in archaeological survey and site testing techniques. Hendrick Island is entirely wooded and is typically accessed via canoe. To date, three large prehistoric sites have been identified on the island. Artifact deposits are found on the surface and through five feet of buried deposits dating to about 3000 BC. Sites of an earlier age are anticipated to occur on the island and will be one focus of the ongoing survey. More detailed excavations will focus on previously identified sites. The sites include the remains of seasonal hunting, gathering, and fishing camps, and possibly agricultural farmsteads or villages. Although there will be some classroom meetings, the majority of time is spent outdoors doing fieldwork, and visiting other archaeological sites and the excavations of archaeologists working in the region.

PENNSYLVANIA
Location: Ephrata
Site: Ephrata Cloister
Period: Prehistoric; AD 1732–1813

Field School:
Dates: June 8–July 31
Application deadline: April 17
Academic credit: 6 or 9 credits from Elizabethtown College
Cost: $1350 (6 credits) or $1980 (9 credits) tuition, $1000 for lodging and meals, and all other expenses.

Bibliography: Alderfer, Everett Gordon, *The Ephrata Commune: An Early American Counterculture,* Pittsburgh: University of Pittsburgh Press, 1985. Reichmann, Felix, and Eugene E. Doll, *Ephrata as Seen by Contemporaries (Vol. 17)*, Allentown: The Pennsylvania German Folklore Society, 1953. Warfel, Stephen G., *Historical Archaeology at Ephrata Cloister* (a series of annual reports describing results of 1993–96 investigations), Harrisburg: Pennsylvania Historical and Museum Commission, 1993–1996.

Sponsors: The State Museum of Pennsylvania; Elizabethtown College; Ephrata Cloister Historic Site
Director and
Contact: Stephen G. Warfel, Senior Curator
Section of Archaeology
The State Museum of Pennsylvania
PO Box 1026
Harrisburg, PA 17108-1026
(717) 783-2887 (day); (717) 774-5559 (evening)

Founded in 1732, Ephrata Cloister was one of America's earliest communal societies and was well known throughout the Colonies for its production of high-quality paper and printed goods, fraktur (finely lettered manuscripts), musical composition, and mystical literature.

Preserved and interpreted in commemoration of the Penn government's dedication to religious freedom and diversity, the Cloister contains 11 original buildings, including some of unique medieval style. Ongoing archaeological research is designed to discover and mark the location of former structures, determine their age and function, and re-interpret lifestyles of community members. This research also seeks to better understand the nature and operation of communal societies. Excavations will continue to uncover and delineate remains associated with the first communal building complex, built in 1735.

The 1998 Historical Archaeology Field School is designed to provide students with training in excavation techniques, record-keeping, mapping, artifact identification, processing, cataloging, and classification.

PENNSYLVANIA
Location: Greene County
Site: Hughes H. Jones (36Gr4)
Period: Late Prehistoric (post AD 1000)

Field School:
Dates: May and June
Application deadline: mid-April
Academic credit: 3 or 6 credits from California University of Pennsylvania
Cost: $570 or $1083 tuition for Pennsylvania residents (inquire about non-residents). Other expenses to be determined. Inquire for details.

Bibliography: Issues of *Pennsylvania Archeologist*. The 1995 *Annual Volume of Archaeology of Eastern North America*. Hart, John P., "Monongahela Subsistence—Settlement Change: The Late Prehistoric Period in the Lower Upper Ohio River Valley," *Journal of World Prehistory*, 7(1), pp. 71-120.

Director, Sponsor, and
Contact: Dr. John P. Nass, Jr.
California University of Pennsylvania
Social Sciences Department
250 University Avenue
California, PA 15419
(412) 938-5726
E-mail: Nass@cup.edu

The Hughes H. Jones Site (36Gr4), a Late Prehistoric habitation site, has not been dated using radiocarbon, but ceramic decoration places the site early within the Monongahela Tradition, ca. AD 1100. On the basis of five field seasons, substantial settlement data have been obtained. Most notable are the presence of below-ground storage facilities, maize residues, and the structure of the community, which does not exhibit a preconceived plan. These discoveries, together with its believed early age, indicate the site will play an important role in helping to understand the development of Monongahela and its ultimate dependence on maize horticulture.

The field school is designed so that each student receives training in the various methodological techniques and procedures used in investigating prehistoric sites, including designing a site grid, sampling procedures, test unit and feature excavation, data recording methods, site mapping, and laboratory procedures for processing and analyzing artifacts. Field trips to nearby museums and other archaeological sites are also planned.

PENNSYLVANIA
Location: Lancaster
Site: Lancaster Brick Yards
Period: AD 1919–1979

Volunteers:
Dates needed: June 22–July 15
Application deadline: May 15
Minimum age: 16, younger persons are welcome but require prior approval of the director.
Experience required: None.
Academic credit: Credit, if desired, may be arranged through volunteer's own institution.
Cost: Volunteers are responsible for their own lodging, meals, and transportation around Lancaster. Contact the director for details.

Bibliography: Scarlett, Timothy J., "Quaker Brick in Amish Country: The Lancaster Brick Company, 1919–1979," paper presented at the 1997 Annual Meeting of the Society for Historical Archaeology in Corpus Christi, Texas, 1997.

Sponsor: Johns Hopkins University Institute for the Academic Advancement of Youth, Center for Academically Talented Youth; Franklin and Marshall College, Department of Geology
Director and
Contact: Timothy J. Scarlett, MA
Department of Anthropology/096
University of Nevada, Reno
Reno, NV 98557
(702) 784-1781
FAX: (702) 784-1988
E-mail: scarlett@scs.unr.edu

Entering into its seventh season of field research, conducted in conjunction with a class in American Archaeology at Franklin and Marshall College, the project involves recording the remains of industrial facilities on the property of the Lancaster Brick Company. Research topics include: the cultural construction of landscape, gender in the workplace, technology transfer, culture of children and homelessness, and optimality theory. Students in the past have completed measured drawings of industrial foundations, used transits to create topographic maps, taken tree ring samples, drawn detailed feature maps, recorded hobo and homeless camps in the woods, and conducted oral history investigations in the community. New this year, the project will welcome volunteers to help in all aspects of the research.

PENNSYLVANIA
Location: Southwestern PA
Site: Various
Period: Various

Internships: Internship positions in various fields.
Dates needed: Summer
Application deadline: February
Experience required: Each internship is unique and will require experience in different fields.
Salary: Undergraduate interns: $2000, Graduate interns: $3000
Cost: Lodging is located for all interns at an approximate cost of $500 each. All other expenses are the responsibility of the intern.

Director: Dr. T. Allan Comp
Sponsor: Sponsoring institutions change from year to year.
Contact: Erin Powers
Allegheny Heritage Development Corporation
PO Box 565, 105 Zee Plaza
Hollidaysburg, PA 16648
E-mail: epowers@allegheny.org
WWW: http://www.allegheny.org/intern/

The Allegheny Heritage Development Corporation (AHDC) Summer Internship Program is an innovative regional program which matches the expertise of student interns with the needs of a wide variety of organizations within the nine-county region which it serves. Interns are placed in organizations throughout the region to take on projects which encourage economic revitalization, build community and agency strength in heritage tourism and seek to improve the quality of life in southwestern Pennsylvania.

RHODE ISLAND
Location: Narragansett Bay
Site: Various
Period: Various

Volunteers:
Dates needed: Summer and Fall
Application deadline: Spring
Minimum age: 17
Experience required: None, but SCUBA certification preferred.
Cost: Volunteer responsible for all expenses.

Sponsors: Rhode Island Marine Archaeology Project; Rhode Island Historical Preservation and Heritage Commission
Director and
Contact: D.K. Abbass
Rhode Island Marine Archaeology Project
Box 1492
Newport, RI 02840

The Rhode Island Marine Archaeology Project (RIMAP) was established to determine those submerged cultural resources in Rhode Island waters that are historically important; to develop programs by which they may be protected from damage; and to develop programs by which the submerged cultural resources of Rhode Island may be shared with the diving and non-diving public in a non-destructive manner. RIMAP needs volunteers to assist in locating and identifying submerged cultural resources, including shipwrecks, debris fields, submerged man-made structures and inundated terrestrial sites; and to study these resources in a manner consistent with appropriate underwater archaeology practices.

SOUTH CAROLINA
Location: Allendale County, Smith's Lake Creek
Site: Charles site (38AL135) and Big Pine Tree (38AL143)
Period: Paleoindian

Volunteers:
Dates needed: May 5–May 30
Application deadline: April 1
Minimum age: 18; under 18 must be accompanied by an adult.
Experience required: None, but able to do some physical labor.
Cost: $366 for five days covers two prepared meals per day and camping near the site at a facility which has a screened-in dining area and kitchen along with hot showers. Each participant must provide their own camping equipment and bedding. Motels and restaurants are available within 25 minutes of the sites.

Bibliography: Goodyear, Albert C., James L. Michie, and Tommy Charles, *The Earliest South Carolinians, The Paleoindian Occupation of South Carolina*, Occasional Paper 2, The Archaeological Society of South Carolina, Inc., Columbia, 1992. Goodyear, Albert C., "Archaeological and Pedological Investigations at Smith's Lake Creek (38AL135), Allendale County, South Carolina," *Current Research in the Pleistocene*, 9, 1992, pp. 18–20; "The Allendale

Paleoindian Expedition—The Search for South Carolina's Earliest Inhabitants," *PastWatch*, Newsletter of the Archaeological Research Trust, SCIAA, University of South Carolina, Vol. 4, Nos. 1–2, 1995, pp. 2–5, 9; "Site Near Savannah River Yields Clues to Paleoindians," *The Mammoth Trumpet*, Vol. 11, No. 1, Center for the Study of the First Americans, Corvallis, 1996, pp. 10–12; "Savannah River Quarry Site," *The Mammoth Trumpet*, Vol. 12, No. 2, Center for the Study of the First Americans, Corvallis, 1997, pp. 11–12.

Director, Sponsor, and
Contact: Dr. Albert C. Goodyear
SC Institute of Archaeology & Anthropology
University of South Carolina
321 Pendleton Street
Columbia, SC 29208
(803) 777-8170
E-mail: goodyeara@garnet.cla.sc.edu

The 1998 field season of the Allendale Paleoindian Expedition will continue excavations at two alluvially buried Paleoindian quarry/habitation sites located along Smith's Lake Creek in Allendale County. The sites, the Charles site (38AL135) and the Big Pine Tree site (38AL143), have been tested and partially excavated in recent years as part of a long-term study of the Paleoindian occupation in the Savannah River Valley. Excavation strategies will focus on opening up larger areas to discover activity zones. Big Pine Tree has what appears to be a Clovis occupation followed by Dalton. The Charles site seems to have a post-Clovis Suwannee or Dalton occupation. Both sites have prismatic blades and their cores. The archaeological integrity for the sites is great, and the stratigraphy of the Pleistocene-Holocene transition is very clear. A dense preceramic Middle Archaic occupation also occurs at both sites, with one exhibiting a midden. The approach to excavation and analysis is interdisciplinary, emphasizing sedimentology and soil science. Underwater archaeology will also be conducted by SCIAA staff in the creek to investigate drowned chert quarries. Lectures by various archaeologists who work in the Savannah River valley will be provided in the evening.

SOUTH CAROLINA
Location: Camden
Site: Mulberry (38KE12)
Period: Mississippian, AD 1250–1650

Field School:
Dates: Graduate Program: May 12–June 17. Undergraduate Program: May 19–June 20.
Application deadline: April 10
Academic credit: 6 credits from University of South Carolina
Cost: Tuition depends on student status. Lodging, meals, supplies, books, insurance and travel are additional. Inquire for details.

Volunteers:
Dates needed: May 26–June 20. Minimum stay of one week.
Application deadline: April 17
Minimum age: 17, younger persons may be considered if accompanied by an adult.
Experience required: None, but must be in good physical shape.
Cost: $200 per week participation fee and all other expenses. Volunteer responsible for arranging own lodging, meals, and daily commute to the site. Local lodging list is available on request, and arrangements may be made to help with local commute.

Bibliography: Anderson, David G., "The Mississippian in South Carolina," *Studies in South Carolina Archaeology*, A. C. Goodyear,

III, and G. T. Hanson (eds.), Anthropological Studies 9, Occasional Papers of the SCIAA, 1989, pp. 101–132. Blanding, William, "Remains on the Wateree River, Kershaw District, Carolina," *Ancient Monuments of the Mississippi Valley*, E. G. Squier and E. H. Davis (eds.), Smithsonian Contributions to Knowledge 1, 1848, pp. 105–108. DePratter, Chester B., "The Chiefdom of Cofitachequi," *The Forgotten Centuries: Indians and Europeans in the American South, 1521–1704*, C. Hudson and C. C. Tesser (eds.), Athens: The University of Georgia Press, 1994, pp. 197–226. Hally, David J., "An Overview of Lamar Culture" in *Ocmulgee Archaeology 1936–1986*, D.J. Hally (ed.), Athens: University of Georgia Press, 1994, pp. 144–174. Hally, David J., "Platform Mound Construction and the Instability of Mississippian Chiefdoms" in *Political Structure and Change in the Prehistoric Southeastern United States*, J.C. Scarry (ed.), Gainesville: University of Florida Press, 1996, pp. 92–127.

Director, Sponsor, and
Contact: Dr. Gail E. Wagner
          Department of Anthropology
          University of South Carolina
          Columbia, SC 29208
          (803) 777-6548/6500
          FAX: (803) 777-0259
          E-mail: wagnerG@garnet.cla.cs.edu

This season marks the first of a five-year project to study the history of a central South Carolina chiefdom by looking at the interplay of the cultural and natural landscapes. The Mulberry site is a large late prehistoric mound and village site thought to be Cofitachequi, a major Native American town visited by Hernando de Soto in 1540 and by other Spanish and English explorers up through AD 1670. In 1806 as many as ten mounds were observed, but now only two are visible. Until now, little attention has been paid to the village portion of the site. One goal of the 1998 season is the complete excavation of the house features (postmolds and pits) of an AD 1500 Indian house, uncovered in previous seasons. The house is a square, single-post structure, with a central fired clay hearth and a wall trench door facing the mounds. Recovery of information on diet will be emphasized.

Students and volunteers will participate in excavation, mapping, note-taking, and laboratory processing. The project work week will run from Tuesday through Saturday, with public lectures on Friday nights. Participants may also wish to visit nearby projects, including Revolutionary/Colonial era excavations in historic Camden and Paleoindian excavations in Allendale County.

SOUTH CAROLINA
Location: Camden
Site: Historic Camden Revolutionary War Site
Period: Historic, AD 1500–1830

Volunteers:
Dates needed: June 1–27. Minimum stay of one week.
Application deadline: April 10
Minimum age: 18
Experience required: None, but must be in good physical shape. Excavation, mapping, cataloging, cleaning, curation, and survey experience helpful.
Cost: $125 fee per five-day week. Volunteers need to arrange for lodging, meals, and daily transportation. A local lodging list is available on request.

Bibliography: Lewis, Kenneth E., "Camden: A Frontier Town in Eighteenth Century South Carolina," *Studies in South Carolina Archaeology,* Anthropological Studies 2, Occasional Papers of the

SCIAA, 1976. Lewis, Kenneth E., *The American Frontier: An Archaeological Study of Settlement Pattern and Process*, Orlando: Academic Press, 1984.

Director: Dr. Kenneth Lewis, Michigan State University
Sponsor: Camden Historical Commission;
          Historical Camden Revolutionary War Site
Contact: Joanna Craig, Director
          Historical Camden Revolutionary War Site
          PO Box 710
          Camden, SC 29020
          (803) 432-9841
          FAX: (803) 432-3815

This is the third season of a project conducted on the western portion of the 18th-century town of Camden, occupied by the British in 1780–1781. A map of Camden, made just after American forces captured the town, shows several structures in this area. Sampling and excavations in 1996 revealed the location of at least four structures, and excavations in 1997 focused on intensive examination of two of the buildings and the testing of a third. This project will explore the area where a particular structure, the "Blue House," is believed to have been located. Purportedly American General Baron Johann de Kalb, wounded in the battle of Camden on August 16, 1780, died in the house several days later and was buried on vacant land behind it. Volunteers will participate in excavating, mapping, and assisting in laboratory processes. The project work week will run Monday through Friday, with public lectures offered on Friday nights. Volunteers will also have the opportunity to work at or visit the Mulberry site and Paleoindian excavations in Allendale County (see previous entries).

TENNESSEE
Location: Hermitage, near Nashville
Site: The Hermitage, Home of Andrew Jackson
Period: AD 1804–1890

5-Week Internships:
Dates: Session I: June 1–July 5; Session II: July 13–August 16
Application deadline: April 10
Prerequisites: The program is intended for advanced undergraduates and early-phase graduate students who have had some training and are looking for more experience in a research-oriented setting.
Academic credit: None
Cost: Program provides lodging, meals, and $1000 stipend. Travel to Hermitage and personal expenses not included.

2-Week Internships:
Dates: Session A: June 22–July 5; Session B: July 20–August 2; Session C: August 3–16
Application deadline: April 10
Prerequisites: 2-week internships are intended for students in related fields (not archaeology) who are interested in gaining exposure to the archaeological study of the recent past. Such fields include African-American studies, American studies, folklore, and geography.
Academic credit: None
Cost: Program provides lodging, meals, and $200 per week stipend. Travel to Hermitage and personal expenses not included.

Director, Sponsor, and
Contact: Dr. Larry McKee
          The Hermitage, 4580 Rachels Lane
          Hermitage, TN 37076-1331
          (615) 889-2941
          E-mail: LMCKEEHERM@aol.com

Earthwatch Volunteers:
Dates: Team 1: June 22–July 6; Team 2: July 20–August 2; Team 3: August 3–16.
Application deadline: 90 days prior to departure. (Applications will be accepted after that time if space is available.)
Minimum age: 16
Experience required: None
Cost: $1245 covers all expenses except travel to staging area (The Hermitage) and insurance.

Sponsor and
Contact: Earthwatch
                 See page 7 for contact information.

The Hermitage has hosted an archaeological internship program every summer since 1989. Participants work on excavation and laboratory tasks in connection with ongoing archaeological research into life at this antebellum cotton plantation. This year's project will concentrate on excavations around several structures that once housed African-American slaves. Earthwatch volunteers will participate in the full array of archaeological tasks, from survey to excavation.

TEXAS
Location: Lubbock
Site: Lubbock Lake Landmark
Period: Clovis (11,500 BP)–Historic (AD 1930s)

Volunteers: 40 volunteers needed.
Dates needed: June 15–August 16. US residents must commit to full nine-week season; others must commit to a minimum of six weeks.
Application deadline: None
Minimum age: 18
Experience required: None, but willingness to learn and work as part of a team. Crew members are expected to help with daily kitchen and camp chores.
Cost: Program provides lodging (six-person tents with wooden floors, electricity, and showers), meals, and major equipment and field supplies. Transportation, hand tools and personal field supplies, insurance, and personal expenses not included.

Bibliography: Johnson, Eileen, *Lubbock Lake: Late Quaternary Studies on the Southern High Plains*, College Station: Texas A&M University Press, 1987. Johnson, Eileen, and Vance T. Holliday, "Lubbock Lake: Late Quaternary Cultural and Environmental Change on the Southern High Plains, USA," *Journal of Quaternary Sciences*, 4(2), 1989, pp. 145–165. Johnson, Eileen, and Vance T. Holliday, "Archeology and Late Quaternary Environments of the Southern High Plains," *Bulletin of the Texas Archeological Society*, 66, 1995, pp. 519–540. Baxevanis, Susan, Eileen Johnson, Briggs Buchanan, and William Shannon, "Test Excavations Within the Plow Zone at the Hogue Site (41TY2), a Playa Site on the Southern High Plains of Texas," *Bulletin of the Texas Archeological Society*, 68, 1997, pp. 337–386.

Director: Dr. Eileen Johnson
Sponsor and
Contact: Lubbock Lake Landmark
                 Museum of Texas Tech University
                 Box 43191
                 Lubbock, TX 79409-3191
                 (806) 742-2481 (Museum office)
                 (806) 742-1117 (Landmark office)
                 FAX: (806) 742-1136
                 E-mail: mxegj@ttacs.ttu.edu

Lubbock Lake, a 300+ acre archaeological preserve, is a National Historic Landmark and State Archaeological Landmark. The multi-component, geologically stratified site contains evidence of human occupation from Clovis through Historic periods. Current excavations focus on the Paleoindian and late Quaternary records. Work will concentrate on three bison kill and butchering areas in the valley axis, two earlier ones around ponds, and a later one on the edge of what was a marsh stream. Work will continue at a late Ceramic–Protohistoric camp and plant processing area where shallow pits have been discovered. The search for the Singer Store, an 1880s trading post at the Landmark, continues with full-scale excavations at the western edge of the 19th-century lake deposits. As part of the Landmark's regional research program, survey of Pastores sites (1870s Hispanic sheepherders) and playa sites (ephemeral lake basins on the high plains uplands) will occur concurrent with the work at the Landmark. The Landmark is open to the public on a daily basis, through exhibits in the Interpretive Center and guided tours of the excavation areas.

TEXAS
Location: San Saba County
Site: Various
Period: Paleoindian to Historic

Field School:
Dates: June 2–July 11
Application deadline: May 15
Academic credit: 6 hours of credit from Texas Tech University
Cost: ca. $630 tuition for Texas residents, ca. $1400 for non-residents and all expenses except lodging (free camp-site) and local commute.

Director, Sponsor, and
Contact: Grant D. Hall, PhD
                 Texas Tech University
                 Dept. of Sociology, Anthropology, & Social Work
                 Box 41012
                 Lubbock, TX 79409-1012
                 (806) 742-2400

Ten counties making up the San Saba region have river and stream valleys supporting thousands of acres of native pecan groves. A major problem to be addressed through the activities of this and subsequent field schools in the region involves the ways in which the availability of pecan food resources influenced local prehistoric settlement systems and inter-regional interaction, especially with people inhabiting the Southern Plains. The field school will stress basic archaeological field techniques such as site survey, test excavation, record keeping, mapping, and collection documentation. The primary emphasis will be on investigation of prehistoric sites and collections.

UTAH
Location: Bluff
Site: Chacoan Great House
Period: AD 900–1150

Field School:
Dates: June 2–July 3
Application deadline: March
Academic credit: Up to 6 undergraduate or graduate credits from the University of Colorado
Prerequisites: At least one course in anthropology or archaeology and good physical condition.
Cost: Tuition (ca. $846 undergraduate resident, $3012 non-resident; $1032 graduate resident, $2970 non-resident) and $1100 fee for lodging, meals, local commute, and supplies.

Sponsors: University of Colorado; SW Heritage Foundation
Directors: Catherine M. Cameron and Stephen H. Lekson
Contact: University of Colorado
Department of Anthropology
Campus Box 233
Boulder, CO 80309
(303) 492-0408
FAX: (303) 492-1871
E-mail: cameronc@colorado.edu

The field school will investigate the nature of the Chacoan regional system at the Bluff Great House site. The near-urban center at Chaco Canyon in northwestern New Mexico dominated southwestern Pueblo prehistory between AD 900–1150. Monumental Great Houses and Great Kivas were constructed at Chaco, and over 150 smaller Great Houses, built with the same masonry and geometric formality as those in Chaco Canyon, represented Chaco's influence over more than 40,000 square miles. Then, in ca. AD 1150, Chaco and its regional system came to an end. The Bluff site is one of the northernmost Great Houses, and the project will explore the relationship between this site and the 10th–12th century "Chaco Phenomenon." Students receive training in archaeological field methods and artifact analysis, as well as instruction in Southwestern archaeology. Lectures and field trips will explore the Four-Corners area and its Native American cultures.

UTAH
Location: Dry Fork Canyon
Site: McKonkie Petroglyphs
Period: Freemont (ca. AD 500–1000)

Dates of excavation and field school: July 10–August 6
Application deadline: April 30

Field School:
Academic credit: 3 credits from University of Texas-Arlington
Cost: $244 tuition for Texas residents, $672 tuition for non-residents, and $500 fee for lodging, meals, and local commute.

Volunteers:
Minimum age: 25
Experience required: One year of archaeological fieldwork, rock art recording and graphing, photography, drawing skills preferred.
Cost: $500 fee for lodging, meals, local commute, and training.

Bibliography: Cole, Sally, J., *Legacy on Stone*, Boulder, CO: Johnson Books, 1990. Madsen. David B., and David Rhode, *Across the West: Human Population Movement and the Expansion of the Numa*, Salt Lake City: University of Utah Press, 1994. Schaafsma, Polly, *The Rock Art of Utah*, Salt Lake City: University of Utah Press, 1971; *Indian Rock Art of the Southwest*, Albuquerque: University of New Mexico Press, 1980. Shimkin, Demitri, "Eastern Shoshone" in *Handbook of North American Indians*, Vol. 11: Great Basin, pp. 308–334.

Sponsor: University of Texas-Arlington, Center for Research and Fieldwork in Anthropology
Director and
Contact: Jeffery R. Hanson
University of Texas-Arlington
Department of Sociology/Anthropology
Box 19599
Arlington, TX 76019
(817) 272-2661
FAX: (817) 272-3759
E-mail: Hanson@uta.edu

The research project consists of an archaeological and ethnographic study of prehistoric petroglyphs and pictographs in Dry Fork Canyon. The project contains an archaeological component in attempting to fit the Dry Fork Canyon petroglyphs into the regional prehistory, and an ethnographic component that views the petroglyphs as contemporary sacred places. During the past two field seasons, over 123 panels of prehistoric rock art have been recorded and documented through photographs, sketches, illustrations, and meticulous graphing. In addition, over 40 of these panels have been interpreted by a spiritual practitioner of the Eastern Shoshone tribe.

Students and volunteers contribute to the aims of the project by surveying and recording more panels, mapping, developing a database for each panel, and transcribing interviews. In addition, field school students will be expected to read assigned literature and complete exercises in archaeological and ethnographic methods.

UTAH
Location: Four Corners School of Outdoor Education
Site: Various sites in southeast Utah and southwest Colorado
Period: Archaic–Pueblo III (Anasazi)

Volunteers:
Dates of programs: April–November
Application deadline: Depends on program.
Academic credit: College credit is available for all Four Corners School programs. Inquire for details
Minimum age: 16
Experience required: None
Cost: Depends on program, but fee covers lodging, meals, supplies, insurance, and travel to the site from the closest city.

Sponsors: US Forest Service; Denver Museum of Natural History; National Park Service, Bureau of Land Management; Anasazi Heritage Center; Navajo Nation; Ute Tribal Park
Director and
Contact: Janet Ross
Four Corners School of Outdoor Education
PO Box 1029
Monticello, UT 84535
(800) 525-4456 or (435) 587-2156
FAX: (435) 587-2193
E-mail: fcs@igc.apc.org
WWW: http://olmkt.com/fourcorners/

The Four Corners School of Outdoor Education offers a variety of archaeological experiences from survey work to excavation through hands-on fieldwork opportunities and educational programs. Research participants are needed for a wide range of activities in the canyonlands of southern Utah, Cedar Mesa, Anasazi Heritage Center, Chaco Canyon, San Juan River, San Juan National Forest, Lake Powell, Grand Gulch, and the Ute Tribal Park (at the foot of Mesa Verde). Call or write to receive a free catalog of programs offered.

UTAH
Location: Price
Site: Nine Mile Canyon Survey
Period: Prehistoric–Historic

Volunteers:
Dates needed: Saturdays and Sundays in September and October
Application deadline: August
Minimum age: 16
Experience required: None, but willingness to hike and climb.
Cost: Volunteer responsible for all expenses.

Sponsors: Carbon County; Castle Valley Chapter of USAS
Project Archaeologists: Dr. Ray Matheny, Brigham Young University; Dr. Deanne Matheny, Pam Miller, College of Eastern Utah; and Blaine Miller, Bureau of Land Management
Director and
Contact: Pam Miller
    College of Eastern Utah
    Prehistoric Museum
    College of Eastern Utah
    451 East 400 North,
    Price, Utah 84501
    (801) 637-5060

This survey of historic and prehistoric sites in Nine Mile Canyon has been on-going for the past eight years. Evidence of Fremont Culture is found in the form of pictographs and petroglyphs as well as some village and dwelling areas. Evidence for historic cultures includes axle grease pictographs and signatures as well as freight building remnants and ranch buildings. The survey is usually done in the fall of the year during weekends of September and October. Survey members meet in a pre-decided area of the canyon, and various groups survey different levels of the cliff face and vicinity. IMACS forms are used, including measurements, photos, sketches, etc.

UTAH
Site/Location: Southern Utah
Period: Anasazi Pueblo II

Field School:
Dates: Session I: June 8–July 4; Session II: July 8–August 3
Application deadline: June 1
Academic credit: 6 quarter hours from Southern Utah University
Cost: $400 tuition and $650 for lodging and meals at field camp and daily transportation to the site. Insurance (mandatory) not included.

Bibliography: Cordell, Linda S., *Prehistory of the Southwest*, Orlando, Florida: Academic Press, 1984.

Director: Barbara W. Frank
Sponsor and
Contact: Georgia B. Thompson
    Southern Utah University
    Archaeology Field School
    351 W. Center Street
    Cedar City, UT 84720
    (435) 586-7870
    FAX: (435) 865-8393
    E-mail: thompson@suu.edu

The field school provides a hands-on experience as students work at excavation assignments or with the field survey crew carrying out archeological reconnaissance. They will be trained in excavation techniques, note-taking, mapping, diagramming, and some photography. During the evening, there are lectures on southwestern prehistory, general archaeological theory, and cultural history topics; and laboratory work, including cleaning, initial preservation techniques for artifacts, cataloguing, identifying artifacts, and labeling. Students share in camp chores—getting drinking water to the site, assisting the cook, doing dishes, clean-up activities, etc.

VIRGINIA
Location: Alexandria
Site: Shuter's Hill
Period: Pre-Civil War and Civil War

Field School:
Dates: May 26–May 30 and June 2–June 6 (Tuesday–Saturday)
Application deadline: May 20
Academic credit: 3 undergraduate or graduate credits from The George Washington University
Cost: Tuition (inquire for details), $30 fee, and all other expenses.

Volunteers:
Dates needed: Ongoing
Application deadline: None
Minimum age: 16
Experience required: None, training provided. Field and lab skills welcome.
Cost: Volunteer responsible for all expenses.

Sponsors: Alexandria Archaeology; The George Washington University
Director and Field School
Contact: Dr. Pamela Cressey
    Alexandria Archaeology
    105 N. Union Street #327
    Alexandria, VA 22314
    (703) 838-4399
    E-mail: alexarch@gwis2.circ.gwu.edu
    WWW: http://ci.alexandria.va.us/

Volunteer
Contact: Ruth Reeder
    same as above

Alexandria Archaeology studies and preserves archaeological sites in the city and interprets them to the public through museum exhibitions, publications, seminars, workshops, and tours. Archaeological excavations in Alexandria have brought to light a wide range of sites, and volunteers and students have participated in the excavation and study of African-American neighborhoods, the Alexandria Canal, the Lee family homes, Fort Ward, and other sites. Shuter's Hill is the site of a Civil War fort and barracks, 18th and 19th-century mansions, and number of prehistoric artifacts have also been recovered. The Field and Laboratory Research in Historical Archaeology program will train students in survey and excavation techniques, the use of the transit, field record keeping, artifact identification, and laboratory processing, in addition to techniques for on-site public interpretation. Lectures will be given on the history of Alexandria and its urban development, and archaeological theory and methods.

VIRGINIA
Location: Charlottesville
Site: Monticello
Period: ca. AD 1770–1825

Field school:
Dates: June 15–July 26 (6 credits)
Application deadline: April 15
Academic credit: 6 undergraduate or graduate credits from the University of Virginia
Financial aid: All participants receive a Monticello Archaeological Scholarship which covers half of the total tuition charge.
Cost: ca. $425 resident, $625 non-resident tuition and all other expenses. Room and board can be arranged through the University.

Director: Dr. Fraser D. Neiman
Sponsors: Thomas Jefferson Memorial Foundation;
    University of Virginia

Contact: Derry Voysey
Monticello Archaeological Field School
PO Box 316
Charlottesville, VA 22902
(804) 984-9864
FAX: (804) 296-1992

The Monticello Archaeological Field School teaches the fundamentals of excavation techniques in historical archaeology, their methodology, and issues in Virginia social history addressed by archaeological evidence. In the summer of 1998, fieldwork will focus on the greater Monticello plantation complex, including domestic sites that were the homes of enslaved African-American workers. Archaeological research at Monticello is part of an ongoing effort to better understand Thomas Jefferson, the individuals, both enslaved and free, who labored at Monticello, and the plantation society they created.

Students will learn basic archaeological excavation and recording techniques. Technical topics covered include recovery methods and analysis of ceramics, faunal remains, plant phytoliths and pollen, deposits and the sediments they contain, and soil chemistry. On-site instruction, lectures, and discussion sessions at Monticello will be complemented by field trips to related sites. Participants will attend classes 40 hours per week, with the bulk of that time spent on site where physical endurance is essential.

VIRGINIA
Location: Mount Vernon, home of George Washington
Site: Carpenter's Shop
Period: Late 18th century AD

Volunteers:
Dates needed: Field: June–August; Lab: all year
Application deadline: None
Minimum age: 16
Experience required: None
Cost: All expenses

Bibliography: Pogue, Dennis J., "The Archaeology of Plantation Life: Another Perspective on George Washington's Mount Vernon," *Virginia Cavalcade*, October 1991.

Director, Sponsor, and
Contact: Christy Leeson
Mount Vernon Ladies' Association
Mount Vernon, VA 22121
(703) 799-8626

The Mount Vernon Archaeology Department conducts research pertaining to a wide range of questions that remain about the daily lives of the occupants of the 18th-century plantation. The results of such studies are disseminated through a variety of sources, including on-site tours of the excavations in progress, exhibits, and publications.

VIRGINIA
Location/Site: Thomas Jefferson's Poplar Forest
Period: Late 18th–20th century AD

Position(s): Excavators
Dates needed: June–August
Application deadline: April 1
Experience required: Must have completed a field school at a historic site. Preference given to those with more experience.
Salary: $7.50–$8.00 per hour
Cost: Employee responsible for all expenses.

Field School:
Dates: June 7–July 10
Application deadline: April 24
Academic credit: 5 credit hours from the University of Virginia
Financial aid: Half tuition stipends available to for-credit students.
Cost: $141 per credit for Virginia residents, $215 per credit for non-residents, and all other expenses. Non-credit option for flat fee also offered. Inquire for details.

Volunteers:
Dates needed: April–November
Application deadline: None
Minimum age: 18
Experience required: None.
Cost: Volunteer responsible for all expenses.

Director: Dr. Barbara Heath, Thomas Jefferson's Poplar Forest
Sponsors: Corporation for Jefferson's Poplar Forest; University of Virginia
Contact: Thomas Jefferson's Poplar Forest
PO Box 419
Forest, VA 24551
(804) 525-1806

Poplar Forest was a 4800-acre plantation owned by Thomas Jefferson from 1773–1826. The property was one of his principal farms and the site of his octagonal house, built from 1806–1809. Designed as a private retreat, the house and ornamental landscape reflect the private side of Jefferson. The surrounding acreage preserves important features of Jefferson's plantation, including the sites of slave quarters and farm outbuildings. Students at the 1998 field school in historical archaeology will work in the field, learning excavation and record-keeping techniques, and in the on-site lab, learning artifact identification, processing, and analysis. Work in 1998 will focus on the ornamental landscape. Lectures and field trips round out the experience.

VIRGINIA
Location: Williamsburg
Site: Historic Area, Williamsburg
Period: 17th- and 18th-century British-American

Field School:
Dates: Session I: June 1–July 3; Session II: July 6–August 7
Application deadline: Session I: June 1; Session II: July 6
Academic credit: 6 undergraduate or graduate credits from The College of William and Mary
Cost: $153 per credit for Virginia residents, $450 per credit for non-residents, and $450 fee for lodging. Student responsible for all other expenses. (Tuition costs are subject to change.)
Director: Marley R. Brown III
Contact: Gregory J. Brown, Department of Archaeological Research, (757) 220-7335, at the address listed below.

Volunteers:
Dates needed: June–September; must commit to at least 20 hours for fieldwork.
Application deadline: None
Minimum age: 18
Experience required: Prior experience at North American sites. No experience required for lab work.
Cost: Volunteer responsible for all expenses except field supplies.
Contact: Meredith Poole, Department of Archaeological Research, (757) 220-7334, at the address listed below.

Dates: June 22–July 3, August 31–September 11, September 21–
October 2; two-week sessions May–October.
Application deadline: None
Minimum age: 16, unless accompanied by an adult participant.
Experience required: None
Cost: $625 tuition for two weeks or $390 for one week. (Tuition
subject to change.) Participant responsible for all other expenses.
Contact: Williamsburg Institute, (757) 220-8631, at the address
listed below.

Bibliography: Deetz, James, *In Small Things Forgotten*, 2nd edition,
Anchor Books, 1996. Hume, Ivor Noel, *Historical Archaeology*,
Alfred Knopf, 1969.

Sponsor: Colonial Williamsburg Foundation
                 PO Box 1776
                 Williamsburg, VA 23187-1776

Two five-week courses in archaeological field techniques, along with
several two-week sessions of the educational program "Learning
Weeks in Archaeology," emphasize excavation, laboratory skills, and
the interpretation of archaeology to the public. Experience will be
gained in archaeological methods, including one of the most extensive programs in computer-assisted data gathering in the country.

VIRGINIA
Location: Sweet Briar, Franklin County
Site: Sweet Briar Historic District and Booker T. Washington Na-
tional Monument
Period: 19th century

Field School:
Dates: Session 1: June 1–26, Session 2: June 29–July 24. Students
may participate in one or both sessions.
Application deadline: April 1
Academic credit: 3 credits per session from Sweet Briar College
Cost: $1000 per session tuition and ca. $475.00 for lodging, meals,
and local commute.

Bibliography: Fagan, Brian, and Charles Orser, *Historical Archaeology*. Campbell, Edward, and Kym Rice (eds.), *Before Freedom
Came*.

Sponsor: Sweet Briar College; National Park Service
Director and
Contact: Amber Bennett Moncure
                  Department of Anthropology
                  Sweet Briar College
                  Sweet Briar, VA 24595
                  (804) 381-6127
                  FAX: (804) 381-6173
                  E-mail: moncure@sbc.edu

The Sweet Briar College Summer Field School in Historical Archaeology will focus on locating 19th-century sites near the original
plantation home of Sweet Briar and on the excavation of a contemporary site at the Booker T. Washington National Monument. Both
properties were working plantations in the 19th century, and both
were home to both free whites and enslaved African-Americans. The
goal of the project is the regional understanding of the lives of both the
black and white inhabitants of the plantations.

The field school will expose students to both the method and
theory of historical archaeology, and offer participants the opportu-

nity to conduct reconnaissance survey, excavation, and laboratory
processing of artifacts. The fieldwork will be augmented by field trips
to historic sites within the region, lectures from prominent archaeologists and historians, and seminar discussions of assigned readings.
Each student will have the opportunity to conduct directed research on
a relevant topic of his or her choice.

VIRGINIA
Location: Westmoreland County
Site: Stratford Hall Plantation
Period: AD 1740–1920s

Field School:
Dates: May 26–July 3
Application deadline: April 27
Academic credit: 6 credits from Mary Washington College
Cost: ca. $700 tuition for Virginia residents, $1500 for non-residents,
ca. $120 for lodging, and all other expenses. Students will reside on
the plantation within an easy walk of the site, and can either prepare
their meals individually or cooperate on a group basis.

Bibliography: Neiman, Fraser, *The "Manner House" before Stratford*,
1980. Kelso, William M., and Rachel Most (eds.), *Earth Patterns:
Essays in Landscape Archaeology*, 1990.

Director, Sponsor,
Contact: Dr. Douglas W. Sanford
                  Department of Historic Preservation
                  Mary Washington College
                  1301 College Avenue
                  Fredericksburg, Virginia 22401-5358
                  (540) 654-1041/1314
                  FAX: (540) 654-1068
                  E-mail: dsanford@mwc.edu

Stratford Hall, the 18th-century home of the Lee family, is located on
a 1700 acre tract along the Potomac River, approximately 40 miles
southeast of Fredericksburg. Well-known as the birthplace of Robert
E. Lee, the Stratford mansion is one of the best known examples of
Georgian architecture in America. Stratford Hall's long-term research program includes archaeological analysis of the plantation's
historical landscape, in association with ongoing architectural and
historical studies.

The Field School allows participants to gain proficiency in
excavation, recording, and field interpretation, and will include
instruction in the method and theory of historical archaeology. Field
research focuses on the yards and gardens that surround the manor
house, an area where many historic outbuildings survive, but little
written information exists for other structures, formal and informal
gardens, and yards utilized by members of the Lee family and the
plantation's large African American community. The Field School's
overall goal has been to examine the structure and evolution of this
landscape, as well as its cultural use and historical meaning. Field trips
and presentations by regional scholars will augment daily instruction.

WASHINGTON
Location: Central Washington
Site: Various
Period: 12,000 BP–Historic

Field School:
Dates: Summer
Application deadline: April 15
Academic credit: Up to 10 credits from Central Washington University

49

Cost: Tuition (to be determined) and all expenses except local commute.

Director, Sponsor, and
Contact: Patrick T. McCutcheon
             Central Washington University
             Department of Anthropology
             Ellensburg, WA 98926-7544
             (509) 963-3489
             E-mail: mccutchp@cwu.edu

The field school continues as part of a long-term project begun in 1991 to document human history in central Washington State, particularly along the eastern drainages of the Cascade Range. Students will be trained in archaeological survey, excavation, and lab analyses. Lectures and field trips provide a general background in archaeological method and theory, modern and ancient environments, and the legal and ethical issues attached to cultural resources.

WASHINGTON
Location: Okanogan NF
Site: Mt. Hull Site Survey
Period: Early Historic

Volunteers:
Dates needed: April 6–10. Must commit to 2 days.
Application deadline: February 15
Minimum age: 18
Experience required: Hiking in steep, rugged, rocky terrain on primitive trails required. Archaeological site survey and recording skills desirable.
Cost for participant: Contact PIT for details.

Sponsor: USDA Forest Service
Contact: Passport in Time Clearinghouse (PIT)
             See page 8 for contact information.

For the past two field seasons, volunteers have surveyed the west face of Mt. Hull, searching for isolated pits and depressions that likely represent Native American storage features dating to the early historic period. Volunteers will assist archaeologists in surveying, recording, photographing, and mapping additional features.

WISCONSIN
Location: Throughout Wisconsin
Site: Several sites and numerous survey projects
Period: Archaic/Woodland

Position(s): Crew members
Dates needed: April–November. Shorter periods of are available.
Application deadline: Inquire.
Experience required: Archaeological field school.
Salary: $7.50–$10.00 per hour, depending on experience
Cost: Program provides lodging and meals, Monday–Friday. Weekend expenses and insurance not included.

Director: Jennifer Kolb, Museum Archaeology Program
Sponsor and
Contact: Kelly Hamilton, Field Coordinator
             State Historical Society of Wisconsin
             Museum Archaeology Program
             816 State Street
             Madison, Wisconsin 53706
             (608) 264-6562 or (608) 271-9097

The Museum Archaeology Program of the State Historical Society of Wisconsin is hiring field archaeologists for the 1998 season. The Program conducts surveys, evaluations, and excavations for the Wisconsin Department of Transportation throughout the state.

WISCONSIN
Location: Southwest WI
Site: To be determined
Period: To be determined

The Mississippi Valley Archaeology Center (MVAC) at the University of Wisconsin-La Crosse conducts a variety of field schools for college students, high school students, interested adults, and teachers, as detailed below.

University Field School:
Contact: Connie Arzigian, (608) 785-8452, E-mail: arzigian@mail.uwlax.edu, or write to the address listed below.
Dates: June 8–July 17
Application deadline: May 18
Academic credit: 6 credits from University of Wisconsin-La Crosse
Cost: $656.50 tuition for Wisconsin residents, $740.50 for Minnesota residents, $2024.50 for all others. Student responsible for all other expenses except local commute.
   The program consists of the practical application of the basic skills used in the excavation of archaeological sites, including surveying techniques, methods of excavation, compilation of field data, and laboratory analysis.

Public Field School
Contact: Bonnie Christensen, (608) 785-8454, E-mail: christen@mail.uwlax.edu, or write to the address listed below.
Dates: July 13–17
Application deadline: May 18
Experience required: None
Cost: $200 fee and all expenses except local commute. Camping and dorm facilities are available at reasonable rates.
   Participants work alongside professional archaeologists at small-scale excavations (test units) and survey work. The program offers in-depth training in archaeological field techniques.

Field School High School Students
Contact: Bonnie Christensen, (608) 785-8454, E-mail: christen@mail.uwlax.edu, or write to the address listed below.
Dates: July 13–17
Application deadline: May 18
Experience required: None
Cost: $200 fee and all expenses except local commute. Information on dorm facilities is available on request.
   High school students work alongside professional archaeologists at small-scale excavations (test units) and survey work. The program offers in-depth training in archaeological field techniques.

Archaeology for Teachers Class
Director and Contact: Bonnie Christensen, (608) 785-8454, E-mail: christen@mail.uwlax.edu, or write to the address listed below.
Dates: June 23–July 1
Application deadline: June 8
Academic credit: 2 graduate or undergraduate credits (optional) from University of Wisconsin-La Crosse
Cost: Tuition (to be determined), $30 fee, and all expenses except local commute. Camping and dorm facilities are available.
   "Archaeology for Teachers" begins with a brief introduction to the science of archaeology and an overview of the pre-European

cultures that lived in the Wisconsin/Minnesota areas. Teachers participate in hands-on activities that can be applied to the regular classroom. Ideas for lesson plans and an introduction to available resources are presented to assist teachers in incorporating archaeology into various classroom subjects. There will be presentations by members of the MVAC staff and a field trip, weather permitting.

Field School for Teachers
Director and Contact: Bonnie Christensen, (608) 785-8454, E-mail: christen@mail.uwlax.edu, or write to the address listed below.
Dates: July 6–17
Application deadline: May 18
Prerequisite: Teachers who wish to obtain credit for the field school must have taken or be enrolled in the prerequisite "Archaeology for Teachers" described above.
Experience required: None
Academic credit: 2 graduate or undergraduate credits (optional) from University of Wisconsin-La Crosse
Cost: Tuition (to be determined), $100 fee, and all expenses except local commute. Camping and dorm facilities are available.

Participants work alongside professional archaeologists and participate in small-scale excavations (test units) and survey work. A portion of the class will focus on relating the archaeological field experience to the classroom. The program offers in-depth training in archaeological field techniques.

Sponsor and
Contact: Mississippi Valley Archaeology Center
University of Wisconsin-La Crosse
1725 State Street
La Crosse, WI 54601

CANADA

CANADA
Location: Grandes-Bergeronnes (near Tadoussac), Quebec
Site: Falaise
Period: 2000 BCE–AD 1900 AD

Volunteers: 6 volunteers needed.
Dates needed: July or August.
Application deadline: April 15.
Minimum age: 18.
Experience required: One field season (minimum 4 weeks) at a prehistoric site.
Cost: Program provides lodging, equipment, and local commute. Participant pays for meals (ca. CDN$200 per month), insurance, and travel to project.

Bibliography: Wright, J.-V., *Quebec Prehistory*, Toronto: Van Nostrand Reinhold Ltd., 1980.

Director: Michel Plourde, Doctoral student, University of Montreal, E-mail: Michel_Plourde@cmq.qc.ca
Sponsor and
Contact: Marie-Thérèse Bournival, Director
Centre Archéo-Topo
498, rue de la mer
Grandes-Bergeronnes
Québec G0T 1G0, Canada
(418) 232-6286
FAX: (418) 232-6695

The Centre Archéo-Topo is located in the heart of an exceptional marine environment where different species of whales and seals can be observed all year long. The research done in the Grandes-Bergeronnes area since 1995 has produced data on subsistence patterns of prehistoric Amerindians. The Falaise site has been occupied from 2000 BP–19th century AD by marine mammal hunters who may be related to the Montagnais people. Artifacts exeavated consist mainly of flint tools and ceramic objects found in association with fireplaces, bone deposits, and enigmatic gravel floors. A new archaic site (6000 BP) will also be excavated in 1998. A Montagnais community (Essipit) is located near the Centre Archéo-Topo, and there is an interpretation center for visitors, who may visit the site for an introduction to archaeology and even join the digging team for a day.

LATIN AMERICA

CARIBBEAN

BAHAMAS
Location: San Salvador Island
Site: Pigeon Creek
Period: AD 1100–1200

Dates of excavation and field school: May 24–June 19.
Application deadline: April 30.

Field School:
Academic credit: 4–8 undergraduate or 3–6 graduate credits from Wake Forest University.
Cost: $900 tuition (4 undergraduate or 3 graduate credits); $1623 fee for lodging at the Bahamian Field Station, meals, insurance, airfare from Fort Lauderdale to Bahamas and return; and $275 field and lab fee. Travel to Fort Lauderdale not included.

Volunteers: Minimum stay of 8 days.
Minimum age: 20.
Experience required: None, but one course in anthropology or archaeology, maturity, and good general health recommended.
Cost: $50/day for lodging at the Bahamian Field Station, meals, and insurance; $300 for airfare from Fort Lauderdale to Bahamas; and $120 field and lab fee. Travel to Fort Lauderdale not included.

Bibliography: Berman, Mary Jane, "A Chert Microlithic Assemblage from an Early Lucayan Site on San Salvador Island," *Proceedings of the 15th International Congress for Caribbean Archaeology*, R.E. Alegria and M. Rodriguez (eds.), San Juan: I.A.C.A., 1995, pp. 111–119. Gnivecki, Perry L., "Rethinking 'First' Contact," *Proceedings of the 15th International Congress for Caribbean Archaeology*, R.E. Alegria and M. Rodriguez (eds.), San Juan: I.A.C.A., 1995, pp. 209–217. Berman, Mary Jane, and Perry L. Gnivecki, "The Colonization of the Bahama Archipelago: A Reappraisal," *World Archaeology*, 26(3), 1995, pp. 421–441. Berman, Mary Jane, and Perry L. Gnivecki, "The Colonization of the Bahama Archipelago: A View from the Three Dog Site," *Proceedings of the 14th International Congress of the Association for Caribbean Archaeology*, A. Cummins and P. King (eds.), Barbados: I.A.C.A., 1991, pp. 170–186. Keegan, William F., *The People Who Discovered Columbus: The Prehistory of the Bahamas*, Gainesville: The University Press of Florida, 1992. Rouse, Irving, *The Tainos: Rise and Decline of the People Who Greeted Columbus*, New Haven: Yale University Press, 1992.

Directors: Dr. Mary Jane Berman and Dr. Perry L. Gnivecki

Sponsor and
Contact: Dr. Mary Jane Berman
Museum of Anthropology
Department of Anthropology
Box 7267 Reynolda Station
Wake Forest University
Winston-Salem, NC 27109-7267
(910) 759-5827
FAX: (910) 759-5116
E-mail: berman@wfu.edu

The 14th season of archaeological research on San Salvador Island will take place as part of the Lucayan Ecological Archaeology Project, a long-term study of aboriginal Lucayan adaptation to the island ecosystems of the Bahamas Archipelago. Research topics include site chronology; paleo-ethnobotany; zooarchaeology; geoarchaeology; lithic, ceramic, basketry, and shell technology; and site formation processes. During the 1998 field season excavations will continue at the Pigeon Creek Site, a large multicomponent site, which in previous seasons, has yielded a high density of artifacts, many of which are of non-local origin.

The field school will concentrate on survey, mapping, excavation, macrobotanical and archaeozoological recovery, artifact and ecofact analysis, and the anthropological interpretation of archaeological data. Class lectures will cover Caribbean archaeology, ethnohistory, geography, and ecology. Laboratory sessions are supplemented by lectures and field trips.

BERMUDA
Location: St. Georges Island
Site: Paget Fort, Smith Fort, and/or Southhampton Fort
Period: AD 1612–late 18th century

Volunteers:
Dates: July and/or August.
Application deadline: April 15.
Minimum age: College student or older.
Experience required: Some fieldwork or coursework preferred.
Academic credit: By arrangement with student's university.
Cost: Student responsible for all expenses except lodging.

Bibliography: Barka, Norman F., and Edward C. Harris, "The 1993 Archaeological Excavations at Castle Island, Bermuda," *Bermuda Journal of Archaeology and Maritime History*, vol. 6, pp.1–80. Barka, Norman F., Edward C. Harris, and Heather M. Harvey, "Archaeology of the King's Castle, Castle Island, Bermuda," *Bermuda Journal of Archaeology and Maritime History*, vol. 8, pp.1–29.

Directors, Sponsors, and
Contacts: Dr. Norman F. Barka
College of William and Mary
Dept. of Anthropology
Williamsburg, VA 23187
(757) 221-1059
FAX: 757/221-1066
E-mail: nfbark@mail.wm.edu

Dr. Edward Harris, Director
Bermuda Maritime Museum
P.O. Box MA 133
Mangrove Bay, Bermuda MA BX
(441) 234-1333
FAX: (441) 234-1735
E-mail: drharris@ibl.bm

The Bermudas were colonized by the British in 1612. By 1622, 11 forts had been built near the town of St. Georges. These forts represent the earliest English masonry forts in the Americas. Six of these forts survive as archaeological sites; they are an almost unparalleled collection of the earliest English military works in the New World. In July and August, archaeological research will be carried out at one or two of these early fort sites, as part of a long-term study, begun in 1993, of the early English settlement of Bermuda. Underground archaeological features likely to be encountered include fortification ditches, passageways, and significant artifact/ecofact deposits. The upstanding remains of buildings will be recorded in three-dimensional detail by measured drawings and photographs. Any later 18th–19th century features will also be carefully excavated.

WEST INDIES
Location: Nevis
Site: Coconut Walk Estate
Period: 19th century AD

Volunteers:
Dates: Team I: July 4–17, Team II: July 19–August 1
Application deadline: 90 days prior to departure (Applications will be accepted after that time if space is available.)
Minimum age: 16
Experience required: None, but must be willing to work in intense heat with little shade.
Cost: $1695 covers all expenses except travel to staging area (Coconut Walk Estate, Nevis) and insurance.

Directors: James A. Chiarelli, Center for Field Research and Massachusetts Institute of Technology; Michael K. Trimble, US Army Corps of Engineers; Nicola J. Longford, Missouri Historical Society
Sponsor and
Contact: Earthwatch
See page 7 for contact information.

Coconut Walk Estate, a 19th-century sugar plantation, was owned by Edward Huggins, the wealthiest planter on Nevis in the late 1700s and early 1800s; at Emancipation, he owned 900 slaves, whom he was known for mistreating. Through the investigation of this estate, volunteers will help document the history of plantation slavery in the Caribbean, which is largely unwritten. Volunteers will be involved in all aspects of excavation, survey, and laboratory work at the site. Tasks include site mapping with theodolite and stadia; field walking and surface reconnaissance; measuring and recording standing architecture; digging; screening; sketching; photographing; artifact collection, processing, and cataloging; and note-taking.

MEXICO

MEXICO
Site/Location: Ensenada, Baja California
Period: Various

Field School:
Dates: Session I: June 15–July 10; Session II: July 13–August 7. (Admission to Session II requires participation in Session I.)
Prerequisites: College-level; preference is given to students with anthropology backgrounds, Spanish skills, and who enroll in both sessions.
Application deadline: March 1.
Academic credit: 7–14 credits from Arizona State University.

Cost: $1800 for one session or $3000 for both covers tuition and fees, lodging (with Mexican families in Ensenada), one meal per day, and round-trip travel between Ensenada and San Diego. Travel to San Diego, local travel, other meals, and personal expenses not included.

Director, Sponsor and

Contact: Dr. Michael Winkelman
             Anthropology Dept., Box 872402
             Arizona State University
             Tempe, AZ 85287-2402
             (602) 965-6213/0101
             E-mail: michael.winkelman@asu.edu

This ethnographic field school offers intensive Spanish classes and both undergraduate and graduate instruction in ethnographic field study, research methods, and local cultures. In addition to classes in Spanish and cultural anthropology, students carry out their own research projects which may be archaeological in content. Previous projects have included studies of rock art, pottery traditions, and the pre-Columbian Native American cultures of the region.

MEXICO
Location: Oaxaca
Site: Instituto Cultural Oaxaca
Period: Various

Field School:
Dates: 6 weeks in November/December.
Application deadline: July 11. Session is limited to 20 students.
Academic credit: 9 credits (6 in anthropology, 3 in Spanish) from Red Deer College.
Cost: CDN$3500 covers tuition, lodging (with Mexican host families), breakfast, insurance, and local commute. Travel to Oaxaca and meals other than breakfast not included.

Director: Dr. Shawn Haley
Sponsor and
Contact: Anne Brodie, Administrator
             Red Deer College
             P.O. Box 5005
             Red Deer, Alberta T4N 5H5, Canada
             (403) 342-3130
             FAX: (403) 347-0399
             E-mail: anne.brodie@rdc.ab.ca

Students accepted into this intensive six-week educational program will take three Red Deer College courses for credit (Introductory Conversational Spanish, Introduction to Social and Cultural Anthropology, and Peoples and Cultures of Mexico) while experiencing true Mexican lifeways. The program combines classroom instruction at the Instituto Oaxaca, housed in a 19th-century mansion, with frequent field trips to archaeological sites (Monte Alban and Mitla) and museums, and cultural sites such as a small village and a typical market. In addition, special workshops in backstrap weaving, Mexican ceramics, and Oaxacan cooking will be available.

CENTRAL AMERICA

BELIZE
Location: Cayo District, Roaring Creek River Valley area
Site: Actun Tunichil Muknal, Actun Uayazba Kab, and various recently discovered cave sites
Period: Classic Maya (AD 250–900)

Dates of excavation and field school: June 1–June 12; Session II: June 15–June 26; Session III: July 6–July 17; Session IV: July 20–July 31. Two weeks is the suggested minimum length of stay, however, any combination of weeks is available.
Application deadline: April 30. Contact the project early for information and application materials as space is limited; applications are processed in the order received.

Field School:
Academic credit: 4 credit hours for one session or up to 8 credit hours for two sessions from the University of New Hampshire. Undergraduate credit may also be arranged with student's own institution.
Cost: Tuition (inquire for details) and $950 fee for lodging, meals, transportation from airport, and daily travel to and from the site. Travel to Belize, insurance, and optional field trips not included.

Volunteers:
Minimum age: 18
Experience required: Due to the strenuous and dangerous nature of cave reconnaissance, it is imperative that volunteers be in excellent physical condition. Prior spelunking experience is preferred.
Cost: $950 for lodging, meals, transportation from airport, and daily travel to and from the site. Travel to Belize, optional field trips, insurance, and personal items not included.

Bibliography: Stone, Andrea, *Images from the Underworld: Naj Tunich and the Tradition of Maya Cave Painting*, Austin: University of Texas Press, 1995. Bassie-Sweet, Karen, *From the Mouth of the Dark Cave: Commemorative Sculpture of the Late Classic Maya*, Norman: University of Oklahoma Press, 1991. Brady, James E., and George Veni, "Man-made and Pseudo-Karst Caves: The Implications of Subsurface Features within Maya Centers," *Geoarchaeology* 7(2), pp. 149–167, 1992.

Director and
Sponsor: Dr. Jaime Awe, University of New Hampshire
Contact: Cameron Griffith, Assistant Director
             Belize Valley Archaeological Reconnaissance
             (705) 748-2770
             E-mail: BelizeMaya@aol.com
             WWW: http://php.indiana.edu/~casgriff/Belize/
                     CAVE.html

The Western Belize Regional Cave Project will be conducting archaeological research in caves previously investigated in the 1996 and 1997 seasons, including Actun Tunichil Muknal (Stone Sepulchre), Actun Uayazba Kab (Handprint Cave), and a number of caves recently discovered. Material under investigation includes burials, stone monuments, and cave art and carving. Work will involve extensive exploration of cave sites, survey, mapping of rooms and artifacts, typing of pottery, artifact tabulation, data recording, and excavation. In the laboratory, participants will be exposed to ceramic and lithic analyses and preliminary analysis of human remains. Lectures will provide an overview of Maya civilization with a particular focus on ideology and cosmology relating to the use of caves by prehistoric Maya.

BELIZE
Location: Cayo District, Upper Belize River Valley area
Site: Baking Pot
Period: Late Formative–Postclassic Maya (300 BC–AD 1200)

Dates of excavation and field school: Session I: June 1–26; Session II: July 6–July 31

Application deadline: April 30. Contact the project early for information and application materials as space is limited; applications are processed in the order received.

Field School:
Academic credit: 4–8 credits from the University of New Hampshire. Undergraduate credit may also be arranged with student's own institution.
Cost: Tuition (contact the project for credit fees and details) and $1600 fee for lodging, meals, transportation from airport, and daily travel to and from the site. Travel to Belize, insurance, and optional field trips not included.

Volunteers:
Minimum age: 18
Experience required: None
Cost: $1600 for lodging, meals, transportation from airport, and daily travel to and from the site. Travel to Belize, optional field trips, insurance, and personal items not included.

Bibliography: Awe, J.J., and P.F. Healy, "Flakes to Blades?: Middle Formative Development of Obsidian Artifacts in the Upper Belize River Valley," *Latin American Antiquity*, 5(4), 1994. Awe, J.J., M.D. Campbell, and J.M. Conlon, "Preliminary Spatial Analysis of the Site Core at Cahal Pech, Belize, and its Implications to Lowland May Social Organization," *Mexicon*, 13(7), 1991, pp. 25–30. Bullard, W.R., Jr., and M. Ricketson-Bullard, *Late Classic Finds at Baking Pot, British Honduras*, Art and Archaeology Occasional Paper 8, Royal Ontario Museum, Toronto, 1965. Coe, M.D., *The Maya* (5th edition), New York: Thames and Hudson Inc., 1993.

Director and
Sponsor: Dr. Jaime Awe, University of New Hampshire
Contact: Cameron Griffith, Assistant Director
 Belize Valley Archaeological Reconnaissance
 (705) 748-2770
 E-mail: BelizeMaya@aol.com
 WWW: http://php.indiana.edu/~casgriff/Belize/
 BVAR.html

Since 1998, Belize Valley Archaeological Reconnaissance Project (BVAR) will investigate Baking Pot, the site of an ancient Maya ceremonial center. Investigations will concentrate on survey and reconnaissance of neighboring groups and widespread mapping of the area, as well as excavation of pyramids and other structures in the peripheral site groups. Volunteers will have the opportunity to take educational excursions to other Maya sites in the area.

The BVAR field school is designed to familiarize students with fundamental approaches to the practice of archaeology and to provide training in a variety of techniques, including research design, site survey, excavation, data recording, and laboratory skills. Lectures will highlight the archaeology of the Maya and modern archaeological research within Belize. In the laboratory, students employ various techniques of analysis and illustration.

BELIZE
Location: Cayo District, Chiquibul Forest Reserve
Site: Caracol Archaeological Reserve
Period: Maya

Field School:
Dates: Session 1: March 1–31, Session 2: April 1–30, Session 3: May 1–31, Session 4: June 1–30
Application deadline: Inquire.

Academic credit: Through the project's affiliated university or per student's own institution. Inquire for details.
Cost: Tuition (to be determined) plus $2000 for lodging in screened bunkhouses, meals while in camp, and local commute. Travel to Belize not included.

Sponsor and
Contact: Department of Archaeology
 Ministry of Tourism and the Environment
 Government of Belize
 Belmopan, Belize, Central America
 (501) 8 22106; (501) 8 22227
 FAX: (501) 8 23345
 E-Mail: ceibelize@btl.net
 WWW: http://www.belize.gov.bz/doa/doafschl.htm

The field school of the Belize Caracol Regional Research Project is designed to give students a hands-on archaeological experience at one of the premier Maya sites. The project allows students to participate in an archaeological dig, gaining practical experience through excavation and laboratory analysis. There will be weekly assigned readings and lectures on Ancient Maya Civilization and the Archaeology of Belize. In addition, specialists from various disciplines will lecture on pertinent topics such as: Forest Management, Belizean History, and Environment and Conservation Issues in Belize.

BELIZE
Location: Cayo District, north of San Ignacio, on the western border
Site: El Pilar Archaeological Reserve for Maya Flora and Fauna
Period: 450 BC–AD 1000

Volunteers:
Dates: March 1–June 30
Application deadline: February 30
Minimum age: 18
Experience required: None, but preference is given to those with experience and skills needed by the research team. At this time the program needs people interested in ceramics, drafting, computers, and photography, as well as those with archaeological field experience. Graduate students are given preference in student applicants.
Cost: $2000 for lodging (in modern accommodations with bathroom and showers), meals (Monday–Saturday), and local commute. Travel to Belize and Sunday meals not included.

Bibliography: Fedick, Scott, and Anabel Ford, "The Prehistoric Agricultural Landscape of the Central Maya Lowlands," *World Archaeology* 22, 1990, pp. 18–33. Ford, Anabel, and Scott Fedick, "Prehistoric Maya Settlement Patterns in the Upper Belize River Area," *Journal of Field Archaeology* 19, 1992, pp. 35–49

Director: Dr. Anabel Ford
Sponsor and
Contacts: ISBER/Mesoamerican Research Center
 University of California
 Santa Barbara, CA 93106
 FAX: (805) 893-2790
 E-mail: ford@alishaw.ucsb.edu
 WWW: http://alishaw.sscf.ucsb.edu/~ford/index.html
 or
 D. Clark Wernecke
 1002 Huntridge Drive
 Austin, TX 78758
 E-mail: 102402.2332@compuserve.com
 After February 7, E-mail: elpilar@btl.net

El Pilar is a major ancient Maya center straddling the Belize-Guatemala border. Inhabited for more than 15 centuries, its monumental structures cover more than 100 acres and form the core of the new El Pilar Archaeological Reserve for Maya Flora and Fauna. The 1998 program will concentrate on three major projects: 1) the survey of the nine-square-kilometer Belizean park and preliminary survey of monuments in Guatemala, 2) continuation of the professional conservation work on monuments already excavated, and 3) continued excavation to examine construction chronology. The Program operates out of the Santa Familia Benedictine Monastery in San Ignacio.

BELIZE
Location: Cayo District, near Cristo Rey Village
Site: X-ual-canil
Period: AD 300–900, Early to Late Classic Maya

Field School
Dates: Session 1: May 9–June 6; Session 2: June 6–July 4; Session 3: July 4–August 1. (In addition, students may enroll for an extra two-week session prior to the four-week session. This period of directed preparatory study will entail the writing of a term paper based on a short list of topics, and a reading list. The topics are specifically chosen to provide additional background to the project's research. The papers will be due upon arrival in Belize.)
Application deadline: April 1 (Early application is advised, as enrollment is limited to 12 students per session.)
Academic credit: Optional 3 credits from Trent University
Minimum age: 18
Cost: Optional tuition fee (to be determined) for those enrolling for academic credit; $1300 fee per session for lodging, meals, internal travel to and from the Belize airport, and local commute. Travel to Belize, personal expenses, and insurance not included.

Sponsor: Social Archaeology Research Program (SARP), Trent University
Director and
Contact: Dr. Gyles Iannone
     Dept. of Anthropology
     Trent University
     Peterborough, Ontario K9J 7B8, Canada
     (705) 748-1453
     E-mail: giannone@TrentU.ca
     WWW: http://www.trentu.ca/academic/anthro/
      Belize1.html

The Social Archaeology Research Program (SARP) is a long-term project aimed at investigating ancient Maya social organization. The primary emphasis of the program is on the exploration of rural complexity, in particular, the more complex rural settlements, often dubbed "minor centers," which remain virtually unexplored. Situated on a high hill above the Macal River, X-ual-canil is a relatively large "minor center." The site consists of a main public plaza, a residential group, a ball court, and a causeway which terminates at a small shrine with an associated stela and altar. Surrounding the site core are a number of solitary house mounds associated with ancient reservoirs. The latter are components of what appears to be a complex irrigation system. These features suggest that X-ual-canil may have been the locus of intensive agricultural production, and, more specifically, may have functioned to administer agricultural production for the larger center of Cahal Pech.

The 1998 excavations will focus on the exploration of rooms within both the administrative and residential components of the site. The goal is to uncover evidence of the activities carried out within these architectural features and to round out the chronology of the site.

The SARP field school covers all significant archaeological methods and is suitable for both beginners and more advanced students. Participants will engage in the following activities: unit set-up; general excavation; data recording; plan and profile drawing; pace-and-compass, tape-and-compass, and theodolite surveying; general site reconnaissance; and lab work, consisting of artifact processing, drawing, photography, analysis, and cataloging. These activities will be supplemented by lectures, site tours, and other field trips.

BELIZE
Location: Crooked Tree Bird Sanctuary, northern Belize
Site: Chau Hiix
Period: 1200 BC–AD 1500

Field School:
Dates: mid-January–early May, 1999.
Application deadline: Inquire. Limited to 20 students.
Prerequisites: Students at accredited universities with at least junior standing and 3.0 GPA.
Academic credit: 15 undergraduate or 12 graduate credits from Indiana University. Students must be able to engage in strenuous activity in the heat and be willing to share rustic field accommodations without amenities.
Cost: Tuition is subject to change; that listed was current in 1997. Resident undergraduate: $3225, nonresident: $6995, resident graduate: $3225, nonresident $6450 covers tuition, lodging, meals, field trips, and insurance in Belize. Lodging and meals in Bloomington, personal expenses, international airfare, and travel unrelated to program not included.

Director: Prof. Anne Pyburn
Sponsor and
Contact: Office of Overseas Study
     Indiana University
     Franklin Hall 303
     Bloomington, IN 47405
     (812) 855-9304
     WWW: http://ezinfo.ucs.indiana.edu/~apyburn

Chau Hiix was first occupied ca. 1200 BC, and the occupation sequence of the site is complete, extending through the Post Classic to the time of the Spanish Conquest. The site is covers at least ten kilometers, and associated lagoons show evidence of enormous dams and canals suggesting that Chau Hiix may have had one of the largest controlled hydrological systems in the ancient New World.

The Maya Archaeological Field School begins with seven weeks of study on campus at Indiana University, Bloomington, introducing students to archaeological method and theory and the culture history of the Maya. The second seven weeks will take place on site at Chau Hiix where students will apply their academic skills to excavation, survey, and data analysis. In addition, field trips to Caracol and Copán or Tikal are planned.

Chau Hiix lies within the Crooked Tree Wildlife Sanctuary. Animals commonly seen or heard in camp and on site include: jaguar, jaguarundi (the Maya word for jaguarundi is *chau hiix*), ocelot, howler monkey, spider monkey, kinkajou, arboreal anteater, arboreal porcupine, coatimundi, deer, agouti, peccary, crocodile, tree frogs, arachnids, reptiles of all types, and an extraordinary variety of birds, including rare species such as jabiru, guans, trogons, and currasow.

BELIZE
Location: Hill Bank sector, Programme for Belize Reserve
Site: Satal K'an
Period: Maya

The New River Lagoon Settlement Study Project is an ongoing research project devoted to understanding the regional development and decline of Maya polities. The region being studied is significant because it links settlements along the New River with major centers further east and was integral to coastal-inland trade networks. Its position demonstrates the nature of the shifting frontier between the territory of dynastic kingdoms and the evidently non-dynastic Classic states of the eastern margin.

The focus of this year's excavation is the newly discovered site of Satal K'an. In pristine condition, Satal K'an can aid in understanding of the political dynamics in the region as it is situated approximately midway between the two larger centers of La Milpa and Lamanai. The goals for 1998 are 1) to commence testing of Satal K'an in order to determine a preliminary occupational history of the site; 2) to survey the site in order to define its extent; 3) to produce a map of the ceremonial center and its residential zone; and 4) to locate other settlements in the surrounding area.

The following Field Schools are being conducted by the New River Lagoon Settlement Study Project as a part of its 1998 field season.

Sponsors: Department of Sociology and Archaeology, University of Wisconsin-La Crosse; Mississippi Valley Archaeological Center, University of Wisconsin-La Crosse; University of Texas at Austin
Contact for all programs:
> Dr. Kathryn Reese-Taylor
> Department of Sociology and Archaeology
> University of Wisconsin-La Crosse
> La Crosse, WI 54601
> 608-785-6772
> E-mail: reese_kv@mail.uwlax.edu

College-Level Archaeological Field School in Hill Bank
Dates: June 1–28
Application deadline: April 1
Minimum age: 18 years
Academic credit: Up to six hours of undergraduate or graduate credit from the University of Wisconsin-La Crosse.
Cost: To be determined.

This program is a college credit course for undergraduate and graduate students who are interested participating on a regional research project in the Maya lowlands. The field school will include instruction in archaeological field techniques, laboratory methods, as well as survey and mapping procedures. Lectures will be provided by the staff on various aspects Maya civilization. Also included in the program are field trips to nearby archaeological sites, such as Lamanai and La Milpa.

Field School for Pre-Collegiate Teachers at Hill Bank (runs concurrently with the Public Field School)
Dates: July 20–29
Application deadline: April 1
Minimum age: 18 years
Academic credit: Up to 3 hours of undergraduate or graduate credit from the University of Wisconsin-La Crosse or the University of Texas at Austin.
Cost: Tuition (to be determined) and $1250 fee for lodging, meals, and all travel within Belize. Tuition, airfare to/from Belize, and personal expenses not included.

This program provides an opportunity for pre-collegiate teachers to participate in an archaeological excavation. Although the focus of the program will be on field excavation and laboratory processing of artifacts, special lectures and projects will be offered that give the professional educator insight into ways to incorporate Maya archae-

ology into their grade-specific curriculum. Also included in the program will be four field trips: two to the nearby archaeological sites of Lamanai and La Milpa, one to the howler monkey sanctuary, and an excursion into the Programme for Belize Reserve area to study the flora and fauna of the rainforest.

Public Field School at Hill Bank (runs concurrently with the Teachers Field School)
Dates: July 20–29
Application deadline: April 1
Minimum age: 18 years
Cost: $1250 fee for lodging, meals, and all travel within Belize. Tuition, airfare to/from Belize, and personal expenses not included.

This program provides an opportunity for the general public to participate in an archaeological excavation. The focus of the program will be on field excavations and laboratory processing of artifacts. In addition, special lectures and projects will be offered that give avocational archaeologist further insight into Maya civilization. Also included in the program will be four field trips: two to the nearby archaeological, one to the howler monkey sanctuary, and an excursion into the Programme for Belize Reserve area to study the flora and fauna of the rainforest.

BELIZE
Location: Progresso and Honey Camp Lagoons
Site: Caye Coco and Laguna de On Islands
Period: Postclassic/Colonial AD 900–1500

Position(s): Crew supervisors.
Dates needed: June–August
Application deadline: March
Experience required: Excavation, mapping, writing
Salary: None or modest stipend depending on budget.
Cost: Program provides lodging, meals, local commute, and, on occasion, travel to Belize. Insurance and field trips not included.

Field School:
Dates: June 23–July 23
Application deadline: April 15
Academic credit: Optional 6–9 graduate or undergraduate credits from SUNY-Albany
Cost: $1200 (in-state) tuition and $1000 fee for lodging, meals, and local commute. Travel to Belize, optional field trips, and insurance not included.

Earthwatch Volunteers:
Dates: Team I: June 21–July 5, Team II: July 5–19, Team III: July 19–August 2
Application deadline: 90 days prior to departure.
Minimum age: 16
Experience required: None, but willingness to work outdoors in a tropical environment. Skills in Spanish language, illustration, and photography are welcome.
Cost: $1595 covers all expenses except travel to staging area (Belize City, Belize) and insurance.

Bibliography: Masson, Marilyn A., "Cultural Transformation of the Maya Postclassic Community of Laguna de On, Belize," *Latin American Antiquity*, 8(4), 1997. Masson, Marilyn A., "Understanding the Stratigraphic Context of the Maya Postclassic in Belize," *Geoarchaeology* 10(5), pp. 389–404, 1995. Masson, Marilyn A., and Robert M. Rosenswig, *The Belize Postclassic Project: Laguna de On Island Excavations 1996*, Occasional Publication No. 1, Institute for Mesoamerican Studies, SUNY-Albany, New York, 1997.

Field School Director, Sponsor, and
Contact: Dr. Marilyn Masson
Department of Anthropology
Social Science 263
The University at Albany - SUNY
Albany, NY 12208
(518) 442-5i99
E-mail: massonma@cnsvax.albany.edu

Earthwatch Volunteers
Contact: Earthwatch
See page 7 for contact information.

The 1997 season of the Belize Postclassic Project will focus on the island Maya sites of Laguna de On and Caye Coco, located on freshwater, inland lagoons of Honey Camp and Progresso in northern Belize. Investigations of these island Maya are providing information about the survival and adaptations of populations that survived the collapse of Classic period civilization. The project research is tracking the transformations and revitalizations of Maya culture that continued through 600 years of poorly documented Postclassic period culture history from the Classic period collapse at AD 900 until the arrival of the Spanish in 1518.

Three seasons of work have focused on the agrarian village community of Laguna de On Island (an original indigenous name, meaning Lake of the Alligator Pear). In 1998, the project will begin to place this island village in regional context by investigating a large island Postclassic center called Caye Coco, located on a neighboring lagoon. By studying these two island sites, perspectives on Postclassic adaptations will be gleaned from an agrarian village and a regional center. Both the field school and Earthwatch volunteer programs provide a "hands on" approach to learning Maya archaeology through fieldwork, laboratory work, lectures, and site tours.

BELIZE
Location: Southern coastal Belize
Site: Wild Cane Cay
Period: Maya

Volunteers:
Dates: Team I: July 8–22, Team II: July 24–August 7, Team III: August 7–21
Application deadline: 90 days prior to departure (Applications will be accepted after that time if space is available.)
Minimum age: 16
Experience required: None, but the work may involve strenuous walking through mangrove swamps or bush. Volunteers must bring life jackets and be able to swim. Artistic, drafting, mechanical, and surveying skills welcome. Persons with medical expertise are especially welcome due to the remote location.
Cost for participant: $1695 covers all expenses except travel to staging area (Punta Gorda Airstrip, Belize) and insurance.

Director: Dr. Heather McKillop, Louisiana State University
Sponsor and
Contact: Earthwatch
See page 7 for contact information.

For centuries the Maya were Central America's primary coastal merchants, with posts stretching from Guatemala to Costa Rica, trading everything from Honduran copper to Mexican green obsidian. Since 1989, Dr. McKillop and teams of Earthwatch volunteers have been investigating the archaeological evidence for maritime trade and cultural adaptations on Wild Cane Cay, off southern Belize, and how local adaptations and local trade fit in with larger, more long distance trade networks. In 1998, investigations will focus on salt production in this area. Volunteers will participate in all aspects of the field research, from excavation of coral architecture and middens, to screening and flotation of excavated soil, to recording and mapping, and washing, sorting, and cataloging material; as well as exploration of the coastal environment in search of new sites.

BELIZE
Location: Stann Creek District
Site: Mayflower
Period: Late Classic Maya

Field School:
Dates: June 17–July 8
Application deadline: April 1
Academic credit: 3 credits from College of Lake County, Illinois
Cost: $2300 covers in-state tuition, lodging, meals, local commute, and airfare from Chicago (other departure points may be considered). Accommodations will be in the coastal Garifuna village of Hopkins Bay, in hotel rooms with running water, electricity, and telephone. Insurance and incidentals, including all beverages, not included.

Bibliography: Graham, Elizabeth, *The Highlands of the Lowlands: Environment and Archaeology in the Stann Creek District, Belize, Central America*, Monograph in World Archaeology No. 19, Madison: Prehistory Press, 1994.

Director: Richard Williamson
Sponsor and
Contact: Wendy L. Brown
College of Lake County
Social Sciences Division, A237a
19351 West Washington Street
Grayslake, IL 60030
(847) 223-6601 ext. 2608
FAX: (847) 223-0882
E-mail: soc393@mail.clc.cc.il.us

The ancient Maya site Mayflower was continually occupied from the Preclassic to Post Classic Periods, with its zenith in the Classic Period. The site's location near the Caribbean indicates that it may have been used as a trading post between inland sites and the sea. Twenty years ago Elizabeth Graham conducted a survey of the region, but little other research was conducted until 1996, when the Mayflower Archaeology Project began. This season students will be able to continue in the initial investigation of a relatively unknown region in the Maya area. Students will conduct survey, mapping, and excavations of the site as well as analysis of material uncovered. Fieldwork is conducted Monday–Friday with occasional lectures at night. One weekend will include an overnight field trip to visit other archaeological sites in Belize with the other weekends free for the students to explore the country on their own. The site is located approximately ten kilometers inland on the edge of the tropical rainforest.

GUATEMALA
Location: Mirador Basin
Site: Nakbe
Period: Preclassic Maya (ca. 2000–3000 BP)

Volunteers:
Dates: Session 1: March 14–27, Session 2: March 29-April 11.
Application deadline: Inquire.
Minimum age: 16.

Experience required: None, but adaptability, good physical stamina, previous wilderness camping experience, and a hearty sense of adventure a must. Spanish helpful.
Cost: $1195 covers all lodging, meals, and local commute. Travel to assembly point (Flores, Guatemala) not included.

Director: Dr. Richard Hansen, UCLA
Sponsor and
Contact: University Research Expeditions Program (UREP)
See page 7 for contact information

Nakbe, one of the largest and earliest ancient Maya cities, was a center of Preclassic Maya civilization with more than 80 pyramids, temples, and other structures. The elaborate and sophisticated structures discovered at Nakbe are among the earliest such finds of the Maya civilization. Beneath the visible ruins of Nakbe, archaeologists have also found the remnants of an even earlier village, making it possible to investigate the development of this most sophisticated pre-Columbian city and the culture that produced it. Participants will excavate Preclassic Maya residences, burials, and terraces; help create maps; collect artifacts; record data; and gather comparative information on ancient and contemporary agricultural systems.

HONDURAS
Location/Site: Copan
Period: 1100 BC–AD 1000

Field School:
Dates: June 27–July 25
Application deadline: April 15
Academic credit: 8 credits from Harvard University Summer School
Cost: $3950 covers tuition/fees, lodging, meals, insurance, and local commute. Travel to and from Honduras not included.

Bibliography: Fash, William L., *Scribes, Warriors, and Kings: The City of Copan and the Ancient Maya*, Thames and Hudson, 1993. Sharer, Robert J., *The Ancient Maya*, 5th edition, Stanford University Press, 1994. Sabloff, Jeremy A., and John S. Henderson, *Ancient Maya Civilization in the 8th Century AD*, Dumbarton Oaks, 1993.

Sponsor: Harvard University Summer School
Director: William L. Fash, Harvard University; Co-Director: David Stuart, Maya Corpus Project
Contact: Harvard University
Department of Anthropology
11 Divinity Avenue
Cambridge, MA 02138
(617) 496-4884
FAX: (617) 496-8041
E-mail: wfash@fas.harvard.edu

During the program, students will learn about all aspects of archaeological investigation at Copan through on-site training. This will involve lectures and fieldwork at residential sites in the Copan Valley, in the site-core at the Acropolis, and at the extensive laboratory facilities of the Honduran Institute of Anthropology and History. The program provides field and laboratory instruction in the methods employed in Maya archaeology, the body of theory that generates those methods, and the substantive results of field research at the site of Copan. Emphasis is placed on practical instruction in site surveying; mapping with various instruments; grid and excavation set-up; excavations and recording of same in photographs, scale drawings, and notes; artifact analysis; sculpture documentation and reconstruction; hieroglyphic decipherment; iconographic studies; archaeologi-

cal conservation; and museography. Students will be given a broad background in the cultural ecology and anthropological archaeology of the ancient Maya and will be exposed to a wide variety of learning experiences in different parts of the valley and urban core. The course will also explore the interplay between archaeology and history.

NICARAGUA
Location: Ometepe Island
Site: Various
Period: Various

Volunteers:
Dates needed: January–February 1999. Minimum stay of two weeks.
Application deadline: December 1, 1998
Minimum age: 18
Experience required: Some background in archaeology. Drawing skills welcome. Must like sun (hot) in winter, very hard work, basic living, jungle experience (complete with howler monkeys), and interesting sites and people.
Cost: ca. $250–300 per week will cover lodging, meals, and local commute. Travel to Nicaragua and insurance not included.

Director, Sponsor, and
Contact: Suzanne Baker/Culturelink
Archaeological/ Historical Consultants
609 Aileen Street
Oakland, CA 94609
Tel. and FAX: (510) 654-8635
E-mail (James Martin):73220.3636@compuserve.com
WWW: http://ourworld.compuserve.com/
homepages/jrmartin

Ometepe Island, an important pre-Columbian center in Lake Nicaragua, contains numerous ceramic sites and thousands of petroglyphs. There has been little archaeology done on the island and virtually no systematic inventory. The island is also becoming a focus of pot hunting and the illegal antiquities trade, and is seeing increasing impacts from tourism. The Departamento de Archaeología of the Patrimonio Cultural de Nicaragua is struggling mightily with little or no money and few trained personnel to deal with the situation. Archaeological/Historical Consultants of Oakland, California, has organized a five-year volunteer program of site inventory and petroglyph recording to assist the Patrimonio Cultural. The first field season began in March 1995.

SOUTH AMERICA

ARGENTINA
Location: San Salvador de Jujuy
Site: Museo Arqueologico Provincial
Period: All the periods in the cultural development of the South Andean Region, including Formative, Tiawanaco, and Inca

Museum Internship/Field Volunteers:
Dates needed: All year
Application deadline: None
Minimum age: 18
Experience required for internship: Drawing, translation, and computers skills, library experience, and an ability to work as part of a team as well as independently.
Experience required for volunteers: Interest in rock art, photography, and GPS.
Academic credit: Inquire.

Cost: Program provides lodging. Participant responsible for all other expenses.

Bibliography: Fernandez Distel, Alicia Ana, "Aplicacion en el Noroeste Argentino del Sistema Rowe para la denominacion de sitios arqueologicos," *Boletin 5*, Sociedad de Investigacion del Arte Rupestre de Bolivia, La Paz, 1991, pp. 18–20. Rowe, John, "Site designation in the Americas," *American Antiquity*, (36)4, 1971, pp. 477–480. Willey, Gordon, "An Introduction to American Archaeology," *South America*, Vol. II, New Jersey: Prentice Hall, 1974, Chapter 4.

Sponsor: Museo Arqueologico Provincial, Provincial de la Direccion, Provincial de Cultura

Director and
Contact: Dr. Alicia A. Fernandez Distel
            Lavalle 434
            4600 S.S. de Jujuy, Argentina
            Tel/FAX: (54) 88 221343

The Museo Arqueologico Provincial seeks assistance on two projects as follows: 1) The museum internship involves laboratory and desk work to prepare the "Archaeological Map of the Province of Jujuy," and curation of the Museum's archaeological holdings; 2) The program for volunteers involves recording petroglyphs and rupestrian art in the field.

ARGENTINA
Location: Provincia de Catamarca, Departamento de Santa Maria, Valle de Santa Maria del Yokavil (Valles Calchaquies)
Site: La Gruta de Shiquimil (The Cavern of Shiquimil)
Period: 9th–16th centuries AD

Volunteers:
Dates needed: Session 1: March 15–30, Session 2: April 1–15, Session 3: April 17–May 2
Application deadline: February 1
Minimum age: 18
Experience required: None
Cost: $300 per session covers meals and local commute. all expenses except travel to San Salvador de Jujuy and insurance.

Bibliography: Quiroga, Adan, *Petrografias y pictografias de Calchaqui*, Ed. post-morten por Universidad de Tucuman, 1931. *Calchaqui*, Re-impresion y actualizacion por Dr. Raffino, Ed. TEA, Buenos Aires, 1992. Cigliano et al, *Investigaciones arqueologicas en el valle de Santa Maria*, Publicacion No. 4, Instituto de Antropologia, Facultad de Filosofia y Letras, Universidad Nacional del Litoral, Rosario, 1960.

Director, Sponsor, and
Contact: Lic. Jorge A. Sosa
            Museo Etnografico
            Facultad de Filosofia y Letras
            Universidad de Buenos Aires
            Bartolome Mitre 2296, Piso 9 Dto. "C"
            C.P. 1039, Buenos Aires, Argentina
            FAX: (54) 1 9543233 or (54) 1 7170190
            E-mail: jsosa@ethnik.filo.uba.ar

Located in the arid Argentinian northwest, the Valley of Yokavil is the site of 65-million-year-old colorful sedimentary formations, rich paleontological deposits, and the archaeological remains of the Calchaqui culture, which flourished at the same time that the Maya civilization was breaking down. The Calchaqui people thrived for over seven centuries, resisting the encroachment of both the Inca and the Spaniards. The archaeological remains of houses, cultivated fields, and ceremonial sites are dispersed throughout the valley, however, they are now threatened by looting, modern development, and natural processes. Work planned for 1998 includes a survey to rediscover a set of caverns with hundreds of petroglyphs known as "La Gruta de Shiquimil" (The Cavern of Shiquimil), first described in 1899 by a pioneer of Argentine archaeology, Adan Quiroga. Objectives for the season are to locate the cavern in a topographical map, make a photographic record of the petroglyphs, and evaluate the potential for future excavations. In addition to the survey, there will visits to nearby archaeological sites and indigenous villages.

CHILE
Location: Atacama Desert, Region 1, N Chile
Site: Ramaditas
Period: ca. 500 BC–AD 500

Dates of excavation and field school: June 1–July 20

Field School:
Application deadline: April 2
Academic credit: 8 credits from Beloit College
Cost: $3300 covers tuition, lodging, meals, insurance, and local commute. Travel to Chile not included.

Volunteers:
Application deadline: April 15
Minimum age: 16
Experience required: Any excavation, survey, soil analysis, geology experience welcome.
Cost: Program provides lodging, meals, and local commute. Travel to Chile and insurance not included.

Bibliography: Graffem, G., Mario Rivera, and Alvaro Carevic, "Ancient Metallurgy in the Atacama: Evidence for Copper Smelting During Chile's Early Ceramic Period," *Latin American Antiquity*, Vol. 7, No. 2, 1996, pp. 101–113. Graffem, G., Mario Rivera, and Alvaro Carevic, "A Copper-Manufacturing Site of the Late Formative Period from the Desert Rim of Northern Chile: A View Towards Elite Emergence," *Journal of the Steward Anthropological Society*, 1992 (also due to appear in somewhat modified form in *Geoscience and Man*, Vol. 33). Meighan, C., and D. True, "Prehistoric Trails of Atacama," *Monumenta Archaeologica 7*, Institute of Archaeology, UCLA, 1980. Rivera, Mario A., "The Prehistory of Northern Chile: A Synthesis," *Journal of World Prehistory*, 5:1, 1991, pp. 1–14. Shea, Daniel E., "The View From Ramaditas," *Minutes of Central States Anthropological Association*. Shea, Daniel E., "Restricted Percolation and Reticulate Irrigation, a Pseudo-Oasis Niche," paper presented at the 60th annual meeting of the Society for American Archaeology, May 3–7, 1995. Shea, Daniel E., "Reticulate Irrigation in the Atacama," *Chungara*, U. de Tarapaca, Arica, Chile.

Directors: Daniel E. Shea and Mario A. Rivera
Sponsor and
Contact: Beloit College
            Department of Anthropology
            Box 167, 700 College Street
            Beloit, WI 53511-5595
            Prof. Shea: (608) 363-2204
            Prof. Rivera: (414) 768-0272

This will be the seventh year of research at the early agricultural site of Ramaditas. Early immigrants, apparently from Wankarani, Bolivia, moved into the area before ca. 500 BC. Agriculture was practiced on an extensive scale with the aid of an unusual irrigation system. Local copper, nitrates, and marine shell were apparently shipped back to the Bolivian highlands. Field school activities include excavation, survey, GPS, soil sampling, and elementary geomorphology. Some field trips to local sites and fiestas are also planned.

CHILE
Location/Site: Easter Island
Period: 1300 BP

Volunteers:
Dates and cost: Contact Earthwatch for details.
Application deadline: 90 days prior to departure (Applications will be accepted after that time if space is available.)
Minimum age: 16
Experience required: None

Director: Dr. Christopher Stevenson
Sponsor and
Contact: Earthwatch
          See page 7 for contact information.

For a tenth season, Dr. Stevenson will continue his investigation into the 1300-year evolution—and dissolution—of the enigmatic Easter Island culture. Volunteers shovel, trowel, map, photograph, and organize data at each excavation site. Teams will use flotation methods to recover small botanical and faunal remains from soil samples, and laboratory work will include washing and sorting artifacts as well as processing and cataloging finds.

ECUADOR
Location: Southern Manabi province, Pacific coast
Site: OMJ-PLP-170, "Rio Chico"
Period: Valdivia–Contact

Field School:
Dates: Term A: May 11–June 12, Term B: June 29–August 1
Application deadline: March 2
Academic credit: 6 credits from Florida Atlantic University
Cost: Tuition and fees (to be determined) will cover lodging, meals, and local commute. Travel to Ecuador and insurance not included.

Volunteers:
Dates needed: May 11–August 1
Application deadline: March 2
Minimum age: 22
Experience required: At least 3 years previous fieldwork. Those with geology, photography, and drawing skills preferred.
Cost: Program provides lodging, meals, and local commute. Travel to Ecuador and insurance not included.

Bibliography: Damp, J. "Environmental variation, agriculture, and settlement processes in coastal Ecuador," *Current Anthropology* 25(l), pp. 106–111, 1984. Lathrap, D., *Ancient Ecuador: Culture, Clay and Creativity*, Chicago Field Museum of Natural History, 1975. Norton, P., "El Senorio de Salangone y la Liga de Mercaderes," *Miscelania Antropologica Ecuatoriana, Boletin de los Museos del Banco Central del Ecuador*, Vol. 1, pp. 136–154, 1986. Stahl, P., "Arid landscapes and environmental transformation in ancient southwestern Ecuador," *World Archaeology* 22(3), pp. 346–359, 1991.

Directors: Prof. Wm. J. Kennedy, Project Coordinator; Prof. Valentina L. Martinez, Project Field Director

Sponsors: Florida Atlantic University, Boca Raton, Florida; ESPOL University, Guayaquil, Ecuador; Salango Research Center, Manabi Province, Ecuador; Pro-Pueblo Foundation, Ecuador; Norton Foundation, Ecuador
Contact: Florida Atlantic University
          Department of Anthropology
          Boca Raton, FL. 33431
          (561) 367-3230
          E-mail (Wm J. Kennedy): kennedy@acc.fau.edu
          E-mail (Valentina L. Martinez): vmartine@acc.fau.edu
          WWW: http://www.fau.edu/divdept/anthro/home/
          fldschl.htm

During the late Pleistocene and early Holocene, the Pacific coast of southern Manabi province was part of a large tropical forest spreading from the eastern flank of the Andes down to the coastal plain. Today, the region is characterized by deep and shallow water bays, alluvial valleys, and mountains. Around 5000 years ago there were permanent settlements based on a mixed economy (horticulture, fishing, and hunting). Over time, agricultural communities with significant transoceanic long-distance trade networks emerged. By the time of Spanish arrival, ranked societies with complex socio-political organizations were in existence. The goal of FAU's program is to reconstruct the prehistory and paleoecology of the region. Investigations focus on the systematic survey of alluvial valleys and on the excavation of a multicomponent site. Preliminary investigations report cultural components from Valdivia (3500 BC) until the Contact period.

FAU's field school will provide hands-on training in archaeological field and laboratory methods, while weekly lectures will focus on the process and theory of archaeological research and the prehistory of coastal Ecuador. The following general research issues are addressed through the fieldwork: chronology, environmental reconstruction, site formation processes, resource exploitation, bioarchaeology, technological organization, and culture change. Students are trained in the excavation of well defined cultural contexts, collection of special samples (i.e. charcoal, pollen, phytoliths, macroflora, microfauna, etc.), and identification of depositional and post-depositional formation processes. Survey focuses on the identification of geomorphological features within the alluvial valleys and the identification of other prehistoric sites.

ECUADOR
Location: Pimampiro District
Site: Shanshipampa
Period: ca. AD 600–1400

Field School:
Dates: June 6–July 19. (Intensive Spanish: June 6–20; Field School: June 21–July 19)
Application deadline: April 15
Academic credit: 5 credits from Wayne State University
Cost: $689–$1459 tuition depending on residency; ca. $2200 fee for lodging, meals, local commute, and Spanish course. Travel to Ecuador and insurance not included.

Bibliography: Bray, Tamara L., "Pimampiro y Puertos de Comercio: Investigaciones Arqueológicas Recientes en la sierra Norte del Ecuador," *Perspectivas Regionales en la Arqueologia del Suroccidente de Colombia y Norte del Ecuador*, Cristobal Gnecco (ed.), pp. 30–47, Editorial Universidad del Cauca, Popayan , Colombia, 1995; "The Panzaleo Puzzle: Non-Local Pottery in Northern Highland Ecuador," *Journal of Field Archaeology* 22(2), pp. 137–148, 1995; "Vínculos Andinos-Amazónicos en la Prehistoria Ecuatoriana: La Conexión Pimampiro," *Sarance* 20, pp. 135–146, Otavalo, Ecuador, 1994.

Director, Sponsor, and
Contact: Dr. Tamara L. Bray
                 Wayne State University
                 Department of Anthropology
                 137 Manoogian Hall
                 Detroit, MI 48202
                 (313) 577-3056
                 FAX: (313) 577-5958
                 E-mail: TBRAY@cms.cc.wayne.edu

This is the second field season of excavations at the remote site of Shanshipampa, situated in the northern Andes at an elevation of 9000+ feet above sea level. A constellation of archaeological and ethnohistoric data provides strong evidence that Shanshipampa operated as an important port-of-trade between ethnic groups who occupied the tropical forests of the eastern lowlands and societies of the Andean highlands and Pacific coast. Recent finds of carved stone monuments with images of tropical forest animals offer further testimony of the importance of the ancient socioeconomic ties between these diverse ecological zones.

The field school will provide students with a basic introduction to the fundamentals of archaeological field methods, a solid background in the culture history of the northern Andean region, and the experience of living and working in a different culture. Students will learn archaeological mapping, survey, and excavation techniques; note-taking skills; and basic laboratory procedures, including artifact processing and identification. A two-week intensive Spanish language class is offered in conjunction with the field school. The language class is required for those without basic conversational skills in Spanish and strongly recommended for those who wish to improve their speaking abilities.

PERU
Location: Chicama Valley
Site: Mocollope
Period: Moche (AD 200–700)

Volunteers:
Dates: June 25–August 25 (two 2-week sessions).
Application deadline: None.
Minimum age: 16.
Experience required: None, but drawing, mapping, and photography skills welcome.
Cost: $1365 per 2-week session covers lodging, meals, and local commute. Travel to assembly point (Trujillo Airport, Peru) and insurance not included.

Director: Dr. Glenn Russell, UCLA Fowler Museum
Sponsor and
Contact: University Research Expeditions Program (UREP)
                  See page 7 for contact information

Chicama Valley lies in a vast flat expanse between the shore of the Pacific ocean and the distant peaks of the Andes mountains. Crisscrossed by a patchwork of irrigated fields, this coastal desert region harbors the prehistoric remnants of the renowned Moche civilization. The pyramid-centered ceremonial site at Mocollope and an adjacent ceramic workshop at Cerro Mayal contain valuable clues to understanding the development of Moche society. Ornate effigy bottles and other finely-crafted ceremonial vessels are among the remarkable artistic and architectural achievements that define Moche culture, however, the insight these artifacts can reveal about Moche ideology is in peril as a result of ongoing looting. In addition to rescuing ceramic artifacts and preserving architectural features against further damage, excavations at these sites also aim to answer questions regarding economic and political sources of power and to unravel Moche ideology as it is expressed in the ornate decorative ceramics for which the Moche culture is known. Peruvian volunteers will join UREP participants in both site excavation and lab work. Site excavation involves trowels and brush work, taking field notes, labeling samples, drawing maps and photographing the site. Lab activities involve inventorying and cataloging artifacts and analyzing soil samples for botanical and faunal remains.

PERU
Location: South Coast of Peru
Site: Acari Valley and Atiquipa Region
Period: 1200 BC–AD 1600

Field Schools or Study Tours
Dates: 2-week programs, March–April and June–August
Application deadline: 90 days prior to each 2-week program
Academic credit: Optional. May be arranged through individual universities.
Experience required: None, but good health, flexibility, and physical stamina essential.
Cost: $675 per week covers training, lodging, meals, transportation from Lima, and local commute. Travel to Peru and meals while not at research center not included.

Bibliography: Contact CIPS for a list of publications.

Director, Sponsor, and
Contact: Sandy Asmussen, Coordinator
                 California Institute for Peruvian Studies (CIPS)
                 45 Quakie Way
                 Bailey, CO 80421
                 (800) 444-1285 or (303) 838-1215

The California Institute for Peruvian Studies (CIPS) together with Universidad Catolica Santa Maria in Arequipa, Peru, are conducting archaeological expeditions in the Acari River Valley of south coastal Peru. The arid south coast contains some of the world's most well-preserved mummies, textiles, pottery, and architecture. To date over 100 sites have been located, however, few sites have been collected, mapped, photographed, and documented. The archaeological work left to do is enormous. CIPS has scheduled several two-week-long archaeological field schools (or study tours for those who do not desire academic credit) for 1998. Each field school is taught by a specially selected professional, and topics include excavation, textile and pottery analysis, field methods, cultural history, physical anthropology, museology, and more. Optional tours before or after each two-week session may be arranged. Museum internships are also available; contact the Director for details.

PERU
Location: North coastal Peru
Site: Santa Rita (Aguas Alientes)
Period: 1000 BC–AD 1530

Dates of excavation and field school: Session 1: June 28–July 12, Session 2: July 13–August 3. (Participants may select either one or two three-week-long sessions.)
Application deadline: May 10

Field School:
Academic credit: 3–6 credits from Metropolitan State College of Denver

Cost: $25 application fee, $68 per credit tuition (in state), $268 per credit (out of state), plus $2650 fee for 3 weeks, $2950 for 6 weeks, for lodging, meals (at the site), and local commute (including airfare from Trujillo, Peru, to the site and return). Travel to Peru and insurance (mandatory travel and health) not included.

Volunteers:
Minimum age: 17
Experience required: None, but prior fieldwork, mapping, illustration, geology (especially hydrology), photography, auto mechanics, and Spanish language experience welcome.
Cost: $2650 for 3 weeks, $2950 for 6 weeks covers lodging, meals (at the site), and local commute (including airfare from Trujillo, Peru, to the site and return). Travel to Peru and insurance (mandatory travel and health) not included.

Bibliography: Lumbreras, Luis G., *The Peoples and Cultures of Ancient Peru*, Smithsonian Institution Press, 1974. Donkin, R.A., *Agricultural Terracing in the Aboriginal New World*, Wenner-Gren Foundation and University of Arizona Press, 1979. Moseley, Michael E., *The Incas and Their Ancestors*, Thames & Hudson Inc., 1992. Donnan, Christopher, *Ceramics of Ancient Peru*, Fowler Museum of Cultural History, UCLA, 1992. Haas, Jonathan, Sheila Pozorski, and Thomas Pozorski (eds.), *The Origin and Development of the Andean State*, Cambridge University Press, 1987.

Director, Sponsor, and
Contact: Dr. Jonathan D. Kent
Campus Box 28
Metropolitan College of Denver
Denver, CO 80217-3362
(303) 556-2933
or
California Institute for Peruvian Studies (CIPS)
1985 S. Poplar Street
Denver, CO 80224
(303) 504-4463

The Santa Rita site is located in the Andean foothills of northern Peru, approximately 20 miles from the beaches of the Pacific coast, and covers at least 640,000 square meters. The site has evidence of very extensive stone construction, including corrals for camelids (llamas and alpacas), public plazas and platforms, residential structures, and complex water control systems. Also, there is evidence of human burials and elaborately decorated pottery and textiles. Its various occupants span more than 2500 years—from Cupisnique of ca. 1000 BC through Inca, until the arrival of Europeans in the 16th century AD. Because of its strategic location at a point where major drainages emerge from the Andes on their way to the sea, the site has enormous potential to address questions of economic, political, and perhaps military importance in Andean prehistory.

To date the site has only been briefly described by the Peruvian archaeologists who registered it, and no systematic excavation has ever been conducted here. The 1998 field season will begin the process of defining the site's boundaries, mapping the structures and other features, and carrying out systematic surface collections and test excavations. Project participants will work side by side with Peruvian professionals and student archaeologists. Field instruction will include survey methods, mapping, illustration, and excavation techniques. Evenings will be devoted to recording the days discoveries and lectures on both archaeological methods and theories and Peruvian archaeology.

EUROPE (Continental Europe, United Kingdom, & Republic of Ireland)

European Archaeological Research Projects (EARP)
http://archeonet.cilea.it/cgi-bin/archeosite/Webdriver
The Web site, EARP, is part of the European project Archeonet—Archaeology towards the third millennium. One of the major tasks of the Archeonet project, developed in collaboration with the European Association of Archaeologists and headed by the University of Bristol, is to help students and researchers take part in archaeological projects in Europe. EARP puts students as well as researchers directly in contact with European universities and institutions promoting fieldwork and surveys. Institutions may post information, and potential participants can select the work in which they are interested and send a participation form by e-mail.

CONTINENTAL EUROPE

BELGIUM
Location: Stavelot, Province of Liège
Sites: Stavelot Abbey
Period: Medieval

Volunteers:
Dates needed: June and July (possibly August and part of September). Minimum stay of one week.
Application deadline: May
Minimum age: 18
Experience required: Background in historic excavations.
Cost: 1000 BF (ca. $32) tuition fee and travel to Belgium. Program provides lodging, meals, and insurance.

Director: Marcel Otte, Université de Liège
Sponsors: Université de Liège; Ministére de La Region Wallonne
Contact: Marcel Otte
Centre de Recherche Archéologique
Université de Liège
Place du XX Août, 7 Bât. A1
B-4000 Liège, Belgium
(32) 43 665341
FAX: (32) 43 665551
E-mail: marcelotteAulg.ac.be
or
Brigitte Evrard-Neuray and Bernard Lambotte
Centre Stavelotain D'Archeologie
Abbaye de Stavelot
B-4970 Stavelot, Belgium
Tel. & FAX: (32) 80 864113

The Abbey Church of Stavelot was founded in 651 by Saint Remacle, destroyed in 881 by the Normans, and rebuilt in Ottonian style during the 11th century. In 1501, the church was reconstructed in Gothic style and remained so until the end of the 18th century. During the French Revolution, it was completely destroyed. The goal of the excavation is to reconstruct the plan of the 11th-century church. The emphasis of the program is on archaeological techniques, especially those useful for the medieval period.

BELGIUM
Location: Sclayn, Andenne
Site: Scladina Cave
Period: Middle Paleolithic (130,000 BP)

Volunteers:
Dates needed: June 22–July 31
Application deadline: None
Minimum age: 18
Experience required: Some experience working at an archaeological site.
Cost: $1500 BF (ca. $40) per week for meals. Program provides lodging in tents and insurance. Travel to Belgium not included.

Bibliography: Bonjean, Dominique, Marcel Otte, Michel Toussaint, "L'homme de Sclayn," *Archéologia*, No. 299, mars 1994, pp. 26–30. Otte, Marcel, "Recherches aux grottes de Sclayn, le contexte," ERAUL 27, Liège, 1991. Otte, Marcel, "L'occupation moustérienne de Sclayn (Belgique)," EAZ 31, 1990, pp. 78–101. Otte, Marcel, Michel Toussaint, Dominique Bonjean, "Découverte de restes humains immatures dans les niveaux moustériens de la grotte Scladina à Andenne (Belgique)," *Bull. et Mém. de la Société d'Anthropologie de Paris*, n.s., t. 5, 1993, pp. 327–332. Toussaint, Michel, Dominique Bonjean, Marcel Otte, "Découverte de fossiles humains du paléolithique moyen à la grotte Scladina à Andenne," *Deuxième journée d'archéologie namuroise*, Facultés universitaires Notre Dame de la Paix, Namur, 26, Février 1994, pp. 19–33.

Director: Marcel Otte, Université de Liège
Contact: Dominique Bonjean
Rue de Marche en Pré, 51
B-5300 Sclayn, Belgium
Tel/FAX: (32) 81 580851

Discovered about 25 years ago, Scladina Cave is excavated throughout the year, but specifically during the last week of June and the month of July with students from the University of Liège, who, under the direction of Prof. Marcel Otte, are learning techniques of excavation at prehistoric sites in caves. The program is able to accept approximately ten students or archaeologists from abroad.

FRANCE
Location: Nationwide
Site: Various
Period: Various

Contact: Ministère de la Culture, Direction du Patrimoine
Sous-direction de l'Archéologie
Documentation, 4, rue d'Aboukir
75002 Paris, France
(33) 1 40 15 80 00
FAX: (33) 1 40 15 77 00
WWW: http://www.culture.fr/
(go to: "Découverte de la France" then "Chantiers de fouilles pour bénévoles")

Every year in May the French Ministry of Culture publishes a comprehensive directory, *Chantiers Archéologiques Pour Benevoles*, of excavations in France which accept volunteers. The directory also includes a current list of archaeological districts (Service Regional de l'Archéologie) with contact names and addresses to write to for more information about excavations in particular regions. Contact the Ministry of Culture to receive a copy or access it on the World Wide Web at the site listed above.

FRANCE
Location: Nationwide
Site: Various
Period: Various

Volunteers:
Dates needed: Summer
Application deadline: None
Minimum age: 14
Experience required: Basic ability to speak French. No particular skills, but goodwill and motivation are essential. Volunteers are expected to help with cooking and domestic chores on a rotating basis.
Cost: 220FF (ca. $45) for application fee and insurance plus ca. 40FF/ $10 per day for lodging, meals, local commute, and on-site insurance. Volunteers should bring sleeping bag, work clothes, strong work boots, a swimsuit, and pocket money.

Sponsor and
Contact: REMPART
1, rue des Guillemites
75004 Paris, France
(33) 1 42 71 96 55
FAX: (33) 1 42 71 73 00

REMPART (Réhabilitation et Entretien des Monuments et du Patrimoine Artistique) organizes archaeological and restoration projects for volunteers of all ages and national origins. Volunteers are trained in traditional restoration techniques and may become involved in a variety of projects, including the restoration and/or excavation of castles, churches, abbeys, chapels, villages, forts, etc. REMPART organizes some 140 work camps throughout France every year. Every work camp is different, each having its own schedule and rules, but the guidelines delineated above apply to most.

FRANCE
Location: Aisne, Oise, Indre, and other locations, N France
Site: Château-fort de Guise (Aisne), Abbaye Royale du Moncel a Pont-Point (Oise), Chateau d'Argy (Indre), and other sites.
Period: Various

Volunteers:
Dates needed: All year. Minimum stay of 15 days.
Application deadline: 15 to 30 days prior to arrival. Space is limited.
Minimum age: Chateau-fort de Guise, center for basic instruction: 14. Abbaye Royale du Moncel a Pont-Point, center for instruction in the restoration of monuments: 15. Chateau d'Argy, center for instruction in the restoration of ancient monuments, upon invitation only: 17. No age limit.
Experience required: None, but must be in excellent health, be adaptable, hard-working, and have an enthusiastic team spirit. Medical certificate required.
Cost for participant: 90FF per day (ca. $15) for lodging, meals, and local commute, and 90FF for insurance. There is sheltered lodging during the winter, in tents after Easter. The Club provides tents but no other camping gear. Meals are prepared by the participants. For volunteers, 17 years of age and over, who wish to make an extended stay during any period other than the summer, lodging and meals are free after a 15-day trial period.

Director: Monique Dine
Sponsor and
Contact: Club du Vieux Manoir
10, rue de la Cossonnerie
75001 Paris, France
(33) 1 45 08 80 40
Include stamped self-addressed envelope with inquiry.

The Club du Vieux Manoir, founded in 1953, is a volunteer association for young people who want to spend some of their spare-time doing rescue and restoration work (under direction) on ancient monuments and sites. The program has two basic aims: 1) that the historic monuments and places which form part of the national heritage are restored; and 2) that the participants are offered an activity where they can work with their hands, learning different techniques. Volunteers receive instruction in archaeology, architecture, handicrafts, and history. On-site activities depend on the nature of the monument and the treatment that it requires.

Three of the Club du Vieux Manoir sites are permanent and open year round: Guise, Argy, and the Moncel du Pont-Point, and there are no set arrival or departure dates. At these permanent sites young people have the possibility of staying for several months. The other sites function during school holidays and the summer for specific lengths of time. During the summer, arrivals take place on the 2nd and the 16th of each month, and volunteers stay a minimum 15 days with the possibility of an extension.

FRANCE
Location: Aix-en-Provence, near Marseilles
Site: Various sites in and around Aix-en-Provence
Period: mainly Roman–Medieval

Field School:
Dates: Academic year. Students may attend for one or both semesters.
Application deadline: Potential students should contact the IAU as soon as possible. Courses listed may not be offered if student numbers are too low.
Prerequisites: Applicants should have completed a minimum of one year of college or university. No prior French is required.
Academic credit: 15 or more units per semester from IAU, Northern Illinois University, Eckerd College, or the College Consortium for International Studies (CCIS). Inquire for details.
Cost: $4930 tuition for one semester, $9860 for two; $45 fee for archeology courses; and $3440 for one semester, $6880 for two, for lodging with French host families on a half board basis (breakfast and dinner with the family seven days a week). (Adult students may wish to rent their own studio apartments.)

Sponsors: Institute for American Universities; Centre Camille Jullian, Université d'Aix-Marseille I
Contact: Institute for American Universities
IAU United States Office
PO Box 592
Evanston, IL 60204
(800) 221-2051
FAX (847) 864-6897
or
IAU France
27, place de l'Université
13625 Aix-en-Provence, France
(33) 4 42 23 39 35
FAX: (33) 4 42 21 11 38
E-mail: iauadm@univ-aix.fr
WWW: http://www.univ-aix.fr/iau/iau.html

The Institute for American Universities (IAU) in Aix-en-Provence offers an undergraduate program in archaeology with instruction in English in collaboration with the Centre Camille Jullian, one of the top archaeology research centers in Western Europe. The courses offered at le Centre d'Aix are designed for students with or without a background in archaeology. The full program will consist of three courses per semester in archaeology and two courses in French language. The Aix center offers French language courses at all levels. At present the following courses are proposed for the academic year

1998-99: Archaeological Methods and Theory: Approaches to Mediterranean Landscape Archaeology; Mediterranean Prehistory; Ancient Art and Archaeology in Southern France; and Ancient Mediterranean Civilization.

The program takes place in Aix-en-Provence, founded in 122 BC by the Romans and the first Roman settlement in present-day France, superseding the Celto-Ligurian capital of Entremont a mile to the north. Many vestiges of Aix's pre-Roman, Roman, Medieval, and more recent 17th and 18th century past are still visible today. Students learn to place artifacts and monuments as they exist in the landscape in context and will acquire a solid background in the theoretical and practical sides of the discipline of archaeology.

FRANCE
Location: Cantal, Volcanic Massif, S central France
Site: Velzic
Period: Mesolithic (9000 BP)

Volunteers:
Dates needed: July 1–31. Minimum stay of two weeks.
Application deadline: April 1
Minimum age: 18
Experience required: Experience preferred but not required. Volunteer should be self motivated. Basic ability to speak and understand French.
Cost: $200 registration fee covers lodging (in tents), local commute, weekday meals, and insurance. Travel to France and weekend meals not included.

Bibliography: Surmely, F., J-Ph., "Cors, une halte de chasse magdalenienne sur les contreforts du Massif Cantalien," BSPF, t. 90, No. 2, 1993, pp. 137–138. Surmely, F., A. Delpuech, "L'impact du volcanisme dans le Cantal à la fin des temps glaciaires," BSPF, t. 91, No. 2, 1994, pp. 123–129.

Sponsor: Ministère de la Culture; University of Clermont-Ferrand, National Center for Scientific Research
Director and
Contact: Frédéric Surmely, Conservateur
3 rue Gregoire de Tours
63000 Clermont-Ferrand, France
(33) 4 73 41 27 23
FAX: (33) 4 73 41 27 69

The basic objective of the project is to study the dynamics and conditions of settlement in the Volcanic Massif of Cantal from the end of the last Ice Age to the beginning of the post-glacial period. Since 1993, excavations have taken place at an important Mesolithic site in the Jordanne Valley at Velzic. Previous studies have revealed that the site was used by a group of hunters as a campsite; there are also several rockshelters adjacent to the site which were occupied at the same time. Microlithic arrow-points are very numerous. In addition to excavation, there will also be a survey of the geographic sector to find other prehistoric sites and flint deposits.

FRANCE
Location: Cote d'Or, E France
Site: Mâlain
Period: Gallo-Roman and Medieval

Volunteers:
Dates needed: June 28–August 9. Minimum stay of one week
Application deadline: May
Minimum age: 17

Experience required: None, but basic ability to speak and understand French. Drawing and photography skills welcome.
Cost: Program provides lodging (camping), meals (ca. 100FF/$20 per week), and on-site insurance. Travel to France not included.

Director, Sponsor, and
Contact: M. Louis Roussel
Groupe Archeologique du Memontois
52 rue des Forges
21000 Dijon, France
(33) 3 80 30 05 20

Located in the heart of Burgundy, the site includes a prehistoric cave, a Gallo-Roman and Celtic town, and a medieval village with a castle. In 1998, work will focus on the Château de Mâlain, the site of important excavations and restoration since 1985. Volunteers are involved in all aspects of the work, including excavation, restoration, conservation, and recording, and are expected to contribute to domestic chores. Group field trips guided by the Director are regularly organized, and Saturday afternoons and Sundays are free.

FRANCE
Location: Charente, Rozet, Combiers, W France
Site: Priory of Rauzet
Period: 12th–16th century AD (monastic), 17th–18th century AD (church parochial)

Dates of excavation and field school: July 25–August 21
Application deadline: March 1

Field School:
Academic credit: 1–3 credits from Western Michigan University
Cost: Tuition (to be determined) and all other expenses except on-site insurance and local commute.

Volunteers:
Minimum age: 21
Experience required: None, but persons who do not wish to handle skeletal remains should not apply. Drawing and ceramic skills welcome.
Cost: All expenses except for on-site insurance and local commute.

Bibliography: Greene, J. Patrick, Medieval Monasteries, Leicester University Press, 1992. Hutchison, C.A., *The Hermit Monks of Grandmont*, Kalamazoo: Cistercian Publications, 1989. Lawrence, C.H., *Medieval Monasticism, Forms of religious life in Western Europe in the Middle Ages*, London: Longman, 1984. Lackner, B., *Eleventh-Century Background of Cîteaux*, Kalamazoo: Cistercian Publications, 1972.

Director and Volunteer Program
Contact: Carole A. Hutchison
27 The Cedars, Brook Road,
Buckhurst Hill,
Essex IG9 5TS, England, UK

Educational Program
Contact: Dr. E. Rozanne Elder
Institute of Cistercian Studies,
Western Michigan University
Kalamazoo, Michigan 49008

The priory of Rauzet was built in the mid 1160s for a small community of Grandmontine monks. Its north-sited church and three conventual buildings were grouped around a square cloister. Two arched doorways from the west range (which formed part of the monastic kitchen) remain. The very simple, typically Grandmontine church presents a rare and particularly fine example of Romanesque architecture. The remains of the buildings alongside are important archaeologically. Only one other Grandmontine monastery has been excavated, so Rauzet will form the basis of a comparative study, as well as increasing scholars' knowledge of concealed features such as the water supply and drainage system.

This project is worked mainly by volunteers but is linked to the summer course for students from Western Michigan University. In 1998, the project will be excavating the exterior wall of the east range and continuing to excavate the cloister area which was used in the 17th century as a village cemetery following the departure of the monks.

FRANCE
Location: Deux-Sèvres, near Poitiers, W central France
Site: Rom
Period: AD 50–400

Volunteers:
Dates needed: June 15–July 10. Minimum stay of 3 weeks.
Application deadline: April 15
Minimum age: 18
Experience required: Basic ability to speak French and at least one month archaeological fieldwork.
Cost: Program provides lodging, weekday meals, local commute, and insurance. Travel to Poitiers and weekend meals not included.

Sponsor: Université de Poitiers; Ministère de la Culture; Conseil Général des Deux-Sèvres
Director and
Contact: Nadine Dieudonné-Glad
Université de Poitiers
Faculté de Sciences Humaines
8 rue René Descartes
86022 Poitiers Cedex, France

Rom is a small Gallo-Roman town, inhabited from at least the 1st–4th centuries AD. The Rom excavation is designed as a field school for students at the University of Poitiers, but it is also open to non-student volunteers. In 1996 and 1997, excavations focused on the town's housing areas, especially a 300-meter-square building along the main road. In 1998, the Director expects to be able to study the occupation levels in the area around this building. Activities will include excavation and cleaning of finds. All volunteers will be introduced to data recording.

FRANCE
Location: Hautes-Alpes, l'Argentière-la-Bessée, SE France
Site: Fournel Silver Mines
Period: Medieval and 19th century AD

Volunteers:
Dates needed: July
Application deadline: June 1
Minimum age: 18
Experience required: At least one experience working on a dig, physical fitness, fluency in French. Specialists with a knowledge of underground pumping systems are particularly welcome.
Cost: Program provides lodging at a campsite, meals, local commute, and insurance. Anti-tetanus vaccination obligatory. Travel to France not included.

Bibliography: Ancel, B., *Les Anciennes Mines d'Argent des Gorges du Fournel*, CCSTI de l'Argentière, 1994. Cowburn, I., *Valorisation du Patrimoine et Développement Local: l'Exemple du CCSTI de l'Argentière-la-Bessée*, CCSTI de l'Argentière, 1993. Kinchin-Smith, R.M., *The Surface Facilities at the Fournel Silver Mines, 1785–1905*, Masters Thesis in Industrial Archaeology, Ironbridge Institute, Great Britain, 1994.

Directors:	Mr. Ian Cowburn and Mr. Bruno Ancel
Sponsor and	
Contact:	Centre de Culture Scientifique, Technique et Industrielle (CCSTI)
	Château Saint-Jean
	05120 l'Argentière-la-Bessée, France
	(33) 4 92 23 04 48
	FAX: (33) 4 92 23 02 99

Situated at an altitude of 1400 meters in a mountain gorge of great natural beauty, the site was the most important metal-bearing mine in the Alps. Surface remains include a 19th-century mining village, ore-dressing workshops, forges, offices, and traces of medieval workshops. Underground remains include argentiferous lead workings, medieval exploitation chambers and air conduits, and 19th-century exploitation chambers, hydraulic installations, and narrow-gauge railway transports. The specific objective for 1998 is to continue underground evacuation, clearance, and access amelioration. 1997 finds include a complete 19th-century underground pumping system, and work will continue on this feature.

FRANCE
Location: Hautes-Alpes, l'Argentière-la-Bessée, SE France
Site: Fournel Silver Mines
Period: Medieval and 19th century AD

Field School: Fournel Silver Mines Research and Interpretation Project
Dates: Summer
Application deadline: June 1
Minimum age: 18
Academic credit: Certificate available from the Centre de Culture Scientifique.
Cost: Program provides lodging, mid-day meals, local commute, and insurance. Anti-tetanus vaccination obligatory. Travel to France and meals other than mid-day not included.

Bibliography: See bibliography for previous entry.

Director:	Mr. Ian Cowburn
Sponsor:	IDEM (Local Authority Resource Center)
Contact:	Centre de Culture Scientifique, Technique et Industrielle (CCSTI)
	Château Saint-Jean
	05120 l'Argentière-la-Bessée, France
	(33) 4 92 23 04 48
	FAX: (33) 4 92 23 02 99

The mission of the CCSTI, created in 1992, is to foster quality tourism based on local heritage with the aid of scientific research. The interpretation project is linked to the study of the Fournel silver mine (see previous entry) with the aim of developing the site as a tourist attraction. To date, the Château St. Jean has been restored and serves as a visitor center. The old stable buildings are now the Silver Mines Museum. From the Museum visitors walk up the Fournel gorge and tour a mining village and take an underground tour in the "Old Workings." The overall goal of the project is to recreate the site as it appeared in the later 19th century. In 1998 work will continue on reconstructing buildings for the presentation of reconstituted machinery, and on the 19th-century pumping system discovered in 1997.

Students in heritage development, earth sciences, cultural tourism, and human geography are particularly welcome as active contributors to the project. Students follow a three-month program comprised of source research, fieldwork, and report preparation. They also contribute to the Centre's activities and usually produce a particular document aimed at the Centre's needs in a particular field. One field of particular concern is socio-historical investigation into local industrial growth, translated into geographical representation.

FRANCE
Location: Lot, Thémines, S cen. France
Site: Doline de Roucadour
Period: Neolithic and Bronze Age

Volunteers:
Dates needed: July
Application deadline: June 1
Minimum age: 18
Experience required: None
Cost: Program provides lodging, meals, and local commute. Travel to France and insurance (ca. 50FF/$10) not included.

Bibliography: Niederlander A., R. Lacam, J. Arnal, "Le gisement néolithique de Roucadour, *Gallia Préhistoire*, III, supp., Paris, 1967. Arnal, J., L. Couchard, M. Lorblanchet, "La grotte de Roucadour (Thémines, Lot)," *Archivo de Prehistoria Levantina*, XII, 1969, pp. 55–91. Bailloud, G., "Signification de Roucadour C, Données stratigraphiques et évolution interne du Chasséen, Du Néolithique récent au début de l'Age du Bronze," *Les civilisations néolithiques de la France*, Actes du Colloque de Narbonne, 1970, pp. 25, 47–48, 89–9.

Director, Sponsor and	
Contact:	Jean Gascó
	Chargé de Recherche au CNRS (UPR 150)
	Montpellier-Village
	106–72 Rue de la Cadoule
	34070 Montpellier, France
	(33) 5 67 42 84 05

Excavation of Doline de Roucadour, a Neolithic site in southern France, resumed in 1996 after a hiatus of 30 years, and will continue in 1998. The new study will focus on the houses and culture of the indigenous population.

FRANCE
Location: Lozère, St. Germain de Calberte, S France
Site: Castrum de Calberte
Period: 13th–14th centuries AD

Volunteers:
Dates needed: July 13–August 8
Application deadline: May
Minimum age: 18
Experience required: None.
Cost: Program provides lodging, meals, and local commute. Travel to France and insurance not included.

Bibliography: Darnas, Isabelle, "Le Castrum de Calberte, Quartier nord-ouest," *Archéologie du Midi Médiéval*, 1992.

Sponsor: Ministry of Culture
Director and
Contact: Isabelle Darnas
La Colombeche - Le Born
48000 Mende, France
(33) 4 66 65 30 16

The site is a castle and medieval deserted village, built in the 11th century and deserted in the 14th. In 1998, study will focus on the entrance of the village. The site, located in the National Park of Cevennes, is quite isolated, and travel outside of the area is not possible without a car. Volunteers are accommodated in the castle and will work with French students, excavating and drawing.

FRANCE
Location: Moselle, NE France, on French/German border
Site: Bliesbruck-Reinheim, European Archaeological Park
Period: 1st–15th centuries AD

Volunteers:
Dates needed: Inquire.
Application deadline: Inquire.
Minimum age: 18
Experience required: None, but previous experience preferred.
Cost: Inquire.

Sponsor: Département Moselle-Ministère de la Culture
Director and
Contact: Jean Paul Petit
Centre Archéologique Départemental
1 rue Robert Schumann
57200 Bliesbruck, France
(33) 3 87 02 22 32
FAX: (33) 3 87 02 24 80
E-mail: pbrunella@imaginet.fr

Excavation in the area of Bliesbruck-Reinheim has revealed a dense concentration of archaeological sites, spanning 6000 years of occupation—from the Early Stone Age to the Early Middle Ages. The European Archaeological Park at Bliesbruck-Reinheim is a joint French-German effort to preserve the area from destruction and make it accessible to the public. Work at the site will include excavation; conservation and restoration of structures; reconstruction of parts of the settlement; establishment of an on-site museum for exhibitions, lectures, and demonstrations of ancient craft techniques; establishment of a research center; and the development of tourism though the installation of an archaeological/educational foot path.

FRANCE
Location: Nord, Douai, N France
Site: Douai
Period: Medieval

Volunteers:
Dates needed: July 7–August 28
Application deadline: June 15
Minimum age: 18
Experience required: None, but drawing, mapping, and digging skills welcome. Basic ability to speak and understand French.
Cost: Program provides weekday lodging and weekday meals. Travel to France, insurance (150FF, ca. $20), and weekend lodging and meals not included.

Sponsor: Musée de Douai

Director and
Contact: Pierre Demolon
Service Archéologique due Musée de Douai
191, Rue Saint Albin
59500 Douai, France
(33) 3 27 71 38 90
FAX: (33) 3 27 71 38 93
E-mail: Arkeos@wanadoo.fr

Excavations will continue in Douai, one of the most important towns in medieval Flanders. The excavation of an early medieval abbey will continue; the church will be excavated in 1998. Topics covered by the program include excavation techniques, stratigraphy, registration of finds, publication, and administration.

FRANCE
Location: Pas-de-Calais, Arras, N France
Site: Baudimont
Period: Roman, 1st–5th centuries AD

Volunteers:
Dates needed: July and August
Application deadline: May 31 (no exceptions)
Minimum age: 20
Experience required: None, but basic ability to speak and understand French. Tetanus immunization mandatory.
Cost: 60FF registration fee. Program provides lodging, meals, and insurance. Travel to France not included.

Contact: Mr. Alain Jacques
82, Rue Méaulens Prolongée
62000 Arras, France
(33) 3 21 50 86 32

The excavations at Baudimont have revealed the presence of Near Eastern cults, in particular that of Cybele, the great mother goddess of Anatolia, and her youthful lover Attis. This year's excavations will continue at a sanctuary dedicated to Cybele and Attis.

FRANCE
Location: Pas-de-Calais, Hermies Valley, N France
Site: Le Tio Marché
Period: Middle Paleolithic

Volunteers:
Dates needed: July 1–August 28. Minimum stay of two weeks.
Application deadline: June 5
Minimum age: 18
Experience required: Excavation at a prehistoric site. Tetanus immunization mandatory.
Cost: Program provides lodging, meals, insurance, and local commute. Travel to France not included.

Director, Sponsor, and
Contact: Luc Vallin
Service Régional de l'Archéologie
Avenue du Bois
F-59650 Villeneuve d'Ascq, France
(33) 3 20 91 38 69
FAX: (33) 3 20 91 41 81
E-mail: cpn@nordnet.fr
WWW: http://home.nordnet.fr/~cpn

The Centre de Préhistoire du Nord-Pas-de-Calais and the Service

Régional de l'Archéologie have been excavating at Mousterian settlements in the Hermies Valley since 1993. From 1993–1996, excavations at "Hermies le Champ Bruquette" revealed two levels dating back to the Early Glacial Weichselian. The upper layer has yielded more than 4500 flint artifacts from a very well-preserved flint knapping workshop, specializing in the production of Levallois flakes. About one kilometer away from "le Champ Bruquette," test cores have brought to light a well-preserved Mousterian site ("le Tio Marché"), and excavation began there in 1997. Several levels have been recognized, a little younger than those at "le Champ Bruquette," and the flint artifacts belong to the Levallois debitage and there are many refittings. Volunteer work involves minute excavating with three-dimensional recording, sketching stratigraphic profiles, inventory and computer analysis, and refitting lithic artifacts.

FRANCE
Location: St. Cesaire, SE France
Site: Rockshelter
Period: Middle-Upper Paleolithic

Field School:
Dates: July
Application deadline: April 15
Academic credit: 4 credits from Western State College
Cost: Tuition (ca. $350 resident or $1200 non-resident) and ca. $3000 for travel, lodging, and meals.

Volunteers: Contact the Director for details.

Director, Sponsor, and
Contact: Dr. Anna Backer
    Department of Anthropology
    Western State College of Colorado
    Gunnison, Colorado 81231
    E-mail: abacker@western.edu

The Western State College of Colorado field school at the rockshelter site of St. Cesaire will stress proper field excavation techniques such as mapping, recording, note-taking, sketching, photographing, and interpreting stratigraphy. Students will explore the transition from Neandertals to anatomically modern humans through faunal and lithic artifact remains in a deeply stratified rockshelter.

FRANCE
Location: Vaucluse, Gorges de la Nesque, SE France
Site: Bau de l'Aubésier rockshelter
Period: Middle Paleolithic (40,000–100,000 BP)

Dates of excavation and field school: July–August
Application deadline: May 30

Field School:
Academic credit: 3 credits from the Université du Québec à Montréal
Cost: Cost (to be determined) will cover tuition and fees for lodging, meals, and insurance. Travel to France not included. Inquire for details.

Volunteers:
Minimum age: 21
Experience required: None
Cost: Cost (to be determined) will cover lodging, meals, and insurance. Travel to France not included. Inquire for details.

Director: Dr. Serge Lebel

Sponsor: CRSH (Canada); French Government; Université du Quebec à Montréal
Contact: Université du Quebec à Montréal
    Département des Sciences de la Terre
    Laboratoire d'Archéologie
    Case postale 8888, Succursale Centre-ville
    Montréal, Québec H3C 3P8 Canada
    (514) 987-4194
    FAX: (514) 987-7749

Since 1989, an international team has been excavating at the important Middle Paleolithic rockshelter, Bau de l'Aubésier. To date, 12 meters of cave deposits have yielded more than eight archaeological layers. The lower human occupation layer has been radiometrically dated to ca. 200,000 BP, and the first evidence (numerous teeth) for a Neandertal fossil population has been found in layer IV. Two areas with traces of fire were found associated with numerous animal remains, including equus, bos, rangiver tarandus, rhinoceros, etc., and more than 80,000 stone tools and Levallois flakes provide an overview of the Mousterian technology and lithic reduction sequence. Each summer, the site receives 30 students and volunteers from many countries. Students experience excavation in a particular geological environment and learn current techniques used at Paleolithic sites.

FRANCE
Location: Vaucluse, S France
Site: Dolmen de l'Ibac
Period: Neolithic (3500 BC)

Volunteers:
Dates needed: July. Minimum stay of 15 days.
Application deadline: None
Minimum age: 18
Experience required: Background in archaeology and prehistory. Basic ability to speak and understand French.
Cost: Program provides lodging, meals, insurance, and local commute. Travel to France not included.

Bibliography: Whittle, A., *Neolithic Europe: A Survey (Cambridge World Archaeology)*, Cambridge University Press, 1988.

Director, Sponsor, and
Contact: Jacques Buisson-Catil
    Service Départmental de l'Archéologie de Vaucluse
    84000 Avignon, France
    (33) 4 90 16 11 88

The program involves the excavation of a megalithic tomb in southern France, the second found in the Vaucluse Department. Volunteers will participate in excavation, artifact studies, and recording the plan of the monument.

GREECE
Location: Athens
Site: Various
Period: Various

College Year in Athens Academic Year Session:
Dates: Fall and/or Spring semesters; open to single semester and full year students.
Application deadline: May 15 for Fall; October 15 for Spring
Academic credit: Credit for a full-time program (4 courses per semester) arranged through student's own institution.
Cost: $9900 per semester covers tuition, lodging, study trips, and one

main meal, six days per week. Travel to and from Greece, insurance, and personal expenses not included.

College Year in Athens is an independent study abroad program, providing a university-level education focused on Greece and the world of the Eastern Mediterranean. The language of instruction is English and the majority of students come from North America. The courses cover ancient times to the present and represent the disciplines of: Archaeology, Art History, Classical Languages, Ethnography, History, Literature, Modern Greek Language, Philosophy, Political Science, and Religion. The program includes classroom study and study trips to a variety of sites throughout Greece.

College Year in Athens 6-week Summer Session:
Dates: June 9–July 17
Application deadline: April 1
Academic credit: 6–8 credits (2 courses) arranged through student's own institution
Cost: $3500 covers tuition, lodging, study trips, and course materials. Travel to Greece, insurance, meals, and personal expenses not included.

During the College Year in Athens summer program in Greece, students enroll in two courses concentrating on developments in archaeology, art, mythology, and religion in the Greek world from the Bronze through the Classical Age. The courses are closely interwoven with a program of field trips which take students to almost all the important sites in Crete, the Peloponnese, and Central Greece.

College Year in Athens 3-Week Summer Session:
Dates: June 9–June 26
Application deadline: April 1
Academic credit: 3–4 credits (one course) arranged through student's own institution.
Cost: $1550 covers tuition, lodging, and course materials. Travel to Greece, insurance, meals, and personal expenses not included.

During the course "Ancient Athens in its Living Context" students will experience the monuments of ancient Athens and environs within the context of the modern city. Classes meet in the shadow of the Parthenon and other monuments on the Acropolis, in the Agora, and the Kerameikos. The course will provide students with an understanding of the concepts and physical expression of 5th century BC Athens and enable them to recognize its influence on and continuity into modern Athens. The instructor is Karelisa Hartigan.

Director: Alexis Phylactopoulos
Sponsor and
Contact: College Year in Athens, North American Office
432 Columbia Street, 28C
PO Box 390890
Cambridge, MA 02139
(617) 494-1008
FAX: (617) 494-1662
E-mail: cyathens@aol.com
WWW: http://www.cyathens.org

GREECE
Location: Various
Site: Various
Period: Various

ASCSA Summer Sessions:
Dates: Session I: June 15–July 29; Session II: June 22–August 5
Application deadline: February 15
Academic credit: Credit may be arranged through student's own institution.

Prerequisites: Open to graduate and advanced undergraduate students, and high school and college teachers.
Requirements: The program is strenuous, there is extensive walking and some climbing, and Greece is quite hot in the summer. Participants need to be in good physical condition. Those who are concerned about their health and stamina (including special dietary or medication requirements) should not apply. Upon acceptance, a medical checkup certificate is required.
Cost: ca. $2950 covers tuition, lodging, some meals, domestic travel within Greece, and museum and site fees. International airfare, some meals, and incidental expenses not included. A limited number of scholarships are available through the School and are awarded on the basis of answers to questions on the application.

Co-Directors: Session I: Prof. Sarah Pierce, Fordham University, and Prof. Ann Steiner, Franklin and Marshall College. Session II: Prof. Robert F. Sutton, Jr., Indiana University- Purdue University at Indianapolis
Sponsor and
Contact: American School of Classical Studies at Athens
Committee on the Summer Sessions
6-8 Charlton Street
Princeton, NJ 08540-5232
(609) 683-0800
FAX: (609) 924-0578
E-mail: ascsa@ascsa.org
WWW: http://www.ascsa.org

The ASCSA Summer Sessions are an intense introduction to the topography and monuments of Ancient, Byzantine, and Modern Greece, designed for those who wish to become acquainted with Greece in a limited time and to improve their understanding of the relationship between the country (its monuments, landscape, and climate) and its history, literature, and culture. Each session is divided almost equally between the study of sites, monuments, and museums in Attica, and trips to places in Central Greece, the Peloponnese, Macedonia, Northwest Greece, and the islands, according to itineraries set by each Director. Participants are required to deliver oral reports on assigned topics, usually presented at the different sites appropriate to the reports.

GREECE
Location: Various
Site: Various
Period: Various

Study Tour: "On-Site with the American School"
Dates and cost: Inquire

Sponsor and
Contact: American School of Classical Studies at Athens
Committee on the Summer Sessions
6-8 Charlton Street
Princeton, NJ 08540-5232
(609) 683-0800
FAX: (609) 924-0578
E-mail: ascsa@ascsa.org
WWW: http://www.ascsa.org

"On-Site with the American School" provides an annual two-week, in-depth archaeological and historical survey of a specific region in the ancient Greek world, designed specifically for a lay audience. The price will be in the $4800 range, excluding international airfare. For more information, contact the American School of Classical Studies.

GREECE
Location: Various
Site: Various
Period: Various

Study Tour: Ancient Greece
Dates: May 20–June 20
Application deadline: February 27. Applications received after February 27 will be processed on a space-available basis. Maximum enrollment is 25.
Academic credit: One course credit from Duke University.
Prerequisites: Courses in Greek civilization, history, or art history, or special permission of the instructor. Non-Duke students must be in good academic standing and submit a transcript and letter of recommendation from a professor.
Cost: $1560 for tuition and $2500 program fee for lodging, some meals, and excursions. Travel to Greece, some meals, and personal expenses not included. Students must make their own travel arrangements to and from Greece.

Bibliography: Rossiter, S., *The Blue Guide to Greece*. Burn, A.R., *A History of Greece*. Both are in paperback. Students may also wish to purchase and study guidebooks available at the various archaeological sites.

Director, Sponsors, and
Contacts: Prof. John Younger
                 Department of Classical Studies
                 Duke University, Box 90103
                 (919) 684-2082
                 FAX: (919) 681-4262
                 E-mail: jyounger@acpub.duke.edu
                      or
                 Office of Foreign Academic Programs
                 Duke University
                 121 Allen Building, Box 90057
                 Durham, NC 27708-0057
                 (919) 684-2174
                 FAX: (919) 684-3083

Through readings, on-site walking lectures, and tours of the important sites and museums, students in Duke University's program on Ancient Greece will study the development of the Preclassical, Classical, Roman, and Byzantine cultures in Greece, concentrating on Athens, southern Greece, and the Cycladic islands. The itinerary includes: Athens, Corinth, Mycenae, Epidauros, Tiryns, Lerna, Mystra, Pylos, Olympia, Delphi, Thebes, Mykonos, Delos, Thera, and other sites. Careful attention will be given to the methods by which archaeological, literary, and other evidence can be combined and interpreted to form a picture of an ancient culture. There is a final exam, one prepared oral report, and two textbooks. By the end of the program, students will have visited the National Museum in Athens and most of the other important sites and museums in southern Greece.

GREECE
Location: Various
Site: Various
Period: Various

Summer Programs at Greek Universities: A final list of participating universities, courses offered, and costs will be available in January 1998.
Dates: July 6–August 11
Application deadline: Inquire.

Academic credit: 6–9 credits (equivalent of 1–2 courses) from student's own institution.
Cost: Cost ($1900 in 1997) will cover tuition, lodging, meals, and local commute. Travel to Greece and insurance (mandatory) not included.

Sponsors: Greek Ministry of Education; General Secretariat of Crete; DIAS International Academic Studies; and participating institutions.
Contact: DIAS International Academic Studies
                 c/o Dr. John Nathenas
                 18 West View Drive
                 Upper Brookville, NY 11771
                 (516) 624-9015
                 FAX: (516) 624-9050
                 E-mail: 74261.710@compuserve.com
                      or
                 Elita Charalambous
                 Tel/FAX: (516) 746-4590
                      or
                 Dr. Angelos Chaniotis
                 (212) 998-8590
                 FAX: (212) 995-4209
                 E-mail: chaniots@is@.nyu.edu

DIAS is a non-profit educational organization dedicated to making the necessary arrangements for students from all over the world to attend accredited courses at Greek universities during the summer. The courses are offered in English. Possible participating universities include: Aegean University, Athens University, University of Ioannina, University of Crete, University of Thessaloniki, and University of Cyprus. Courses under consideration are: field archaeology (with excavation component), Minoan and Mycenaean history, ancient history of the eastern Mediterranean, Byzantine studies, ancient and modern Greek language, ancient drama, and philosophy.

GREECE
Location: Various
Site: Various
Period: Various

Study Tour: Classical Studies Abroad
Dates: May. Exact dates to be determined.
Application deadline: Inquire.
Academic credit: One term course (Classical Studies 390) from the University of Waterloo. Inquire for details.
Prerequisite: Minimum of three term courses in Classics, Latin, or Greek, or permission of the Department.
Cost: ca. CDN$3000–$3200 includes airfare from Toronto, all transportation in Greece, lodging, breakfast, entrance fees, and tips. Lunch, most dinners, and spending money not included.

Director, Sponsor, and
Contact: Dr. Maria Liston
                 Department of Anthropology and Classical Studies
                 University of Waterloo
                 (519) 885-4567, ext. 2553
                 E-mail: mliston@watarts.uwaterloo.ca

The course features a combination of academic study and firsthand investigation of museums and ancient sites in Greece. The course material will concentrate on the archaeology, history, and art of Bronze Age and Classical Greece, but will also include Byzantine art and modern Greek culture. The trip begins in Athens, followed by a tour of the Greek mainland and a tour of the island of Crete. The itinerary includes the Acropolis, Agora and National Museum in Athens, Eleusis, Corinth, Mycenae, Epidaurus, Olympia, and Delphi. Students will be expected to participate in a number preliminary sessions before departure (arrangements will be made to accommodate distance learning students). Requirements for the course are: 1) preliminary readings and classes, 2) participation in all required activities while in Greece, 3) a research project resulting in an on-site presentation to the group while in Greece or a final paper based on research and personal observations in Greece, and 4) a final exam.

GREECE
Location: Isthmus of Corinth, NE Peloponnese
Site: Isthmia, 12 km from Ancient Korinth
Period: Classical–Byzantine

Field School:
Dates: April 15–June 2
Application deadline: February 1
Academic credit: 15 quarter hours from The Ohio State University
Cost: $2700 covers tuition, lodging, some meals, local commute, field trips, and insurance. Airfare to Athens (ca. $1000), weekend lunches and Saturday dinner (ca. $120), and one week of independent travel (ca. $200) not included.

Volunteers:
Dates needed: June 29–August 1. Minimum stay of four weeks.
Application deadline: May 1
Minimum age: 16
Experience required: None
Cost: Program provides some meals and local commute. Travel to project, lodging, some meals, and insurance not included.

Bibliography: Publications may be found in the *Isthmia* series (Princeton) and in the journal *Hesperia*.

Director, Sponsor, and
Contact: Timothy E. Gregory
           The Ohio State University
           Department of History
           230 West 17th Avenue
           Columbus, OH 43210
           (614) 292-2674/1949
           FAX: (614) 292-2282
           E-mail: gregory.4@osu.edu
           WWW: http://www.acs.ohio-state.edu/history/
               isthmia/teg
               or
           The Ohio State University
           Excavations at Isthmia
           Ancient Korinth GR 200 07, Greece
           (30) 741 31209/37219
           E-mail: isthmia@compulink.gr

Isthmia was the site of the Sanctuary of Poseidon and the Isthmian Games. In the Middle Ages it was transformed into a stronghold on the military fortifications that protected southern Greece from invasion from the north. The University of Chicago excavated at the site beginning in 1952, and they continue their work today in the center of the sanctuary. This project, however, is a continuation of one begun in 1967 by UCLA and continued since 1987 by The Ohio State University.

The OSU Study-Abroad Opportunity will provide a first-hand introduction to classical archaeology by visiting archaeological sites and working at Isthmia. Sites to be visited include Athens and the island of Aegina; the Argolid and sites such as Mycenae, Tiryns, and Nauplion; and the ancient cities of Paphos and Kition and the medieval castles of Cyprus. At Isthmia, students will work as a team in the investigation of the site and in the restoration of the large monochrome mosaic that has been excavated over the past two years. Participants will learn proper archaeological techniques and analysis and they will give reports and work on projects based on their own interests. All participants will learn the rudiments of the Modern Greek language, however, no previous knowledge is assumed, and basic language classes are part of the program.

A limited number of volunteers will be accepted by The OSU Excavations at Isthmia to assist in the 1998 program, which will continue to focus on the conservation and re-laying of a great monochrome mosaic in the Roman Bath, as well as cleaning and exploration in other areas of the site. Volunteers work with experienced staff members in a revolving series of tasks, many of them involving some physical labor, but it should be noted that the program does not use volunteers as laborers, but as archaeological apprentices, and the whole program is educational in nature.

GREECE
Location: Pylos
Site: Iklaina
Period: Late Bronze Age (Mycenaean) ca. 1600–1100 BC

Dates of excavation and field school: July 6–20
Application deadline: March 1

Field School/Study Tour:
Academic credit: 6 credits from University of Manitoba
Cost: CDN$650 for tuition and ca. CDN$800 for lodging, meals, and local commute. Travel to Greece and insurance not included.

Volunteers:
Minimum age: 18
Experience required: None.
Cost: ca. CDN$1300 covers lodging, meals, local commute, and training. Travel to Greece and insurance not included.

Director: Prof. Michael Cosmopoulos
Sponsor and
Contact: University of Manitoba
           Department of Classics
           Winnipeg, Manitoba R3T 2M8, Canada
           (204) 474-9171
           E-mail: cosmopo@ccu.umanitoba.ca

Iklaina has been identified one of the district capitals of the Mycenaean kingdom of Pylos, known from the Linear B tablets as *a-pu2*. The objective of the project is to study the mechanisms of state formation in Mycenaean Greece, specifically, to examine the processes of integration of regional centers of power into centralized states, through a thorough study and analysis of one of these regional centers (Iklaina).

The goal of the 1998 season is to survey the site and its major area in preparation for excavation. Students and volunteers will participate in the fieldwork (fieldwalking, and artifact and data collection and analysis) and visits to nearby sites and museums. Those attending for academic credit attend seminars and classes in the evenings.

GREECE
Location: Thasos Island
Site: Agora and Necropolis of Thasos, and Archaeological Museum
Period: Classical

Dates of excavation and field school: June 4–30
Application deadline: May 1

Field School:
Academic credit: 6 credits from Adelphi University
Cost: $2500 covers tuition, fees, lodging, 50% of meals, and local commute. Travel to Greece and insurance not included.

Volunteers:
Minimum age: 18
Experience required: None.
Cost: $1500 covers lodging, 50% of meals, and local commute. Travel to Greece and insurance not included.

Bibliography: Koukouli-Chrysanthaki, C.H., M. Sgourou, and A. Agelarakis, *Archaeological Investigations in the Necropolis of Ancient Thasos*, paper presented at the 1996 symposium "Greek Archaeology in Macedonia and Thrace" (available from the Director).

Sponsors: Adelphi University; Greek Archaeological Service
Director and
Contact: Prof. Anagnosti P. Agelarakis
Adelphi University
Department of Anthropology
Garden City, NY 11530
(516) 877-4112
FAX: (516) 877-4191
E-mail: agelarakis@adlibr.adelphi.edu

The project combines laboratory analyses and, to a lesser extent, excavation, to study the paleodemography of the ancient population of Thasos, a generation after it was visited by Hippocrates. There will also be an attempt to relate findings to Hippocrates' Book III on Epidemics. The Adelphi team will consist of 5–7 people, including the Director, and will work in conjunction with a European team. The focus is on skeletal biology, paleopathology, archaeological forensics, taphonomy, and paleoenvironments. The project provides a singular opportunity for hands-on experience, behind the scenes at the Thasos Archaeological Museum and at archaeological sites.

HUNGARY

Location: Greater Danube region, north-central Hungary
Site: Szarvasgede
Period: Neolithic–Modern

Volunteers:
Dates: Project 1, Hungarian Country Manor: Team I: June 21–July 4, Team II: June 6–July 20. **Project 2, Ancient Foods and Future Farming:** Team I: June 21–July 4, Team: II: July 5–18, Team III: July 20–August 2, Team IV: August 5–18

Application deadline: 90 days prior to departure. (Applications will be accepted after that time if space is available.)
Minimum age: 16
Experience required: None
Cost: $1695 per session covers all expenses except travel to staging area (Szarvasgede, Hungry) and insurance.

Director: Project 1: Dr. Lauren Sickels-Taves, Dr. Michael Sheehan, and Ms. Jenny Bjork. Project 2: Dr. Irwin Rovner and Dr. Ferenc Gyulai, North Carolina State University
Sponsor and
Contact: Earthwatch
See page 7 for contact information.

The Biohistory Habitat and International Research Center is dedicated to experimental archaeology pertaining to the origins of agriculture, the preservation and propagation of living examples of ancient seed crops, and experimentation with the reintroduction of ancient cultigens into modern agricultural contexts. One long-term objective of this effort is to re-create the medieval farm that occupied the site.

Project 1: Hungarian Country Manor: The ultimate goal of this project is the restoration of an 18th-century manor house that stands within the limits of the proposed experimental farm. The plan is for the manor house to become the core of the research center. Volunteers in architecture/historic preservation will assist in the documentation of the structure's condition and its unique features; identify and make note of existing threats to its preservation; make a photographic record; and take measurements. Volunteers in archaeology will conduct controlled excavation; map and recover cultural materials and features; screen sediment removed during excavation; and assist in laboratory processing and preliminary analysis of cultural materials and features.

Project 2: Ancient Foods and Future Farming: This project is part of the Biohistory Habitat and Research Center research on paleoecology, paleoenvironment, paleobotany, archaeology, agricultural history, and ancient farming practices and methods. The first phase of the project is an extensive survey of the on-site historical and prehistoric resources, employing near-surface remote sensing technology. Volunteers will conduct controlled stratigraphic excavation of archaeological units, expose artifacts and features, map and record data, recover artifacts, and collect soil and microfossil samples. Volunteers will also assist in the lab with washing, labeling, and cataloging collected materials, and flotation processing to recover macrofossil remains, e.g. seeds, charcoal and plant fragments, small bones, hair, etc.

ITALY
Location: Various
Site: Various
Period: Various

Study Tour: The Making Of The Roman World
Dates: June 27–July 24
Application deadline:
Academic credit: 3–6 credits from Hunter College. Program open to both undergraduate and graduate students
Cost: Tuition ($135 per credit for New York residents, $325 per credit for non-residents) plus $2750 for round-trip airfare, transfers, lodging, breakfasts, and some dinners. Lunches and some dinners not included.

Directors: Professors Tamara M. Green and Robert J. White
Sponsor and
Contact: Gary Braglia
Hunter College Study Abroad
Hunter College
695 Park Avenue
New York, NY 10021
(212) 772-4983
or
Tamara Green
E-mail: tgreen@shiva.hunter.cuny.edu
(212) 772-5061

This program is a concentrated study of the various cultures that shaped the foundations of Roman civilization in Italy. Umbrians, Etruscans, Oscans, Sicels, and Greeks flourished in Italy long before Rome expanded beyond a small village. The recognition of their multicultural foundations and inheritances made the Romans perhaps more receptive to the varieties of cultures within the boundaries of the Italian peninsula and Sicily, as they borrowed and adapted political, religious, and literary traditions, even as they shaped their own distinctive civilization. The itinerary includes: Rome, with visits to Cerveteri and other Etruscan sites; Naples and environs, with visits to Pompeii and Herculaneum, and Capri; and Sicily with visits to all major Greek sites. Students will be expected to attend lectures four afternoons a week and to write a series of essays.

ITALY
Location: Calabria, 7 km SW of Oppido Mamertina, S Italy
Site: Contrada Mella (ancient *Mamertion* [?])
Period: ca. 300 BC–AD 50

Volunteers:
Dates needed: June 15–August 1
Application deadline: May 2
Minimum age: 20
Experience required: None, but drawing and recording skills preferred.
Cost: Volunteer responsible for all expenses except local commute.

Bibliography: Lomas, K., *Rome and the Western Greeks 350 BC–AD 200*, London and New York, 1993, pp. 59–97. Visonà, P., *American Journal of Archaeology*, 92, 1988, p. 264; 95, 1991, pp. 311–312; 97, 1993, p. 320; 99; 1995, p. 347. Visonà, P., "Gli scavi americani a contrada Mella (Oppido Mamertina), 1987–1991: risultati e prospettive," *Klearchos*, 32 (1990) [1992] pp. 69–103. Costamagna, L., and P. Visonà (eds.), *Oppido Mamertina 1*, Rome, 1997.

Sponsor: The Mamertion Foundation; Soprintendenza Archeologica della Calabria
Director, and
Contact: Dr. Paolo Visonà
The Mamertion Foundation
12542 W. Mississippi Avenue
Lakewood, CO 80228
Tel/FAX: (303) 989-7748

Unlike most Italic sites in Calabria, Contrada Mella flourished after the Second Punic War and was continuously occupied until the 1st century BC. The finds cast light on the architecture and material culture of a Hellenized Oscan town, possibly to be identified as ancient *Mamertion*, during the Romanization of Magna Graecia. In the 1998 season, a new city block in the central area of habitation will be investigated, in addition to a Roman house built upon a street intersection after the destruction of the Italic settlement. Participants will be trained in excavation and recording techniques, and will visit Greek and Oscan sites in the region.

ITALY
Location: Latium, Viterbo, near Rome
Site: Various
Period: Mainly Etruscan

Living History Tours: The Mystery of the Etruscans (and others). A variety of guided tour options are offered.
Dates: Inquire. Tours and excursions range from 1–14 days.
Application deadline: Inquire.
Academic credit: Credit may be arranged through participant's own institution. Participants receive Certificates of Attendance upon completion of the tour.
Cost: Inquire.

Director, Sponsor, and
Contact: Joanna B. Bulgarini, Executive Director
The Foundation for International Educational and
     Cultural Exchange
via di Grottarossa 296
00189 Rome, Italy
Tel/FAX: (39) 6 33261796
E-mail: Bulgarin@isinet.it

The Foundation for International Educational and Cultural Exchange Living History Tours focus on providing hands-on experience in exploring the lives and customs of past civilizations and cultures. They are designed to meet the interests and needs of professional groups, middle and high school groups, university students, and senior citizen and special interest groups.

"The Mysterious Etruscan Peoples of Italy" study tour consists of lectures and on-site tours with historians and archaeologists who present the evolution of the Etruscans in Italy from their beginnings as agrarian tribes of prehistory, through their growth into politically and culturally sophisticated confederations of 12 city states, to their integration into the Roman Empire. The tour begins at The Center for Experimental Archeology, situated in the Etruscan Aisna Tuti Tamna, (Sacred Valley of the Horses), a protected European Archeological Park Reserve. The Center re-creates the life, customs, and skills practiced by the Etruscans of the Villanovan Period (9th–8th centuries BC) and provides a hands-on experience in the arts of bronze-casting, archery, potting and open-hearth firing, weaving, grinding farro wheat, making rustic spelt bread and other foods, constructing ancient systems of water purification, and building hut-dwellings and walls. Techniques of excavation in simulated digs and restoration of antiquities are practiced to prepare travelers for their visits to museums, archeological excavations, and ancient ruins throughout the tour.

The Living History Tours Series is just one of many programs offered. The Center's School of Equestrian Sciences and Horseriding (in the style of the ancient Butteri horsemen), provides guided excursions into the surrounding valley to visit archeological digs and museums. Trips are planned in accordance with the personal needs and physical stamina of participants and can be from half-day excursions to ten-day camping expeditions.

ITALY
Location: Molise, Isernia, central Italy
Site: San Vincenzo al Volturno
Period: Medieval

Students/Volunteers:
Dates: June–August
Application deadline: Inquire.
Minimum age: Inquire.
Experience required: None.
Cost: Inquire.

Coordinator, Sponsor, and
Contact: Oliver Gilkes
The Prince of Wales's Institute of Architecture
14 Gloucester Gate
Regent's Park
London NWI 4HG, England, UK
(44) 171 9167380
FAX: (44) 171 916 7381

The Princes of Wales's Institute of Architecture is running a series of archaeological and architectural projects for which there are places for students and volunteers. These will take place over the course of 1998 and subsequent years. At San Vincenzo al Volturno, the great early medieval abbey, the Institute will continue their ongoing excavations, and offer a course on excavation methodology. The Institute also has projects in Pompeii (see below) and in Norfolk, England. Contact the coordinator for more information.

ITALY
Location/Site: Pompeii
Period: Roman

Students/Volunteers:
Dates: September
Application deadline: Inquire.
Minimum age: Inquire.
Experience required: None.
Cost: Inquire.

Coordinator, Sponsor, and
Contact: Oliver Gilkes
The Prince of Wales's Institute of Architecture
14 Gloucester Gate
Regent's Park
London NWI 4HG, England, UK
(44) 171 9167380
FAX: (44) 171 916 7381

The Princes of Wales's Institute of Architecture is running a series of archaeological and architectural projects for which there are places for students and volunteers. These will take place over the course of 1998 and subsequent years. In Pompeii, the project involves documentation and reconstruction based on the study of one of the long excavated villas near the city. There will be a concurrent course in the analysis and reconstruction of ancient buildings. The Institute is also running one other project in Italy at San Vincenzo and one in Norfolk, England. Contact the coordinator for more information.

ITALY
Location/Site: Pompeii, Regio VI, Insula 1, near Naples, S Italy
Period: Middle 1st millennium BC–AD 79

Field School: Maximum of 15 students.
Dates: July 5–August 8
Application deadline: March 1
Academic Credit: 3 credits from Hunter College or the University of Bradford.
Cost: $2500 covers tuition, lodging, meals, insurance, and local commute. Travel to Italy not included.

Bibliography: Bon, Sara, and Rick Jones (eds.), *Sequence and Space in Pompeii*, Oxbow Books, 1997. Wallace-Hadrill, Andrew, *Houses and Society in Pompeii and Herculaneum*, Princeton University Press, 1994. Laurence, Ray, *Roman Pompeii—Space and Society*, Routledge, 1994. Etienne, Robert, *Pompeii: The Day a City Died*, Thames and Hudson Inc., 1992. La Rocca E., M. De Vos, and A. De Vos, *Pompei*, Guide Archeologiche Mondadori, Milano, 1994. Arthur, P., "Problems of the urbanization of Pompeii: excavations 1980-1," *Antiquaries Journal*, 66, 1986, pp. 29-44.

Directors: Dr. Rick Jones, Damian Robinson, University of Bradford; Sara Bon, University of North Carolina at Chapel Hill; Bernice Kurchin, Hunter College, CUNY
Sponsors: Department of Archaeological Sciences, University of Bradford, UK; Department of Anthropology, Hunter College, CUNY

Contact: Bernice Kurchin
Department of Anthropology
Hunter College, CUNY
695 Park Avenue
New York, NY 10021
(212) 772-5672 or (914) 478-3423
FAX: (212) 772-5423
E-mail: bkurchin@aol.com
or
Rick Jones
Bradford Pompeii Research Laboratory
Department of Archaeological Sciences
University of Bradford
Bradford BD7 1DP, UK
(44) 1274 383536
FAX: (44) 1274 385190
E-mail: archsci-pompeii@bradford.ac.uk
WWW: http://www.brad.ac.uk/acad/archsci/
field_proj/anampomp/anampomp.html

In 1998, 250 years of excavation at Pompeii will be celebrated with its designation as a World Heritage Site, and there are many new research initiatives that are adding fresh perspectives to our understanding of this classic site, and major new programs for the conservation and presentation of Pompeii. The Anglo-American Project in Pompeii plays a substantial role in all these areas, working in collaboration with the Soprintendenza Archeologica di Pompei. The project's aim is to discover how the city came to be the place that was destroyed by Vesuvius in AD 79. The focus is on recovering in full detail the history of changing occupation in one complete block of the city (Regio VI, insula 1). Situated in the northwest corner of the city, immediately inside the Herculaneum Gate on one of the city's main thoroughfares, Insula VI,1 had a range of types of buildings, bars, and workshops as well as two large houses, the House of the Vestals and the House of the Surgeon, often considered one of the oldest structures still standing at Pompeii in AD 79.

In 1998, the fourth full field season, excavation will continue in the House of the Vestals, one of the largest houses of the city. It became an imposing residence with extensive mosaics and elaborately painted walls. Much has been lost during the two centuries since the house was first exposed, but painstaking research has revealed much about the late house and its development over three centuries, as well as recognizing earlier earth-built structures dating to the third century BC.

The field school has a ratio of one staff member to two students, and all students are trained in excavation, standing building analysis, finds processing, and environmental archaeology. Throughout the program students take a direct part in interpreting the archaeology and maintaining detailed records, all under close supervision. The program also includes guided visits to other sites on the Bay of Naples, such as Herculaneum, Oplontis, and the National Museum in Naples.

ITALY
Location: Potenza, Oppido Lucano, S Italy
Site: Roman Villa
Period: 1st century BC–5th century AD

Volunteers:
Dates needed: July
Application deadline: April 30
Minimum age: 21
Experience required: Basic training in field archaeology.
Cost: Volunteer responsible for all expenses except local commute and insurance.

Bibliography: Gualtieri, M., and H. Fracchia, "Excavations and Survey at Masseria Ciccotti, Oppido Lucano: Interim Report 1989–92," *Echos Classiques/Classical Views* 37, 1993, pp. 313–38; "Excavations at Oppido Lucano (Potenza, Italy): Interim Report 1993–94," *Echos Classiques/Classical Views* 39, 1995, pp. 61–95.

Sponsors: University of Alberta, Edmonton, Canada; University of Perugia, Italy
Director and:
Contact: M. Gualtieri
University of Perugia
via Armonica 3
Perugia 06123 Italy
FAX: (39) 755 854941
E-mail: mgualt@unipg.it

The large villa site at Oppido Lucano is located at the center of a fertile agricultural area along the upper/middle Bradano valley in south Italy. The buildings so far excavated belong to the central residential area of the villa and indicate a sustained level of wealth (as evidenced by mosaic and marble floors in particular) and architectural sophistication in inland Lucania throughout the Roman period. Research plans for 1998 include continuing exploration of selected areas of the *pars rustica* (the productive sector of the estate) and surface survey of the middle Bradano valley, to collect more specific archaeological and environmental data on systems of land exploitation in the region. The ultimate goal is to provide new evidence on the economy of the site as the basis for a more general study of rural south Italy under the Roman Empire. The evidence so far recovered contradicts the conventional, and still widely accepted, view of the decline and impoverishment of the region after the Roman conquest.

ITALY
Location: Rome and immediate environs

American Academy in Rome Classical Summer School
Dates: June 22–August 1
Application deadline: March 1
Prerequisites: Open to high school teachers and graduate students of Latin, ancient history, and the classics.
Academic credit: Graduate credit is available from SUNY-Buffalo.
Financial aid: Scholarships are available. Application deadlines for these awards range from October 1997–May 1998. Candidates are advised to consult the list sent with summer school application packages and to contact the associations as early as possible.
Cost: ca. $4000 will cover tuition, fees, lodging, and meals. Travel to Italy not included. (Tuition only is $1400.)

Sponsor: American Academy in Rome
Director and
Contact: Prof. Stephen Dyson
Classics Department
712 Clemens Hall
SUNY-Buffalo
Buffalo, NY 14260
(716) 645-2154, ext. 1114
FAX: (716) 645-2225
E-mail: cldyson@acsu.buffalo.edu
or
American Academy in Rome
7 East 60th Street
New York, NY 10022-1001
(212) 751-7200
WWW: http://www.aarome.org

The Classical Summer School is designed to provide the student with an understanding of the growth and development of the ancient city of Rome and its immediate environs from the earliest times to the age of Constantine, through a careful study of material remains and literary sources. The daily visits to sites and museums will be preceded and accompanied by lectures intended to offer an introduction to the material and to place it within its context. Besides frequent excursions within Rome, the group takes field trips to major sites in Latium and Etruria such as Tivoli, Palestrina, Gabii, the Alban Hills, Ostia, Cerveteri, Tarquinia, Cosa, and Veii. Summer School students should be aware of the Vergilian Society's two-week program on Campanian sites, including Pompeii and Herculaneum, which immediately follows the Summer School. For details, contact Prof. John A. Dutra, Dept. of Classics, Miami University, Oxford, OH 45056.

ITALY
Site/Location: Rome and immediate environs, and other sites

American Academy in Rome Summer Program in Italian Archaeology
Dates: To be determined, generally May 31–August 1
Application deadline: February 15
Prerequisites: Graduate students in all fields of classical studies; recent PhD's may also apply.
Academic credit: Inquire.
Financial aid: Through the generosity of the Packard Foundation financial assistance is available to qualified applicants.
Cost: $2200 covers tuition, fees, lodging, and meals six days per week, and travel within Italy. Travel to Italy not included.

Sponsor: American Academy in Rome
Directors: Elizabeth Fentress, Russell T. Scott
Contact: Dr. Elizabeth Fentress
American Academy in Rome
Via Angelo Masina 5
00153 Rome, Italy
(39) 6 584 6431
FAX: (39) 6 581-0788
E-mail: fentress@librs6k.vatlib.it
or
American Academy in Rome
7 East 60th Street
New York, NY 10022-1001
(212) 751-7200
WWW: http://www.aarome.org

The American Academy in Rome Program in Archaeology in Italy introduces students to the problems and methods of archaeological research. A three-week session in Rome consisting of site visits and classes is followed by a five-week assignment to an archaeological project in Italy. The Rome session emphasizes issues involved in the study and interpretation of the topography and monuments of the city, as well as an introduction to archaeological methods.

    Participating archaeological projects have included the Academy's own excavations at Cosa in southern Etruria, on the Palatine Hill in Rome, and in the Temple of Vesta in the Roman Forum; the University of Virginia excavations at Morgantina in Sicily; the field survey of the island of Jerba, Tunisia, conducted by the Academy and the University of Pennsylvania; the field survey of the territory of Metapontion in southern Italy, conducted by the University of Texas at Austin; and excavations conducted by the École Française de Rome at Musarna in southern Etruria, by the British School at Rome at San Vincenzo a Volturno in Molise, by the University of Rome La Sapienza at a villa north of the city walls, and by the University of Perugia at Fregellae in Southern Latium at the Roman villa of Ossaia near Cortona and at Oppido Lucano. Information regarding the participating excavations or surveys will be sent after acceptance into the program. Choice of field project will be left as much as possible to the individual student.

ITALY
Site/Location: Rome and immediate environs

Intercollegiate Center for Classical Studies in Rome (ICCS)
Dates: The Center operates for two sessions of approximately 15 weeks each per year. Fall sessions commence on or about September 1 and terminate on or about December 15. Spring sessions commence on or about February 1 and terminate on or about May 15.
Application deadline: Inquire.
Academic credit: Inquire.
Institutions offering credit: The ICCS is operated by a consortium of more than 80 American and Canadian colleges and universities. Member institutions define the academic program, set policy, and select faculty and students. Contact the ICCS for details.
Cost: Inquire.

Director: Dr. Francesco Sgariglia
Sponsor: Duke University, Foreign Academic Programs
Contact: Intercollegiate Center for Classical Studies in Rome
via A. Algardi 19
00152 Rome, Italy
(39) 6 5817036
FAX: (39) 6 5809306
E-mail: iccsrome@nexus.it

The ICCS provides undergraduate students the opportunity to study Greek and Latin literature, ancient history, archaeology, and ancient art in Rome. The core of the curriculum is the "Ancient City" course, which counts as two of the four courses of the total academic load. The "Ancient City" is intended to supplement and complement a classics major by structuring the experience of being in Rome around literature and history which are normally taught at the students' home institutions. This course allows the student to explore the ancient world, both physically and intellectually, in a comprehensive and integrated fashion. In addition to the "Ancient City" course, students can choose two other courses from the following: Intermediate or Advanced Latin, Intermediate or Advanced Greek, Renaissance and Baroque Art History, and Elementary Italian. All site visits and major field trips (Sicily and Campania) are integral parts of the curriculum.

ITALY
Location: Near Rome
Site: Rossilli di Gavignano
Period: Roman–Medieval

Volunteers:
Dates needed: August (Two 2-week sessions).
Application deadline: July 15
Minimum age: 16
Experience required: None, but basic ability to speak and understand Italian.
Cost: Volunteer is responsible for all expenses

Sponsor and
Contact: Gruppo Archeologico Milanese
via Bagutta 12
20121 Milano, Italy
(39) 2 796372

The site consists of a Benedictine Abbey built over a Roman villa. The program includes excavation seven hours per day, five days per week, plus visits to historical and archaeological sites in the area.

ITALY
Location: Sardinia, Borore
Site: Duos Nuraghes
Period: ca. 2000 BC–AD 1000

Volunteers:
Dates needed: June 15–July 24
Application deadline: March 15
Minimum age: 18
Experience required: None, but should be in good physical health, and exhibit maturity, adaptability, and self-discipline. Italian language proficiency, while an asset, is not required.
Academic credit: By arrangement with student's own institution. All students who successfully complete the program will receive a letter of acknowledgment from the Penn State Sardinia Program.
Cost: $1260 ($30 per day) covers lodging in the hotel Ulmos (double/triple occupancy), half-board (breakfast and one main meal), and the educational program. Travel to Italy, other meals, weekend travel, and personal expenses not included. (On past experience the total cost per student for the program will be around $2500.)

Bibliography: Webster, G., *A Prehistory of Sardinia, 2300 to 500 BC*, Monographs in Mediterranean Archaeology 5, Sheffield, 1996. Teglund, M., and G. Webster, "Report of the Excavations at Duos Nuraghes-Borore (NU) 1992," *Old World Archaeology Newsletter* 16(2), 1993, pp. 19–23. Webster, G., "Duos Nuraghes: Preliminary Results of the First Three Seasons of Excavation," *Journal of Field Archaeology* 15, 1988, pp. 465–472.

Sponsor: Pennsylvania State University; National Geographic Society; Office of the Superintendent of Antiquities for the Provinces of Sassari and Nuoro; Italian Ministry of Culture
Directors and
Contact: Gary and Maud Webster
Sardinia Program
Penn State University - Mont Alto
Campus Drive
Mont Alto, PA 17237-9703

The Bronze-Iron Age Nuragic civilization has been long regarded for its unique monumental stone towers, megalithic tombs, and bronze figurines; only recently has research started to reveal details of its ancient lifeways. Duos Nuraghes is a small village site with standing masonry architecture including defensive circuit walls. The principal architectural features are two nuraghi, monumental stone towers with domed interior chambers unique to the island. The nuraghi are surrounded by a still unknown number of round stone-walled huts and other features. Duos is perhaps the oldest continuously occupied Nuragic settlement known, and the long-term aims of the project are to investigate a sufficient number of structures to enable a reconstruction of its exceptionally long history in terms of layout, residential and subsistence patterns, native industries, trade, and local cult practices.

The Field School provides training in excavation and field-laboratory techniques within the context an on-going professional research program. As members of a small research team of fewer than 15, students will be trained to excavate, document the provenance of the finds, and conduct preliminary lab analyses of artifacts recovered. Through lectures, assigned readings, and field trips students will further explore the significance of the project's findings within larger cultural, historical, and theoretical contexts.

ITALY
Location: Sicily
Site: Isle of Ustica
Period: Prehistoric–Roman

Field School: Lessons in Maritime Archaeology
Dates: August 29–September 7
Application deadline: August 10
Minimum age: Inquire.
Experience required: Inquire.
Academic credit: A certificate of attendance is provided.
Cost: ƒ1500 (ca. $865) for divers or ƒ800 (ca. $465) for non-divers covers lodging in hotel, breakfast, one main meal per day, local commute, instruction, and tanks and weights. Travel to Italy, other meals, insurance, and other equipment not included.

Director: Piero Pruneti, *Archeologia Viva* magazine
Sponsors: *Archeologia Viva*; International Academy of Underwater Sciences and Techniques; Ustica Marine Reserve
Contact: *Archeologia Viva*
            Via Bolognese 165
            50139 Florence, Italy
            FAX: (36) 55 6679298
            or
            Claire Calcagno, Course Instructor
            University of Oxford, Institute of Archaeology
            36 Beaumont Street
            Oxford OX1 2PG, UK
            (44) 1865 278240
            FAX: (44) 1865 278254

Since ancient times the Isle of Ustica has been a fixed point on the routes of those sailing the Mediterranean. "Lessons in Maritime Archaeology" will consist of two courses, one theoretical and the other practical. The theory course will include an introduction to the history of maritime archaeology in the Mediterranean; underwater survey and excavation techniques; ancient ship technology and seafaring; conservation; geomorphology, coasts and harbors; and a case study of Uluburun, a Late Bronze Age merchant ship. The practical course (eight dives) will include guided visits to underwater areas of archaeological and naturalistic significance around Ustica.

ITALY
Location: Tuscany, Arezzo, near Cortona, central Italy
Site: Ossaia/La Tufa
Period: 1st century BC–5th century AD

Field School: Enrollment limited to 25.
Dates: May 26–June 26
Application deadline: February 20
Academic credit: 6 from the University of Alberta
Cost: CDN$700 for tuition plus CDN$750 covers lodging, breakfast and lunch (Monday–Friday), tea break, an evening meal (Monday–Thursday). Travel to Italy, weekend travel, and Friday evening and weekend-meals not included.

Director and Sponsor: Prof. H. Fracchia, University of Alberta
To receive information packet and application materials,
contact: Department of History and Classics
            University of Alberta
            2-28 H.M. Tory Building
            Edmonton, Alberta T6G 2E5, Canada
            (403) 492-3270
            FAX: (403) 492-9125

Send completed applications
to: Professor H. Fracchia
            University of Alberta in Italy
            via Mecenate 6-8
            Chiusi (Siena) 53043, Italy

The project involves the excavation of a Roman villa, as part of an overall study of the Romanization of Etruria. Based on the evidence of brick stamps, the villa belonged to C. VIBIUS, a Roman consul of 43 BC who then willed his property to Gaius and Lucius Caesar; a brick stamp bearing the word CAESARUM indicates that the complex was part of an estate of the Roman Imperial family. To date, well preserved mosaics, wall paintings, rooms, and drainage systems have been uncovered. All the basic archaeological techniques will be taught, and field survey is an integral part of the program. Weekends are free for trips to nearby sites. Ossaia is within an hour of Perugia, Assisi, Chiusi, Arezzo, Florence, Siena, and Rome.

ITALY
Location: Tuscany, Murlo, W Italy
Site: Poggio Civitate
Period: Early Etruscan, 7th–6th centuries BC

Field School:
Dates: Session 1: June 10–July 3, Session 2: July 6–August 1. Students may attend one or both sessions.
Application deadline: April 30
Academic credit: 3 or 6 credits (1 or 2 sessions) from the University of Evansville
Cost: $1900 for one session or $2900 for both covers tuition, lodging, most meals, and local commute. Travel to project, meals on non-working days, and insurance not included.

Bibliography: Nielsen, E., and K. M. Phillips, *American Journal of Archaeology*, 1967–1975, (preliminary reports on the site; includes bibliography). Nielsen, E., "Some preliminary thoughts on new and old terracottas," *Opuscula Romana* XVI:5, 1987. Nielsen, E., "Recent Excavation at Poggio Civitate," *Studi e Materiali* VI, 1990.

Co-Directors: Dr. Anthony Tuck, University of Evansville; Dr. Erik Nielsen, Franklin College
Sponsors: University of Evansville and Franklin College
Contact: Dr. Anthony Tuck
            University of Evansville
            Department of Archaeology
            1800 Lincoln Avenue
            Evansville, IN 47722
            (812) 488-1019
            E-mail: tt4@evansville.edu
            WWW: http://www.evansville.edu/~murloweb

The Murlo summer program introduces undergraduate and graduate students to both the practical and theoretical aspects of Etruscan archaeology. The program, conducted as a field school, consists of seminars, visits to archaeological sites in Etruria, and visits to regional museums with Etruscan collections. Approximately seven weeks are spent in fieldwork at the Etruscan site of Poggio Civitate. The Web site provides a history of the site, interesting photographs, and an on-line application form that can be sent directly to Dr. Anthony Tuck.

ITALY
Location: Tuscany, San Mario near Dalmazio, W Italy
Site: Etruscan Farm, Cecina River Valley
Period: ca. 6th century BC–6th century AD

Volunteers:
Dates: Team I: August 16–29, Team II: August 30–September 12, Team III: September 13–26
Application deadline: 90 days prior to departure (Applications will be accepted after that time if space is available.)
Minimum age: 16
Experience required: None, but willingness to work under a hot sun.
Cost: $1995 covers all expenses except travel to staging area (San Dalmazio) and insurance.

Directors:	Nicola Terrenato, Laura Motta, University of Rome
Sponsor and	
Contact:	Earthwatch, Box 403
	See page 7 for contact information.

Teams will continue to explore the social, structural, productive, and ecological development of the long-lived rural settlement of San Mario as part of a wider research program aimed at investigating the region from Etruscan times to the Middle Ages as . Working with staff and archaeological students, volunteers identify, clean, dig, and photograph excavation layers as well as collect artifacts and sediment samples for analysis. In the laboratory, team members wash, mark, and identify pottery and other artifacts.

ITALY
Location: Tuscany, Vicchio, 22 miles NE of Florence
Site: Poggio Colla
Period: Etruscan, 7th–3rd centuries BCE.

Field School:
Dates: June 16–July 29
Application deadline: March 1 or until filled.
Academic credit: 6 credits from Southern Methodist University.
Cost: $4000 covers tuition, lodging, meals (Monday–Friday), and local commute. Travel to Italy and week-end meals not included.

Directors:	Greg Warden, Southern Methodist University
Sponsor and	
Contact:	Southern Methodist University
	Division of Art History, OAC 1630
	Dallas, TX 75275
	(214) 768-2783
	FAX: (214) 768-3998
	E-mail: gwarden@mail.smu.edu
	WWW: http://www.oberlin.edu./~scarrier/Poggio_Colla/Intro.html

Poggio Colla is an Etruscan site that seems to have been the political and ceremonial center of the scenic Mugello and Sieve valleys. The site spans most of Etruscan history, from the 7th century until its destruction by the Romans at the end of the 3rd century BCE. The first three seasons of excavation have revealed two major phases: an extraordinarily rich Orientalizing and Archaic phase that includes the remains of a monumental temple, and a 4th and 3rd century BCE phase when the site was turned into a fortified stronghold. The 1998 season will continue to define the monumental architecture of the "acropolis" area, as well as to open up new areas on the lower slopes of the site. A survey is also planned.

Field School participants will receive training in Etruscan archaeology as well as in the theoretical and practical aspects of fieldwork. Lectures supplement on-site learning. The site's proximity to Florence allows for week-end visits to major museums and archaeological sites.

ITALY
Location: Tuscany, near Siena
Site: La Piana
Period: Late Etruscan (mid 4th century–late 3rd century BC)

Dates of excavation and field school: June 26–August 7

Position(s): Flotation/Ethnobotanist
Application deadline: April 15
Experience required: Yes.
Salary: Negotiable.
Cost: Programs provides travel to project, local commute, lodging, and meals. Insurance, weekend activities, and equipment not covered.

Field School:
Application deadline: May 1
Academic credit: 3 or 6 credits from Cornell University
Cost: $3085 or $4785 (depending on number of credits) covers tuition, lodging, meals, and local commute. Travel to Italy, insurance, and weekend activities not included.

Volunteers:
Application deadline: May 1
Minimum age: 18
Experience required: None. Drafting and photography skills preferred.
Cost: $2600 covers lodging, meals, and local commute. Travel to Italy, insurance, and weekend activities not included.

Bibliography: Whitehead, J.K., "Survey and Excavations of the Etruscan Foundation, 1989–1991: La Piana, Mocali and Ripostena," *Etruscan Studies* 1, 1994, pp. 123–160; "New Researches at La Piana, 1991–95," *Etruscan Studies* 3, 1996, pp. 105–146.

Sponsor:	Etruscan Foundation
Director and	
Contact:	Jane K. Whitehead
	Classics Department
	Colby College
	Waterville, ME 04901
	Tel/FAX: (207) 872-0344

La Piana is located on the flat summit of a high ridge overlooking the rolling Tuscan hills. Thirteen previous excavation seasons have produced evidence that an orthogonally-gridded Etruscan settlement flourished here in the 4th–late 3rd centuries BC. Two large structures of monumental proportions have so far emerged; their fieldstone foundation walls are almost a meter thick. Artifacts and pottery found within the rooms attest to the domestic activities of an agricultural settlement. The 1998 season will excavate the cistern, five meters in diameter, which should encapsulate the entire history of the habitation and destruction of the site.

The program combines fieldwork with visits to major Etruscan sites. Students will be instructed in excavation techniques and strategies, drafting, surveying, objects conservation, and recording methods. Participants will reside in the villa of Spannocchia, which is built into a massive castle that dates back to the Middle Ages and is fully equipped with all necessary facilities, including a library, classrooms, laboratory, museum, and swimming pool.

ITALY
Location: Tuscany
Site: Various
Period: Etruscan

Study Tour I: "Etruscan Culture"
Dates: May 29–June 8
Application deadline: April 15
Cost: $1400 covers tuition, lodging, meals, and local commute. Travel to Italy, insurance, museum entrance fees and personal activities not included.

Study Tour II: "Etruscan Art"
Dates: June 9–19
Application deadline: April 15
Cost: $1400 covers tuition, lodging, meals, and local commute. Travel to Italy, insurance, museum entrance fees and personal activities not included.

Sponsor: Etruscan Foundation
Director and
Contact: Jane K. Whitehead
Classics Department
Colby College
Waterville, ME 04901
Tel/FAX: (207) 872-0344
or
Etruscan Foundation
Fisher Mews, Suite D-2
377 Fisher Road
Grosse Pointe, MI 48230
Tel/FAX: (313) 882-2462

Writers from Hesiod to D.H. Lawrence and George Dennis have regarded the Etruscans as a mysterious people. Two courses, offered by the Etruscan Foundation and taught by Jane K. Whitehead, director of excavations at the site of La Piana, explore this important civilization. Participants will learn of the Etruscans through lectures as well as through visits to the ruins of their major centers.

Study Tour I: "Etruscan Culture" involves a combination of lectures in a classroom setting and excursions to ancient sites. The places to be visited include the necropoleis of Vetulonia, Sovana, and Populonia; the important settlements of Roselle, Marzabotto, Lago dell'Accesa; the museums of Grosseto, Bologna, Massa Marittima, Murlo, and Volterra; and archaeological sites currently under excavation, as time and weather permit.

Study Tour II: "Etruscan Art" involves a combination of lectures in a classroom setting and excursions to ancient sites. The places to be visited include the sites of Tarquinia, Volterra, San Gimignano, Fiesole, Chiusi, and Orvieto; the museums of Florence, Arezzo, Cortona, and Murlo; and archaeological sites currently under excavation, as time and weather permit.

Participants will reside in the villa of Spannocchia, which is built into a massive castle that dates back to the Middle Ages. The villa is fully equipped with all necessary facilities, including a library, classrooms, archaeology laboratory, museum, and swimming pool. Count Cinelli, founder of the Etruscan Foundation, has also invited all participants to dine with him at the Circolo degli Uniti.

ITALY
Location: Val Camonica and Val Tellina, Alpine regions near the Swiss border
Sites: Grosio and Paspardo
Period: Neolithic–Medieval

Volunteers: Vacancies for 20 volunteers at each site.
Dates: Grosio: July 20–July 30. Paspardo: August 1–10. Minimum stay one week.
Application deadline: June 20

Minimum age: 18
Experience required: None, but an interest in prehistoric art and archaeology. Drawing, photography, and registry skills helpful.
Cost: ƒ440 (ca. $295) per week covers lodging, meals, local commute, and training. Travel to project and insurance not included.

Bibliography: Arca, A., A. Fossati, E. Marchi, and E. Tognoni, *Rupe Magna. La roccia incisa piu grande delle Alpi*, Sondrio, 1995. A. Fossati, Mila Simões de Abreu, and Ludwig Jaffe, *Rupestrian Archaeology—Techniques and Terminology*, Cerveno, 1990. A. Fossati, Mila Simões de Abreu, and Ludwig Jaffe, *Etched in Time—The Petroglyphs of Val Camonica*, Cerveno, 1990. Fossati, A., "Il complesso petroglifico di Grosio, (So)," *Valtellina e Mondo alpino nella preistoria*, R. Keller Poggiani (ed) Modena, 1989.

Sponsor: Società Cooperativa Archeologica "Le Orme dell'Uomo," member, International Federation of Rock Art Organizations (IFRAO)
Director and
Contact: Dr. Angelo Fossati
Coop. Archeologica Le Orme dell'Uomo
Piazzale Donatori di Sangue, 1
25040 Cerveno (Brescia) Italy
(39) 364 433983
FAX: (39) 364 434351
WWW: http://www.geocities.com/Athens/5806/
or
Mr. Andrea Arcà
Coop. Archeologica Le Orme dell'Uomo
E-mail: aarca@mailer.inrete.it

Paspardo is in Val Camonica, a 70-km-long Alpine valley, and Grosio is in Val Tellina, a 100-km-long Alpine valley. Both valleys contain large concentrations of rock engravings spanning 10,000 years of prehistory. Students, scholars, and rock art enthusiasts come from many different countries to participate in both projects. At both Paspardo and Grosio, the project consists of surveying, recording, and tracing engraved rocks. In addition to fieldwork, there will be lectures on rock-art sites throughout the world, and visits to museums and other localities with rock engravings. The program will also involve the group in preparing rock art related Web pages and papers.

ITALY
Location: Val Camonica, Alpine region near the Swiss border
Site: Capo di Ponte
Period: Paleolithic–Medieval.

Positions: Research Assistants
Dates needed: All year
Application deadline: 3 months prior to arrival date.
Experience required: BA and references, background in archaeology, knowledge of two European languages, and computer skills.
Cost: $80 registration fee plus ca. $400 per month for lodging and meals. Tutoring available on request. Travel to Italy not included.
Work: Laboratory and research work, focusing on one of the projects being conducted by the CCSP, especially Har Karkom (see entry under Israel) or World Archive of Rock Art (WARA).

Field school:
Dates: July–September
Application deadline: 3 months prior to start of program.
Academic credit: Credit from student's own institution or diploma from the CCSP.
Cost: $350 registration fee plus ca. $400 per month for lodging and meals. Travel to Italy not included.

Volunteers:
Dates needed: All year
Application deadline: 3 months prior to arrival date.
Minimum age: 20
Experience required: Background in art history, archaeology, drawing, photography, languages, computer processing, translation, editing, and public relations preferred.
Cost: $80 registration fee plus $600–$900/month for lodging and meals. A limited amount of free rooms with cooking facilities are available. Travel to Italy not included.

Bibliography: Anati, E., *Camonica Valley*, New York: Alfred A. Knopf, 1961; *La Préhistoire des Alpes*, Paris: Payot-Weber, 1987; *Evolution and Style*, Capo di Ponte: Edizioni del Centro, 1989; *World Rock Art: The Primordial Language*, Capo di Ponte: Edizioni del Centro, 1993.; *Valcamonica Rock Art: A History for Europe*, Capo di Ponte: Edizioni del Centro, 1994; *Har Karkom: In the Light of New Discoveries*, Capo di Ponte: Edizioni del Centro, 1994.

Director, Sponsor, and
Contact: Emmanuel Anati
        Centro Camuno di Studi Preistorici (CCSP)
        25044 Capo di Ponte
        Valcamonica, Brescia, Italy
        (39) 364 42091
        FAX: (39) 364 42572
        E-mail: ccsp@globalnet.it
        WWW: http://www.globalnet.it/ccsp/ccsp.htm

The main focus of research at the CCSP is on prehistoric and tribal art, especially rock art. Val Camonica is one of the most important sites of European rock art; over 250,000 figures are engraved on rocks in a 70-km-long mountain valley. The program includes recording rock art on site, the study and analysis of rock art, analithic research, and individual studies. The research conducted by the CCSP has led the site to be included in the "World Heritage List" of UNESCO.

MALTA
Location: Marsaxlokk
Site: Tas-Silg
Period: Prehistoric–Early Christian

Field School:
Dates: June 15–July 24
Application deadline: April 18
Academic credit: 2 credits from University of Malta.
Cost: $2100 for six weeks or $1500 for four weeks covers tuition, lodging, breakfast and dinner, local commute, field trips. Travel to Malta and insurance not included.

Bibliography: Yearly reports of the Italian expedition: *Missione Archeologica Italiana a Malta. Rapporto Preliminare della Campagna 1964–1970*, Rome: Istituto di Studi del Vicino Oriente, 1965–1972.

Directors: Prof. Anthony Bonanno, Dr. Anthony Frendo
Sponsor and
Contact: University of Malta
        Foundation for International Studies
        Summer School in Archaeology, Attn: Jean Killick
        St. Paul Street
        Valletta VLT 07, Malta
        (356) 234121 or 234122
        FAX: (356) 230538
        E-mail: intof@cis.um.edu.mt

or
The OTS Foundation
P.O. Box 17166
Sarasota, FL 34276
(941) 918-9215
FAX: (941) 918-0265
E-mail: otsf@aol.com

The Tas-Silg site, first excavated by an Italian expedition from the University of Rome between 1964 and 1970, is an extremely important one for Maltese archaeology. The results of the excavation, revealed an early prehistoric megalithic temple and a Phoenician conversion of this temple which, in successive ages, continued to expand to include monumental altars, gateways, and porticoes, at times utilizing features of the original prehistoric temple.

The field school is intended to introduce participants to the theory and practice of archaeology in general and to Mediterranean and Maltese archaeology in particular. It will consist of lectures explaining the general principals and methods of archaeological practice, including field archaeology, and excavation sessions at the University of Malta's dig. The course will also include a number of excursions to important sites in Malta and Gozo.

LUXEMBOURG
Location: Goeblange, Forest of Miecher
Site: Gallo-Roman rural estate
Period: 1st–4th century AD, Gallo-Roman

Volunteers:
Dates needed: August 3-15
Application deadline: May 1
Minimum age: 18
Experience required: None, reasonable physical fitness and a willingness to get their hands dirty. Tetanus immunization mandatory.
Academic credit: None, but students may obtain an official certificate, issued by the Luxembourg National Museum, attesting their participation.
Cost: 3000 Luxembourg/BF per week (ca. $100) covers all on-site meals (including evenings), local commute, lodging (on-site camping), and accident insurance. Volunteers may bring their own tents, but the program will provide large army tents. There are toilet facilities on site and transport to and from shower facilities will be organized each day. Travel to Luxembourg, health insurance, and off-site expenses not included.

Bibliography: Complete bibliography is on the program's Web site.

Sponsor: Archaeological Society D'Georges Kayser Altertumsfuerscher; Luxembourg National Museum
Contact: Jos Thiel
        11, rue Principale
        L-8365 Hagen, Luxembourg
        (352) 499871309
        E-mail: 74171.2152@compuserve.com
        or thiel@cetrel.lu
        WWW: http://ourworld.compuserve.com/homepages/
        G_K_A

The 3rd International Archaeological Camp Luxembourg will take place at a Gallo-Roman farmstead, situated in the forest of Miecher, a few miles from the Roman route from Arlon (Belgium) to Trier (Germany). This excavation is part of a long-term project, which began in 1965 with the farmstead's residential buildings. Previous excavations in the vicinity of Miecher have revealed tombs of Treverian knights and a necropolis from Early Imperial times, built on the foundations of a Late Bronze age settlement. The main site in Miecher is the Roman estate, where so far six buildings have been discovered; three have been excavated, and the restoration of cellars, cisterns, heating systems, and walls is complete in buildings I and II. This summer, work will concentrate on one of several subsidiary buildings within the enclosed farmstead compound. Work involves digging, carrying buckets of soil, pushing wheelbarrows, taking measurements, drawing, photography, cleaning and describing finds, and updating the excavation journal. Everyone will be expected to take part in all tasks, which will be rotated, as widely as possible, taking into account levels of fitness and personal interests wherever possible.

PORTUGAL
Location: Côa Valley, Trás-os-Montes, NE Portugal
Sites: Various
Period: Pleistocene and Holocene

Dates of programs: June–September and special teams throughout the year.
Application deadline: June, late applications will be considered.

Position(s): Research consultants and tutors
Minimum age: 18
Experience required: Background in the research of rock art and attendant skills (e.g., conservation, protection, management), ethnology, folklore, music, geomorphology, photography, etc. Aptitude for training students and volunteers. Team spirit essential.
Salary: Possible, pending funding.
Cost: Program provides lodging, meals, and local commute. Travel to Portugal and insurance not included.

Volunteers:
Minimum age: 18, but younger volunteers may be accepted.
Experience required: None, but team spirit essential. Useful interests include archaeology, rock art, ethnology, anthropology, folklore, music, geography, geology, drawing, and photography.
Academic credit: Optional. Diploma available from Associção Portuguesa de Arte Rupestre (APAR), International Federation of Rock Art Organizations (IFRAO). Number of credits earned is determined by student's own institution.
Cost: Tuition (if credit is desired) and contribution to program (to be determined) will cover lodging, meals, and local commute. Travel to Portugal and insurance not included.

Bibliography: Abreu, Mila Simões de, and Ludwig Jaffe, "Southern Europe: Recent Discoveries of post-Paleolithic Rock Art in Portugal" in *Rock Art Studies: News of the World*, Paul Bahn and Angelo Fossati (eds.), Owbow Monograph 72, Oxford, 1996, pp. 29–33. Abreu, Mila Simões de, Angelo Fossati, and Ludwig Jaffe (eds.), *Rupestrian Archaeology—Techniques and Terminology—A Methodological Approach: Petroglyphs*, Richerche Archeologiche, Vol. I, Tomo I, Cerveno (Italy), Cooperativa Archeologica Le Orme dell'Uomo, 1990. Bahn, Paul G., and Jean Vertut, *Images of the Ice Age*, New York: Facts on File, 1988. Bahn, Paul G., "Paleolithic Engravings Endangered in Côa Valley," *La Pintura*, Vol. 21, No. 3, Winter 1995, pp. 1–3. Bahn, Paul G., "Portuguese Scandal," *Archaeology*, Vol. 48, No. 2, March/April 1995, pp. 18–19.

Sponsors: Grupo de Antropogénese (GA-UTAD), Unidade de Universidade de Trás-os-Montes e Alto Douro (UNARQ-UTAD); Arqueologia da Associação Portuguesa de Arte Rupestre (APAAR); International Federation of Rock Art Organizations (IFRAO)

Directors and Contacts: Dr. Mila Simões de Abreu,
Unidade de Arqueologia, Secção de Geologia
Universidade de Trás-os-Montes e Alto Douro.
Apartado 202
5001 Vila Real Codex, Portugal
(351) 59 320179
FAX: (351) 59 320480
E-mail: msabreu@utad.pt
or
Ludwig Jaffe
Associção Portuguesa de Arte Rupestre
The Etched in Time Project
Av D José I - n.53.
2780 Oeiras, Portugal
Tel/FAX: (351) 14 579524
E-mail: luwig.mila@mail.telepac.pt
WWW: http://www.utad.pt/~origins

When, in 1706, Padre António Carvalho da Costa published notes on paintings in the rockshelter at Cachão da Rapa, he was the first scholar to document prehistoric art in Portugal, one of the first enterprises of this kind in Europe. Despite this notable fact, information about Portugal's early rock art is far from complete and needs to be systematically reviewed. Furthermore, time is running out for gathering folklore often associated with these vestiges; each passing year sees the loss of the only people able to recount and transmit their knowledge to the present and future generations, thus it is increasingly urgent that all aspects of this legacy be collected and registered.

The Etched in Time Project is a multi-disciplinary investigation of Portugal's PRE ART (Paintings on Rock and Engravings, and Analogous or Related Tradition). Research during 1998 will focus on the Côa Valley, the natural setting for a unique arrangement of open-air rock engravings. Dated to ca. 10,000–30,000 BP, it is the largest of only six known open-air assemblages of Ice Age rock art in the world. A controversial dam that was being built on the Côa River threatened to submerge the site, however, an international campaign led to the suspension of the dam project for as long as it takes for scholars to fully document the region. Teams will survey the area and record rock art, using a blend of conventional and innovative methods. In addition, team members will meet village storytellers and record their narratives—in writing, on tape, and on film. The Project's diverse facets reflect an integrated approach, affirmed by the project's motto: "Man and Nature Together!"

SPAIN
Location: Arrazua, 4 km away from Guernica (Gernika in Basque language), Vizcaya, Basque Country
Site: Gastiburu Protohistoric Sanctuary
Period: Iron Age (2nd century BC)

Volunteers:
Dates needed: Summer
Application deadline: June
Minimum age: 20. Younger people are welcome if they are enrolled in a university.
Experience required: Archaeology student, two previous fieldwork experiences, knowledge of Spanish, French, or English preferred.
Cost: $170 per week covers lodging, meals, insurance, local commute, and training, if necessary, (drawing with a pantograph, drawing profiles, photography, etc.)

Bibliography: *Arkeoikuska*, from 1986 (reports about archaeological sites in the Basque Country published by the Basque Government).

Director: Dr. Luis Valdes (Gastiburu S.L.)
Sponsor: Diputacion Foral de Bizkaia (Biscay Province Council) and Gastiburu S.L.
Contact: Jose Manuel Mates Luque
5 Wester Drylaw Row
Edinburgh EH4 2SF, Fife, Scotland, UK
or
Apdo de Correos 6003
48080 Bilbao, Bizkaia, Spain
E-mail: jmml@st-andrews.ac.uk
(if no response, use: itloh@arrakis.es)

Excavations in the Gastiburu Protohistoric Sanctuary started in 1985 and will continue in 1998. The site has a social and, possibly, religious character, and contains four large and two small barrows, each with stone benches on them. The benches are situated in such a way that they appear to have served some ceremonial purpose, and may have been placed in accordance with astronomical alignments. Near it, there is a 2nd–1st century BC protohistoric settlement ("castro" in Spanish) occupied by the Caristian people, a pre-Roman people who lived in northern Spain, according to Classical sources. During the 1997 field season, half of the eastern barrow was excavated. The outer wall and several inner ones were discovered, providing information about how the barrow was constructed. A great quantity of charcoal was found, but no animal or human remains or artifacts, supporting the idea the construction served a ceremonial purpose, and was not a cemetery, military structure, or residence.

SPAIN
Location: Costa Brava, Catalonia
Site: Empúries
Period: Greek–Roman

Field School:
Dates: May 20–June 27
Application deadline: March 15
Academic credit: 8 credits from Boston University
Cost: $4500 covers tuition, lodging, meals, local commute, and insurance. Travel to Spain not included.

Bibliography: Boardman, John, *The Greeks Overseas: The Archaeology of their Early Colonies and Trade,* 2d edition, Harmondsworth: Penguin, 1973. Curchin, L.A., *Roman Spain: Conquest and Assimilation*, London: Routledge, 1991. Harrison, R.J., *Spain at the Dawn of History: Iberians, Phoenicians and Greeks,* New York: Thames and Hudson, 1988. Keay, S.J., *Roman Spain,* Berkeley: University of California Press, 1988. MacKendrick, P.L., *The Iberian Stones Speak: Archaeology in Spain and Portugal,* New York: Funk and Wagnalls, 1969. Marcet i Barbe, Roger and Enric Sanmarti, *Empúries*, Barcelona: Diputacion de Barcelona, 1989.

Director: Prof. Murray C. McClellan
Sponsor and
Contact: Boston University
International Programs
232 Bay State Road
Boston, MA 02215
(617) 353-9888
FAX: (617) 353-5402
E-mail: abroad@bu.edu
World Wide Web: http://www.bu.edu/abroad

Around 650 BC Greek colonists landed on what is now the Catalan coast of Spain and founded the westernmost Greek settlement in the Mediterranean. The city, known in antiquity as Emporion (the trading post) thrived as the Greek settlers interacted with native Celtiberian peoples. In later centuries it became the entry point of the Roman conquest of Iberia and, later still, it witnessed invasions by Visigoths and Arabs, and an impressive Medieval resurgence. Today the site is an innovative archaeological research center located on one of the most beautiful spots of the Costa Brava.

Students on the Empúries Field School will participate on a joint Catalonian-American excavation investigating the process of urbanization in the Greek section of Empúries. Students will gain hands-on experience in all aspects of the project, from excavation, field recording, and geophysical prospection, to laboratory processing, computer database entry, site presentation, and museum design. In addition, daily seminars and excursions to nearby sites will introduce students to the archaeology of Greek and Roman Spain.

SPAIN
Location: Deya, Mallorca, Balearic Islands
Site: Various prehistoric settlements
Period: ca. 2800–123 BC

Position(s): Site and lab assistants, cook
Dates needed: June–September (5 two-week sessions, with a lab week between each)
Application deadline: Apply after April 1 and before 15 May.
Experience required: Yes. Assistants: previous experience at Copper, Bronze Age sites, knowledge of western Mediterranean prehistory. Cook: experience cooking or catering for large group home. References required for all.
Salary: Assistants: lodging and meals. Cook: small salary, lodging, and meals.
Cost: Program provides lodging, meals, local commute, and insurance. Travel to Mallorca and personal expenses not included.

Earthwatch Volunteers:
Dates: Team I: June 17–July 1, Team II: July 8–22, Team III: July 29–August 12, Team IV: August 19–September 2. There will also be sessions in December and January. Inquire for details.
Application deadline: 90 days prior to departure. (Applications will be accepted after that time if space is available.)
Academic credit: 3–4 from student's own institution.
Minimum age: 17
Experience required: None, but photography, drawing (mechanical, topographical, or illustrative), ceramics, chemistry, and computer skills helpful.
Cost: $1895 covers all expenses except travel to staging area (Palma, Mallorca) and insurance.

Bibliography: Perico Garcia, Luis, *Balearic Islands*, Thames and Hudson, 1967. Waldren, William, et. al. (eds.), "Balearic Prehistory, Ecology, and Culture," *BAR*, 1982. Waldren, William, "The Balearic Pentapartite Division of Prehistory," *BAR International Series*, No. 282, 1986. Waldren, William, et. al. (eds.), "Rites, Rituals, and Religion in Prehistory," *Tempus Reparatum*, 1995.

Director: Dr. William Waldren, Oxford University
Sponsor and Volunteer
Contact: Earthwatch, Box 403
See page 7 for contact information.
Staff Position
Contact: Dr. Jacqueline Waldren, Administrator,
E-mail: damarc@redestb.es

The Deya Project is a long-term, multidisciplinary archaeological research program devoted to illuminating the prehistory of the Balearic Islands, the western Mediterranean, and the history and culture of the mysterious "Beaker People," named after their etched drinking vessels. This year, research will continue at the 4000-year-old Sanctuary of Son Mas to document the site's various phases of construction, occupation, and abandonment, and the social, religious, and economic activities which took place during those phases. Fieldwork and lab work assignments will be rotated, taking into consideration weather and other priorities. Volunteers will be instructed in techniques necessary to perform any research assignment. A typical day includes a mid-day break for lunch and rest, with work resuming in the afternoon. Late evening dinners, following the Spanish custom, will often be accompanied by guest lectures, films, or slide presentations.

SPAIN
Location: Murcia, SE Spain
Site: Sima de las Palomas de Cabezo Gordo and Cueva Negra de la Encarnción
Period: Middle Paleolithic

Volunteers:
Dates: Team I: July 10–24, Team II: July 24–August 7, Team III: August 7–21
Application deadline: 90 days prior to departure. (Applications will be accepted after that time if space is available.)
Minimum age: 16
Experience required: None, but this project is not suitable for the severely physically disabled or for those with cardiovascular ailments.
Cost: $1,795 covers all expenses except travel to staging area (Murcia National Airport) and insurance.

Director: Dr. Michael Walker, Murcia University
Sponsor and
Contact: Earthwatch
       See page 7 for contact information.

Excavations will continue in 1998 at two Neandertal cave sites, Cueva Negra and Cabezo Gordo. Excavations at the rockshelter called Cueva Negra ("Black Cave") in the mountains of southeastern Spain have so far revealed Neandertal teeth, remnants of extinct animals, and stone tools. The second site, Cabezo Gordo ("Big Hill"), was discovered accidentally when a speleologist descending a natural shaft called Sima de las Palomas (Hole of the Doves) noticed bones jutting from the cavern wall. The bones turned out to be the upper and lower jawbones of a Neandertal. Subsequent excavations of this site have yielded the remains of 20 Neanderthals, their tools, and the bones of now-extinct animals, including lions and panthers. Volunteers will be assigned to task groups and by rotation will have the opportunity to work on all aspects of the project. Morning assignments involve excavation and removing excavated material for sieving. Afternoon assignments include washing and drying excavated materials from the morning's work and preliminary classification of the dry materials from the previous day.

UNITED KINGDOM & THE REPUBLIC OF IRELAND

UNITED KINGDOM/England
Location: Worldwide
Site: Various
Period: Various

Archaeology Abroad
31-34 Gordon Square
London WC1H OPY, United Kingdom
(44) 0171 387-7050, ext. 4750
FAX: (44) 0171 383-2572
E-mail: arch.abroad@ucl.ac.uk
WWW: http://britac3.britac.ac.uk/cba/archabroad.html

Archaeology Abroad provides information about opportunities for archaeological fieldwork and excavation outside Britain. Three bulletins are issued annually—in March, May, and October—and are available by subscription. These include details of projects overseas for which volunteers or staff are requested. For further details, contact *Archaeology Abroad*. See listing under "Worldwide Opportunities" for a more detailed description.

UNITED KINGDOM/England
Location: Nationwide (England, Scotland, Wales, and Republic of Northern Ireland)
Site: Various
Period: Various

Council for British Archaeology (CBA)
Bowes Morrell House
111 Walmgate
York Y01 2UA, England, UK
(44) 1904 671417
FAX: (44) 1904 671384
E-mail: archaeology@compuserve.com
WWW: http://britac3.britac.ac.uk/cba/

The Council for British Archaeology publishes *CBA Briefing* five times a year. This publication lists excavations in the United Kingdom which take volunteers. The *Briefing* also gives notice of training excavations, archaeological courses, conferences, and tours. The majority of digs occur during the summer months, and there is usually a minimum age limit of 16. The *Young Archaeologists' Club* is specifically for those aged between 9 and 16. For more information contact the CBA.

UNITED KINGDOM/England
Location: Nationwide
Site: Various
Period: Various

Current Archaeology
9 Nassington Road
London NW3 2TX, England, UK
(44) 171 4357517
FAX: (44) 171 9162405
E-mail: selkirk@cix.compulink.co.uk
WWW: http://www.archaeology.co.uk/index.htm

Current Archaeology is a full color, bimonthly magazine, approximately 40 pages long, with no advertisements, and devoted mainly to

British archaeology. The "Directory of British Archaeology," a special supplement to the Spring issue of the magazine, lists over 500 names and addresses of societies, professional organizations, universities, and other organizations in Great Britain, including details of research and fieldwork undertaken. As a subset of this, the "Directory of British Excavations" lists those organizations offering fieldwork opportunities in Britain. Both directories may be accessed through *Current Archaeology*'s Web site at the address listed above. The price for a subscription to *Current Archaeology* is £15 (UK rate) or £18 (world-wide rate, approximately $30) a year, including free postage, anywhere in the world. To order by Visa or MasterCard, call, fax, or e-mail to the numbers listed above, or subscribe through the Web site.

UNITED KINGDOM/England
Location: Cambridgeshire, Peterborough, central England
Site: Flag Fen Excavations
Period: Late Bronze Age–Iron Age

Field School:
Dates: May–October
Application deadline: March
Academic credit: Inquire.
Cost: Tuition and program fee (to be finalized) will cover lodging and insurance. Meals, travel, and equipment not included.

Volunteers:
Dates needed: April–October
Application deadline: March
Minimum age: 18
Experience required: None, but any practical skills (e.g. drawing, surveying, photography, etc.) are welcome.
Cost: Program fee (to be determined) will cover lodging and insurance. Meals, travel, and equipment not included.

Bibliography: *Antiquity*, Vol. 66, No. 251, June, 1992. Parker-Pearson, Michael, *Bronze Age Britain*, English Heritage, Batsford, 1993. Pryor, Francis, *Flag Fen*, English Heritage, Batsford; *Fengate Monographs*, Royal Ontario Museum; *Fengate*, Shire Publications. Taylor, M., *Wood in Archaeology*, Shire Publications.

Director: Dr. F.M.M. Pryor
Sponsor and
Contact: Miss S. Foster
Flag Fen Excavations
Fourth Drove, Fengate
Peterborough, PE1 5UR
Cambridgeshire, England, UK
(44) 0173 331 3414
FAX: (44) 0173 334 9957

Flag Fen is a well-known Late Bronze Age religious site which is largely composed of very well-preserved waterlogged timbers. These timbers are part of a very large wooden monument which the Fenland Archaeological Trust has been researching for the last ten years in order to fully appreciate the archaeology of Flag Fen and Fengate. It is a working excavation which trains archaeology students in the excavation and processing of wet timbers. Most aspects of field archaeology are addressed at the site, including excavation, drawing, photography, surveying, etc.

UNITED KINGDOM/England
Location: Cumbria, Esk Valley, NW England
Site: Low Birker
Period: ca. AD 600–900

Volunteers:
Dates: Team I: July 1–15, Team II: July 15–29, Team III: July 30–August 13
Application deadline: 90 days prior to departure (Applications will be accepted after that time if space is available.)
Minimum age: 16
Experience required: None
Cost: $1695 covers all expenses except travel to staging area (Ravenglass, England) and insurance.

Director: Dr. Carl Blair, University of Wisconsin
Sponsor and
Contact: Earthwatch
See page 7 for contact information.

The project at Low Birker involves the excavation of one of the first iron-smelting furnaces in England. This mid-shaft furnace, made of clay and sand and fired with charcoal, is a type that is not well known, so work here will add important information about this crucial development in English history. Research results will be used to illuminate how iron was made here and what role it played in the larger economy and culture. Staff, students, and volunteers will excavate the site in one-meter-square blocks, looking for iron slag, ore, furnace parts, and other evidence of smelting; screen the soil; map the site; make a photographic record; and collect and process paleo-environmental samples.

UNITED KINGDOM/England
Location: Devon, SW England
Site: Dartington Hall
Period: Medieval/post-Medieval

Field School:
Dates: July 12–18
Application deadline: Inquire.
Cost: £98 (ca. $160) tuition for adults, £68 (ca. $110) for full-time students, for one-week session, including on-site insurance. (The Project will assist in arranging accommodations, which range from one's own study room with all modern facilities and full meals, down to a self-catering campsite for those on a limited budget.)

Bibliography: Currie, C.K., and M. Locock, "An evaluation of the archaeological techniques used at Castle Bromwich Hall Gardens, 1989–90," *Garden History*, No. 19.1, 1991, pp. 77–99. Emery, A., *Dartington Hall*, Oxford, 1970. Platt, C., "Excavations at Dartington Hall, 1962," *Archaeological Journal*, 119, 1962, pp. 208–224.

Director: Christopher K. Currie
Sponsor and
Contact: Gardens Archaeology Project
71 Upper Barn Copse
Fair Oak, Eastleigh
Hants SOS0 8DB, England, UK
(44) 0703 558500

Dartington Hall is considered by Nicholas Peusner, author of *The Buildings of England*, to be the finest example of medieval domestic architecture in the southwest of England. For many years it had reputedly been the site of a tournament ground built by John Holand, half brother of Richard II. Archaeological evidence has called this into question, and the so-called "Tiltyard" is now thought to be part of an elaborate historic garden. The project will help to confirm this thesis.

The Gardens Archaeology Project runs an annual training excavation which caters to the individual needs of both beginners and experienced archaeologists wishing to learn more about the new discipline of garden archaeology. The extensive medieval remains found also make this excavation highly suitable for those interested in medieval studies. Among the many finds is the "Dartington Pin," recently exhibited in the "Treasures of Devon" exhibition at the Royal Albert Museum, Exeter, UK.

UNITED KINGDOM/England
Location: Devon, Welsh Borderlands, SW England
Sites: Various
Period: Various

Field Training and Courses:
Dates: All year.
Application deadline: Inquire.
Cost: £62 for weekend courses, £93 for three-day courses, £150 for five-day courses covers tuition, handouts and book lists, transport on visits, morning and afternoon tea or coffee, and a light lunch on full days but not on half days. Lodging, most meals, and travel to UK not included. Courses are non-residential and participants must make their own housing arrangements; a list of hotels, bed-and-breakfasts, and camping accommodations will be supplied upon enrollment. Some visits may involve entrance fees or donations to churches which are not included but will be minimal.

Director: Margaret Worthington, AIFA
Sponsor and
Contact: Porth y waen Study Centre
The Paddocks
Porth y waen, Oswestry
Shropshire SY10 8LX, UK
(44) 1691 828900

Porth y waen Study Centre offers a range of non-residential short archaeology courses, some of which are practical and include on-site excavation and survey. Visits to local archaeological and historical sites form a part of many of the courses. The Centre aims to give visitors a warm welcome and an opportunity to learn in a relaxed atmosphere as part of a small group. Weekend and longer courses are offered. All courses take place in the Welsh Borderlands, the site of Iron Age hillforts, ancient churches dedicated to early Celtic saints, and the two great earthworks of Offa's Dyke and Wat's Dyke.

UNITED KINGDOM/England
Location: Devon, Welsh Borderlands, SW England
Sites: Lifton Earthwork Fortification, Offa's Dyke
Period: Early Medieval

Field Training:
Dates: July 25–August 8 for Lifton. Inquire about Offa's Dyke.
Application deadline: July 15
Cost: £150 per week covers lunch, on-site insurance, and local commute. Travel to UK, lodging, and meals other than lunch not included. Participants must make their own housing arrangements; a list of hotels, bed-and-breakfasts, and camping accommodations will be supplied upon enrollment.

Bibliography: Campbell, James, et al, *The Anglo-Saxons*, London, 1982. Hill, D.H., and A.R. Rumble, *The Defense of Wessex*, Manchester, 1996. Fox, Cyril, *Offa's Dyke*, Oxford, 1955.

Directors and Sponsors: Dr. David Hill, FSA, University of Manchester; Margaret Worthington, AIFA, Porth y waen Study Centre

Contact: Porth y waen Study Centre
The Paddocks
Porth y waen, Oswestry
Shropshire SY10 8LX, UK
(44) 1691 828900

Lifton: The Lifton earthwork is probably one of the fortifications built on the instructions of Alfred the Great or his son as a defense against the Vikings. This will be the first archaeological investigation of the site apart from exploratory excavations last year to determine if the area warranted further investigation. A range of excavation, survey, and post-excavation techniques will be taught and practiced on site.
Offa's Dyke: Offa's Dyke is an 8th century earthwork on the border between England and Wales. Survey and excavation on this 89 mile bank and ditch have been carried out by the directors for 25 and 18 years respectively. The emphasis will be on survey and geophysical techniques appropriate to the site, and on the landscape and its effect on the choice of siting of the earth work.

UNITED KINGDOM/England
Location: Isle of Man, north of Castletown
Site: Billown Neolithic Landscape Project
Period: Mesolithic, Neolithic, Bronze Age (ca. 7000–1000 BC)

Volunteers:
Dates: Weekly sessions, June 15–July 14.
Application deadline: End of May. An application form to join the Project will be available with an information sheet in February.
Minimum age: 18
Experience required: None, training is provided. A Certificate of Attendance will be given to all volunteers. All participants are required to bring evidence of current tetanus inoculation.
Cost: £80 per week for volunteers not resident on the Isle of Man (includes training, tea and coffee, lunch, and transport from Castletown to site and return); £10 per week for volunteers resident on the Isle of Man (includes training and tea and coffee, but not lunch or transport). Lodging, travel to the Isle of Man, and insurance not included. The Director will send a list of bed-and-breakfast establishments situated in and around Castletown to those planning to participate.

Bibliography: Clark, J.D.G., "The prehistory of the Isle of Man," *Proceedings of the Prehistoric Society* 1, 1935, pp. 70–92. Cubbon, A.M. (ed.), *Prehistoric sites in the Isle of Man*, Douglas, The Manx Museum and National Trust, 1986. Darvill, T., *Prehistoric Britain*, London & New York: Batsford & Yale University Press, 1987. Darvill, T., *Billown Neolithic Landscape Project, Isle of Man, 1995*, Bournemouth and Douglas, Bournemouth University and Manx National Heritage, 1996. Darvill, T., "Billown," *Current Archaeology* 13:6 (no. 150), 1996, pp. 232–237. Davey, P. (ed.), *Man and environment in the Isle of Man* (BAR 54), Oxford: British Archaeological Reports, 1978.

Sponsors: School of Conservation Sciences, Bournemouth University; Manx National Heritage
Director and
Contact: Professor Timothy Darvill
Billown Neolithic Landscape Project
School of Conservation Sciences
Bournemouth University, Talbot Campus
Fern Barrow, Poole, Dorset BH12 5BB, UK
(44) 1202 595536
FAX: (44) 1202 595478
E-mail: tdarvill@bournemouth.ac.uk

The Billown Neolithic Landscape Project combines research into the Neolithic and Bronze Age of the Isle of Man, rescue of an important site prior to destruction by quarrying, and training through a field school for undergraduate students of Archaeology and Heritage Conservation at Bournemouth University. Volunteers are welcome to join the field school on a weekly basis. In addition to work on site, including training in field methods, volunteers will participate in the University's program of seminars and lectures.

The Billown area north of Castletown in the Isle of Man, due to be destroyed by quarrying over the next few years, is now the focus for a wide-ranging landscape investigation aimed at developing an understanding of the way the area was used during prehistoric times. The area is extremely rich in prehistoric remains, including a stone circle, numerous standing stones, and four round barrows. Previous seasons of excavation have revealed Mesolithic flints and features; a Neolithic enclosure and leaf-shaped flint arrowheads; a Bronze Age mini-henge and a crematorium. In 1998 work will focus on the area west of the Neolithic enclosure where it is hoped to find more Neolithic features, part of a Bronze Age field system, and later Bronze Age industrial areas. Surveys and excavations will also be carried out at adjacent sites.

UNITED KINGDOM/England
Location: London and sites in the USA and continental Europe

International Academic Projects Summer Schools in Conservation/Museum Studies and Archaeology
Dates: Mainly during July
Application deadline: June
Experience required: None
Academic credit: By arrangement with student's own institution.
Cost for participant: ca. $35–$800, depending on courses taken, and all other expenses. Lodging can be arranged.

Director, Sponsor, and
Contact:　　James Black, Coordinator
　　　　　　　International Academic Projects Summer Schools
　　　　　　　31–34 Gordon Square
　　　　　　　London WC1H OPY, England, UK
　　　　　　　Tel: (44) 171 3879651
　　　　　　　FAX: (44) 171 3880283
　　　　　　　E-mail: james.black@ucl.ac.uk

The International Academic Projects Summer Schools runs approximately 40 courses in Conservation/Museum Studies and Archaeology. Most courses are held in London during July, however, several are held in the United States and continental Europe; there are also two correspondence courses. Contact Mr. Black at the above address to reserve a space (without obligation), and/or to receive a 1998 Summer Brochure. Course offerings for 1998 include, among others: Archaeological Techniques, Drawing Archaeological Finds, Surveying Archaeological Sites, Identification of Fibers, Identification of Wood, Glass Vessel Restoration, and Metallography of Ancient Metals.

UNITED KINGDOM/England
Location: London, England
Site: To be determined
Period: To be determined

Field School:
Dates needed: Summer, probably late June, July. Minimum stay of one week
Application deadline: Inquire.
Minimum age: 18

Experience required: None.
Cost: ca. £125 (ca. $200) tuition and all other expenses.

Director, Sponsor, and
Contact:　　Lesley Hannigan
　　　　　　　Birbeck College
　　　　　　　Centre for Extra-Mural Studies
　　　　　　　26 Russell Square
　　　　　　　London WC1B 5DQ, England, UK
　　　　　　　(44) 0171 631 6627
　　　　　　　FAX: (44) 0171 631 6688

The Centre will be running a training excavation in the summer of 1998. The course will be held in London and will be non-residential. Complete details will be available from the contact in January. In addition to the training excavation, the Centre hopes to offer several non-residential summer schools in Egyptology, consisting of lectures and museum visits during July. Each school will last one week and each week will be stand-alone; students may to attend for more than one week. Full details will be available in the spring of 1998, and those interested should contact Anna Colloms at the address listed above.

UNITED KINGDOM/England
Location: Newcastle on Tyne, South Shields, NE England
Site: Arbeia Roman Fort
Period: Iron Age and Roman

Volunteers:
Dates: Two-week sessions, June–September
Application deadline: 90 days prior to departure. (Applications will be accepted after that time if space is available.)
Minimum age: 16
Experience required: None
Cost: $1795 covers all expenses except travel to staging area (South Shields) and insurance.

Directors: Paul Bidwell, Nicholas Hodgson, Graeme Stobbs, Tyne and Wear Museums
Sponsor and
Contact:　　Earthwatch
　　　　　　　See page 7 for contact information.

The site, on a flat-topped hill overlooking the mouth of the River Tyne, is a multi-period Roman fort with occupation ranging from AD 80 until the 5th century. Special interest surrounds the use of the site as a supply depot throughout the 3rd century, initially to serve an army campaign in Scotland and subsequently for the frontier system of Hadrian's Wall. Over three centuries, the fort became one of the busiest in the northern Empire. In addition, the remains of a Late Iron Age site underlie the Roman outpost. Volunteers will participate in excavating, surveying, and mapping the site; cleaning and recording the finds; and making the site an educational attraction.

UNITED KINGDOM/England
Location: Norfolk, E England
Site: Melton Constable
Period: Medieval–present

Students/Volunteers:
Dates: June
Application deadline: Inquire.
Minimum age: Inquire.
Experience required: None.
Cost: Inquire.

Coordinator, Sponsor, and
Contact: Oliver Gilkes
The Prince of Wales's Institute of Architecture
14 Gloucester Gate, Regent's Park
London NWI 4HG, England, UK
(44) 171 9167380
FAX: (44) 171 916 7381

The Princes of Wales's Institute of Architecture is running a series of archaeological and architectural projects for which there are places for students and volunteers. These will take place over the course of 1998 and subsequent years. In Norfolk, a landscape archaeology project at Melton Constable trace the development of a typical English manor and estate. The Institute is also running two projects in Italy, one at San Vincenzo and one in Pompeii. Interested parties should contact the coordinator for more information.

UNITED KINGDOM/England
Location: Sussex, Bignor near Pulborough, S England
Site: Bignor Roman Villa
Period: 1st–4th centuries AD

Field School:
Dates: July and August (series of five- and two-day courses)
Application deadline: June
Academic credit: Optional credit from The University of Sussex. Contact the program for details.
Cost: ca. £100–£110 (ca. $165–$175) tuition for five-day course, £45 (ca. $75) for two-day course. Students responsible for all additional expenses. Details of local bed and breakfast accommodations available on request.

Bibliography: Aldsworth, F., and D. Rudling, "1995 Excavations at Bignor Roman Villa, West Sussex, 985–90," *Sussex Archaeological Collections* 133, pp. 103–88. Black, E. W., "The Roman Villa at Bignor in the Fourth Century," *Oxford Journal of Archaeology* 2, No. 1, 1983, pp. 93–107. Drewett, P., D. Rudling, and M. Gardiner, *The South-East to A.D. 1000* (Longmans), 1988.

Director: David R. Rudling, MA, BSc, FSA, MIFA, Director, Field Archaeology Unit
Sponsor: Institute of Archaeology, University College London
Contact: Mrs. Sheila Maltby
Field Archaeology Unit
1 West Street
Ditchling, Sussex BN6 8TS, England, UK
(44) 1273 845497
FAX: (44) 1273 844187
E-mail: tcrndrr@ucl.ac.uk

The Roman villa at Bignor is one of the largest and best-known in Britain. The site was discovered and extensively excavated in the early 19th century. After the excavations, cover-buildings were erected over the principal mosaics, and most of the rest of the villa was reburied. During 1991 a program of excavations was started to re-excavate parts of the villa. This work will continue in 1998. During July and August of 1998 a number of Archaeology Summer Schools will be based at the Bignor Villa. The Excavation Schools, which are suitable either for beginners or for those with some experience, cover excavation techniques, recording plans and sections, on-site surveying/leveling, photography, sieving and flotation, and finds-processing. There will also be two- and five-day courses concerned with archaeological surveying, planning and section drawings, and timber-framed buildings.

UNITED KINGDOM/England
Location: Winchester, S England, 65 miles southwest of London
Site: Hyde Abbey
Period: Medieval

Volunteers:
Dates: Team I: July 12–25, Team II: July 26–August 8
Application deadline: 90 days prior to departure. (Applications will be accepted after that time if space is available.)
Minimum age: 16
Experience required: None, but volunteers must be physically able to carry out both the strenuous excavation work and the precise, methodical processing of finds.
Cost: $1745 covers all expenses except travel to staging area (Hyde Abbey, Winchester, England) and insurance.

Directors: Dr. Eric Klingelhofer, Mercer University; Kenneth Qualmann, Winchester Museum
Sponsor and
Contact: Earthwatch
See page 7 for contact information.

The project involves the excavation of Hyde Abbey. Alfred the Great, the first King of England, is supposed to be buried in the abbey, but the location of his tomb remains unknown. If excavation reveals Alfred's tomb it will be a discovery of international significance, however, if it does not, it will still provide valuable information about the original plan and structure of the abbey, and shed light on the birth of the English monarchy. Volunteers will be involved with all excavation and finds processing work. In the field volunteers will assist with measuring for basic site recording. Those with drafting or artistic experience may be asked to record site data; those with mathematical skills may help with surveying; and those with relevant experience may do finds illustration or process of soil samples. Volunteers may also be asked to assist with public relations tasks that will help disseminate information about the project.

UNITED KINGDOM/Scotland
Location: Borders Region, Scotland
Site: Lilliesleaf
Period: Late Iron Age/Roman

Field Training:
Dates: 3 weeks in July
Application deadline: May 1
Cost: £80 per week covers lodging, local commute, field training, field school handbook, and 2 field trips. Meals (kitchen facilities provided in lodging), insurance, and travel to Scotland not included.

Bibliography: Hanson, W.S., and E.A. Slater (eds.), *Scottish Archaeology: New Perceptions*, Aberdeen: Aberdeen University Press, 1991.

Directors: Alicia Wise, University of York, Simon Clarke, Bradford University; John Dent, Borders Regional Archaeologist
Sponsor and
Contact: Alicia Wise
Department of Archaeology
University of York
York YO1 2EP, England, UK
(44) 1904 433954
FAX: (44) 1904 433939
E-mail: aw25@york.ac.uk

In 1998 the Lilliesleaf Project will focus on excavation of a Late Iron

Age/Roman Period enclosure in the Scottish Borders. The goals of this excavation are to understand the site's paleoenvironment, as recorded in pollen and sediment deposits in ditches, and the inhabitants' interactions with the Roman empire, as recorded by artifacts. The enclosure at Lilliesleaf is of great interest because it is a small rural enclosure located in a fairly indefensible location. Unusually, numerous finds of 1st and 2nd century AD Roman coins and Samian potsherds have been made there in the last three years. Geophysical survey completed in 1993 suggests the preservation of round houses within the rectilinear enclosure.

UNITED KINGDOM/Scotland
Location: Edinburgh
Site: Various
Period: Various

Field School:
Dates: July 4–17
Application deadline: June 1
Academic credit: 10 (optional) credits from University of Edinburgh.
Cost for participant: ca. £400 (ca. $655) tuition will cover course materials and weekend field trip. Student pays for travel to Scotland, insurance, and lodging and meals (the Centre will provide assistance in making arrangements).

Bibliography: Ritchie, G. and A., *Scotland: Archaeology and Early History*, Edinburgh University Press, 1991. Renfrew, C., and P. Bahn, *Archaeology: Theories, Methods and Practice*, Thames and Hudson, 1991.

Director, Sponsor, and
Contact: Bridget M. Stevens, Administrative Director
International Summer Schools
Centre for Continuing Education
University of Edinburgh
11 Buccleuch Place
Edinburgh EH8 9LW, Scotland, UK
(44) 131 650 4400
FAX: (44) 131 662 0738
E-mail: b.stevens@ed.ac.uk
WWW: http://www.ed.ac.uk/~cce/summer

Scotland has a long history with settlement remains that go back 10,000 years. These remains include fortified forts and castles, stone circles, chambered tombs, and rock art sites. To take advantage of this resource, the University of Edinburgh Centre for Continuing Education International Summer School developed the course "Archaeology in Scotland." Students will be introduced to the basic developments in the settlement of Scotland, from the earliest times to the end of the Viking Age, and there will be visits to typical sites from the various different ages. Classes are taught by archaeologists working in the many different fields of Scottish archaeology, and there will be an introduction to archaeological techniques. A highlight of the course is a weekend trip to Kilmartin Glen, an important Stone Age ritual center.

UNITED KINGDOM/Scotland
Location: Galloway, SW Scotland
Site: Botel Bailey
Period: Prehistoric–Medieval

Volunteers:
Dates needed: June–September. Minimum stay is two weeks.
Application deadline: February

Minimum age: 18
Experience required: None, but excavation skills welcome.
Cost: Volunteer responsible for all expenses. Project may be able to arrange some accommodations.

Bibliography: Botel Bailey Excavation Interim Reports, 1991–94, 1995, 1996. MacLeod, Innes, *Discovering Galloway*.

Director and
Contact: Alistair Penman, PIFA, FSAScot.
Kingston, Rhonehouse
Castle Douglas
Kirkcudbrightshire DG7 1SA, Scotland, UK

The project is an ongoing excavation of an Anglo/Norman motte and bailey and medieval burgh which had been constructed on an earlier, multi-period site, ca. 4500 BC–AD 1370. This site was twice the royal court of Scotland (AD 1292–96 and 1332–56) under the Balliol kings. The project offers instruction in excavation techniques and introduces participants to the history of Galloway, 8000 BC to the present.

UNITED KINGDOM/Scotland
Location: Outer Hebrides
Site: Milton on South Uist
Period: ca. AD 1746

Volunteers:
Dates: Team I: July 4–18, Team II: July 18–August 1
Application deadline: 90 days prior to departure. (Applications will be accepted after that time if space is available.)
Minimum age: 16
Experience required: None, must be able to work long hours out of doors, sometimes in wind and rain.
Cost: $1795 covers all expenses except travel to staging area (South Uist) and insurance.

Directors: James Symonds, University of Sheffield
Sponsor and
Contact: Earthwatch
See page 7 for contact information.

Through survey and excavation at Milton on South Uist, a post-medieval baile, or town, the project aims to fill in some historical blanks in Highland Scottish culture. Volunteers will excavate two traditional longhouses believed to date from the time of Flora MacDonald, the legendary Scottish Highlander. The work will include digging, collecting, recording, drawing, and photographing artifacts and other samples.

UNITED KINGDOM/Scotland
Location: Portmahomack, Easter Ross, Scotland
Site: Tarbat Discovery Programme, Easter Ross, Scotland
Period: AD 200–1600

Field School:
Dates: August 3–21
Application deadline: February 2
Academic credit: 10 credits from the University of York
Cost: £300 covers tuition, lodging, meals, equipment, field trips, and on-site insurance. Travel to UK not included.

Volunteers:
Dates needed: July 6–29
Application deadline: June 1

Minimum age: 18
Experience required: None, but excavation experience helpful.
Cost: £30 per week covers on-site lodging and meals. Travel to UK and insurance not included.

Bibliography: *Bulletin of the Tarbat Discovery Programme*, No 1 (1995) and No 2 (1996).

Sponsors: University of York; Tarbat Historic Trust
Director and
Contact: Justin Garner-Lahire
Tarbat Discovery Programme
Field Archaeology Unit, University of York
The King's Manor
York YO1 2EP, England, UK
(44) 1904 433903
(44) 1904 433902
E-mail: arch18@york.ac.uk

The Tarbat Discovery Programme is a major archaeological project which aims at discovering the earliest kingdom of the Northern Picts. The archaeological site has so far shown evidence of 1) a late Iron Age (Pagan Pictish) enclosure, 200–700; 2) a Pictish monastery, 700–900; 3) a Norse settlement, 900–1100; and 4) a medieval settlement 1100–1600. There is more than half a meter of stratification and finds of pottery and sculpture are unusually frequent. The old church of St. Colman (Tarbat Old Church), situated outside the small fishing port of Portmahomack, is now being converted into a Museum and Visitor Centre designed to display the work of the Tarbat Discovery Programme, which is scheduled to continue until 2001.

UNITED KINGDOM/Wales

Location: Gwynedd, off Aberdaron, NW Wales
Site: Bardsey Island
Period: Prehistoric–present

Field School:
Dates: July 11–18
Application deadline: May 30
Academic credit: 10 credits from University College of Wales
Cost: £180 (ca. $290) covers tuition, lodging (in Victorian farmhouses), meals, local commute, ferry, and insurance.

Bibliography: Jones, P.H., *The Natural History of Bardsey*, National Museum of Wales, Cardiff, 1988.

Director, Sponsor and
Contact: Dr. Chris Arnold
Department of Continuing Education
University College of Wales
10–11 Laura Place
Aberystwyth, Dyfed SY23 2AU, Wales, UK

Bardsey Island lies three miles off the tip of the Lleyn Peninsula in northwest Wales. It has been inhabited since prehistoric times, was a major place of pilgrimage in the medieval period, supported pirates in the 17th century, and in Victorian times was home to up to 100 fishermen and farmers. The island is owned and managed by a trust, and as well as having a rich variety of archaeological sites, it is also a national nature reserve and has a bird observatory. It is quite isolated and has no electricity or telephones. The course aims to teach excavation techniques as well as to provide background on the island's archaeology. Students will spend the day working on the excavation, and there will be lectures in the evenings.

UNITED KINGDOM/Wales and IRELAND

Location: SW Wales and S Ireland
Site: Castell Henllys (Wales), Clonmacnoise/Monasterboice (Ireland)
Period: Iron Age, Roman, Early Christian, Historic

Field School: (Maximum of 22 students)
Dates: July 4–August 15
Application deadline: May
Academic credit: Credit equivalent to one UK term's work from the University of York.
Cost: £950 (ca. $1550) tuition plus £500 (ca. $800) fee for lodging (campsite in Wales, house in Ireland), meals, on-site insurance, and local commute; and £150 (ca. $220) for travel to and from Ireland.

Bibliography: Cunliffe, B.W., *Iron Age Communities of Britain*, Routledge, 1991 (earlier editions: 1976, 1978). Mytum, H.C., "Castell Henllys: Iron Age Fort," *Fortress*, No. 9, 1991, pp. 3–11. Mytum, H.C., *The Origins of Early Christian Ireland*, Routledge, 1992. Mytum, H.C. "Language as symbol in churchyard monuments: the use of Welsh in 19th and 20th century Pembrokeshire," *World Archaeology*, No. 26:2, 1994.

Director: Dr. Harold C. Mytum
Sponsor and
Contact: Department of Archaeology
University of York
The King's Manor
York YO1 2EP, England, UK
(44) 1904 433929
FAX: (44) 1904 433902
E-mail: hcml@york.ac.uk
WWW: http://www.york.ac.uk/depts/arch/staff/sites/
henllys/hcmfield.htm

This intensive field school is based in the Pembrokeshire Coast National Park at Castell Henllys, the most extensively excavated Iron Age fort in Wales and noted for its experimental reconstructions of buildings and earthworks. Excavations at this site and an adjacent native Roman-period settlement and a nearby historic farm site will continue in 1998.

The course consists of three parts, each of two weeks duration: 1) Data Capture: Excavation at the Iron Age, Roman, or historic site with training in basic excavation, recording, and preliminary processing of finds and environmental samples; 2) Data Capture: Survey in Ireland, concentrating on the world famous Early Christian monasteries of Clonmacnoise and Monasterboice, with training in surface and geophysical survey and recording monuments such as gravestones; 3) Data Analysis: Based at Castell Henllys, students work on a project of their choice derived from 1) or 2). Work is six days per week with optional trips to nearby prehistoric and historic sites on days off.

The course is intensive, with a maximum of 22 students. The group will be split in half for parts 1) and 2), with one group doing 1) then 2), the other doing 2) then 1), ensuring small group teaching. Assessment will be based on practical work and written assignments. Instruction can be geared to undergraduate or graduate needs.

UNITED KINGDOM/Wales

Location: Near Port Talbot, S Wales; Llanllyfni, N Wales
Site: Site 1: Margam Park, Site 2: Cae Mawr
Period: Prehistoric/Roman/post-Medieval

Volunteers:
Dates needed: January–November
Application deadline: Ongoing; last date to apply is September 1.

Minimum age: 16

Experience required: BA in archaeology or survey and/or excavation experience.

Cost: £7.50 per day for training; £10–£15 per day for lodging, £5 per day for meals. Program provides local commute and on-site insurance. Travel to Wales not included.

Bibliography: Will be sent on application.

Director: Karl-James Langford
Sponsor and
Contact: Archaeology Cymru
Cae Mawr
Tan Yr Allt, Llanllyfni
Gwynedd LL54 6RT, Wales, UK
(44) 1446 749747
or
Archaeology Cymru
The Old Custom House
41 Dock View Road
Barry, Wales, UK
(44) 1446 749747

Archaeology Cymru will have several fieldwork opportunities in 1998. Amateurs and professionals who are interested in gaining experience, on a voluntary basis, at sites in Wales, are invited to apply. Work at Site 1 involves the excavation and recording of a Roman roan in Margam, South Wales; at Site 2 it involves the excavation and recording of a prehistoric and post-Medieval site at Llanllyfni in North Wales. More details are sent upon application.

IRELAND

Location: Aran Islands
Site: Mainistir Chiarain
Period: Medieval, AD 1000–1500

Volunteers:
Dates needed: June 27–August 15, three two-week sessions.
Application deadline: None
Minimum age: 16
Experience required: None, but mapping, drawing, and photography skills welcome.
Cost: ca. $1365 (1997 cost) covers lodging, meals, and local commute. Travel to Aran Islands not included.

Director: Sinead Ni Ghabhlain, UCLA Institute of Archaeology
Sponsor and
Contact: University Research Expeditions Program (UREP)
See page 7 for contact information.

The three Islands of Aran were renowned for their monasteries in Medieval times. A limited historical record exists for these monasteries and little is known about how they functioned in their heyday. Recent excavations at the monastery of Mainistir Chiarain have revealed domestic structures within the inner monastic enclosure in addition to a range of domestic artifacts. Continued excavation and mapping of this 12th century church will provide insight into the changing functions of the island monasteries over the period AD 1000–1500. Team members will be trained in stratigraphic excavation methods and will assist with post- excavation processing of discoveries. Those with drafting skills can produce illustrations of artifacts recovered during excavation, while those interested in photography can assist in site documentation with cameras. Irish students will also participate.

IRELAND

Location: County Mayo, Achill Island
Site: Deserted Village, Slievemore
Period: AD 1200–1900

Field School:
Dates: June 29–August 15
Application deadline: May 30
Academic credit: 6 credits from Achill Archaeological Summer School.
Minimum age: 18
Cost: $1750 covers tuition, lodging, and local commute. Meals, insurance, and travel to Ireland not included.

Volunteers:
Dates needed: June 29–August 15
Application deadline: April 30
Minimum age: 25
Experience required: MA in Archaeology/Anthropology, and supervisory and computer skills.
Cost: Volunteer responsible for all expenses.

Bibliography: McDonald, T., *Achill Island*, 1997; *Achill: 5000 BC to 1900 AD: History, Archaeology, and Folklore*, 1992. Cooney, G., and E. Grogan, *Irish Prehistory: A Social Perspective*, 1994. Edwards, Nancy, *The Archaeology of Early Medieval Ireland*, 1990. Barry, Terry B., *The Archaeology of Medieval Ireland*, 1987. Kingston, B., *The Deserted Village at Slievemore*, 1990.

Sponsor: Mayo County Council
Director and
Contact: Theresa McDonald, MA
Achill Archaeological Summer School
St. O'Hara's Hill
Tullamore, Co. Offaly, Ireland
(353) 506 21627
FAX: (353) 506 22975
E-mail: theresa@iol.ie
WWW: http://www.iol.ie/~theresa/index.html

The Deserted Village site, on the slopes of Slievemore Mountain, consists of some 74 upstanding buildings and an associated field system of lazy beds, a farming practice used in the system of booleying (transhumance), where livestock is moved from a lowland, permanent village, to summer pasture, frequently in the mountains. The houses and field systems represent the last phase of settlement on the mountainside. There is also evidence of activity dating back some 5000 years, including Megalithic tombs from the Neolithic Period, Bronze Age hut platforms, the remains of an Iron Age caher (fort), and Early Medieval remains.

The Achill Archaeological Summer Field School specializes in a hands-on approach, and students experience all aspects of survey and excavation methodology. This is backed up by lectures and seminars, which cover the main features of Irish archaeology. Guided field trips and on-site lectures allow students to view various monument types of all periods from the Neolithic to the Late Medieval. In 1998, there will be a special, four-day field trip to sites and monuments in other parts of Ireland. There is also an introduction to local folklore, and to the botany and geology of the island, some features of which are unique to Achill.

IRELAND

Location: County Roscommon, Strokestown
Site: Ballykilcline, Aughamore Village
Period: AD late 1700s–1847

Field School:
Dates: June 29–July 31
Application deadline: March 15, or until maximum enrollment is reached.
Academic credit: 6 credits from Illinois State University. The field school is open to students from any university. Students must first enroll at Illinois State University, but this is an easy process and does not affect enrollment elsewhere.
Cost: ca. $3500 covers tuition, lodging, meals, insurance, and local commute. Travel to Ireland not included.

Bibliography: Orser, Charles E., Jr., "Probing County Roscommon," *Archaeology* 50:5, pp. 72–75, September/October, 1997; (1997) "Archaeology and Nineteenth-Century Rural Life in County Roscommon," *Archaeology Ireland* 11:1, pp. 14–17, 1997; "Archaeology and Modern Irish History," *Irish Studies Review* 18, pp. 2–7, 1997; "Of Dishes and Drains: An Archaeological Perspective on Irish Rural Life in the Great Famine Era," *New Hibernia Review* 1:1 pp. 120–135, 1997; *A Historical Archaeology of the Modern World*, Plenum Press, New York, 1996. Scally, Robert James, *The End of Hidden Ireland: Rebellion, Famine, and Emigration*, Oxford University Press, New York, 1995.

Director: Prof. Charles E. Orser, Jr.
Sponsor and
Contact: Illinois State University
Anthropology, Campus Box 4640
Normal, Illinois 61790-4640
(309) 438-2271
FAX: (309) 438-7177
E-mail: ceorser@ilstu.edu

This research constitutes year five of a long-term effort to study the peasant villages located on the old Mahon estate in County Roscommon. To date, students have excavated two villages: Gortoose and Muliviltrin. In 1998, the program will investigate the village of Aughamore, located on the townland of Ballykilcline, subject of Robert Scally's *The End of Hidden Ireland*. This is the first project of this kind ever to be conducted in the Republic of Ireland, and the research promises to change the way we think about the men and women who lived in the Irish countryside before 1850. Many of these men and women, forced from their homes by starvation and want, left Ireland for the United States, Britain, Canada, Australia, and elsewhere. Students spend their days working at the archaeological site. Evenings are spent washing artifacts or listening to lectures. Friday evenings and weekends are free for traveling.

IRELAND
Location: Various
Site: Various
Period: Prehistoric–Medieval

Study Tour: Ancient Ireland (Maximum tour group size is 25)
Dates: June 20–July 1
Application deadline: None
Cost: Cost (to be determined) will cover lodging in 3 and 4 star hotels, most meals, air transportation on scheduled major airlines, all land transportation, entrance fees to all museums and listed stops, guided tours and lectures, and taxes and gratuities for hotels and meals. Lunches and two evening meals not included.

Bibliography: Cahill, Thomas, *How the Irish Saved Civilization*, Doubleday, 1995. Cooney, Gabriel, and Eoin Grogan, *Irish Prehistory: A Social Perspective*, Wordwell, Dublin. Harbison, Peter, *Pre-*

Christian Ireland, Thames and Hudson Inc., 1988. Ryan, Michael (ed.), *The Illustrated Archaeology of Ireland*, Country House, Dublin, 1991. Scherman, Katharine, *The Flowering of Ireland*, Barnes and Noble, 1996.

Sponsor: Mississippi Valley Archaeology Center, University of Wisconsin-La Crosse
Director and
Contact: Jim Gallagher
Archaeological Studies Program
University of Wisconsin-La Crosse
La Crosse, WI 54601-3788
(608) 785-8463
FAX: (608) 785-8486
E-mail: galla_jp@mail.uwlax.edu

This study tour will focus on the prehistoric and Medieval remains of Ireland's past. The tour begins in Dublin and proceeds north to the Boyne Valley megalithic tombs of Newgrange and Knowth. From there the tour will proceed north around the coast of Ireland, and down the east coast to Galway. Participants will visit archaeological remains, including stone circles, megalithic tombs, Celtic forts, the ruins of castles and cathedrals, plus there will be visits to ongoing excavations. The tour will feature presentations by some of the leading figures in Irish archaeology.

COMMONWEALTH OF INDEPENDENT STATES

REPUBLIC OF GEORGIA
Location: W Georgia, SW of Kutaisi, 2 hours drive from Black Sea
Site: Vani
Period: 7th–2nd centuries BC

Volunteers:
Dates needed: July 11–August 1
Application deadline: May 1
Minimum age: 18
Experience required: None, but drawing skills and some knowledge of the history of the region welcome. (Reading list provided.)
Academic credit: The Georgian Academy of Sciences Center for Archaeological Studies will present certificates of participation to students who successfully complete the Field School Program. Students should consult their own universities regarding additional documentation necessary to secure academic credit.
Cost: $900 covers tuition, lodging, meals, local commute, and travel to project from Tbilisi. Travel to Georgia and insurance not included.

Bibliography: Braund, David, *Georgian Antiquity—A History of Colchis and Transcaucasian Iberia, 550 BC–AD 562*, Oxford: Clarendon Press, 1994.

Director: Dr. Otar Lordkipanidze, Centre for Archaeological Studies, Georgian Academy of Science
Sponsor and
Contact: Georgian Academy of Science
c/o GAS-J. Elliott
102 Woodside Avenue
Metuchen, NJ 08840
(908) 549-3322
FAX: (732) 205-9737
E-mail: elliott@aesop.rutgers.edu

Located between the Black and Caspian Seas, Georgia stands at the crossroads between Europe and Asia. Rich and substantial remains of numerous ancient and medieval cultures continue to be discovered. Recent finds include the oldest human remains found in Europe, a Bronze Age golden lion, the 5th-century BC tombs of Vani, and artifacts of ancient Colchis (home of Medea and the Golden Fleece). The Field School will participate in excavations at a number of Classical, Hellenistic, and Byzantine sites. Daily lectures will focus on methodology and particular issues concerning specific problems and sites. Participants will prepare reports for presentation during site visits. The program also includes a tour of principal archaeological excavations, historic sites, museums, churches, and other important monuments of Georgian culture.

REPUBLIC OF GEORGIA
Location: 85 km SW of Tbilisi
Site: Dmanisi
Period: Paleolithic and Medieval

Volunteers:
Dates needed: July 11–August 1
Application deadline: May 1
Minimum age: 18
Experience required: None.
Academic credit: The Georgian Academy of Sciences Center for Archaeological Studies will present certificates of participation to students who successfully complete the Field School Program. Students should consult their own universities regarding additional documentation necessary to secure academic credit.
Cost: $900 covers tuition, lodging, meals, local commute, and travel to project from Tbilisi. Travel to Georgia and insurance not included.

Bibliography: Dean, D. Delson, "E. Homo at the gates of Europe," *Nature*, 373, pp. 472–473, 1995. Gabunia, L., and A.A. Vekua, "Plio-Pleistocene hominid from Dmanisi," *Nature*, 373, pp. 509–512, 1995.

Director: Dr. Otar Lordkipanidze, Centre for Archaeological Studies, Georgian Academy of Science
Sponsor and
Contact: Georgian Academy of Science
c/o GAS-J. Elliott
102 Woodside Avenue
Metuchen, NJ 08840
(908) 549-3322
FAX: (732) 205-9737
E-mail: elliott@aesop.rutgers.edu

The site is on the surface of a basaltic lava flow, cut by the rivers Pinezauri and Mashavera, creating a triangular promontory of lava which towers 90 meters above the present level of the rivers. The medieval town of Dmanisi is located on this promontory. In addition, a paleolithic site was uncovered here during the excavation of cellars of medieval houses. Since 1991, the paleolithic site has been investigated within the framework of an international research project by a joint team of the Georgian Centre for Archaeological Studies and the Romish-Germanishes Zentralmuseum (Mainz, Germany) and has yielded a well-preserved mandible of *Homo erectus* directly associated with a non-Acheulean lithic industry and abundant vertebrate fauna; Dmanisi is a strong candidate for one of the earliest Euro-Asian archaeological localities.

RUSSIA
Location: Caucasus, near the city of Gelenjik
Site: Zhane, a group of dolmens
Period: 3rd millennium BC

Field School:
Dates: 3 weeks between August 10 and September 10
Application deadline: July 1
Academic credit: 1 credit from Institute for Study of Material Culture History or Saint Petersburg State University
Cost: $840 for tuition and fees, and all other expenses except local commute.

Volunteers:
Dates needed: August 10–September 10
Application deadline: July 1
Minimum age: 18
Experience required: None, but photography, drawing, and topography equipment experience welcome.
Cost: All expenses except local commute.

Bibliography: Mohen, J.-P., *The World of Megaliths*, 1993.

Director, Sponsor, and
Contact: Dr. V. Trifonov
Institute for Study of Material Culture History
Russian Academy of Science
Dvortsovaya nab., 18
Saint Petersburg 191186, Russia
(7) 812 3121484 or (7) 812 1437338
FAX: (7) 812 3116271 or (7) 812 1437338
E-mail: trifonov@reuters.spb.ru

The project is a part of long-term (1996–1999) program, "Caucasian Megaliths in Cultural, Social and Ecological Context." The "Zhane" group of dolmens are unique in terms of design and architecture, consisting of three megalithic tombs, two circular and one rectangular. In 1997, one of the dolmens was excavated and re-assembled by an international archaeological team from Russia, the US, Australia, and Italy.

RUSSIA
Location: Central Russian plain, Bryansk Region, Khotylevo Village
Site: Khotylevo II
Period: Upper Paleolithic, Gravettian (24,000 BP)

Volunteers:
Dates needed: July 1–August 25
Application deadline: April 1
Minimum age: 18
Experience required: None
Cost: $100 per week covers lodging, meals, field training, and local commute. Travel to Russia not included.

Bibliography: Soffer, Olga, *The Upper Paleolithic of the Central Russian Plain*, Academic Press Inc., 1985.

Director, Sponsor, and
Contact: Konstantin N. Gavrilov
Institute of Archaeology
Department of Stone Age Archaeology
Russian Academy of Sciences
Dm. Ulyanov St. 19
117036 Moscow V-36, Russia
(7) 095 1269454
FAX: (7) 095 1260630
E-mail: kg@iaras2.msk.su

Khotylevo II is a well-known Gravettian site with unique geological stratigraphy, including sediments from the Mousterian to Holocene periods, and good conditions for bone preservation. A large collection of lithics and bone artifacts as well as female figurines were uncovered during previous excavations in the 1970s. A new complex was found during reconnaissance fieldwork in 1993, and traces of a new living horizon dating to the Upper Pleistocene were studied in 1994–1997. The 1998 project will include archaeological, paleoecological, and geological investigation of Khotylevo II as well as visits to the Upper Paleolithic site of Yudinovo, which contains a dwelling constructed of mammoth bone, and local museums.

RUSSIA
Location: Central Russian plain, Kursk Region, Avdeevo Village
Site: Avdeevo
Period: Upper Paleolithic (ca. 21,000–20,000 BP)

Volunteers:
Dates needed: July 1–September 10
Application deadline: May 1
Minimum age: 18
Experience required: None
Cost: $96 per week covers lodging, meals, field training, and local commute. Travel to Russia not included.

Bibliography: Soffer, Olga, and N.D. Praslov (eds.), *From Kostenki to Clovis: Upper Paleolithic-Paleo-Indian Adaptations*, New York and London: Plenum Press, 1993. Gvozdover, M.D., *Art of the Mammoth Hunters. The Finds from Avdeevo*, Oxbow Monograph, 1995. Gvozdover, M.D., "Ornamental decoration on artifacts of the Kostenki culture" and "Typology of Female Figurines of the Kostenki Paleolithic Culture," *Soviet Anthropology and Archeology*, 27(4), pp. 8–31 and 32–94, 1989.

Director, Sponsor, and
Contact: Ms. Eugenia Bulotchnikova
                  Moscow State University
                  Research Institute and Museum of Anthropology
                  Mokhovaya St. 11
                  103009 Moscow, Russia
                  FAX: (7) 095 4821013
                  E-mail: root@escape.zgrad.su

The site of Avdeevo, one of the most interesting and important Upper Paleolithic sites on the Russian Plain, has yielded an extremely rich collection of stone and bone implements as well as unique examples of Paleolithic art. The site is also significant because its rich artifactual materials permit researchers to trace clear connections between Upper Paleolithic sites of Central and Eastern Europe, such as Willendorf, Dolni Vestonice, and Pavlov in Central Europe as well as with the similar Russian site at Kostenki. Research at the site was conducted from 1946–1949 (old complex) by Voevodskij and Rogachev, and from 1972 at a new complex by Gvozdover and Grigor'ev. In 1998, investigations will be carried out on the field between the old and new complexes.

RUSSIA
Location: Moscow
Site: Various sites in the historical center of Moscow
Period: 16th–19th centuries AD

Volunteers:
Dates: August
Application deadline: Inquire.
Minimum age: 18

Experience required: None, all training is in English and suitable for either beginners or those with some experience.
Cost: $1800 (single occupancy), $1600 (double occupancy), $1100 (student dormitory), covers training, lodging, meals, local commute in Moscow, and visits to museums and historical/archaeological sites.

Bibliography: Prevost-Logan, Nicole, "Moscow Reclaims its Past," pp. 26–35; Veksler, Alexander G., "The Manege Dig," pp. 32–33; Beliaev, Leonid A., "Mystery Monasteries," pp. 36–38, *Archaeology* 50(4) July/August, 1997. Beliaev, Leonid, "Excavation and Restoration of Kazan Cathedral," *Science in Russia*, 1993. Berton, Kathleen, *Moscow, An Architectural History* (reprint in paperback). Brumfield, William, C., *Gold in Azure, A Thousand Years of Russian Architecture*, 1983. Kelly, Laurence, *Moscow, A Traveller's Companion*. Massie, Robert, *Peter the Great*.

Directors and Sponsors: Leonid Beliaev, Head, Department of Moscow Archaeology, Institute of Archaeology, Russian Academy of Sciences; Alexander Veksler, Director, Centre for Archaeological Investigations of Moscow
Contact: Ada Beliaev
                  Project Coordinator at Moscow, Russia
                  (7) 095 2002846
                  FAX: (7) 095 2000689
                  E-mail: labeliaev@glasnet.ru

Training excavations will continue in 1998 at the center of medieval Moscow. Previous excavations have revealed several hundred years of history, starting with Moscow's foundation in AD 1147; possible sites to be investigated in 1998 include occupational layers dating back to the 12th century. Volunteers will learn archaeological techniques, including the use of stratigraphy, dating methods, typology, and restoration of pottery.

RUSSIA
Location: Near Nedvigovka village, in the area of the Don River delta, S Russia
Site: Kamennaya Balka II and III
Period: Upper Paleolithic (ca. 15,000 BP)

Volunteers:
Dates needed: July 5–August 25
Application deadline: April 1
Minimum age: 18; maximum age: 50
Experience required: None.
Cost: $400 fee covers lodging, meals, and local commute. Travel to Russia not included.

Bibliography: Leonova, N.B., "The Upper Paleolithic of the Russian Steppe Zone," *Journal of World Prehistory*, Vol. 8, No. 2, 1994. *From Kostenki to Clovis. Upper Paleolithic, Paleo-Indian Adaptations*, Plenum Press, New York, 1993.

Sponsor: Moscow State University; National Geographic Society
Director and
Contact: Dr. N. Leonova
                  Moscow State University
                  Department of Archaeology
                  Petchatnikov per., 5-6
                  103045 Moscow, Russia
                  (7) 095 2085492
                  E-mail: aleon@chair.cogsci.msu.su

The area of the Don River delta and the adjacent coast of the Azov Sea is rich in Upper Paleolithic sites; those of the Kamennaya Balka culture are the most well studied. These sites were discovered in 1957 and excavations by Moscow State University's archaeological expedition to the Don over the past 37 years have proven instrumental in establishing new methodological approaches useful in determining the length of time that sites have been occupied. Finds from these sites are stored in the collections of the Moscow State University Anthropology Museum.

RUSSIA
Location: Primorie Province, near Vladivostok, Russian Far East
Site: Boisman II, shell midden
Period: Early Neolithic (ca. 6000–6500–7000)

Field School:
Dates: July 2–August 3
Application deadline: April 15
Academic credit: 3 credits (400-level anthropology course) from University of Alaska Anchorage
Requirements: An ability to endure sometimes rugged field conditions, in terms of food and living arrangements, is a necessity for participation in this project. An introductory course in archaeology is also useful.
Cost: $225 tuition, $1050 fee for lodging, meals, and local commute. Travel to Russia, insurance, excavation kit, and personal effects not included.

Bibliography: Chard, Chester S., *Northeast Asia in Prehistory*, Madison, Wisconsin: University of Wisconsin Press, 1974. Kononenko, N.A., *Ancient Cultures of Primorye in the Late Pleistocene and Early Holocene: Origins and Adaptations*, Tokyo, 1993. Michael, Henry N., *The Archaeology and Geomorphology of Northern Asia*, Toronto: University of Toronto Press, 1964. Okladnikov, A.P., *The Soviet Far East in Antiquity: An Archaeological and Historical Study of the Maritime Region of the U.S.S.R.*, Toronto: University of Toronto Press, 1965.

Sponsor: University of Alaska, Anchorage, Department of Anthropology; Russian Far East State University; Russian Academy of Sciences
Director and
Contact: Dr. David Yesner
                 University of Alaska
                 Department of Anthropology
                 3211 Providence Drive
                 Anchorage, AK 99508
                 (907) 786-6845 or (907) 786-6840
                 FAX: (907) 786-6850
                 E-mail: AFDRY@uaa.alaska.edu

The Boisman site, south of Vladivostok, is the oldest coastal site in the Russian Far East, dating to the Early Neolithic period. The earliest people there hunted sea-lions, seals, deer, and wild pigs, and collected large oysters in an ancient estuary. They developed an elaborate stone and bone tool industry, with a variety of harpoons and other implements, many of which are similar to early Alaskan industries dating to around the same or slightly later time period. This is particularly intriguing, since a series of human burials from the site have been labeled "proto-Chuckchi/Eskimo" by physical anthropologists and clearly have northern affinities. At the same time, a type of pottery was developed that has its closest affinities with China and Korea, and agriculture eventually came in from that area as well. Thus, a series of influences from a broad region to the north and south amalgamated to produce this earliest maritime culture.

The site is located in a beautiful embayment adjacent to a modern tourist resort. During the project, students will learn techniques of archaeological excavation and the recovery, processing, and analysis of archaeological materials. There will be guest lectures in Russian and English. Some knowledge of Russian language is desirable, but not essential. Informal classes in Russian language will be part of the field program.

RUSSIA
Location: St. Petersburg
Site: Catherine Park of Tsarskoe Selo
Period: 18th–19th centuries AD

Field School:
Dates: July 1–20
Application deadline: April 30
Academic credit: 1 credit from Institute for Study of Material Culture History, Russian Academy of Sciences
Cost: $940 tuition and fees, and all other expenses except local commute.

Volunteers:
Dates needed: June 1–July 30
Application deadline: April 30
Minimum age: 18
Experience required: None, but photography, drawing, remote sensing, and topography equipment experience welcome.
Cost: All expenses except local commute.

Bibliography: Radzinsky, Adward, *The Last Tsar*. Massie, Leon, *Nicholas and Alexandra*. Biographies of Peter the Great and Catherine the Great. Books on St. Petersburg and the palaces at Tsarskoe Selo and Pavlovsk.

Sponsors: WAC Foundation; Tsarskoe Selo State Museum; Institute for Study of Material Culture History
Director and
Contact: Dr. V. Trifonov
                 Institute for Study of Material Culture History
                 Russian Academy of Science
                 Dvortsovaya nab., 18
                 St. Petersburg 191186, Russia
                 (7) 812 3121484 or (7) 812 1437338
                 FAX: (7) 812 3116271 or (7) 812 1437338
                 E-mail: trifonov@reuters.spb.ru

Old St. Petersburg parks and gardens of 18th–19th centuries are an integral part of Russian cultural heritage. The preservation and restoration of these cultural legacies depends upon research into the landscape architecture of the period. Modern methods of archaeological field research have greatly improved and assisted in the preservation and restoration of previously lost park elements. The main aim of the Project is to locate and document the material remains and traces of lost buildings, such as pavilions, booths, and other historical structures and, through archaeological fieldwork and archival research, develop plans for their restoration.

Structures to be studied during the 1998 field season include the Swiss House and the Turkish Booth. Both buildings were destroyed by fire during World War II. Goals for 1998 are to excavate and measure preserved foundations, explore their condition, and reintroduce these structures into the Park plan. In addition, the project seeks to locate and unearth marble sculpture that was hidden in the Park by museum staff prior to the German army occupation of Tsarskoe Selo in 1942.

RUSSIA
Location: Siberia, Khabarovsk Province, Tyr Village
Site: Buddhist Temple of Tyr
Period: 15th century AD

Volunteers:
Dates: Team I: July 5–18, Team II: July 19–August 1, Team III: August 2–19
Application deadline: 90 days prior to departure. (Applications will be accepted after that time if space is available.)
Minimum age: 16
Experience required: None
Cost: $1795 covers all expenses except travel to staging area (Kharbarovsk International airport) and insurance.

Director: Dr. Alexandr R. Artemiev, Russian Academy of Sciences
Sponsor and
Contact: Earthwatch
See page 7 for contact information.

The Buddhist temple at Tyr, named "Eternal Calm," was erected on Tyr Cliff overlooking the Amur in ca. AD 1415 to introduce Chinese Buddhism to the local populations. By AD 1434 the temple was in ruins and a second temple was built and a second stela erected and inscribed. Though the history of the temple from this point on is unknown, it was most probably destroyed again. It was rediscovered in the 1600s by Russian explorers. Dr. Artemiev began research at the site in 1995 and has since discovered that the second temple was not built upon the ruins of the first, but ca. 56 miles away. Therefore the remains of two 15th-century Buddhist temples exist in the area.

Volunteers will be given the opportunity to take part in all stages of archaeological fieldwork, including digging with hand tools, screening excavated matrix for artifacts, processing artifacts on-site and in the lab, and documenting each excavation unit through photography, sketches and plotted drawings, and detailed field notes. In the evenings the volunteers may take part in the reconstruction of ceramics.

RUSSIA
Location/Site: Siberia, Lake Baikal, about 300 km east of Irkutsk
Period: Neolithic, ca. 4000–6000 BP

Field School: Enrollment limited to 10.
Dates: June 3–July 18
Application deadline: March 1
Academic credit: Credit from the University of Alberta. Inquire for details.
Requirements: Previous digging experience is not necessary, but priority will be given to students with archaeology or physical anthropology as a major and experience in camping under rugged conditions. Students will be required to sign a liability waiver, and the site is at least a day's travel away from the nearest medical attention.
Cost: ca. CDN$700 tuition for students registered in a University of Alberta degree program and ca CDN$4500 (1997 cost) for airfare, ground travel, field trips, food, health insurance (mandatory) and vaccination, lodging in Irkutsk, excavation supplies, and visa. Lodging at the site will be in tents, and students need to bring their own all-weather tents, with wind resistance being an important criterion. Camping gear and personal expenses usually amount to no less than CDN$300.

Directors: Dr. Andrzej Weber and Dr. Olga I. Goriunova
Sponsors: University of Alberta, Edmonton, Canada; Irkutsk State University, Russia

Contact: Department of Anthropology
University of Alberta
Edmonton, Alberta T6G 2H4, Canada
(403) 492-3879
FAX: (403) 492-5273

The second annual Field School in Mortuary Archaeology at Lake Baikal, Siberia, will involve the excavation of a Neolithic grave site that features good preservation of skeletal remains and grave goods characteristic of a hunting-gathering culture. Students will receive training in a variety of subjects, including topographic survey, burial excavation and documentation, data collection, and elements of human osteology. Field trips will allow students to learn more about the area's geography, ethnography, history, and archaeology.

Participants should expect very simple living conditions with regard to personal hygiene (although there will be plenty of remarkably clean but rather cold water in Lake Baikal and a sauna once a week), food (although there will plenty of fresh fish from the lake), and entertainment. All students will be expected to assist with kitchen and camp duties on a rotating basis.

RUSSIA
Location: Urals, Trans-Urals, Kurgan and Chelyabinsk Districts
Site: Burial grounds at Kazakbajevo
Period: Iron Age, 4th–3rd centuries BC

Application deadline for all programs: May 1. Potential participants should FAX or e-mail their passport data (name, date of birth, address, citizenship, etc.) to the director by the deadline to expedite the preparation of visas.

Study Tour:
Dates: August 1–8
Cost: ca. $500 for lodging (with host families while in Ekaterinburg, and camping), meals, and local commute. Must supply own tent and sleeping bag. Travel to Russia and insurance not included.

Field School:
Dates: July 5–August 5
Academic credit: 4 credits from Ural State University.
Experience required: None, but must be comfortable in group environment in exotic setting.
Cost: ca. $200 per week for tuition, lodging (with host families while in Ekaterinburg, and camping), meals, and local commute. Travel to Russia and insurance not included.

Volunteers:
Dates needed: July 5–August 5
Minimum age: 18
Experience required: Excavation, drawing, and experience working with collections. Must be comfortable in group environment in exotic setting.
Cost: ca. $150 will cover lodging (camping), meals, and local commute within the excavation area. Travel to Russia and insurance not included.

Bibliography: Sulimirski, T., *The Sarmatians*, London, 1970. "The Steppe of the Asiatic Region of the USSR at the Scythian and Sarmatian Periods," *Archaeology of the USSR*, Moscow, 1992 (in Russian).

Directors: Dr. Ludmila Koryakova, Ural State University; Dr. Marie-Yvane Daire (French team)
Sponsor: Russian Academy of Science

Contact: Ural State University, Archaeological Lab
51 Lenin Av.
Ekaterinburg 620083, Russia
(7) 343 2557005 or (7) 343 2454131
FAX: (7) 343 2557401
E-mail: Ludmila.Koryakova@usu.ru

"Kurgans and Fortresses of the North Periphery of the Silk Road: Cultural Change in the Contact Zones" is a joint French/Russian project which involves the excavation of burial grounds. Sites to be investigated are significant for understanding the interrelationship between settled and nomadic populations in marginal territory in the 1st millennium BC. The educational and volunteer programs will include lectures on Russian prehistory (Bronze and Iron Ages of the Urals and West Siberia), visits to sites, work on collections, and fieldwork on Iron Age kurgans and fortresses. The study tour will visit sites, including caves, settlements, fortresses, burial grounds, and museums. Participants will also have the opportunity to become acquainted with the people and culture of the region.

RUSSIA

Location: Upper Volga, 40 km from Yaroslavl, 250 km from Moscow
Site: Stanovoye 4
Period: Mesolithic–Early Neolithic

Volunteers:
Dates needed: July
Application deadline: April 1
Minimum age: 18
Experience required: None, but should be willing to live in tents without much comfort.
Cost: ca. $20 per day covers lodging in tents, travel from Moscow to project and return, lectures on the prehistory of western Russia, and simple meals. Excursions to other sites and travel to Russia not included.

Bibliography: Zhilin, M.G., *Bone Weapons of the Ancient Upper Volga Population*, Moscow, 1993.

Director, Sponsor, and
Contact: Mikle G. Zhilin
Institute of Archaeology
Russian Academy of Sciences
Dm. Ulyanov St. 19
117036 Moscow V-36, Russia
(7) 095 1269454
FAX: (7) 095 1260630
E-mail: Zhilin@iaras2.msk.su

Stanovoye 4 is situated at the Podozerskoye peat bog; the Lahost River links the bog to the Upper Volga. The site has 3 cultural layers: Early Mesolithic, Middle or Late Mesolithic, and the upper layer represents the Early Neolithic Upper Volga culture, genetically linked with materials from lower layers of the site. All three layers, in addition to lithics, contain numerous well-preserved bone, antler, and wooden artifacts, and floral and faunal remains. Excavation at the site began in 1995 and has already yielded one of the most beautiful Mesolithic inventories in Eastern Europe, and will certainly reveal much more.

RUSSIA

Location: Voronezh Region, Ostrogozhsk District
Site: Ternovoe and Kolbino villages
Period: Scythian, 5th–4th centuries BC

Volunteers:
Dates needed: July 5–August 5. Minimum stay of 2 weeks.
Application deadline: May 30
Minimum age: 18
Experience required: Excavation and cleaning finds, but must be comfortable in camping environment with no electricity.
Cost: $800 for 2 weeks covers lodging (in tents in wonderful environment), meals (from the general "cauldron" of the expedition), travel to Voronezh from Moscow and return, local commute to sites and museums, and insurance. Travel to Russia not included.

Bibliography: *Archaeology of the USSR*, Vol. 10, Moscow, 1989 (in Russian). Guliaev, V.I., *The Gold of the Scythians*, Moscow, 1977, (in Russian). Liberov, P.D., *The Population of the Middle Don Area in the Scythian Period*, Moscow, 1968 (in Russian). Edwards, Michael, "Searching for the Scythians," *National Geographic*, Vol. 190, No. 3, September 1996, pp. 54–79. Davis-Kimball, Jeannine, V. Bashilov, and L.T. Yablonsky (eds.), *Nomads of the Eurasian Steppes in the Early Iron Age*, Berkeley: Zinat Press, 1995. Piotrovsky, Boris, Ludmila Galanina, and Nonna Grach, *Scythian Art*, Oxford and Leningrad: Phaidon, 1979. Talbot Rice, Tamara, *The Scythians*, New York: The Praeger, 1959.

Director, Sponsor, and
Contact: Dr. Valeri I. Guliaev
Institute of Archaeology
Russian Academy of Sciences
Dm. Ulyanov St. 19
117036 Moscow V-36, Russia
(7) 095 1269443 (secretary) or 1269429 (direct)
FAX: (7) 095 1260630
E-mail: ekozl@online.ru

The Scythian period is a brilliant page in the history of the nomadic and settled tribes who inhabited vast territories of South Russia and Ukraine, between the Don River on the west and the Dniester River on the east. The Don (Classical Tanais) was considered by the Greeks to be the true frontier between Europe and Asia, and Greek colonists on the Black Sea coast established wide trade relations with local barbarians and were a major influence on their culture. The main purpose of the field project is the investigation of archaeological and historical materials pertaining to the territory of South Russia in the Scythian period. The project includes some excavation of Scythian burial mounds in Ternovoe and Kolbino, wide surveys in the mentioned area, laboratory analyses, the study of literature by Classical authors, including Herodotus, and publication of results.

RUSSIA

Location: Zaraysk, ca. 125 km SE of Moscow
Site: Zaraysk
Period: Upper Paleolithic 18,000–24,000 BP

Volunteers:
Dates needed: Session 1: July 19–August 1, Session 2: August 2- 15. Volunteers may participate in one or both sessions.
Application deadline: April 15
Minimum age: 18
Experience required: None, but preference will be given to those with excavation experience and good references. Participants must meet physical and health requirements and demonstrate ability to work and live with a small group of people with varied backgrounds.
Cost: $1700 per two week session covers lodging, meals, local commute, and travel to site from Moscow and return. Travel to Russia, visa, and insurance not included.

Bibliography: References, readings, and a video of previous work will be provided to successful applicants.

Director and Sponsor: Dr. Hizri Amirkhanov, Institute of Archaeology, Russian Academy of Sciences, Moscow, E-mail: hizri@iaras2.msk.su

Contact: Dr. Bruce Bradley
Primitive Tech Enterprises, Inc.
P.O. Box 534
Cortez, CO 81321
(970) 565-7618
E-mail: primtech@juno.com

Zaraysk is a Late Upper Paleolithic site of great significance; it is further north than any other known site of its type and archaeological culture (Kostenki-Avdeevo). The site is a habitation with two known occupations and includes at least one pit structure, mammoth bones and tusks, and numerous other features. The work will include detailed excavation of the living floor and other cultural deposits, laboratory processing, and possibly preliminary analysis of flint tools. Field trips to other nearby archaeological projects are also planned. Educational lectures and demonstrations are an integral part of the program, and there may be a possibility of participating in a Mesolithic site excavation at the White Well site. There will also be ample opportunity to interact with Russian archaeologists, local people, and to experience Russian culture in the post-Soviet era. A knowledge of Russian is not required.

NEAR & MIDDLE EAST

CYPRUS
Location: Athienou, S central Cyprus
Site: Athienou-Malloura
Period: Archaic–Ottoman

Field School:
Dates: May 31–July 18
Application deadline: March 16
Academic credit: 4 credits from Davidson College
Cost: $2200 covers tuition, lodging, meals, and local commute. Travel to Cyprus and insurance not included. Pending approval of an NSF-REU grant, ten undergraduates may be eligible for full scholarships (including airfare).

Bibliography: *American Journal of Archaeology*, 95, 1991, pp. 316–17; 96, 1992, p. 352; 97, 1993, p. 323; 98, 1994, p. 290; 99, 1995, pp. 329–330; 100, 1996, p. 365. *Bulletin de correspondence hellenique*, 115, 1991, pp. 813–16; 116, 1992, pp. 819; 117, 1993, p. 742; 118, 1994, pp. 678–79. *Old World Archaeology Newsletter*, 15.3, 1992, pp. 18–23; 20.1, 1996, pp. 1–8. *Annual Report of the Department of Antiquities of Cyprus*, 1990, pp. 54–55; 1991, pp. 51–52

Director, Sponsor, and
Contact: Dr. Michael K. Toumazou
Department of Classics
Davidson College
Davidson, NC 28036
(704) 892-2281
FAX: (704) 892-2005
E-mail: mitoumazou@davidson.edu

The Athienou Archaeological Project (AAP) is a multi-disciplinary project focusing on the site of Athienou-Malloura and the surrounding valley in south-central Cyprus. The site was used for about 2500 years, encompassing the Archaic, Classical, Hellenistic, Roman, Byzantine, Frankish, Venetian, and Ottoman periods.

Since its inception in 1990, AAP has completed a field survey of the valley, a topographical survey of Malloura, and geophysical prospection of portions of the site. Several buildings of the Roman–Ottoman settlement and some 30 burials dating to the Venetian period (15th–16th centuries) have been excavated. Several rock-cut chamber tombs (Archaic–Roman), an aquifer, and two water cisterns have been excavated at the northern periphery of the site. Moreover, the Archaic–Roman rural sanctuary, initially investigated in 1862 by a French mission, was located in 1991 and is now the main focus of AAP's excavation efforts. Thus far AAP investigations have thrown considerable light on the long-term history and use of this small rural inland site, as compared to larger urban, usually coastal, centers which have traditionally been more intensively investigated.

The site's long occupation, coupled with the diversity of archaeological remains encountered—domestic, religious, and funerary—make it an excellent training ground in archaeological methodology and provide ample evidence for introducing students to the history and material culture of Aphrodite's Isle.

CYPRUS
Location: Dhali
Site: Idalion
Period: ca. 1200 BCE–Roman

Field School:
Dates: June 27–August 8
Application deadline: April 1
Academic credit: 6 undergraduate or graduate credits from the University of Arizona
Cost: $1500 covers tuition, lodging, and meals during work week. Travel to Cyprus, weekend expenses, and insurance not included.

Volunteers:
Dates of excavation and field school: June 29–August 7. Minimum stay of 2 weeks.
Application deadline: June 1
Minimum age: 17
Experience required: None, but excavation experience helpful.
Cost: $600 for two weeks or $1500 for six weeks covers meals during work week and lodging. Travel to Cyprus, weekend expenses, and insurance not included.

Bibliography: Gaber, P., "The History of Ancient Idalion in the light of Recent Excavations" in *Visitors, Immigrants, and Invaders in Cyprus*, Paul Wallace (ed.), SUNY Albany, 1995, pp. 32–39; "In Search of Adonis" in *Cypriote Stone Sculpture*, Institute of Archaeology, University of Belgium, Brussels-Liege, 1994, pp. 161–165; "Idalion" in *Oxford Encyclopedia of Near Eastern Archaeology*, 1996. Gaber, P., and W. Dever, "Idalion, Cyprus: Conquest and Continuity," *Annual of the American Schools of Oriental Research*, 1996, pp. 81–127. Stager, L., and A. Walker (eds.) *American Expedition to Idalion, Cyprus, 1973–1980*, Oriental Institute Press, 1989.

Director: Dr. Pamela Gaber, University of Arizona
Sponsor: Dept. of Near Eastern Studies, University of Arizona
Contact: Linda Clougherty
39 Clear Vista Drive
Rolling Hills Estates, CA 90274-5433
(310) 544-0294
FAX: (310) 377-8897
E-mail: lclougher@aol.com

The ancient city of Idalion, one of the most important and cosmopolitan cities of the ancient Eastern Mediterranean, was probably founded in the 12th century BC, and reached its greatest prosperity and extent in the 7th–6th centuries BC. It was a center of the Cypriote copper trade and of the ancient cult of the Great Mother and her consort, "The Young Lord." These deities came to be known in Roman times as Venus and Adonis, and Idalion was undoubtedly identified as the site of that legend. One of the sites under excavation in 1998 is the Temenos of Adonis, the seat of that cult. The other site under investigation is the "Lower City" domestic and industrial quarter, where an olive oil producing complex, a horn working area, and a *bothros*, or depository for sacred objects were in the process of excavation in the 1997 season..

During the excavation, students will learn how to excavate; process artifacts and ecofacts; do comparative research studies; keep and report excavation records. Undergraduates prepare one oral presentation and take a final exam; graduate students prepare a research paper. All students participate in field trips to other sites and keep a journal of their learning and experiences. A student who successfully completes this field school is qualified to join a stratigraphic excavation as an assistant supervisor.

CYPRUS
Location: Dhali
Site: Idalion
Period: Archaic–Roman (7th–1st centuries BC)

Field School:
Dates: June 27–August 8
Application deadline: April 10
Academic credit: 1 "full" or "year" credit (Canadian), equivalent to 6 semester hours (US), from Brock University
Cost: Tuition (CDN$685 for Canadians citizens and permanent residents; CDN$1845 for others) plus fees (CDN$2000 or US$1600) for lodging, meals, field trips and entrance fees, and local commute. Travel to Cyprus, meals and travel on days off, and insurance not included.

Bibliography: Karageorghis, Vassos, *Cyprus from the Stone Age to the Romans*, Thames and Hudson, 1982. Hunt, Sir David, *Footprints in Cyprus: An Illustrated History*, London: Trigraph, 1982.

Director: Dr. Pamela Gaber, University of Arizona
Sponsors: University of Arizona, ASOR
Contact: Prof. David W. Rupp
Classics Department
Brock University
St. Catharines, Ontario L2S 3A1, Canada
(905) 688-5550, ext. 3575
FAX: (905) 688-2789
E-mail: leslie@spartan.ac.brocku.ca

Idalion, one of the independent city kingdoms of Iron Age Cyprus, straddled two acropoleis on which civic and religious centers and domestic architecture have been excavated. In 1998 the Brock University Archaeological Practicum, as part of the University of Arizona expedition to Idalion (see above entry), will focus its attention on the lower town below the western acropolis (believed to be the city's administrative center), where previous excavation has uncovered evidence for domestic and light industrial use. The Practicum will train the student in field methodology for excavation and primary processing of artifacts. The learning experience is expanded by lectures given by specialists on staff, weekly field trips, and student presentations.

CYPRUS
Location: Dhali
Site: Idalion Survey Project
Period: Early Prehistoric–Modern

Volunteers:
Dates needed: June 6–June 27
Application deadline: Inquire.
Minimum age: 18
Experience required: None.
Cost: CDN$900 covers lodging, meals, and local commute. Travel to Cyprus, insurance, expenses away from the project on days off not included.

Directors: Margaret E. Morden and Sarah T. Stewart
Sponsors: University of Arizona, ASOR
Contact: Margaret E. Morden and Sarah T. Stewart
5-67 Linwell Rd.
St. Catharines, Ontario L2N 7N1, Canada
(905) 938-1935
E-mail: mmorden@spartan.ac.brocku.ca

The Idalion Survey Project is an interdisciplinary investigation of the hinterland of ancient Idalion, one of the more important kingdoms of Iron Age Cyprus. This is the second and final season of survey. The project is run in conjunction with the University of Arizona Expedition to Idalion under the directorship of Dr. Pamela Gaber, and seeks to place ancient Idalion within its historical and environmental framework with special emphasis on locating and analyzing the chert and clay sources available to the inhabitants of the region. Volunteers will be instructed in field-walking strategies (both intensive and extensive), map reading, artifact recognition, and will be involved in artifact and data processing.

CYPRUS
Location: Kourion
Site: Kourion Amathus Gate Cemetery
Period: Hellenistic-Late Roman

Position(s): Area supervisor (possible)
Dates needed: ca. June 22–August 7
Application deadline: February 1
Experience required: Previous field experience
Salary: None
Cost: Program provides lodging, meals, some travel (depending on funding). Insurance and travel (if funding is not forthcoming).

Field School:
Dates: ca. June 22–August 7
Application deadline: March 1. Applications will be dealt with on a first come, first served basis.
Academic credit: Up to 4 credits (negotiable) from the University of Missouri-Columbia.
Cost: Tuition (to be determined, depends on number of hours, residency, etc.) plus a fee for lodging. Travel to Cyprus, meals, and insurance not included.

Volunteers:
Dates needed: ca. June 22–August 7
Application deadline: March 1
Minimum age: 18
Experience required: None
Cost: Program fee (to be determined) covers lodging. Volunteer responsible for all other expenses.

Bibliography: Parks, D.A., "Excavations at Kourion's Amathus Gate Cemetery, 1995," *Report of the Department of Antiquities, Cyprus*, 1996, pp. 127–33; "Excavations at Kourion's Amathus Gate Cemetery, 1996" *Report of the Department of Antiquities, Cyprus*, 1997, (in press). Swiny, H.W., *An Archaeological Guide to the Ancient Kourion Area*, Nicosia: Department of Antiquities, 1982.

Sponsor: Cyprus American Archaeological Research Institute
Director and
Contact: Danielle Parks
Art History and Archaeology
109 Pickard Hall
University of Missouri-Columbia
Columbia, MO 65211 USA
(573) 443-0477
FAX: (573) 884 4039
E-mail: C506075@showme.missouri.edu

The site is the Hellenistic-Late Roman cemetery serving Kourion, one of the largest cities on Cyprus during that period. It offers a rare opportunity to investigate a necropolis not burdened with modern occupation. The project is intensively excavating a portion of the cemetery, and surveying others, in the hopes of reconstructing the ancient funerary landscape—how the cemetery related to the settlement, its layout, and how it changed over time. Individual tombs yield important information on burial rituals, particularly for the Late Roman period. Field School students will participate in both field and laboratory activities. There will also be some evening lectures given by the staff on the archaeology of the area and pertinent specialties, such as physical anthropology. Kourion is convenient to quite a few nearby sites, and field trips will be arranged. Students will also be encouraged to explore on their own.

CYPRUS
Location: Near Kouklia/Palaipaphos, SW Cyprus
Site: Rantidi
Period: Cypro-Archaic–Roman

Position(s): Trench supervisors
Dates needed: June 29–August 3
Application deadline: None
Experience required: One season of excavation experience.
Salary: None
Cost: Program provides lodging, meals, and local commute. Travel to Cyprus, insurance and personal expenses not included.

Field School:
Dates: June 29–July 29
Application deadline: None
Academic credit: 3 credits from University of Indianapolis
Cost: $522 covers tuition, lodging, meals (except on days off), and local commute. Travel to Cyprus and insurance not included.

Volunteers:
Dates needed: June 29–July 29
Application deadline: None
Minimum age: 16
Experience required: None, but good physical condition.
Cost: $400 covers lodging, meals (except on days off), and local commute. Travel to Cyprus and insurance not included.

Bibliography: Hunt, Sir David, *Footprints in Cyprus: An Illustrated History*, London: Trigraph, 1982. Mitford, Terence B., and Olivier Masson, *The Syllabic Inscriptions of Rantidi-Paphos*, 1983.

Directors: Excavation Director: G. Bonny Basemore; Field School Director: Philip H. Young.
Sponsor: University of Indianapolis
Field School and Volunteer
Contact: Dr. Philip H. Young
Krannert Memorial Library
University of Indianapolis
1400 E. Hanna Avenue
Indianapolis, Indiana 46227
(317) 788-3399
FAX: (317) 788-3275
E-mail: pyoung@uindy.edu

Staff Positions
Contact: Bonny Basemore
5214 South Woodlawn, #304
Chicago, IL 60615

The site of Rantidi has produced over 100 syllabic inscriptions, large terracotta statuary, artifacts, and architectural remains identifying the central hilltop as a sanctuary, and there are associated rock-cut tombs and habitation sites. Its proximity to the major Sanctuary of Aphrodite at Palaipaphos is significant. During the 1998 season, the project will sample architecture and tombs, and continue mapping and surveying the sanctuary. Students and volunteers will be involved primarily in excavation and will assist with finds cleaning, study, photography, registration, and conservation. The program also includes lectures on archaeological principles, field and conservation techniques, and topics in Cypriot history and archaeology; and field trips to other sites, museums, and excavations on the island. During free times participants can relax, sightsee, shop, visit nearby beaches and generally experience life and cuisine in the small Cypriot village of Alektora.

CYPRUS
Location: Nicosia District, Agia Varvara-Almyras
Site: Almyras
Period: Iron Age (ca. 600–150 BC)

Volunteers:
Dates: Team I: September 5–19, Team II: September 21–October 4
Application deadline: 90 days prior to departure. (Applications will be accepted after that time if space is available.)
Minimum age: 16
Experience required: None, but photography; computer, drawing, excavating, mapping, and surveying skills helpful. As there is much heavy work to be done, those who enjoy and are accustomed to manual labor will be enthusiastically received.
Cost: $1895 covers all expenses except travel to staging area (Larnaca International Airport) and insurance.

Director: Walter Fasnacht, Curator, Neolithic Collection, Swiss National Museum
Sponsor and
Contact: Earthwatch
See page 7 for contact information.

Almyras is a well-preserved Iron Age copper-mining, ore-processing, and smelting site. Research will focus on how the Cypriot Iron Age mining industry functioned and what its impact was on the habitat. Volunteer tasks include excavating; collecting and mapping finds; documenting and classifying archaeometallurgical objects such as ores, slag, and metals; surveying to identify archaeological remains, metallurgical residues, and evidence of copper mining; and experimentally reconstructing smelting installations and their operation.

ISRAEL
Location: Nationwide
Site: Various
Period: Various

Volunteers: General information
Dates needed: Throughout the year; the main season of excavation runs from May–September, when universities are not in session.
Application deadline: Varies by program.
Minimum age: Usually 18 or older.
Experience required: Usually, no previous experience is necessary, but volunteers should be in good physical condition and able to work long hours in very hot weather. When applying to the director of an excavation volunteers should indicate any previous studies in archaeology or related fields, such as anthropology, architecture, geography, surveying, graphic arts; or experience in excavation work, pottery restoration, or photography.
Academic credit: Some expeditions offer credit courses from sponsoring institutions. Details may be obtained by contacting individual expedition directors.
Cost: Volunteers are responsible for their own travel arrangements/costs to and from Israel. There is usually a fee for food and lodging, although on some excavations these are free. Accommodations for volunteers can range from sleeping bags in the field, to rooms in hostels or kibbutzim, to hotels near a site. Excavations conducted in or near a city often require volunteers to find their own accommodations. In most cases, volunteers must arrange for medical and accident insurance in advance. Even in instances when accident insurance is provided, it is strongly advised that volunteers come fully insured as the insurance offered is minimal.

Contact: The Israel Ministry of Foreign Affairs:
Home Page: http://www.israel-mfa.gov.il/index.html
Archaeology Page:
    http://www.israel-mfa.gov.il/facts/hist/archeo.html
Excavations Page:
    http://www.israel-mfa.gov.il/archdigs.html
E-mail: ask@israel-info.gov.il

Archaeology in Israel has provided a valuable link between the country's present and past, with thousands of years of history unearthed at some 3500 sites. Many archaeologists enlist volunteer help on their digs as volunteers are highly motivated and wish to learn and gain experience, although the work is often difficult and tedious. The work includes digging, shoveling, hauling baskets of earth and sherds, cleaning pottery sherds and more. The work schedule at an excavation is organized according to the conditions at the site. A day on an average dig begins before dawn and ends after noon. There is normally a rest period after lunch. The afternoons and early evenings may be devoted to lectures, additional excavation work, cleaning and sorting of pottery and other finds, or they may be free. Most expedition directors (or other staff members) offer informal lectures covering the history and archaeology of the site and discussions of the type of work involved and organize sightseeing and field trips to sites in the area and to neighboring museums.

A list of archaeological expeditions which accept volunteers is compiled by the Israel Antiquities Authority (IAA) as a service to the public and may be accessed at the World Wide Web site of the Israel Foreign Ministry (see above).

ISRAEL
Location: Nationwide
Site: Various
Period: Various

Israel Antiquities Authority: Programs for Organized Groups
The Israel Antiquities Authority's Department of Education and Information is responsible for educational programs in archaeology and heritage preservation. The department runs three centers for archaeology, offering tours, workshops, activities, enrichment courses and opportunities to participate in excavations. These programs are for organized groups only.

For further information,
contact: The Center for Archaeology in the Galilee
POB 1094
Old Acco, Israel
Tel./FAX: (972) 4 9816569

The Center For Archaeology in Jerusalem
POB 586
91004 Jerusalem, Israel
(972) 2 5602621
FAX: (972) 2 5602628 or (972) 2 6285054

The Center for Archaeology in the Negev
Hen St. 34, POB 497
80750 Arad, Israel
Tel./FAX: (972) 7 9954445

ISRAEL (and Jordan, Syria, Lebanon, and Egypt)
Site/Location: Various
Period: Various

Volunteers:
Dates: June 19–August 1. Volunteers may join from 1–6 weeks.
Application deadline: Up until two weeks prior to departure, if space is available; tour usually reaches capacity by March or April.
Minimum age: College age, families, and senior citizens welcome.
Experience required: None, but enthusiasm.
Academic credit: 4–6 credits from Hebrew University, if desired.
Cost: $2895–$6895 depending on length of stay. Fee covers lodging, most meals, local commute, a Nile Cruise, and airfare New York–Israel and return. The Society will arrange connecting flights from any city in the US or Canada.

Sponsor and
Contact: Arthur D. Greenburg
The Israel Archaeological Society
467 Levering Avenue
Los Angeles, CA 90024-1909
(800) 477- 2358; (310) 472-9449
FAX: (310) 476-6259
E-mail: archaeology@mindspring.com

The program includes one–four weeks of digging and classes in Israel and Jordan plus excursions to other sites in Israel, Jordan, Syria, Lebanon, and Egypt, including a Nile cruise. There will also be a two-week program over the 1998–99 Christmas and New Year holidays. Contact the Society for details.

ISRAEL
Location: Acre, Beth Shean, Caesarea
Site: Various
Period: Various

Field School: Internship Program in Documentation & Conservation
Dates: During the summer for a minimum of 2 weeks up to 3 months.
Application deadline: Throughout the year.

Academic credit: Inquire.

Cost: Program fee (to be determined), travel to Israel, and insurance (medical and accident mandatory; advance proof of coverage required).

Director: Ing. Ya'acov Schaffer

Sponsor and

Contact: Ms. Gail Sussman, Head, Training & Documentation
Israel Antiquities Authority (IAA)
Conservation Department
Rockefeller Museum Bldg., POB 586
91004 Jerusalem, Israel
(972) 2 560-2616/2633
FAX: (972) 2 626-0105
E-mail: gail@israntique.org.il

The Conservation Department of the Israel Antiquities Authority annually conducts an Internship Program in the recording and conservation of archaeological sites at various locations. Contact Ms. Sussman for details.

ISRAEL
Site/Location: Bethsaida, NE coast of Sea of Galilee
Period: Late Bronze Age–Roman

Dates of excavation and field school: Session 1: June 1–June 9, Session 2: June 22–July 10, Session 3: July 13–July 31. Credit and non-credit sessions are three weeks, but a minimum one-week, non-credit session can be arranged.

Application deadline: Rolling admissions began on December 1, 1997. To secure a place, participants must send in a completed application and $200 deposit according to the following deadlines: Session 1: April 15, Session 2: May 1, Session 3: May 15.

Field School:

Academic credit: 3–6 undergraduate or graduate credits from the University of Nebraska at Omaha.

Cost: $86.75 per credit undergraduate, $102.75 graduate tuition for Nebraska residents (inquire about cost for non-residents); and $350 per week for lodging, meals, and local commute. Credit-bearing sessions are three weeks. Additional days (less than a week) are calculated at $50 per night. Travel to Israel, insurance (mandatory), and optional weekend tours not included.

Volunteers:

Minimum age: 18

Experience required: None, but good physical condition.

Cost: $350 per week for lodging, meals, and local commute. Minimum stay is one week. Additional days (less than a week) are calculated at $50 per night. Travel to Israel, insurance (mandatory), and optional weekend tours not included.

Bibliography: Arav, R., and R. Freund, *Bethsaida: A City by the North Shore of the Sea of Galilee*, Thomas Jefferson Press, 1995. Arav, R., and J. Rousseau, *The Archaeology of Jesus*, Fortress Press, 1994. Arav, R., *Israel Exploration Journal*, 38, 3, 1988, pp. 187–188; 39, 1–2, 1989, pp. 99–100; 41, 1–3, 1991, pp. 184–186; 42, 1992, pp. 252–254. Arav, R., *Excavations and Surveys in Israel*, Vol. 9, No. 2, 1989–1990, pp. 98–99. Pixner, B., "Searching for the New Testament Site of Bethsaida," *Biblical Archaeologist*, December 1985, pp. 207–216. Wolff, S.R., "Archaeology in Israel," *American Journal of Archaeology*, Vol. 95, No. 3, July 1991, p. 520.

Directors: Dr. Rami Arav, Dr. Richard Freund

Sponsor and

Contact: Wendi Chiarbos, Coordinator
Dept. of Philosophy and Religion
Arts & Sciences Hall 230
University of Nebraska at Omaha
Omaha, NE 68182-0265
(402) 554-2902
FAX: (402) 554-3681
E-mail: betsaida@cwis.unomaha.edu
WWW: http://www.bethsaida.unomaha.edu

In the classical period of the Bible, Bethsaida and Jerusalem were major cities of King David. In the Greek and Roman conquests of the Near East, Bethsaida and Jerusalem were linked as significant cities of the Herodian families. They were both visited by Jesus and many of the apostles, by the Jewish historian Josephus Flavius, and by important rabbinic figures. Then mysteriously Bethsaida disappeared. Visitors, pilgrims and travelers in the Middle Ages found Jerusalem but searched in vain for Bethsaida. The search for the lost city of Bethsaida re-emerged with the rise of modern biblical research in the 19th century, however, no systematic excavations were undertaken until 1987, when Dr. Rami Arav began a series of probes and excavations to determine the location of Bethsaida. By 1989, the State of Israel had recognized the official location of Bethsaida on Israeli maps, as a result of Dr. Arav's work.

Excavations, ongoing since 1987, have revealed at succeeding levels a city dating from the Early Bronze Age (2700–2400 BC); an Iron Age (1000–600 BCE) city with a massive city wall and impressive public buildings; and a city dating from the Hellenistic period (4th century BCE) that was destroyed in 66 CE during the Jewish-Roman war. In 1998 the site will become a public tourist attraction. The workday begins at 5:30 am with fieldwork done in the morning, lab work in the afternoon, and lectures in the evening. Weekend tours to Galilee and Jerusalem are available for an additional fee.

ISRAEL
Site/Location: Caesarea Maritima, 40 km north of Tel Aviv
Period: 4th century BC–13th century AD

Dates of excavation and field school: Underwater Excavations: May 24–July 23; Land Excavations: May 31–July 23
Application deadline: May 1

Field School:

Academic credit: 3–6 undergraduate credits from the University of Maryland; Brooklyn College of the City University of New York; Temple University, Trinity College, Connecticut; or the University of Oklahoma. Graduate credit also available.

Cost: $500 and up (3 or 6 credits) tuition; $50 application fee; $375 per week dig fee (minimum four weeks for credit) for lodging, meals, insurance, and local commute; and $50 per week surcharge for divers. Travel to Israel not included. All participants must provide their own medical insurance.

Volunteers: There will be openings in the 1998 season for as many as 40 divers and 200 land volunteers. Minimum stay of two weeks; four weeks for divers.

Minimum age: 18

Experience required: None, but drafting and excavation experience welcome, and SCUBA certification required for divers.

Cost: $50 application fee; $375 per week dig fee for lodging, meals, insurance, and local commute; and $50 per week surcharge for divers. Travel to Israel not included. All participants must provide their own medical insurance.

Bibliography: Holum, Kenneth G., Robert Hohlfelder, Robert Bull, and Avner Raban, *King Herod's Dream: Caesarea on the Sea*, New York and London: W.W. Norton, 1988. *Caesarea Papers*, *Journal of Roman Archaeology*, supplementary volume no. 5, Ann Arbor, Michigan, October 1992. *Caesarea Maritima, Retrospective After 2,000 Years: A Symposium of Scholars Held at Caesarea, Israel, January 3–11, 1995*, Avner Raban and Kenneth G. Holum (eds.), Leiden: E.J. Brill, 1996.

Directors:	Kenneth G. Holum, Avner Raban, Joseph Patrich
Sponsors:	University of Maryland; Haifa University
Contact:	Combined Caesarea Expeditions
	Department of History
	University of Maryland
	College Park, MD 20742
	(301) 405-4353
	FAX: (301) 314-9399
	E-mail: caesarea@umail.umd.edu
	WWW: http://www.inform.umd.edu/Caesarea

Caesarea Maritima, located on the Mediterranean coast of Israel, is a major urban site of the Classical period. Founded in 10 BC by King Herod the Great, it became the metropolis of Roman Palestine and was noted for its artificial harbor, an engineering marvel. Marine excavators have been exploring this harbor in recent years, while their terrestrial colleagues have uncovered the ancient city's street plan, a well-preserved aqueduct system, a theater, a circus, a waterfront warehouse complex, several baths, shops and dwellings, and the Temple Platform, with remains of an Early Christian martyr church built over ruins of King Herod's temple to Roma and Augustus. The temple foundations were discovered by Combined Caesarea Expeditions land excavators during the 1995 season. The site has also yielded a rich harvest of sculpture, ceramics, glass, jewelry, coins, Greek and Latin inscriptions, and figured mosaic pavements. Also prominent on the site are ruins of medieval Caesarea, including splendid Crusader fortifications. There are also exiguous remains of Straton's Tower, the Phoenician trading station that preceded Caesarea on the same site. Excavations in 1998 will investigate the harbor, the Temple Platform, and a domestic/mercantile quarter of the ancient city.

ISRAEL
Site/Location: Ein Gedi, on the western shore of the Dead Sea
Period: Roman–Byzantine

Field School:
Dates: December 27, 1998–January 14, 1999
Application deadline: End of November.
Academic credit: 6 credits the University of Hartford
Cost: ca. $3995 (1997 cost) covers tuition, round-trip airfare from JFK, ground transport, field trips, and lodging and meals five days per week. Health insurance (mandatory) not included.

Volunteers:
Dates needed: December 27, 1998–January 30, 1999. Minimum stay of one week, two-week (10-day) stay is recommended.
Application deadline: December 1
Minimum age: 16. There is no age limit, senior citizens are welcome.
Experience required: None, but volunteers are required to be in good physical health and good cheer.
Cost: ca. $225–$450 per 5-day week (depending on accommodations selected) for lodging and meals. Weekend accommodations can be arranged. Travel to Israel and insurance (mandatory) not included.

Bibliography: "Ein Gedi," *New Encyclopedia of Archaeological Excavations in the Holy Land*, Vol. 2, Jerusalem, 1993, pp. 399–409.

Sponsors: Hebrew University, Israel; University of Hartford, Connecticut, Maurice Greenberg Center For Judaic Studies
Director and Volunteer

Contact:	Dr. Yizhar Hirschfeld
	Hebrew University, Institute of Archaeology
	Mount Scopus
	Jerusalem 91905, Israel
	FAX: (972) 2 5825548
	E-mail: hani@actcom.co.il

Field School

Contact:	Hilda Grossman, Director of Winterterm
	University of Hartford, Computer Center 231
	200 Bloomfield Avenue
	West Hartford, CT 06117-1599.
	(800) 234-4412

The excavation of the Roman-Byzantine village site of Ein Gedi is part of a study of rural life on the edge of the Judean wilderness. The village of Ein Gedi covered some 10 acres and had an approximate population of 1200 people. To date, excavations have revealed a series of 3rd–6th century synagogues, with mosaic floors, a village street, the village entrance, multi-storied buildings, shops, a ritual bath, and small finds, including coins, pottery lamps and vessels, jewelry, and glass. The work entails clearing rocks, soil, and debris with shovels, buckets, and wheelbarrows; carefully excavating and sifting human occupation levels with small hand tools; pottery washing; and registering finds. Optional after-work activities include lectures and tours to visit archaeological sites and nature reserves.

ISRAEL
Site/Location: Har Karkom, Negev Desert
Period: Paleolithic, Chalcolithic, Bronze Age

Volunteers:
Dates needed: March–April
Application deadline: January
Minimum age: 18
Experience required: Background or strong interest in archaeology or ethnology, and knowledge of computers, languages, and graphics.
Cost: ca. $2800 for lodging, meals, and local commute. Travel to Israel not included.

Bibliography: Anati, E., *The Mountain of God*, New York: Alfred A. Knopf, 1986; *I Siti a Plaza di Har Karkom*, Capo di Ponte: Edizioni del Centro, 1987; *Har Karkom in the Light of Recent Discoveries*, Capo di Ponte: Edizioni del Centro, 1994.

Director, Sponsor, and

Contact:	Emmanuel Anati
	Centro Camuno di Studi Preistorici (CCSP)
	25044 Capo di Ponte
	Valcamonica, Brescia, Italy
	(39) 364 42091
	FAX: (39) 364 42572
	E-mail: ccsp@globalnet.it
	WWW: http://www.globalnet.it/ccsp/ccsp.htm

Har Karkom was a major religious high place; numerous ceremonial sites have been identified, including altars and caves with geoglyphs. In addition, remains of large campsites from the Chalcolithic and Bronze Ages have been documented around it, and recent finds have verified that the site was also frequented during the Paleolithic era. With over 40,000 engraved figures documented, Har Karkom has the largest concentration of rock art in the Negev and Sinai.

ISRAEL
Site/Location: Gamla, 40 km NE of Tiberias, on the Golan heights
Period: Early Bronze Age (3200–2000 BCE), Hellenistic–early Roman (ca. 200 BCE–67 CE)

Volunteers:
Dates needed: May–September. Minimum stay of two weeks.
Application deadline: Inquire.
Minimum age: 17
Experience required: None, but skilled people may be put in charge of various tasks.
Academic credit: No formal credits offered, but a certificate of participation can be provided for student to achieve credit through own institution.
Cost: Cost is not yet finalized but will cover lodging and meals.

Bibliography: Josephus, Flavius, *War of the Jews*, Book IV, Chapter 1. Syon, D., "Gamla—Portrait of a Rebellion," BAR 18(1), January/February 1992, pp. 20–37

Director: Danny Syon, Israel Antiquities Authority
Sponsor and
Contact: Gamla Excavations
c/o Golan Museum, PO Box 30
Qatzrin 12900, Israel
(972) 6 6961350
FAX: (972) 6 6969637
E-mail: danny@israntique.org.il

Gamla or "Gamala" (Camel) is often is referred to as the Masada of the North. In 67 CE the Roman Army besieged the ancient mountain-top town, and thousands died in the Romans' final assault. Josephus describes Gamla's stand in great detail in "The Jewish War." The site is partially excavated, and ruins include fortified city walls, a synagogue, and guard towers.

ISRAEL
Site/Location: Jerusalem
Period: Various

Archaeology of Jerusalem:
Dates: July 1–30
Application deadline: May 15
Prerequisites: All applicants must have successfully completed at least one year of study at an accredited institution of higher education.
Academic credit: 4 undergraduate or graduate credits from The Hebrew University of Jerusalem
Cost: $745 covers tuition and field trips. Housing is in the University's dormitories. Students should plan to spend US $10–$15 per day for meals. Health insurance coverage (ca. $35) through the Hebrew University Student Health Services is required. Travel to Israel not included.

Sponsor: The Hebrew University of Jerusalem, Rothberg School for Overseas Students
Contacts: The program has special contact addresses for persons applying from the following countries: United States, United Kingdom, Canada, France, Australia, and Israel (and all other countries). Those for the United States and Israel are listed below. For other addresses, contact the Hebrew University or visit their Web site.

United States
Contact: Office of Academic Affairs
The Hebrew University of Jerusalem
11 East 69th Street
New York, NY 10021
(800) 404-8622 or (212) 472-2288
FAX: (212) 517-4548
E-mail: 74542.340@compuserve.com

Israel (and all other countries except those listed above)
Contact: Department of Summer Courses
The Hebrew University of Jerusalem
Rothberg School for Overseas Students
Mount Scopus, 91905 Jerusalem, Israel
(972) 2 5882602
FAX: (972) 2 5827078
E-mail: msroz@pluto.mscc.huji.ac.il
WWW: http://www2.huji.ac.il/www_sfos/top.html

The Rothberg School for Overseas Studies of The Hebrew University of Jerusalem offers broad selection of courses for undergraduate and graduate students through its summer sessions and year-long programs. The course "Archaeology of Jerusalem" investigates how the history this religious center has been revealed through archaeological study. The evolution of Jerusalem into a holy city for three religions will be traced from Canaanite times through the First and Second Temple periods to the Roman, Byzantine, and Early Islamic periods. Topics include an introduction to archaeological sites, chronology, the City of David, the walls of the city, tombs, the water supply, the Temple Mount, Byzantine churches, and the rise of Islam. Field trips will be held at least three times per week beyond class hours.

ISRAEL
Site/Location: Kfar HaHoresh, Lower Galilee, near Nazareth
Period: Pre-Pottery Neolithic B (ca. 9000–8500 BP)

Volunteers:
Dates: June 29–August 6. Minimum stay of three weeks: June 29–July 17 or July 19–August 6.
Application deadline: April 1
Minimum age: 18
Experience required: Previous experience preferred but not vital. Preference is given to archaeology or anthropology majors. Must be willing to work long hours in hot and humid weather.
Academic credit: Available through School of Overseas Studies, Hebrew University of Jerusalem at ca. $75 per credit. Inquire for details.
Cost: ca. $150 per week, exclusive of credits, covers lodging and meals at Kibbutz Kfar HaHoresh guest house (3–4 persons per room). Tuition (if credit is desired), travel to Israel, and insurance (mandatory) not included.

Sponsor: Hebrew University of Jerusalem
Director and
Contact: Dr. Nigel Goring-Morris
Department of Prehistory
Institute of Archaeology
Hebrew University
Jerusalem 91905, Israel
(972) 2 5882424
FAX: (972) 2 5825548
E-mail: goring@hum.huji.ac.il

Kfar HaHoresh is an Early Neolithic mortuary and cult center with a series of lime-plastered burial vaults containing hitherto unique burial practices, including associations of human and animal remains. Part of the site is associated with maintenance and industrial activities such as lime-plaster production. Project staff includes archaeologists, physical anthropologists, an archaeozoologist and a petrographer, and they will provide on-site lectures.

ISRAEL
Site/Location: Khirbet Cana (Cana of the Galilee)
Period: Neolithic, Iron Age, Hellenistic, Roman, Byzantine, Arab, Crusader, Ottoman

Dates of excavation and field school: July 21–August 25 (provisional). There is an optional study tour prior to the excavation. Participants may choose to stay from three–six weeks.
Application deadline: January 30, 1998; late applications accepted at anytime up to April 6, as space is available.

Field School:
Academic credit: 2 units from the University of Puget Sound
Cost: Tuition (to be determined), $50 application fee, and $2450 fee for lodging, meals, local commute, two guided tours of Galilee, and dig expenses. Travel to Israel (ca. $1050 round-trip airfare from New York, ca. $1300 from Seattle), personal expenses (ca. $200–$300), and insurance not included. The fee quoted above is for the full session; other options are available. Contact the Director for details.

Volunteers: Minimum stay of 3 weeks.
Minimum age: 18, unless accompanied by a parent or relative with the special permission of the project director.
Experience required: None, but must be in good health and to be able to work in a hot and strenuous environment. Drafting, surveying, computer (database, autocad, 3-d modeling), drawing skills welcome.
Cost: $50 application fee and $2450 fee for lodging, meals, local commute, two guided tours of Galilee, and dig expenses. Travel to Israel (ca. $1050 round-trip airfare from New York, ca. $1300 from Seattle), personal expenses (ca. $200–$300), and insurance not included. The fee quoted above is for the full session; other options are available. Contact the Director for details.

Study Tour:
Location: Jerusalem and environs (Dead Sea, Masada, Jericho), Jordan Valley, Galilee, Caesarea, and Tel Aviv
Dates: July 13–20
Cost: $1450 covers lodging, meals, and local commute. Travel to Israel (ca. $1050 round-trip airfare from New York, ca. $1300 from Seattle) and insurance not included. The cost for the study tour plus the full season of excavation is $3550. The cost for the study tour plus three weeks of excavation is $3280. Contact the Director for details.

Bibliography: Bagatti, B., *Antichi Villaggi Christianai di Galilea*, Jerusalem, 1971. Strange, James F., "Cana of the Galilee" in *Anchor Bible Dictionary*, Vol. 1, p. 827. Wilkinson, J., *Jerusalem Pilgrims Before the Crusades*, Warminster, 1977.

Director, Sponsor, and
Contact: Dr. Douglas R. Edwards
Cana of the Galilee Archaeology Project
University of Puget Sound, 1500 North Warner
Tacoma, WA 98416
(253) 756-3748
FAX: 253-756-3500
E-mail: dedwards@ups.edu
WWW: http://www.ups.edu/religion/cana/canahome.htm

Never excavated, Khirbet Cana is the most likely of three sites identified as the Cana of the Galilee, mentioned in the Gospel of John as the site of the marriage feast where Jesus turned water to wine. Excavation and survey at Cana have located many building remains, rock-cut tombs, numerous caves, cisterns, large building stones, possibly from a city wall, a very large building composed of many rooms, a dovecote, possibly dating to the Hellenistic period, and pottery, glass, and other artifacts.

The Cana of the Galilee Project trains volunteers and students in the fundamentals of archaeology, and the staff includes experts on geology, zoology, botany, archaeology, and anthropology to reconstruct the environment, culture, society, and landscape of ancient Cana of the Galilee.

ISRAEL
Site/Location: Khirbet el-Maqatir, 10 miles north of Jerusalem
Period: Bronze Age, Late Hellenistic, Early Roman

Volunteers/Study Tour:
Dates needed: Session I: June 10–28; Session II: September 9–27
Application deadline: Session I: payment due by April 1, Session I: payment due by July 1
Minimum age: Inquire.
Experience required: None
Cost: $2600 covers round-trip airfare from New York City, touring, lodging, and meals. The portion of the expense related to the excavation is tax deductible.

Director: Dr. Bryant Wood
Sponsor and
Contact: Associates for Biblical Research
31 East Frederick Street, Suite 468
Walkersville, MD 21793-8234
Tel/FAX: (301) 898-9358

The Associates for Biblical Research are excavating a 15th century BC Canaanite fortress. The site may be the Biblical city of Ai, referred to in Joshua 7 and 8. Two previous seasons have revealed a city wall system and tower or gate complex. Later occupation from the 2nd–1st century BC include defensive walls and industrial installations. The 1998 excavation will continue to focus on these features; the goal is to uncover the plan of the fortress. The program includes two weeks of excavation. When not digging, there are tours to historical and archaeological sites throughout the country. Nightly lectures cover topics related to archaeological technique, pottery typology, the Conquest, and the early Judges period. Accommodations are in the Jerusalem area and participants commute to the site by bus.

ISRAEL
Site/Location: Megiddo, Jezreel Valley
Period: Neolithic–Persian (mainly Bronze and Iron Age)

Field School:
Dates: Session 1: June 15–July 3, Session 2: July 5–July 24
Application deadline: April
Academic credit: 2, 6, or 8 credits from Tel Aviv University
Cost: $100 per credit tuition, plus $900 for three weeks, $1700 for six weeks, or $1900 for seven weeks for lodging, meals, and local commute. Travel to Israel and insurance not included.

Volunteers:
Dates: Four options: three-week sessions: June 15–July 3 or July 5–July 24; six-week session: June 15–July 24, or seven-week session: June 15–July 31

Application deadline: April
Minimum age: 18
Experience required: None.
Cost: $900 for three weeks, $1700 for six weeks, or $1900 for seven weeks covers lodging, meals, training, and local commute. There are discounts for consortium members and previous participants. Those who attend for seven weeks may apply for a scholarship/stipend. Travel to Israel and insurance not included.

Bibliography: Finkelstein, I., and D. Ussishkin, "Back to Megiddo," *Biblical Archaeology Review*, Vol. 20, No. 1, 1994. Kempinski, A., *Megiddo. A City State and Royal Centre in North Israel*, Munchen, 1989. Davies, G.I., *Megiddo*, Cambridge, 1986.

Directors: Prof. Israel Finkelstein, Prof. David Ussishkin, Prof. Baruch Halpern
Sponsor: Tel Aviv University; Pennsylvania State University
Contact: Lynne Koppeser
　　　Pennsylvania State University
　　　Jewish Studies Program, Megiddo Expedition
　　　103 Weaver Bldg.
　　　University Park, PA 16802
　　　(814) 863-8939
　　　FAX: 814-865-6204
　　　E-mail: megiddo@psuvm.psu.edu
　　　WWW: http://squash.la.psu.edu/jst/megiddo/welcome.html
　　　or
　　　Norma Franklin, Expedition Coordinator
　　　Tel Aviv University
　　　E-mail: franklin@zoot.tau.ac.il
　　　WWW: http://www.tau.ac.il/~archpubs/megiddo.html

Excavation at Megiddo has revealed thirty successive cities, from the very beginning of civilization to the end of the Biblical Period. Surrounded by mighty fortifications, fitted out with sophisticated water installations, and adorned by impressive palaces and temples, Megiddo was the queen of the cities of Canaan-Israel. Strategically located, it controlled one of the most important military and trade routes of antiquity—the international road linking Egypt, in the south, with Syria, Anatolia, and Mesopotamia to the north and east. Megiddo features in an abundance of Biblical sources and in texts of the great powers of Biblical times—Egypt, Hatti, and Assyria. Although Megiddo has been excavated three times in the past, the stratigraphy and thus the history of the site has remained elusive; almost every layer and major architectural feature has become the focus of fierce scholarly dispute. This expedition intends to clarify the stratigraphy and chronology of the site, from the Early– Late Bronze Age. Volunteers and students work as part of a multinational team, and the educational program includes an introduction to Biblical archaeology and fieldwork methodology, and guided tours of nearby archaeological sites.

ISRAEL
Site/Location: Sepphoris (Tsippori)
Period: Hellenistic–Arab II

Dates of excavation and field school: June 9–July 14
Application deadline: For staff positions: March 1. For field school and volunteers: April 15.

Position(s): Area Supervisors
Experience required: 1 season's experience at a dig and references.
Salary: None
Cost: Contact the Director for details.

Field School:
Academic credit: 3 or 6 undergraduate or graduate credits from University of South Florida.
Cost: Tuition (ca. $90 per credit) and ca. $3000 for round-trip fare from New York, lodging, meals, two guided trips around Galilee, and local commute. Insurance (mandatory) not included.

Volunteers:
Minimum age: 18
Experience required: None, but ability to relate to others in a high-pressure atmosphere, good health, high motivation, and no sensitivity to sun or insect bites.
Cost: ca. $3000 for round-trip fare from New York, lodging, meals, two guided trips around Galilee, and local commute. Insurance (mandatory) not included.

Bibliography: Strange, James F., "Sepphoris," *Mercer Dictionary of the Bible*, Mercer University Press, 1990, p. 808; "Sepphoris," in *The Anchor Bible Dictionary*, Vol. 5, David Noel Freedman (ed.), New York: Doubleday, 1992, pp. 1090–3; "Six Campaigns at Sepphoris: The University of South Florida Excavations, 1983–89," in *The Galilee in Late Antiquity*, Lee I. Levine, (ed.), New York and Jerusalem: The Jewish Theological Seminary of America, 1992, pp. 339–55. "Notes and News" in *The Israel Exploration Journal*.

Director, Sponsor, and
Contact: Prof. James F. Strange
　　　University of South Florida
　　　Department of Religious Studies CPR 107
　　　Tampa, FL 33620
　　　(813) 974-1859
　　　FAX: 813-974-1853
　　　E-mail: strange@chuma.cas.usf.edu
　　　WWW: http://www.colby.edu/rel/Announce98.html

Sepphoris was one of the most important urban centers in Roman Palestine. It was an administrative capital during the Herodian era, and a mixed population of Romans, Jews, Christians, and Judeo-Christians lived there. The *Mishnah*, the chief Jewish work of the early post-biblical period, was codified at Sepphoris. In Christian tradition, the site is the birthplace of Mary, mother of Jesus; a crusader church dedicated to Mary's mother still stands at the site. The city continued to be a major regional capital until the invasion of the Arabs in AD 640.

The University of Florida began excavations at Sepphoris in the summer of 1983. Since that time, excavations have uncovered one of only four theaters in Roman Palestine, a Roman villa, mosaics, ritual baths, and a peristyle building. Excavation in 1998 will continue at a large basilica type building built in the Early Roman period and destroyed in the middle of the fourth century CE, which has beautiful mosaic floors and painted plaster. The educational program includes a pre-dig orientation, field instruction, evening lectures in history and archaeology of the region, and two weekend tours of the area. Excavation is from 4:30 am–12:30 pm daily, then chores from 4:30–6:00 pm daily except Saturday and Sunday. The excavation team is assembled from institutions throughout the United States.

ISRAEL
Site/Location: Sha'ar Hagolan, Jordan Valley, near the sea of Galilee
Period: Neolithic, 6th millennium BC

Dates of excavation and field school: July 5–August 14
Application deadline: March for staff positions, April 15 for volunteers.

Position(s): Square Supervisor, Lithics Specialist
Experience required: Excavation experience at prehistoric sites
Salary: None
Cost: Program provides lodging, meals, and local commute. Travel to Israel and insurance not included. Travel to Israel for lithics specialist may be provided. Inquire for details.

Volunteers:
Minimum age: 18
Experience required: None but physical stamina. Previous excavation experience preferred but not necessary. Computer database (Excel) and survey experience helpful.
Cost: $160 per week covers lodging, meals, local commute to site, instruction, local tours, and museum lectures. There may also be a one-time non-refundable $50 registration fee for volunteers, to ensure arrival. Travel to Israel and insurance not included.

Bibliography: "Sha'ar Hagolan" in *New Encyclopedia of Archaeological Excavations in the Holy Land.* Garfinkel, Y., "The Yamukian Culture in Israel," *Paleorient* 19:1, 1993, pp. 115–134. 3. Gopher, A., and E. Orrelle, "An Alternative Interpretation for the Material Imagery of the Yamukian, a Neolithic Culture of the Sixth Millennium BC in the Southern Levant," Cambridge Archaeological Journal 6:2, 1996, pp. 255–79.

Directors:	Dr. Yosef Garfinkel, Dr. Michele Miller
Sponsor:	The Hebrew University of Jerusalem
Contact:	Dr. Michele Miller
	29 Claremont Ave.
	Apt. 6N
	New York, NY 10027
	E-mail: Micmil@aol.com

This marks the fifth season of the new excavations at the important Yamukian (Neolithic) site of Sha'ar Hagolan. When the site was first excavated in 1949–52 it was noted for its large assemblage of artifacts, including both clay and pebble figurines, often attributed to a fertility cult, as well as distinctive herringbone-patterned pottery, denticulated sickle blades, arrowheads, limestone bowls, and other cultural material. The new excavations have revealed substantial architectural remains, including a monumental building complex with a large courtyard, a circular building, and surrounding rooms, several of which are paved with flat river pebbles. Important finds include Mediterranean seashells and obsidian artifacts (both signs of long-distance trade), a monumental "goddess" figurine, and several incised cobbles which may have had a ritual function.

In the coming season, the project plans to complete excavation of a similar, but better preserved, building complex. The work week is Monday through Friday. Excavation begins early in the morning and ends by 1:00 pm due to the extreme heat. After lunch, there is free time. In the evening, before dinner, time is devoted to washing finds, data-entry, and sorting and registering the excavated material. Several evenings will be set aside for lectures given in the Kibbutz Museum, which houses the materials from the Sha'ar Hagolan excavations, and there are weekly tours of nearby sites, such as the ancient churches and synagogues along the Sea of Galilee.

ISRAEL

Site/Location: Tel Beth-Shemesh, 16 miles west of Jerusalem
Period: Bronze Age–Iron Age (17th–6th centuries BCE)

Field School: Open to Indiana University students (any campus).
Dates: June 21–July 11 (tentative), with the option to stay an additional three weeks (for no credit).

Application deadline: January 28
Academic credit: 3 credits from Indiana University, Bloomington.
Prerequisites: 3.0 cumulative GPA, and must be able to engage in strenuous physical activity in the heat.
Cost: ca. $1420 (resident), $2120 (non-resident) for tuition, lodging, meals, local commute, afternoon activities, and field trips. Travel to Israel (ca. $1200) and personal expenses not included.

Volunteers: Program for non-IU students and IU students wishing to participate without credit.
Dates: June 21–August 1 (tentative). Three two-week sessions. Volunteers may attend any or all sessions.
Application deadline: March 15
Minimum age: 18
Experience required: None, but must be able to engage in strenuous physical activity in the heat.
Cost: $590 for two-weeks, $1180 for four weeks, or $1770 for six weeks covers lodging, meals, local commute, field training, afternoon workshops, and excavation-related activities. Travel to Israel, personal expenses, and insurance (mandatory) not included. Lunch and evening meal not included.

Directors and
Sponsors: Steven P. Weitzman, Department of Religious Studies, Indiana University, Bloomington; Zvi Lederman, Ben Gurion University; Shlomo Bunimovitz, Bar-Ilan University
Field School

Contact:	Steven P. Weitzman
	Indiana University, Department of Religious Studies
	Sycamore Hall 230
	Bloomington, IN 47405-2601
	(812) 337-3803
	FAX: (812) 855-4687
	E-mail: sweitzma@indiana.edu
	WWW: http://www.indiana.edu/~relstud/shemesh/ shemesh.html
Volunteer	
Contact:	Marc Fratter
	Indiana University
	(812) 339-5491
	E-mail: mfratter@in
	WWW: http://www.indiana.edu/~relstud/shemesh/ non-info.html

Once a major Canaanite city-state and later an Israelite royal administrative center, the site of Biblical Beth-Shemesh and its immediate region was an area of conflict and the meeting point of different cultures, representing different social organizations, ideological concepts, and religions. Beth-Shemesh was an important part of King Solomon's administrative organization and remained an important stronghold until its final destruction during the violent military campaign of the Assyrian emperor Sennacherib. Excavations at the site have revealed fortification systems, industrial installations, one of the earliest known olive-oil production centers, private and public houses, pottery and metal artifacts, jewelry, and seals and tablets with Ugaritic and Paleo-Hebrew scripts.

The excavations are conducted as an integrative multi-disciplinary project to reveal features of the past as well as cultural changes through time. The field school provides instruction in archaeological field methods and techniques, surveying, recording, principles of stratigraphic analysis, and drafting and computerizing archaeological data. The program includes afternoon workshops and a series of lectures. Volunteers participate in the educational program and field trips. Optional weekend tours are also planned.

ISRAEL
Site/Location: Tel Dor, Mediterranean coast
Period: Bronze Age, Phoenician, Persian, Hellenistic, Roman

Dates of excavation, field school, study tour: June 25–August 8
Application deadline: June 1

Field School:
Academic credit: 2–4 credits from the University of California, Berkeley.
Cost: $500 tuition for 2 credits or $700 for 4 credits and $1495 fee (3 weeks) or $2995 fee (full session) for lodging, meals, local commute, insurance, guided tour, and field trips. Other fee payment options are available (depending on length of stay, e.g., 4 weeks, 5 weeks, etc.), and there are some discounts for full-time students. Contact the Director for details. Travel to Israel not included.

Volunteers:
Minimum age: 18
Experience required: None, but should be enthusiastic, physically fit, and willing to work hard and learn.
Cost: $1495 fee (3 weeks) or $2995 (full session) for lodging, meals, local commute, insurance, guided tour, and field trips. Other payment options are available (depending on length of stay, e.g., 2 weeks, 4 weeks, etc.), and there are some discounts for full-time students. Contact the Director for details. Travel to Israel not included.

Bibliography: Stern, Ephraim, *Dor, Rulers of the Seas*, Jerusalem, 1994; "The Many Masters of Dor: Part I," *Biblical Archaeology Review*, Vol. 19, No. 1, 1993, pp. 22–33; "Tel Dor: A Phoenician-Israelite Trading Center" in *Recent Excavations in Israel: A View to the West—Reports on Kabri, Nami, Miqne-Ekron, Dor and Ashkelon*, Seymour Gitin (ed.), Archaeological Institute of America, Colloquia and Conference Papers No. 1, Dubuque, IA: Kendall/Hunt Publishing Co., 1995, pp. 81–93; "Dor," *The New Encyclopedia of Archaeological Excavations in the Holy Land*, E. Stern (ed.), Jerusalem: Carta, 1993, pp. 357–368. Stewart, Andrew, "A Death at Dor," *Biblical Archaeology Review*, 19(2), 1993.

Sponsors: University of California, Berkeley; University of California, Santa Barbara
Director and
Contact: Prof. Rainer Mack
                    UC Tel Dor Archaeological Expedition
                    History of Art and Architecture, 1234 Arts Building
                    University of California, Santa Barbara
                    Santa Barbara, CA 93106
                    (805) 893-7593
                    FAX: (805) 893-7117
                    E-mail: mack@humanitas.ucsb.edu
                    WWW: http://www.qal.berkeley.edu/~teldor/

The UC Tel Dor Archaeological Expedition is part of an international effort, led by Professor Ephraim Stern of the Hebrew University of Jerusalem, to uncover one of the richest sites in coastal Israel. Tel Dor, a major harbor city and trading emporium, was occupied by a variety of cultures, including Canaanites, Egyptians, Sea Peoples, Phoenicians, Israelites, Assyrians, Babylonians, Persians, Greeks, and Romans. This summer, the project will continue the excavation of Greco-Roman areas previously opened, and probably open up a new Persian and earlier area elsewhere on the mound.

Participants will take part in all aspects of fieldwork, so that they may gain an understanding of everything that is involved in the archaeological research process. Morning work may involve any or all of the following: clearing of brush and weeds to prepare an area for excavation; large-scale earth moving with picks, large hoes, and buckets; finer work with small picks, trowels, and brushes to delineate features and artifacts (chiefly pottery); washing pottery; taking levels; and various record-keeping activities. Afternoon work will include sorting pottery, classifying and recording artifacts, and the preparation of daily reports. In addition, there will be a pre-excavation tour of Jerusalem and its environs and field trips to archaeological sites in the Carmel Coast, Jordan Valley, and Galilee.

ISRAEL
Site/Location: Tel Harassim (Nahal Barkai)
Period: Chalcolithic, Bronze Age, Iron Age, Byzantine

Field School/Volunteers:
Dates needed: July 12–August 14
Application deadline: July 1
Minimum age: 18
Experience required: None, but should be in good health.
Academic credit: Credit available from Bar Ilan University. Contact the Director for details.
Cost: $25 registration fee, $25/day for lodging, meals, and local commute. Travel to Israel; and insurance (mandatory) not included. Tuition, if credit is desired, is additional.

Bibliography: *Excavations and Surveys in Israel*, No. 10, 1991, pp. 145–146; *Excavations and Surveys in Israel*, No. 13, 1993, pp. 97–98; *Excavations and Surveys in Israel*, No. 14, 1994, pp. 108–109.

Sponsor: Bar Ilan University, Israel
Director and
Contact: Shmuel Givon
                    113 Bialik Street
                    Ramat Gan 52523, Israel
                    (972) 3 6131840
                    FAX: (972) 3 6132755

During the ninth season at Tel Harassim, excavation will be primarily concerned with exposing the Late Bronze and Iron Age strata. Excavation so far has revealed an open courtyard with an ochre-colored plastered floor, together with quantities of animal bones and cultic vessels; several walls of a public building, in association with additional cultic vessels and scarabs; and remains of structures, installations, courtyards, and lanes that were dated to the Late Bronze period. Finds include pottery, flints, figurines, scarabs, and jewelry pieces. In 1998, there are plans to excavate a public building from Iron Age II and continue to excavate Late Bronze Age building strata.

ISRAEL
Site/Location: Tel Hazor, Upper Galilee
Period: Bronze Age, Iron Age

Volunteers:
Dates of excavation: Session I: June 23–July 14; Session II: July 14–August 4. Minimum stay of 3 weeks.
Application deadline: March
Minimum age: 18
Academic credit: May be arranged through students own institution.
Cost: $25 registration fee and $230 per week for lodging at Gesher House-Safed and meals. Travel to Israel and medical and accident insurance not included.

Bibliography: Aharoni, Yohanan, "Hazor and the Battle of Deborah in Judges 4—Wrong?" *Biblical Archaeology Review*, 1(4), 1975, pp.

3–4, 26. Bienkowski, Piotr, "The Role of Hazor in the Late Bronze Age," PEQ 119, 1987, pp. 50–61. Dever, W.G., "The Water System at Hazor and Gezer," *Biblical Archaeologist* 32, 1977, pp. 71–78. Malamat, A., "Silver, Gold and Precious Stones from Hazor," *Biblical Archaeologist* 46, 1983, pp. 169–174. Yadin, Yigael, *Hazor—The Rediscovery of a Great Citadel of the Bible*, New York: Random House, 1975. Yadin, Yigael, "Hazor and the Battle of Joshua—Is Joshua 11 Wrong?" *Biblical Archaeology Review*, 2(1), 1976, 3 ff. Yadin, Yigael, "Is the Biblical Account of the Israelite Conquest of Canaan Historically Reliable?" *Biblical Archaeology Review*, 8(2), 1982, pp. 25–36.

Sponsors: Israel Exploration Society, Jerusalem; The Selz Foundation, New York; Yad Ha-Nadiv, Rothschild Foundation
Director and
Contact: Professor A. Ben-Tor
Institute of Archaeology
Hebrew University
Jerusalem 91905, Israel
(972) 2 882 403 or 882 404
FAX: (972) 2 825 548 (attn: Ben-Tor)
E-mail: bentor@hum.huji.ac.il

Tel Hazor is the largest Bronze Age site in Israel. The Book of Kings says it was built, together with Megiddo and Gezer, by King Solomon. Its king was also called the "King of Canaan," and the site is referred to by Joshua as the "head of all those kingdoms." Often mentioned in external records, it is the only site in Israel to be mentioned in the Mari archive. It was finally destroyed by the Assyrian Tiglath Pilesser in 732 BC. Work on the excavation begins at 5:00 am and continues for 8 hours. Other work is done from 5:00–7:00 pm. Staff members will present lectures on archaeological topics related to the excavation. Please write for further details. The excavations are a joint project of The Berman Center for Biblical Archaeology at the Hebrew University and Complutense University, Madrid.

ISRAEL
Site/Location: Tel Rehov, near Beth Shean, NE Israel
Period: Iron Age, especially 10th century and 8th century BCE

Dates of excavation and field school: June 28–August 7
Application deadline: March 30

Field School:
Academic credit: 3 or 6 credits from Hebrew University of Jerusalem, or 3 semester hours from William Carey College.
Cost: $300 for three credits, $600 for six credits tuition, plus $250 per week for lodging and meals at nearby kibbutz. Travel to project and insurance not included.

Volunteers: Minimum stay of three weeks.
Minimum age: 18. In 1997, volunteers from 14 different countries participated and their age range was from 18–74. Retired persons are usually very successful as diggers, and are encouraged to apply.
Experience required: None, but must be in excellent health, and willing to work hard in sometimes difficult conditions, including hot weather.
Cost: $250 per week covers lodging and meals at nearby kibbutz, educational programs, and local commute. There is a slight reduction for those who will work more than three weeks. Travel to project and insurance not included.

Bibliography: Mazar, Amihai, *Archaeology of the Land of the Bible*, Doubleday, 1992.

Sponsor: Hebrew University of Jerusalem
Director: Prof. Amihai Mazar, Director, Institute of Archaeology, Hebrew University of Jerusalem
Contact: **North America:**
Dr. Daniel C. Browning
Tel Rehov Excavations
William Carey College
498 Tuscan Avenue
Hattiesburg, MS 39401
(601) 582-6454
FAX: (601) 582-6154
E-mail: browning@wmcarey.edu

Europe and Middle East:
Prof. Amihai Mazar
Tel Rehov Excavations
Hebrew University
Institute of Archaeology
Jerusalem 91905, Israel
FAX: (972) 2 825548
E-mail: rehov@hum.huji.ac.il
WWW: http://www.rehov.org/rehov

The Tel Rehov project, a major new excavation, is part of the continuing Beth Shean Valley Archaeological Project. The Beth Shean Valley was a fertile, densely inhabited region in antiquity, and is the site of numerous tells. Since 1989, the project has focused on Tel Beth Shean, a fabulously productive mound which for several centuries served as the stronghold of the Egyptian New Kingdom in north Israel. In 1997 the excavation of Tel Rehov began.

The first season of excavations revealed successive occupation layers from the Iron Age I; large and well-preserved buildings from two occupation layers dating to the 10th century BCE (the time of the united monarchy of David and Solomon); and remains of the Iron Age II city, which was violently destroyed by the Assyrians in 732 BCE. Finds include abundant restorable pottery vessels from the 10th century BCE, a unique pottery cult stand from the same century, clay figurines, and other objects from the Iron Age II city. A geophysical survey revealed large buildings at certain points on the mound. The goal of the 1998 season is to continue the excavation of the areas which were opened in the 1997 season, with special emphasis on the 10th century BCE layers.

The educational program includes three lectures per week, a weekly guided tour of the excavation areas, two afternoon field trips to neighboring sites, and optional all-day archaeological tours on Sundays, guided by experienced archaeologists (these latter cost ca. $35 per day). The fieldwork includes hand digging with picks and shovels, moving dirt in buckets and wheelbarrows, and sifting, washing, and sorting pottery finds. Fieldwork is done under sheds.

ISRAEL
Site/Location: Tel Rehov
Period: Iron Age

Field School:
Dates: July 13-August 1
Application deadline: May 15
Prerequisites: All applicants must have successfully completed at least one year of study at an accredited institution of higher education. A medical certificate must be submitted with the application, stating that the student is in good health and capable of participating in the dig. The dig involves strenuous work in very hot weather.
Academic credit: 4 undergraduate or graduate credits from The Hebrew University of Jerusalem

Cost: $600 tuition and $350 for 15 nights covers lodging during the dig, meals, and local commute. Students are required to arrange full health insurance coverage (ca. $35) through the Hebrew University Student Health Services. Travel to Israel not included.

Director: Anne Killebrew
Sponsor: The Hebrew University of Jerusalem, Rothberg School for Overseas Students
Contacts: The program has special contact addresses for persons applying from the following countries: United States, United Kingdom, Canada, France, Australia, and Israel (and all other countries). Those for the United States and Israel are listed below. For other addresses, contact the Hebrew University of Jerusalem or visit their Web site (listed below).

United States
Contact: Office of Academic Affairs
The Hebrew University of Jerusalem
11 East 69th Street
New York, NY 10021
(800) 404-8622 or (212) 472-2288
FAX: (212) 517-4548
E-mail: 74542.340@compuserve.com

Israel (and all other countries except those listed above)
Contact: Department of Summer Courses
The Hebrew University of Jerusalem
Rothberg School for Overseas Students
Mount Scopus, 91905 Jerusalem, Israel
(972) 2 5882602
FAX: (972) 2 5827078
E-mail: msroz@pluto.mscc.huji.ac.il
WWW: http://www2.huji.ac.il/www_sfos/top.html

The Rothberg School for Overseas Students of The Hebrew University of Jerusalem offers broad selection of courses for undergraduate and graduate students through its summer sessions and year-long programs. "Excavating Biblical Tel Rehov" is designed for beginners and advanced students in archaeology and Bible studies. The course examines approaches and methods used by archaeologists to reconstruct ancient Canaanite and early Israelite culture and history and consists of a series of lectures and field trips dealing with the archaeological and Biblical evidence, and an archaeological field school at Tel Rehov, the site of a major new excavation in the Beth Shean Valley (see description in previous entry).

The field school includes instruction in excavation, recording methods, processing artifacts, and analysis and interpretation of the archaeological remains. Explanatory lectures take place during the dig period and several evenings a week. The beginner's course is designed for students who have never excavated. They will be taught basic principles of field archaeology through the activity of excavating. Advanced students participate in an advanced field school intended for students of archaeology and Biblical studies who have previously worked on excavations and wish to acquire skills necessary for conducting professional archaeological work.

ISRAEL
Site/Location: Tel e-Safi (Gath of the Philistines/Blanche Garde Castle of the Crusaders) in central Israel
Period: Chalcolithic (5th millennium BCE)–Modern, with strong evidence of Iron Age I–II, Persian, Crusader, and Modern

Dates of excavation and field school: August 2–28
Application deadline: June 1

Field School:
Academic credit: 3 (two weeks) or 6 (4 weeks) credits from Bar Ilan University or Hebrew University.
Cost: $300 tuition for 3 credits or $600 for 6 plus $200 per 5-day week for lodging and meals and local commute. Lodging and meals on weekends are extra. Travel to Israel and health insurance not included.

Volunteers: Minimum stay of one week.
Minimum age: 18
Experience required: None
Cost: $200 per 5-day week for lodging and meals and local commute. Lodging and meals on weekends are extra. Travel to Israel and health insurance not included.

Bibliography: Articles on Tel e-Safi in the *New Encyclopedia for Archaeological Excavations in the Holy Land*, E. Stern (ed.), Jerusalem, 1993; in the *Anchor Bible Dictionary* (listed under Gath). Rainey, A., "The identification of Philistine Gath—a problem in source analysis for historical geography," *Eretz Israel* 12, 1975, pp. 63–76.

Directors: Aren Maeir, Adrian Baos
Sponsors: Bar Ilan University; Hebrew University
Contact: Aren Maeir
Department of Land of Israel Studies
Bar Ilan University
Ramat Gan 52900 Israel
FAX: (972) 2 5825548
E-mail: maeir@hum.huji.ac.il

Tel e-Safi is one of the largest sites in Israel and was settled almost continuously from the Chalcolithic period onwards. During the Iron Age, it was the site of the important Philistine city of Gath, home of Goliath and Achish (known from the Bible). The site was pivotal in the ongoing battles between the Philistines and the Judean kingdom, switching hands several times, and it was apparently captured numerous times by the Assyrians and Arameans as well. Remains from the Iron age include of an immense siege system surrounding the site. In the Persian period (ca. 550–330 BCE) the site was intensively settled, and numerous cultic objects have been found. In the Crusader period a castle was built on the site (Blanche Garde) and historical sources relate it to Richard the Lion-Heart. In the modern period, the site was an Arab village, abandoned in 1948. The excavation this year will concentrate on the Iron Age and Crusader remains, both on and around the tel. The educational program will include both archaeological field experience and lectures on various topics relating to the history and archaeology of the ancient land of Israel.

ISRAEL
Site/Location: Tel Tanninim, on the Mediterranean coast
Period: Persian–Crusader

Volunteers:
Dates needed: May 25–July 3. Minimum stay of two weeks. Orientations will be held on Sunday May 24 and June 14, in the afternoon. Participants arriving on other dates will be oriented individually.
Application deadline: April 1
Minimum age: 18
Experience required: None. Experienced excavators are, of course, welcome, but previous fieldwork is not required. Volunteers are expected participate in all the phases of the work, including excavation, processing and recording.
Cost: Volunteer is responsible for all expenses except local commute to site. Inquire for details.

Bibliography: Volunteers are expected to complete some reading on the history of this region, and ancient Israel in general, prior to their arrival in Israel. A good beginning is: K.G. Holum, et al., *King Herod's Dream: Caesarea on the Sea*, New York and London: W.W. Norton, 1988.

Director, Sponsor, and
Contact: Prof. Robert R. Stieglitz
Classical and Modern Languages and Literature
Rutgers University
Newark, NJ 07102-1814
(973)-353-5233/5498
FAX: (718) 268-1746
E-mail: stieglit@andromeda.rutgers.edu

This is the third season of excavations by the (TAP) at Tel Tanninim, "Crocodiles Mound," located at the outflow of Nahal Tanninim "Crocodiles River." The Project involves the investigation a little-known Phoenician coastal town, presumably founded by the Phoenicians after this part of Palestine was ceded to the king of Sidon at the end of the 6th century BCE. Its native name is unknown, but in the Hellenistic and Roman eras its Greek name was *Krokodeilon Polis* "Crocodiles City" (Strabo 16.2.27), and *Crocodilon* in Latin (Pliny 5.17.75). In the Byzantine era, as a wealthy suburb of Caesarea, the site was called *Migdal Malha* in Aramaic and *Turris Salinarum* in Latin. Excavations in 1996–97 indicate that the site was occupied in the Persian, Hellenistic, Roman, Byzantine and Crusader periods. In the late Byzantine and later periods, the tel was supplied with running water by an aqueduct, now termed Channel E, tapping into the nearby high-level aqueduct of Caesarea Maritima. For those concerned by the repeated references to crocodiles, there were Nilotic crocodiles in the river and in the now drained adjacent Kabbara marsh, but they are no longer there, as the last of the reptiles was killed in 1905.

ISRAEL
Site/Location: Yavneh-Yam, central coastal plain of Israel, 20 km south of Tel Aviv
Period: Middle Bronze Age–Mamluke

Earthwatch Volunteers:
Dates: Team I: July 19–31, Team II: August 2–14, Team III: August 16–28
Application deadline: 90 days prior to departure. (Applications will be accepted after that time if space is available.)
Minimum age: 16
Experience required: None
Cost: $1245 per two-week session covers all expenses except travel to staging area (Ayanot Agricultural School) and insurance.

Volunteer opportunities through Tel Aviv University:
Dates needed: July 19–August 29. Minimum stay of two weeks.
Application deadline: May
Minimum age: 18
Experience required: None, training provided.
Cost: $600 for two weeks covers lodging, meals, and local commute. Travel to Israel and insurance not included.

Bibliography: Aharoni, Y., *Land of the Bible: A Historical Geography*, 1979. Albright, W.F., *From Stone Age to Christianity*, 1940. Avi-Yonah, M., *The Jews of Palestine—A Political History: From the Bar Kokhba War to the Arab Conquest*, 1976. Fischer, M., and B. Dashti, *Yavneh-Yam and its Neighbourhood*, 1991, (in Hebrew). Kaplan, Y., "Yavneh-Yam," *The Encyclopedia of Archaeological Excavation in the Holy Land*.

Director: Dr. Moshe Fischer, Tel Aviv University
Sponsors: Tel Aviv University; Earthwatch
Contact: Tel Aviv University
Department of Classical Studies
Ramat Aviv, 69978, Israel
(972) 3 640 9938
FAX: (972) 3 640 9457
E-mail: fischer@ccsg.tau.ac.il
or
Earthwatch
See page 7 for contact information.

Yavneh-Yam served as a harbor from the Middle Bronze Age up to the Middle Ages. One of the main goals of the excavation will be the examination of relations between Yavneh-Yam and the Mediterranean world during the Classical Greek period, the Hellenistic period, and the Roman-Byzantine period. Finds include fragments of Greek painted pottery, terracotta statuettes representing persons known from Greek history and mythology, and remains of monumental buildings. The project hopes to shed light on how the cultural developments of classical antiquity affected indigenous people on the periphery of the classical world, and use archaeological evidence to reconstruct the diet, economy, leisure activities, and religious beliefs of the port's residents. Volunteers will be trained in standard archaeological methods, including systematic digging, use of a grid plan, and documentation of finds according to stratigraphy.

JORDAN
Site/Location: Abila of the Decapolis, N Jordan, near Irbid
Period: Chalcolithic/Early Bronze Age–Late Islamic (4000 BC–AD 1500)

Dates of excavation and field school: June 13–August 1
Application deadline: March 1

Field School:
Academic credit: 4 credits from Covenant Theological Seminary or student's own institution.
Cost: Tuition ($192 per credit in 1997) plus $1200 fee for lodging and meals. Round-trip airfare to Jordan (ca. $1100), insurance, local commute, and personal and weekend expenses not included.

Volunteers:
Minimum age: 18
Experience required: None, but previous archaeological experience; drawing, photography, architectural, or computer skills helpful.
Cost: $1200 fee for seven weeks covers lodging and meals. Round-trip airfare to Jordan (ca. $1100), insurance, local commute, and personal and weekend expenses not included.

Bibliography: "Archaeology in Jordan Newsletter," *American Journal of Archaeology*, April 1991, 1992, 1993; *Encyclopedia of Archaeological Excavations in the Holy Land*, Oxford University Press, 1991; *The New Encyclopedia of Archaeological Excavations in the Holy Land*, New York: Simon and Schuster, 1993.

Sponsors: Covenant Theological Seminary; The Abila Archaeological Project, Inc.
Director and
Contact: Dr. W. Harold Mare
Covenant Theological Seminary
12330 Conway Road
St. Louis, MO 63141
(314) 434-4044

The site consists of two tells, Tell Abila (north) and Umm el 'Amad (south); with a depression in between, containing ruins of a theater cavea, with evidence of a Roman-period theater; an extended length of street in front; a later Islamic public building; and other civic center buildings, including a bath/fountain complex. Partial restoration (1987–1988) of a 7th-century AD Christian basilica is seen on the south tell, the remains of a 6th-century AD basilica on the north tell, and a newly-found basilica in the civic complex in between the two tells. A large cemetery, dating to Bronze Age, Iron Age, Hellenistic, Roman, Byzantine extends along the wadi; and there is also an extensive underground water tunnel system. Work in 1998 will continue and expand on the work of previous seasons.

The field school provides intensive hands-on training in the essential principles of archaeological excavation and practice. Participants also work in the camp laboratory, registering finds, identifying and labeling pottery, drawing, and performing other tasks. Scholarly lectures are provided twice a week on archaeological and multidisciplinary subjects, including the history of Jordan, ceramic typology, epigraphy, osteology, geology, etc.; and educational weekend field trips to important archaeological sites in Jordan are offered at a minimal, shared cost.

JORDAN
Site/Location: Aila, within Aqaba, Jordan's port on the Red Sea
Period: Roman/Byzantine (1st century BC–7th century AD)

Field School:
Dates: May 16–July 7
Application deadline: February 16
Academic credit: 6 credits from North Carolina State University
Cost for participant: $450 tuition and $1500 fee for lodging (in apartments in the modern city of Aqaba) and meals. Round-trip travel to Jordan (New York-Amman) is ca. $775.

Bibliography: Parker, S. Thomas, "Preliminary Report on the 1994 Season of the Roman Aqaba Projects," *Bulletin of the American Schools of Oriental Research* 305, 1997, pp. 19–44; "The Roman Aqaba Project: The Economy of Aila on the Red Sea," *Biblical Archaeologist* 59:3, 1996, p. 182; "The Roman Aqaba Project" in P. Bikai and V. Egan (eds.), "Archaeology in Jordan," *American Journal of Archaeology* 101, 1997, pp. 525–526. Smith II, Andrew M., Michelle Stevens, and Tina M. Niemi, "The Southeast Araba Archaeological Survey: A Preliminary Report of the 1994 Season," *Bulletin of the American Schools of Oriental Research* 305, 1997, 45–71.

Director, Sponsor, and
Contact: Dr. S. Thomas Parker
       North Carolina State University
       Department of History, Box 8108
       Raleigh, NC 27695-8108
       (919) 515-2484
       FAX: (919) 515-3886
       E-mail: Thomas_Parker@ncsu.edu

Aila is an ancient port city that served as a key transit point for seaborne commerce via the Red Sea from south Arabia, east Africa, and India, and for land travel on camel caravans traveling north into the Roman provinces of Arabia, Palestine and Syria. Aila was the southern terminus of a great Roman road that ran northward through Jordan to Syria and became an important Roman military base, where the famous 10th Fretensis Legion was stationed. Aila fell to Muslim forces in AD 630, when the Prophet Mohammed personally negotiated the city's terms of surrender. The ancient city is now largely covered by sand dunes and palm trees by the sea.

Excavations have uncovered various structures, including the city's fortification wall, domestic complexes, and a possible 4th-century Christian church and associated cemetery. Thousands of recovered artifacts reveal much about the city's history and population. The project is also conducting a surface archaeological survey of the region to learn about the city's hinterland.

After an orientation and training program, students work five days per week, under the supervision of experienced senior staff, in archaeological excavation and recording, keeping a detailed field notebook, and recording and processing artifacts. Weekends are free to travel elsewhere in Jordan, and a trip is planned to Petra, one of the most famous archaeological sites in the world and only three hours from Aqaba. All weekend trips are optional and the financial responsibility of the participant.

JORDAN
Site/Location: Khirbat al Mudayna, 24 miles south of Amman, 9 miles southeast of Madaba
Period: Iron Age II, Early Roman

Dates of excavation and field school: June 19–August 4
Application deadline: February 28

Field School:
Academic credit: 1 undergraduate full year, 1/2 graduate credit from Wilfrid Laurier University
Cost: Tuition (CDN$724 for Canadian residents, CDN$1400 for non-residents) and participation fee (US$1750 or CDN$1900 for Canadian residents) for lodging, meals, local commute, and tours. Travel to Jordan and insurance not included.

Volunteers:
Minimum age: 18
Experience required: Some course work and field experience in archaeology preferred.
Cost: Participation fee (US$1750 or CDN$1900 for Canadian residents) covers lodging, meals, local commute, and tour. Travel to Jordan and insurance not included.

Bibliography: MacDonald, Burton, *Ammon, Moab and Edom: Early States/Nations of Jordan in the Biblical Period.* Glueck, Nelson, "Explorations in Eastern Palestine II," *AASOR* Vol. XV 1934–1935, 1935 ASOR; "Explorations in Eastern Palestine III," *AASOR* Vol. XVIII–XIX 1937–1939, 1939 ASOR; "Explorations in Eastern Palestine IV," *AASOR* Vols. XXV–XXVIII 1945–1949, ASOR 1951.

Sponsor: Wilfrid Laurier University
Directors and
Contacts: Dr. P.M. Michèle Daviau
       Wilfrid Laurier University
       Waterloo, Ontario N2L 3C5 Canada
       (519) 884-1970, ext. 6680
       FAX: (519) 884-8853
       E-mail: mdaviau@mach1.wlu.ca

As part of the Wadi al Thamad Project, excavations at the Iron Age tell of Khirbat al Mudayna have exposed a casemate wall system and a six-chambered gate. Similar in style to gates found at Megiddo, Gezer, and Hazor, the walls of the gate at Mudayna are preserved, 2.5 meters high. The discovery of arrowheads and a piece of armor scale in the western gate rooms suggest a violent end to occupation. Iron Age finds include female and zoomorphic figurines, two large stone basins with inscribed designs, and Moabite inscriptions on pottery sherds and seal impressions.

At the foot of the tell, is a settlement dating to the Nabataean-early Roman period. Excavation began on the Nabataean building, possibly a temple, that was surrounded by a perimeter wall. The most interesting feature was a stairway beside the central podium which turned to the left at a 90° angle, and consisted of a total of ten stairs. A lamp found on the stairway allowed the occupation of the building to be dated to the Herodian era (1st century BC–1st century AD). Other finds include Thamudic graffiti on a door jamb, Nabataean painted wares and terra sigillata pottery. An arched reservoir, located to the south of the temple dates to the same period; finds include stones with Latin and Greek inscriptions.

JORDAN

Site/Location: Sa'ad, highlands of N Jordan
Period: Byzantine

Field School:
Dates: June 19–August 11
Application deadline: March 15
Academic credit: 6 undergraduate credits from University of Arkansas, Fayetteville; graduate credit is available at a higher tuition rate.
Cost: $2950 for tuition, round-trip airfare (Chicago/Amman), lodging, drinking water, and four field trips; $86 for entrance and exit fees; and $80 for two overnight hotel stays on field trips. Daily travel to the site is by bus. Meals and personal expenses not included. Each apartment is equipped with a kitchen and a washer. Previous participants recommend bringing ca. $1500 to cover personal expenses.

Bibliography: Rose, J.C., and M. El-Najjar, "Sa'ad," *ACOR Newsletter* 8(2), 1996, pp. 9–10. Rose, J.C., M. El-Najjar, and S. Sari, "Sa'ad," *American Journal of Archaeology* 101, 1997, pp. 528–529. Other materials will be sent upon acceptance to program.

Directors and Sponsors: Jerome C. Rose, University of Arkansas, Fayetteville; Mahmoud El-Najjar and Saleh Sari, Yarmouk University, Jordan
Contact: Fulbright Institute
Office of Study Abroad
722 West Maple
Fayetteville, AR 72701
(501) 575-7582
FAX: (501) 575-7402
E-mail: dslong@comp.uark.edu, jcross@comp.uark.edu
WWW: http://www.uark.edu/~dgould/rose.html

Sa'ad is a small, but prosperous, village occupied from Late Roman to Islamic times whose location on a road to Jerash made it an ideal location for exporting agricultural products such as wine. Previous seasons of excavation have revealed a Byzantine church with mosaic floor, an Umayyad mosque, industrial buildings, a six-room wine press, and more than 90 Byzantine tombs. The field school focuses upon the excavation of Byzantine period tombs where the techniques of mortuary site archaeology and preliminary osteological laboratory methods are taught. Whenever possible each student is given the opportunity to supervise the excavation of a tomb and has the responsibility for note taking, cataloging, mapping, drawing, and writing the final report. Laboratory sessions focus on cleaning, cataloging and preliminary analysis. There will be four field trips to such sites as Petra, Jerash, Kerak Castle, and desert sites.

JORDAN

Sites/Locations: Tall al-'Umayri, 7 miles S of Amman; Tall Jalul, 3 miles E of Madaba
Period: Paleolithic, Bronze Age, and Iron Age

Dates of excavation and field school: Full season: June 24–August 5; 1st half season: June 24–July 19; 2nd half season: July 15–August 5
Application deadline: March 15 for security forms (no exceptions), April 15 for application forms. Early application is advised.

Field School:
Academic credit: Up to 8 undergraduate or graduate quarter credits from consortium institutions (see below). Because of the size of the Madaba Plains Project, the educational offerings are wide ranging, and credit may be earned in archaeology, anthropology, history, science, and religion.
Cost: Tuition (varies by school, check with chosen consortium school), and dig fee ($1600 for full session and $1000 for half session) covers lodging, meals, field trip, and local commute. Travel to Jordan and insurance not included.

Volunteers:
Minimum age: College age.
Experience required: None, but good health and congenial attitude.
Cost for participant: Dig fee ($1650 for full session and $1000 for half session) covers lodging, meals, field trip, and local commute. Travel to Jordan and insurance not included.

Bibliography: Bibliography sent with application materials.

Directors: Tall al-'Umayri: Dr. Larry G. Herr, Canadian Union College; Tall Jalul: Dr. Randall W. Younker, Andrews University
Sponsors: Andrews University, Canadian Union College, La Sierra University, University of Eastern Africa Baraton, Walla Walla College
Contact: Douglas R. Clark
Madaba Plains Project
Walla Walla College
College Place, WA 99324-1198
(509) 527-2194
FAX: (509) 527-2253
E-mail: clardo@wwc.edu
WWW: http://www.wwc.edu/academics/departments/theology/mpp/

The overall research objective of the Madaba Plains Project is to illuminate the multi-millennial cycles of intensification and abatement in human settlement and land use in the greater Madaba Plans region. The research objective is addressed through three projects as described below.

Tall al-'Umayri: Six seasons of excavation and survey have taken place at Tall al-'Umayri and vicinity. During the biblical period, the Ammonites apparently controlled the city, making it an administrative center. Excavations have revealed Iron Age fortifications including walls over a meter thick, a steep rampart, and a dry moat. All these structures emerged from beneath two meters of burned destruction debris which suggest a rapid and devastating end for the inhabitants somewhere around 1100 BC.

Tall Jalul: Three seasons of excavation and survey have taken place at Tall Jalul. Tall Jalul is the largest and most centrally located site in the entire Madaba Plains area and promises to be a key to better understanding the socio-historical development of central Jordan. To date, excavation has revealed the remains of buildings, walls, roads, and small surface finds, including pottery, jewelry, and figurines.

Hinterland Project: The regional survey in the vicinity of the sites has located well over 100 sites ranging from roads and winepresses to lime kilns, farmsteads, watchtowers and forts, and cities. A picture of complex farming systems is emerging from this study. In addition, in 1996 a new paleolithic site was located and over 500 pieces of worked stone and faunal remains have been recovered.

JORDAN

Site/Location: Tell Abu al-Kharaz, in the northern Jordan Valley, south of Pella
Period: Bronze Age–Islamic

Volunteers:
Dates needed: April–May (6 weeks). Minimum stay of 3 weeks.
Application deadline: Inquire.
Minimum age: 18
Experience required: Inquire.
Cost: $1200 for 3 weeks covers lodging at the Pella Dig House, meals (6 days per week), transportation Amman–Pella, and weekend excursions to Jerash, Umm Quais, Madaba, Mt. Nebo, and Petra. Travel to Jordan not included.

Director and Sponsor: Peter M. Fischer, University of Göteborg, Sweden; Swedish Jordan Expedition
Contact: Peter M. Fischer
        Dorjeskarsgatan 37
        SE-421 60 Vastra Frolunda, Sweden
        FAX: (46) 31 493377
        E-mail: fischer@lls.se.

This will be the 10th season of excavation at Tell Abu al-Kharaz, a possible candidate for the Biblical Jabesh Gilead. Important finds include complete Early Bronze Age assemblages, a Late Bronze Age temple, Early and Late Bronze Age fortifications, Iron Age towers and houses, a silver alloy statuette of a Canaanite God with Egyptian attributes, a bone handle with 2 sphinxes, a stone cosmetic palette, a horse figurine with attached vessels, and imports from Egypt and Cyprus. Goals for 1998 are the excavation of Iron and Bronze Age domestic buildings, and continued excavation of fortifications.

JORDAN

Site/Location: Tell Safut, just NW of Amman
Period: Late Bronze Age–Iron Age/Persian

Volunteers:
Dates needed: July 4–26
Application deadline: March 1
Minimum age: 18
Experience required: None, but attention to detail, regularity in recording helpful. Training provided.
Cost: $990 camp fee covers lodging, and meals at camp. Travel to Jordan, insurance, and lodging and travel on free days not included.

Bibliography: Wimmer, Donald H., "Tell Safut," *Anchor Bible Dictionary*; "Tell Safut," *Near East Encyclopedia of Archaeology*.

Director, Sponsor, and
Contact: Donald H. Wimmer
        Tell Safut Project
        Seton Hall University
        South Orange, NJ 07079
        Tel. & FAX: (201) 761-9608
        E-mail: wimmerdh@shu.edu

Tell Safut, classified as a small site, was probably the administrative center overlooking this valley on behalf of Rabbath Ammon, the capital of the Ammonites. The goal of the coming season is to explore the wider precincts of a sacred area where an idol once wrapped totally in gold, and female figurines of the pillar type that are associated with fertility religions were found. The project's overall goal is to trace developments on the tell from the latest to the earliest times.

OMAN

Location: Coast of Oman
Site: Various
Period: Various

Volunteers:
Dates: Team I: March 23–April 5, Team II: April 9–22.
Application deadline: 90 days prior to departure. (Applications will be accepted after that time if space is available.)
Minimum age: 16
Experience required: None, but must be willing to work in extremely hot temperatures and camp in the desert.

Director: Thomas Vosmer, Western Australia Maritime Museum
Sponsor and
Contact: Earthwatch, Box 403
        See page 7 for contact information.

Four thousand years ago, the Bronze Age Magan Empire, in what now is Oman, controlled sea-trading routes that reached from the Mediterranean to China and the East Indies. Their vessel was the dhow, a ship that still plies the Arabian Sea today. Project research will focus on the design and construction of dhow wrecks along the Omani coast, and the relationship between shipbuilding techniques and seafaring traditions. Volunteers will document vessels using photography, measured drawings, written notes, and EDM; some volunteers on Team II will have the opportunity to SCUBA dive, if certified.

OMAN

Location/Site: Dhofar, S Oman
Period: Iron Age

Volunteers:
Dates needed: February 10–March 20
Application deadline: As soon as possible.
Minimum age: 19
Experience required: Yes, excavation and drawing skills preferred. The project does not take beginners.
Cost: Program provides lodging, meals, local commute, and on-site insurance. Travel to Oman not included.

Bibliography: Yule, P., and M. Kervran, "More than Samad in Oman: Pre-Islamic Pottery from Suhar and Khor Rori," *Arabian Archaeology and Epigraphy* 4, 1993, pp. 69–106. Yule, P., and B. Kazenwadel, "Toward a Chronology of the Late Iron Age in the Sultanate of Oman" in *Materialien zur Archäologie der Seleukiden-und Partherzeit im südlichen Babylonien und Golfgebiet*, Tuebingen, 1993, pp. 251–277. Yule, P., "Grabarchitektur der Eisenzeit im Sultanat Oman," BaM 25, 1994, pp. 519–577. Yule, P., "Die Archaeologie des Sultanats Oman" in *Oman*, G. Popp (ed.), Nuernberg 1996 & 1995, pp. 319–338. Yule, P., and G. Weisgerber, "Die 14, Deutsche Archaeologische Oman-Expedition 1995," MDOG 128, 1996, pp. 135–155.

Sponsor: German Mining Museum, Bochum; Department of Prehistory, University of Heidelberg
Director and
Contact: Dr. Paul Yule
        Am Büchel 77
        53173 Bad Godesberg, Germany
        Tel./FAX: (49) 228 364195
        E-mail: Paul.Yule@t-online.de

Archaeologically speaking, the Sultanate of Oman is one of the least known countries of the Arab world and has been accessible to archaeologists only since the early 1970s. It was a meeting place for traders and settlers from South Asia and East Africa, and much of the research in the Sultanate is devoted to the international trade of the 3rd and 2nd millennia BC. Until recently, the German Archaeological Oman-Expedition focused its research on the history of metals production in Oman. However, in 1996 the emphasis changed to structuring an Iron Age chronology for the Sultanate. Having collected data in central and north Oman in previous seasons, in 1998 the Expedition will work in Dhofar in southern Oman, a region for which very little archaeological data is available. Excavations will focus on graves, and a heavy emphasis will be placed on surveying. The excavation documentation is recorded daily with the help of computers.

SYRIA
Site/Location: Tell Tuneinir
Period: 2500 BC–AD 1401

Dates of excavation and field school: May 18–July 17
Application deadline: February 1

Field School:
Academic credit: 3–9 credits from St. Louis Community College
Cost: Tuition (depends on residency and credits desired) and $1000 camp fee for lodging and meals. Travel to Jordan and insurance not included.

Volunteers: Maximum of 15 serious volunteers needed.
Minimum age: 18
Experience required: At least one college-level class in archaeology or ancient Near Eastern history. Surveying, architectural drawing, photography, and bone analysis skills preferred. Individuals with prior field experience will be given priority.
Cost: $1000 camp fee for lodging and meals. Travel to Jordan and insurance not included.

Bibliography: Fuller, Michael, and Neathery B., "A Medieval Church in Mesopotamia," *Biblical Archaeologist*, Vol. 57, No. 1, 1994, pp. 38–45; "Vessels from Early Christian Church," *Biblical Archaeologist*, Vol. 57, No. 4, 1994, p. 245; "Archaeology in Syria," *American Journal of Archaeology*, Vol. 95, No. 4, 1991, pp. 738–740; "Archaeology in Syria," *American Journal of Archaeology*, Vol. 98, No. 1, 1994, pp. 157–158; "Continuity and Change in the Syriac Population at Tell Tuneinir, Syria," ARAM, Vol. 6, Nos. 1 and 2, 1994, pp. 259–259–277

Directors: Dr. Michael Fuller and Neathery B. Fuller
Sponsor, and
Contact: St. Louis Community College
3400 Pershall Road
St. Louis, MO 63135
(314) 595-4414
E-mail: mfuller@artsci.wustl.edu

This will be the 11th field season at Tell Tuneinir, which rises 60 feet above the flood plain and has a history of occupation that spans from the Bronze Age to the Medieval Period. The site is threatened by a reservoir project that will flood this ancient city, and what cannot be rescued will be pages lost from the history of humanity. The reservoir was completed in 1997 and is beginning to fill.

The first settlement at Tell Tuneinir dates to the Ninevite V Period (2500–2200 BC) based on pottery typology and radiocarbon dates. The deepest deposits are rich in animal bones, flint sickle blades, clay figurines, and clay tokens. Several meters of second millennium deposits accumulated on top of the Ninevite V gray beds.

Evidence for first millennium history at the site includes Neo-Assyrian pottery and a cylinder seal representing a king hunting the winged bull of heaven. Most of the research is focused on the Byzantine and Islamic history of the site. The medieval layers of the city contain houses, markets, a bath, monastery, winery, pottery factory, mosque, and a Syriac Christian Church. Work will continue in the monastery during the summer of 1998. It is an exciting dig with everyone in the field participating in the discovery of important features and artifacts.

TURKEY
Location: Yozgat Province, Turkey
Site: The Alisar Regional Project: Alisar Höyük/Çadir Höyük
Period: 4500 BC–AD 600

Dates of project: ca. Last week of June–last week of August, 1999.
Application deadline: December 1, 1998

Position(s): Excavators, computer analysts, GIS specialists, and illustrators.
Experience required: Previous excavation experience.
Salary: Varies according to position and experience.
Cost: Program provides lodging, meals, local commute, and travel to project. Insurance and personal travel and expenses not included.

Volunteers:
Minimum age: 18
Experience required: Two years of fieldwork preferred. Excavators, supervisors, zooarchaeologist, photographer, and draftsmen welcome.
Academic credit: May be possible through volunteer's own institution.
Cost: Program provides lodging, meals, local commute, and travel from Ankara to project. Travel to Turkey, insurance, and personal travel and expenses not included.

Bibliography: Branting, S.A., "The Alisar Regional Survey 1993–1994: Preliminary Report," *Anatolica* 22, 1996, pp. 145–158. Chernoff, M., and T. Harnischfeger, "Preliminary Report on the Botanical Remains from Çadir Höyük (1994 Season)," *Anatolica* 22, 1996, pp. 159–179. Gorny, R., "Environment, Archaeology, and History in Hittite Anatolia," *Biblical Archaeologist* 52, 1989, pp. 78–96. Gorny, R., "The Biconvex Seals of Alisar Höyük," *Anatolian Studies* 43, 1993, pp. 163–191. Gorny, R., "The 1993 Season at Alisar Höyük," *Anatolica* 20, 1994, pp. 191–202. Gorny, R., "Viticulture in Ancient Anatolia" in *Origins and Ancient History of Wine* (Gordon and Breach History and Anthropology of Food Series), Patrick McGovern, Stuart Fleming, and Solomon Katz (eds.), Newark: Gordon and Breach Publishers, 1995, pp. 133–175. Gorny, R., "Imperial Integration and Anti-Imperial Resistance in Hittite Anatolia: The View From Alisar Höyük," in BASOR 299/300, Ronald L. Gorny and Sharon Steadman (eds.), 1996, pp. 65–89. Gorny, R., G. McMahon, S. Paley, and L. Kealhofer, "The Alisar Regional Project 1994," *Anatolica* 21, 1995, pp. 65–100. Osten, H.H. von der, *The Alisar Hüyük: Seasons of 1930–32*, Parts 1 and 2 (Oriental Institute Publications 28 and 29, Chicago: University of Chicago Press, 1937.

Sponsors: National Geographic Society and private donors. Excavation has ties to the University of Chicago.
Director and
Contact: Dr. Ronald L. Gorny
5454 South Shore Drive, #335
Chicago, IL 60615
(773) 702-8624, (773) 918-2601 (voice mail)
FAX: (773) 702-5846
E-mail: rlg2@midway.uchicago.edu

The Alisar Höyük Project has been planned with the Turkish Department of Monuments and Museums to be a long-term excavation. Preliminary work began in 1993 and continued in 1994. Primary emphasis is currently on chronological issues with excavation taking place in a deep sounding and in a 40-meter-long step trench. Work will also be expanded horizontally in order to facilitate a multidisciplinary examination of the sites' earliest periods.

The Alisar Project's significance lies in the fact that it has the potential to unlock the regional chronology for central Anatolia and illuminate events occurring in Anatolia and across the entire ancient Near East. It can examine environmental and economic changes through time and relate these to wider changes in power and population in central Anatolia. Because of the long sequences (ca. 4500 BC–AD 600) at Alisar and Çadir, the Project has had the opportunity to look for patterns, especially in the relationship between environment and socio-political events, an exercise which is not possible in short-term sites. Alisar and Çadir, therefore, are ideal sites at which to integrate information about soils, vegetation, pollen cores, dendrochronology, bones, seeds, paleoenvironments, and site distribution. This data will be used to build an independent data base with which to compare other sites throughout Anatolia and the Near East. The Project will provide a baseline which will elucidate the rise of social complexity and the emergence of states and empires on the Anatolian plateau, as well as the intricacies of the Hittite Empire.

AFRICA

EGYPT
Location: Cairo, Nile Delta region, southern Egypt
Site: Various
Period: All phases of Egyptian history

Educational Progam:
Dates: September 7–December 11 (Standard course: September 7–October 30; Optional course: November 2–December 11)
Application deadline: March 30
Academic credit: Inquire.
Prerequisites: Fluency in English, a reading knowledge of French and German, and a thorough knowledge of the geography, history, and culture(s) of pre-Islamic Egypt.
Cost: ca. $2000 for tuition and fees; ca. $600 per month living expenses (includes rent); and travel to Cairo.

Sponsor and
Contact: Netherlands Institute for Archaeology
       and Arabic Studies in Cairo (NIAASC)
    P.O. Box 50
    11211 Zamalek, Cairo, Egypt
    20-2-3400076
    FAX: 20-2-3404376
    E-mail: niaasc@frcu.eun.eg

The Netherlands Institute for Archaeology and Arabic Studies in Cairo (NIAASC) program in Archaeology/Egyptology was developed to prepare students for research in Egypt by providing instruction in the fields of archaeology, Egyptology, and material culture within the country of Egypt itself. The program is aimed at advanced undergraduates and graduate students in the fields of Egyptology, Egyptian archaeology, papyrology, and Coptic studies, or students in other academic fields who can demonstrate a significant interest in the study of ancient, Hellenistic, or Coptic Egypt. The program is taught in English, and the maximum number of participants is sixteen. The standard course consists of eight weeks of lectures, seminars, assign-

ments, and excursions in the vicinity of Cairo and in the Nile Delta. The optional course consists of a brief period of fieldwork, the results of which are presented in a paper.

EGYPT (Israel, and Jordan)
Location: Various
Site: Various
Period: Various

Itinerant Seminar in Archaeology and Anthropology:
Dates: March 16–30
Application deadline: 60 days prior to start of tour
Minimum age: 18
Experience required: None
Cost: ca. $100–$120 per day covers training, lodging, meals, and local commute.

Director, Sponsor, and
Contact: Emmanuel Anati
    Centro Camuno di Studi Preistorici (CCSP)
    25044 Capo di Ponte
    Valcamonica, Brescia, Italy
    (39) 364 42091
    FAX: (39) 364 42572
    E-mail: ccsp@globalnet.it
    WWW: http://www.globalnet.it/ccsp/ccsp.htm

Since 1964 the Centro Camuno di Studi Preistorici (CCSP) has organized itinerant seminars, consisting of a trip to an area where a specific topic is being studied; survey, occasional excavation, and practical fieldwork at the site; and lectures, discussions, and debates on the topic. The itinerary of this seminar will attempt to follow the route of the Exodus, from Egypt to the Land of Canaan.

KENYA
Location: Sibiloi National Park, shores of Lake Turkana, N Kenya
Site: Koobi Fora
Period: Pliocene, Pleistocene, and Holocene

Field School:
Dates: Session 1: May 25–July 5, Session 2: July 16–August 26
Application deadline: April 15. Enrollment is limited to 25 students per session; students are encouraged to apply as early as possible.
Academic credit: 8 credits per session from Rutgers University
Cost: ca. $4040 per session for NJ residents, $4390 for non-residents, covers tuition, lodging (dormitory-like accommodations when not in the field), meals, insurance and local commute. Students are expected to bring their own tents. Travel to Kenya not included.

Sponsors: National Museums of Kenya; Program of Human Evolutionary Studies, Department of Anthropology, Rutgers University, Rutgers Study Abroad Program
Contact: Dr. Michael Rogers, Co-Field Director
    Koobi Fora Field School
    Study Abroad Office
    Rutgers, The State University of New Jersey
    102 College Avenue
    New Brunswick, NJ 08901
    (732) 932-7787
    FAX: (732) 932-8659
    E-mail: ru_abroad@emaiL.rutgers.edu
    WWW: http://www.rutgers.edu/Academics/Study_Abroad

The summer field school at Koobi Fora is open to undergraduate and graduate students interested in human origins, archaeology, paleontology, and ecology. Koobi Fora, the site famous for finds of ancient hominids, encompasses about 1000 square kilometers of Pliocene, Pleistocene, and Holocene sediments along the eastern shores of Lake Turkana in one of the most isolated areas of Africa. The program is dedicated to hands-on introductory training in all of the main disciplines within paleoanthropology, paleontology, archaeology, geology, taphonomy, and ecology. Each session includes four weeks at Koobi Fora and a one-week trip to Laikipia on the slopes of Mount Kenya to study savanna landscapes and wildlife ecology. This part of the program will provide students with an understanding of the physical landscapes and plant and animal communities (particularly of nonhuman primates) that make up the savanna ecosystem, an integral part of understanding the early stages of human evolution. Students also benefit from the cultural experience of exposure to the Kiswahili language.

MOROCCO

Location: Near Rissani, a small town in the province of Errachidia, south of the High Atlas Mountains, at the edge of the Sahara Desert
Site: Sijilmasa
Period: Various

Volunteers:

Dates: Team I: May 10–19, Team II: May 19–28, Team III: May 28–June 6
Application deadline: 90 days prior to departure. (Applications will be accepted after that time if space is available.)
Minimum age: 16
Experience required: None, but French language skills, previous archaeological experience, and photographic and artistic skills helpful. Volunteers should bring insect repellent and be prepared for walking in hot weather.
Cost: $1595 covers all expenses except travel to staging area (Errachidia, Morocco) and insurance.

Director: Dr. Ronald Messier, Middle Tennessee State University
Sponsor and
Contact:　　Earthwatch
　　　　　　　See page 7 for contact information.

Sijilmasa was the key port city for caravans carrying gold from West Africa to the Mediterranean and Islamic worlds. During five seasons of excavations, the site has been mapped, seven levels of occupation distinguished, a ceramics typology established, and important architecture including four phases of the central mosque, a bath and public latrine, a residential zone, and possibly the original governmental palace have been identified. During the 1998 season, the project plans to continue excavations at the central mosque and at a lower class residence in order to better describe the typical Sijilmasa house. Volunteers will participate in light digging and sifting of soil, fill out deposit sheets, create sketches and plans of the excavation, sort and wash pottery, bag and label finds, and assist project staff in photographing and sketching artifacts.

SOUTH AFRICA

Location: Tshiendeulu, Soutpansberg Mountains
Site: Mutokolwe
Period: AD 1500–1550

Volunteers:
Dates needed: July–August
Application deadline: End of February
Minimum age: 18

Experience required: None, but good health.
Cost: R600 (ca. $125) per week covers lodging, meals, and local commute. Volunteers must bring their camping equipment and be prepared for camping in very primitive conditions. Travel to South Africa not included.

Bibliography: Huffman, T.N., and E.O.M. Harnisch, "Settlement Hierarchies in the Northern Transvaal, Zimbabwe Ruins and Venda History," *African Studies* 46(1), pp. 79–116, 1987. Loubser, J.H.N., "Archaeology and the Early Venda History," *South African Archaeological Society Goodwin Series* 6, pp. 54–61, 1989.

Director:　　Warren Fish
Sponsor:　　Northern Provinces Heritage Services, South Africa
Contact:　　Magdel le Roux
　　　　　　　Department of Old Testament
　　　　　　　University of South Africa (UNISA)
　　　　　　　PO Box 392
　　　　　　　Pretoria 0003, Republic of South Africa
　　　　　　　(27) 12 4294711

Volunteers are invited to participate in an excavation at Mutokolwe, a site occupied by Singo and Shona peoples from Zimbabwe, in the Soutpansberg Mountains. Participants will meet at the Air Force Base near Louis Trichardt and be transported to the site by helicopter. The daily program consists of excavating, pottery washing, relevant lectures around the campfire, and plenty of time for relaxing. The Soutpansberg area is rich in the archaeology of ancient cultures, and participants will have the opportunity to view other excavation sites and ancient ruins by helicopter.

TUNISIA

Location: Carthage
Site: Bir Ftouha
Period: 5th–7th centuries CE

Position(s): Area Supervisors (3)
Dates needed: May 27–July 30
Application deadline: February 1
Experience required: 1–2 seasons supervisory experience.
Salary: None
Cost: Program provides lodging, meals, and local commute. Dependent on experience, program may provide travel stipend. Insurance not included.

Field School:
Dates: June 14–July 27
Application deadline: February 1
Academic credit: 3 credits from Randolph-Macon Woman's College
Cost: $600 tuition plus $1500 in fees covers lodging, meals, and local commute. Travel to project (ca. $1000) and insurance not included.

Director:　　Dr. Susan T. Stevens
Sponsors:　　Samuel H. Kress Foundation; Randolph-Macon Woman's College; and others
Contact:　　Randolph-Macon Woman's College
　　　　　　　Department of Classics
　　　　　　　Lynchburg, VA 24503
　　　　　　　(804) 947-8533

The 1998 Archaeological Field School at Carthage is an experiential learning program designed to give students the opportunity to learn archaeological techniques and be part of a research team by participating in a working excavation. It is also an opportunity for students to explore the culture of both ancient and modern Tunisia. Students spend most working days at the site, learning the basic skills and methods of stratigraphic excavation and recording. They will also have the opportunity to experience other aspects of the excavation by registering artifacts, entering field data, and helping with surveying, computer-assisted drafting, and artifact analysis.

The excavations are part of the ongoing International Campaign sponsored by UNESCO to preserve the ancient city of Carthage and to develop the area into an archaeological park. The focus of the 1998 excavation is a 5th–7th century CE Christian church complex called Bir Ftouha on the northern outskirts of the ancient city of Carthage. This architecturally rich and unusual Christian site is now threatened by proposed road construction through the field.

During the 1997 season, the team excavated an unusual annex building and basilica constructed after the mid-5th century. The annex building was decorated with mosaic floors, carved and colored marble columns, and fine wall veneer. It was attached in the north to a tile-roofed building with burials cut through its paved floor. On the west, an ambulatory attached the annex building to the apse of a richly decorated, east-west oriented basilica. The goal of the 1998 season is to complete excavation of the annex building and to determine the full width and length of the basilica.

ZIMBABWE
Location/Site: Various prehistoric rock art sites
Period: Various

Itinerant Seminar in Archaeology and Anthropology:
Dates: July 17–31
Application deadline: 60 days prior to start of tour
Minimum age: 18
Experience required: None
Cost: ca. $100–$120 per day covers training, lodging, meals, and local commute.

Director, Sponsor, and
Contact: Emmanuel Anati
        Centro Camuno di Studi Preistorici (CCSP)
        25044 Capo di Ponte
        Valcamonica, Brescia, Italy
        (39) 364 42091
        FAX: (39) 364 42572
        E-mail: ccsp@globalnet.it
        WWW: http://www.globalnet.it/ccsp/ccsp.htm

Since 1964 the Centro Camuno di Studi Preistorici (CCSP) has organized itinerant seminars, consisting of a trip to an area where a specific topic is being studied; survey, occasional excavation, and practical fieldwork at the site; and lectures, discussions, and debates on the topic. This seminar will focus on rock art sites and related living sites, and methods of recording and analyzing rock art.

ASIA, AUSTRALIA, & PACIFIC

CHINA
Location: Beijing and environs
Site: Various
Period: Various

Archaeology Seminar at Beijing University: Earth of Plenty: Discoveries in Chinese Archaeology in the 1990s
Dates: Seminar: June 13–23, Optional Extension: June 23–30
Application deadline: Until filled.

Academic credit: To be arranged through student's own institution.
Cost: Seminar: $3495 (double occupancy), covers roundtrip airfare San Francisco-Beijing, lodging, all breakfasts, two dinners, and all local tours. Optional Extension: $1550 (double occupancy) covers air and bus transport, lodging, all meals except three dinners, and all tours, entertainment, and cultural activities.

Sponsors: Archaeological Institute of America; Department of Archaeology, Beijing University
Scholar/Escort: Dr. David A. Sensabaugh, Curator of Asian Art, Yale University Art Gallery
Contact: Archaeological Institute of America
        656 Beacon Street
        Boston, MA 02215-2010
        (617) 353-9361
        FAX: (617) 353-6550
        E-mail: aia@bu.edu
        WWW: http://csa.brynmawr.edu/aia.html

The Archaeology Department of Beijing University offers an intensive seminar on Chinese archaeology, including the Chinese archaeologists' personal views of excavation sites, artifacts, interpretation, and disputes in the Chinese archaeological world. There will be field trips some of the most important excavation sites near Beijing. Participants will live on campus at Beijing University, and the opportunity to befriend Chinese students and colleagues, many of whom speak English, complements the full schedule of daily activities. Contact the AIA for information on the optional extension.

CHINA
Location: Xian, Shaanxi Province
Site: To be determined
Period: Han

Field School/Study Tour:
Dates: July 10–August 14
Application deadline: Until filled.
Academic credit: 6 transferable credits from Xian Jiaotong University (3 for Fieldwork in Archaeology; 3 for Chinese Cultural History)
Cost: $3950 covers airfare from JFK Airport, New York, to China and return, tuition, fees, lodging (double occupancy), meals, field trips, and local commute.

Sponsor: Xian Jiaotong University, Xian, Shaanxi, China; Fudan Museum Foundation, USA
Director and
Contact: Dr. Alfonz Lengyel, American Director:
        Fudan Museum Foundation
        4206 - 73rd Terrace East
        Sarasota, FL 34243
        Tel/FAX: (941) 351-8208
        E-mail: fmfsafsa@Juno.Com

The Sino-American Field School of Archaeology offers an archaeology practicum supplemented by a course, given in English, on Chinese art and culture and visits to historically important places in and around Shanghai and Xian. The focus of the archaeology practicum is on salvage archaeology and the program includes: fieldwork, lectures, studies of collections in museums, and field trips.

CHINA
Location: Yuanqu County, Shanxi Province
Site: Yuanqu Shang Dynasty Town
Period: Early Shang, ca. 2000–1300 BC

Field School:
Dates: June 8–July 25
Application deadline: April 30
Academic credit: 3-6 from Washington University in St. Louis
Cost: $4050 for 6 credits or $2810 for 3 credits covers tuition, lodging, meals, and local commute. Travel to China and insurance not included.

Directors and
Sponsors: Jim A. Railey, Washington University in Saint Louis; Tong Weihua, National Museum of Chinese History
Contact: Jim A. Railey or David L. Browman
Washington University
Dept. of Anthropology, Campus Box 1114
St. Louis, MO 63130-4899.
314/935-5252
FAX: 314/935-8535
E-mail: jrailey@artsci.wustl.edu
dlbrowman@artsci.wustl.edu

The Yuanqu Shang town is only one of four walled settlements known from the Shang, China's earliest historically verified dynasty. The site is rich in both Shang and pre- and post-Shang archaeological remains, and portions of the Shang town's original pounded earth wall are still visible above ground. The Yuanqu Shang Town Field School provides students with the opportunity to participate in excavations at this important site and to experience rural Chinese life by living for several weeks in a remote, mountainous area normally closed to foreigners. The program includes training in modern excavation techniques plus short study tours of Beijing and Xian.

CHINA
Location: Zhoukoudian (Choukoutian), near Beijing, N China
Site: Locality 26
Period: Lower–Middle Paleolithic (500,000–10,000 BP)

Field School/Study Tour:
Dates: June 7–July 12 (tentative)
Application deadline: April 1
Academic credit: 3–6 undergraduate or graduate credits from The George Washington University
Cost: $3920 (3 credits) or $5195 (6 credits) covers tuition, lodging, meals, local commute, and field trips. Cost is subject to change. Travel to China not included; GWU will try to arrange for discount group flight from Washington, DC.

Bibliography: Wu, Ru-kang, et al., *Palaeoanthropology and Palaeolithic Archaeology in the People's Republic of China.* Zhanxiang, Qiu, and Shikon Takei, *Zhoukoudian: Peking Man Site. Palaeontologica Sinica*, Series D, No. 1; New Series D, No. 10, pp. 1–485. Selections from *Acta Anthropologica Sinica.*

Directors: Shao Xiang-Qing and Alison S. Brooks
Sponsor and
Contact: The George Washington University
Zhoukoudian Field Project
Department of Anthropology
Bldg. WW, 2110 G Street, NW
Washington, DC 20052
(202) 994-6075
FAX: (202) 994-6097
E-mail: anth@gwis2.circ.gwu.edu

Zhoukoudian is located at the foot of the Western Mountains near

Beijing. Since the discovery here of Peking Man (*Homo erectus pekinensis*) in the 1920s, the site has been renowned for its value in understanding human origins. From over 20 localities, scientists have recovered the remains of about 40 individuals who lived between 500,000 and 10,000 year ago, classified as *Homo erectus*, archaic *Homo sapiens*, and *Homo sapiens*. GWU's Paleoanthropological Field Program is the first program for American students at Zhoukoudian. Students will learn excavation and recording techniques, including mapping, surveying, and field photography at Locality 26. There will also be classes on faunal analysis, microscreening, and other laboratory and field methods. Digging takes place six days per week. On Sundays, students will tour other famous sites around Zhoukoudian. Five days are reserved to visit historical and archaeological sites in Beijing, and four days will be spent in Xian, whose massive walls were described by Marco Polo.

MONGOLIA
Location: Northern Mongolia, Bulgan Aimag (closest city Erdenet)
Site: Various sites in the Egiin Gol River Valley
Period: Neolithic–19th century AD

Volunteers:
Dates needed: Session 1: June 6–June 28, Session 2: July 4–July 26 (subject to change due to airline flights, etc.)
Application deadline: March 15
Minimum age: 21
Experience required: None, training will be provided by both American and Mongolian archaeologists, but participants must be able to withstand challenging field conditions.
Cost: Tax deductible $1800 per 3-week session, $3000 per 6 week session covers lodging in Ulan Bator, meals, and local commute from Ulan Bator to site and return. Travel to Mongolia and insurance not included.

Bibliography: Barfield, Thomas, *The Perilous Frontier.* Askarov, A., et al "Pastoral and Nomadic Tribes at the Beginning of the First Millennium BC," in *History of the Civilizations of Central Asia: Dawn of Civilization*, A.H. Dani and V.M. Masson (eds.) Fairservis, Jr., Walter A. (ed.), *Archaeology of the Southern Gobi of Mongolia.* Volkov, V.V., "Early nomads of Mongolia," in *Nomads of the Eurasian Steppes in the Early Iron Age*, J. Davis-Kimball (ed.)

Director, Sponsor, and
Contact: Dr. Mark Hall
American-Eurasian Research Institute, Inc.
(formerly Kazakh/American Research Project, Inc.)
Center for the Study of Eurasian Nomads
1607 Walnut Street
Berkeley, CA 94709
(510) 549-3708
FAX: (510) 849-3137
E-mail: hall@qal.berkeley.edu

The Egiin Gol river valley is located in northern Mongolia about 150 km south of Lake Baikal. Over 100 sq. km of the valley is scheduled to be flooded early in the next century by a large hydro-electric dam project. Archaeological survey and excavation is being conducted there by a joint Mongolian-American team in advance of the flooding. Previous work in the valley has revealed the existence of various types of sites from a variety of time periods. There are extensive lithic and pottery scatters, several large kheregsur complexes, Buddhist monasteries dating to the 18th and 19th centuries AD, and numerous burials dating to the Xiong-nu confederacy and the Mongol Empire.

Volunteers will work with American and Mongolian archaeologists, and Mongolian students in excavating some of these sites. Survey will be conducted further up river to see what sites exist in the valley. Work begins at 8:30 am and continues, with a lunch break, until the evening meal at about 7:30 pm. Volunteers will be expected to work six days a week. On their day off, volunteers can fish or explore the surrounding countryside.

The Egiin Gol river valley is in a wooded steppe zone at an altitude of 1000–1500 m above sea level. The summertime temperature ranges from 40°–80° F, and it usually rains for a few hours several times a week. Volunteers must realize that living conditions in Mongolia will be quite primitive and that they will be over 100 km from the nearest town. Volunteers must be flexible, have a spirit of adventure, and realize that Murphy's Law reigns supreme in Mongolia.

THAILAND
Location: Nakon Ratchasima, N Thailand
Site: Noen U-Loke

Volunteers:
Dates: 2-week sessions in January and February.
Application deadline: 90 days prior to departure. (Applications will be accepted after that time if space is available.)
Minimum age: 16
Experience required: None
Cost: $1895 covers all expenses except travel to staging area (Nakon Ratchasima) and insurance.

Directors: Dr. Charles Higham, University of Otago, New Zealand; Rachanie Thosarat, Thai Fine Arts Department, Bangkok
Sponsor and
Contact: Earthwatch
See page 7 for contact information.

Noen U-Loke, 250 kilometers northwest of Angkor Wat, an exceptionally well-preserved moated settlement. Crews will investigate whether the moat was used for rice irrigation or for defense and will uncover burials where the quantity and quality of grave goods give clues to the rise of complex social hierarchies. Teams will excavate, record finds, restore human skeletal material, restore pottery vessels, and retrieve geomorphological and biological samples.

AUSTRALIA
Location: Mainly Australia
Site: Various
Period: Various

The School of Archaeology at the University of Sydney, Australia, maintains a regularly updated list of fieldwork opportunities on their Web site. They also maintain an extensive set of links to other Web sites devoted to Australian archaeology.

Fieldwork Opportunities:
http://www.archaeology.usyd.edu.au/news/ongoing/fieldwork.html

Australian Archaeology Web Sites:
http://www.archaeology.usyd.edu.au/links/index.html

AUSTRALIA
Location: Training Program 1: Great Barrier Reef; Training Program 2: Victoria

AIMA/NAS Training Program 1:
Dates: 7 days in the end of March
Application deadline: Inquire

Minimum age: Inquire
Experience required: Divers: Participants are required to be classed as an Open Water diver with ten logged dives and have a diving medical certificate, confirming that they are fit to dive. Non-divers are also eligible to participate, and will be involved in learning dry land skills at sites located above low water level.
Cost: ca. $1000–$1500 depending on enrollment and student status. Inquire for complete details.

This seven-day course will be held at sea on the Great Barrier Reef aboard the *Undersea Explorer*.

AIMA/NAS Training Program 2:
Dates: First weekend course will take place in late October.
Application deadline: Inquire.
Academic credit: Certification from the Australian Instate for Maritime Archaeology (AIMA) in conjunction with the British Nautical Archaeological Society (NAS).
Cost: $160 per weekend course covers training lectures, pool training, AIMA/NAS study manual, selected reading material, AIMA membership, and administration fees including presentation of AIMA Certification. Participant responsible for all other expenses

This training program is intended for volunteers interested in maritime archaeology and is run by qualified maritime archaeologists with specialized instructors and diving organizations assisting with lectures and pool training. This is the first part of a four-part training program.

Bibliography: *Archaeology Underwater: The NAS Guide to Principles and Practise*, M. Dean, B. Ferrari, I. Oxley, and M. Redknap (eds.), Dorchester, UK: NAS and Archetype Press, 1992. Green, J., Maritime Archaeology: A Technical Handbook, London: Academic Press, 1990 (No longer in print).

Director: Mark Staniforth, Flinders University, South Australia
Sponsor: The Australian Institute for Maritime Archaeology (AIMA)
Contact: Vivienne Moran
Queensland Museum
GPO Box 3300
South Brisbane, Queensland, 4101 Australia
(61) 7 3840 7675
E-mail: VivM@qm.qld.gov.au

AUSTRALIA
Location: North Queensland
Site: Laura area in North Queensland
Period: 10,000–1,000 BP

Dates of excavation and field school: July 6–24
Application deadline: March 31

Field School: Investigating Australian Rock Art
Academic credit: 4 credits from James Cook University (JCU)
Cost: Tuition fees vary according to academic status. Students should contact the (JCU) admissions office for details. In addition to tuition, there is a $350 fee for equipment, meals, accommodations at the field camp, and local commute. Students must arrange their own accommodation in Cairns, and bring their own sleeping bag, mosquito net, and air mattress for the field camp. Travel to Australia not included.

Volunteers:
Minimum age: 18
Experience required: Bush camping, knowledge of Aboriginal values and rock art. Photography, surveying, and cooking skills welcome.

Cost: Program provides lodging, meals, insurance, and local commute. Lodging in Cairns and travel to Australia not included.

Bibliography: Cole, Nolene A., and Alan Watchman, "Archaeology of White Hand Stencils of the Laura Region, North Queensland (Australia)," *Techne* 3, pp. 82–90, 1996. Cole, Nolene A., and Alan Watchman, "Painting with plants: Investigating fibres in Aboriginal rock paintings at Laura, north Queensland," *Rock Art Research* 9, pp. 27–36, 1992. Flood, Josephine, *Archaeology of the Dreamtime, The Story of Prehistoric Australia and Its People* (revised ed.), New Haven and London: Yale University Press, 1990. Mowaljarlai, D., and Alan Watchman, "An Aboriginal view of rock art management," *Rock Art Research* 6(2), pp. 151–153, 1989. Roughsey, Dick (Goobalathaldin), *The Rainbow Serpent*, Wm Collins Ltd. Sydney, 1975. Utermorrah, Daisy, David Mowaljarlai, et al, *Visions of Mowanjum: Aboriginal writings from the Kimberley,* Rigby Ltd, Adelaide, 1980.

Director, Sponsor, and
Contact: Dr. Alan Watchman
Department of Anthropology and Archaeology
James Cook University
Townsville, Queensland 4811, Australia
E-mail: Alan.Watchman@jcu.edu.au
(61) 77 815155
FAX: (61) 77 815244

Student Admissions Office
1-800-24-6446
FAX: (61) 77 814644

The James Cook University School of Anthropology and Archaeology field school will investigate Australian rock art. The first week of introductory lectures at JCU campus in Cairns will focus on ethical and theoretical considerations concerning the documentation of rock art sites, and equipment used for laboratory analysis of rocks, salts, and microorganisms will be demonstrated. The remaining two weeks will be spent documenting rock art sites near Laura, far north Queensland. Students will be instructed on-site in surveying, photographic recording techniques, measuring environmental and rock surface parameters, and in observing visitor and tourist impacts. A broad range of practical skills will be taught for recording motifs and assessing rock art stability; methods used for sampling, analyzing and dating rock art will be demonstrated; and a range of intervention and non-intervention options for protecting and managing rock art will be taught. Students will gain an understanding of global perspectives, interpretations, and values of rock art and gain an appreciation of the value and significance of rock art sites to Aboriginal people.

FIJI
Location: Viti Levu
Site: Suva campus of the University of the South Pacific and a site near the Sigatoka Sand Dune National Park, on the Coral Coast
Period: 3000–200 BP

Field School:
Dates: Nine weeks, May-July. Inquire for exact dates.
Application deadline: February 20
Prerequisites: 2.5 grade point average, introductory course in Archaeology or other social science, or permission of Director.
Academic credit: 12 credits from Simon Fraser University. Students from other institutions must first gain admission to SFU and must arrange for transfer credit with their own institution. Application forms are available from the SFU admissions office.

Cost: CDN$5200 for Canadian residents, CDN$7000 for non-residents covers tuition and fees, travel to Fiji from Vancouver and return, lodging, field trips, visas, and health insurance. Meals not included.

Director,   Dr. Dave Burley, E-mail: burley@sfu.ca
Sponsor and
Contact: Simon Fraser University
International and Exchange Student Services
Maggie Benston Bldg. #1200
Burnaby, British Columbia V5A 1S6, Canada
(604) 291-4232
FAX: (614) 291-5880
E-mail: sfu_international@sfu.ca

Simon Fraser University's nine-week program in South Pacific Archaeology consists of one week of orientation at SFU followed by five weeks of academic course work at the University of the South Pacific in Suva and three weeks of fieldwork and training on the Coral Coast. Courses include: Fijian Culture, Western Pacific Prehistory, and Introduction of Field Methods in Archaeology. Participants will have the opportunity to tour other archaeological sites on Viti Levu as well as to experience traditional Fijian village life. There will be time for independent travel upon the formal close of the field school.

INDONESIA
Location: Banda Islands
Site: Banda Neira, Banda Besar, Pulau Ai

Volunteers:
Dates: Two-week sessions in January, February, and March.
Application deadline: 90 days prior to departure
Minimum age: 16
Experience required: None, but the following skills will be much appreciated: surveying and mapping, drawing, photography, and previous archaeological excavation experience. Good health and physical condition a necessity.
Cost: $1895 covers all expenses except travel to staging area (Banda Neira Airport) and insurance.

Director,   Peter V. Lape, Brown University
Sponsor and
Contact: Earthwatch
See page 7 for contact information.

The remote Banda Islands were, until the 19th century, the only place on earth where nutmeg was grown, and visiting merchants from Southeast Asia, China, India and the Near East would call there to trade their textiles, foods, and precious metals for the valuable nutmeg and mace. Archaeology has been utilized to understand past ecological systems and to gain insight into a complex, highly developed trade network that encompassed much of the world from the first century AD onward. Excavation and survey will be concentrated on three of the Banda Islands: Banda Neira, Banda Besar, and Pulau Ai. Tasks will include walking surveys, mapping, excavation, and data processing. Generally, team members will spend morning and afternoon work sessions on either survey, mapping, or excavation. Evenings will generally be reserved for data processing. This includes the consolidation of unit data and notes, cleaning and cataloguing of artifacts and ecofacts, and mapping in survey data.

STATE HISTORIC PRESERVATION OFFICERS &
STATE ARCHAEOLOGISTS

Most, if not all, states have an active program of archaeology which is often placed under the jurisdiction of a state's division of cultural resources and historic preservation. State Historic Preservation Officers (SHPOs) administer the national historic preservation program at the state level, review National Register of Historic Places nominations, maintain data on historic properties that have been identified but not yet nominated, and Federal agencies seek the views of the appropriate SHPO when identifying historic properties and assessing effects of an undertaking on historic properties. The Office of the State Archaeologist (OSA) advises the State Historic Preservation Office, other state and public agencies, and private individuals on compliance related activities; coordinates burial preservation; acts as a liaison to Native American tribal entities; and supports the advancement of archaeology within the state, region, and nation. State Archaeologists (SA) can answer questions regarding laws, procedures, current research, educational programs, and other aspects of archaeology for each state and possession. Lists of State Historic Preservation Officers and State Archaeologists may be accessed at the following World Wide Web sites:

National Conference of State Historic Preservation Officers: http://www.achp.gov/states.html
National Association of State Archaeologists: http://www.lib.uconn.edu/NASA/

ALABAMA
Lawerence Oaks, SHPO
Alabama Historical Commission
468 South Perry Street
Montgomery, AL 36130-0900
(205) 242-3184, FAX: (205) 240-3477
E-mail: lawereoaks@aol.com

J. Parker, SA
Archaeological Services Div.
Same as above, except for e-mail.

ALASKA
Judith Bittner, SHPO
Office of History & Archaeology
Div. of Parks & Outdoor Recreation
Dept. of Natural Resources
3601 C Street, Suite 1278
Anchorage, AK 99503-5921
(907) 269-8715, FAX: (907) 269-8908
E-mail: oha@alaska.net

Robert Shaw, SA
Address & FAX same as above.
(907) 269-8727

AMERICAN SAMOA
John Enright, SHPO
Historic Preservation Office
Dept. of Parks & Recreation
Government of American Samoa
Pago Pago, American Samoa, 96799
(684) 633-2384, FAX: (684) 633-2367

David J. Herdrich, SA
Same as above.
E-mail: herdrich@samoatelco.com

ARIZONA
James W. Garrison, SHPO
Arizona State Parks
Office of Historic Preservation
1300 West Washington
Phoenix, AZ 85007
(602) 542-4009, FAX: (602) 542-4180
E-mail: jgarrison@prpo01.pr.state.az.us

Paul Fish, SA
Curator of Archaeology
Arizona State Museum
University of Arizona

Tucson, AZ 85721
(520) 621-2556, FAX: (520) 621-2976
E-mail: archaeo@ccit.arizona.edu

ARKANSAS
Cathryn H. Slater, SHPO
Historic Preservation Program
Tower Bldg., Suite 1500
323 Center Street
Little Rock, AR 72201
(501) 324-9880, FAX: (501) 324-9184
E-mail: info@dah.state.ar.us
WWW: http://www.heritage.state.ar.us

Hester Davis, State Archaeologist
Arkansas Archeological Survey
PO Box 1249
Fayetteville, AR 72702-1249
(501) 575-3556, FAX: (501) 575-5453
E-mail: hadavis@comp.uark.edu

CALIFORNIA
Cherilyn Widell, SHPO
Office of Historic Preservation
Dept. of Parks & Recreation
PO Box 942896
Sacramento, CA 94296-0001
(916) 653-6624, FAX: (916) 653-9824
E-mail: calshpo@cwo.com
WWW: http://www.ceres.ca.gov/parks/ohp.html

William Seidel, SA
Address and FAX same as above.
(916) 653-9623

COLORADO
James E. Hartmann, SHPO
Colorado Historical Society
1300 Broadway
Denver, CO 80203
(303) 866-3395, FAX: (303) 866-4464

Susan M. Collins, SA
Address and FAX same as above.
(303) 866-2736
E-mail: SColl10492@aol.com

CONNECTICUT
John W. Shannahan, SHPO
Contact: David A. Poirier, Staff Archaeologist
State Historic Preservation Office

Connecticut Historical Commission
59 South Prospect Street
Hartford, CT 06106
(860) 566-3005, FAX: (860) 566-5078
E-mail: CTHIST@NECA.com

Nicholas F. Bellantoni, SA
CT State Museum of Natural History
Dept. of Anthropology/U-23
University of Connecticut
Storrs, CT 06269
(860) 486-5248, FAX: (860) 486-1719/6364
E-mail: nbell@uconnvm.uconn.edu

DELAWARE
Daniel R. Griffith, SHPO
Director, Div. of Historical & Cultural Affairs
Hall of Records, PO Box 1401
Dover, DE 19903-1401
(302) 739-5313, FAX: (302) 739-6711

Faye L. Stocum, SA
State Historic Preservation Office
15 The Green
Dover, DE 19901
(302) 739-5685, FAX: (302) 739-5660

DISTRICT OF COLUMBIA
Nancy J. Kassner, SA
Historic Preservation Div.
614 H Street, NW, Room 305
Washington, DC 20001
(202) 727-7360, FAX: (202) 727-7211

FLORIDA
George W. Percy, SHPO
Div. of Historical Resources
R.A. Gray Bldg.
500 S. Bronough Street
Tallahassee, FL 32399-0250
(904) 488-1480
E-mail: flshpo@gteens.com
WWW: http://www.dos.state.fl.us/dhr/

James J. Miller, SA
Address same as above.
(904) 487-2299, FAX: (904) 414-2207
E-mail: jmiller@mail.dos.state.fl.us
WWW: http://www.dos.state.fl.us/dhr/

GEORGIA
Mark Edwards, SHPO
Director, Historic Preservation Div.
Dept. of Natural Resources
500 Healey Bldg.
57 Forsyth Street, NW, Suite 500
Atlanta, GA 30303
(404) 656-2840, FAX: (404) 651-8739
E-mail: mark_edwards@mail.dnr.state.ga.us

John R. Morgan, SA
Address same as above.
(404) 656-2840, FAX: (404) 657-1040

GUAM
Richard D. Davis, SHPO
Historic Resources Div.
Dept. of Parks & Recreation
Bldg. 13-8, Tiyan, PO Box 2950
Agana Heights, Guam 96910
(671) 475-6259, FAX: (671) 477-2822
E-mail: davisrd@ns.gu

Victoriano April, SA
Address and FAX same as above.
(671) 475-6920

HAWAII
Keith W. Ahue, SHPO
Dept. of Land & Natural Resources
Historic Preservation Office
1151 Punchbowl Street
Honolulu, HI 96813
(808) 548-6550

Ross H. Cordy, SA
Dept. of Land & Natural Resources
Historic Preservation Div.
33 South King Street, 6th Floor
Honolulu, HI 96813
(808) 587-0012, FAX: (808) 587-0018

IDAHO
Robert M. Yohe II, SHPO (interim) & SA
Idaho Historical Society
210 Main Street
Boise, ID 83702
(208) 334-3847, FAX: (208) 334-2775
E-mail: rmyohe@ishs.state.id.us

ILLINOIS
William L. Wheeler, SHPO
Illinois Historic Preservation Agency
Div. of Preservation Services
1 Old State Capitol Plaza, 500 E. Madison
Springfield, IL 62701-1512
(217) 785-9045

Mark Esarey, SA
Address same as above.
(217) 785-4999, FAX: (217) 782-8161

INDIANA
Larry D. Macklin , SHPO
Director, Dept. of Natural Resources
402 W. Washington Street, Rm. W-274
Indianapolis, IN 46204
(317) 232-4020
E-mail: dhpa_at_dnrlan@ima.isd.state.in.us

Dr. James R. Jones III, SA
Div. of Historic Preservation & Archaeology
Address same as above.
(317) 232-1646, FAX: (317) 232-0693
E-mail: rick_jones_at_dnrlan@ima.ind.state.in.us

IOWA
Tom Moraine, SHPO
State Historical Society of Iowa
Capitol Complex
East Sixth & Locust Streets
Des Moines, IA 50309-0290
(515) 281-8837, FAX: (515) 282-0502

William Green, SA
University of Iowa
303 Eastlawn Bldg.
Iowa City, IA 52242
(319) 335-2389, FAX: (319) 335-2776
E-mail: bill-green@uiowa.edu
WWW: http://www.uiowa.edu/~osa

KANSAS
Ramon Powers, SHPO
Kansas State Historical Society
6425 Southwest 6th Avenue
Topeka, KS 66615-1099
(913) 272-8681, FAX: (913) 272-8682
E-mail: Rpowers@hspo.wpo.state.ks.us
WWW: http://history.cc.ukans.edu/heritage/kshs/
kshs1.html

Virginia A Wulfkuhle, SA (interim)
Address and FAX same as above.
(913) 272-8681, ext. 268
E-mail: vwulf@hspo.wpo.state.ks.us

KENTUCKY
David Morgan, SHPO
Kentucky Heritage Council
300 Washington Street
Frankfort, KY 40601
(502) 564-7005, FAX: (502) 564-5820
E-mail: dmorgan@mail.state.ky.us

R. Berle Clay, SA
University of Kentucky
Dept. of Anthropology
Lexington, KY 40506-0024
(606) 257-5735, FAX: (606) 257-1034
E-mail: ant131@ukcc.uky.edu

LOUISIANA
Gerri Hobdy, SHPO
Office of Cultural Development
Div. of Archaeology
Capitol Annex Bldg., PO Box 44247
Baton Rouge, LA 70804
(504) 342-8200, FAX: (504) 342-8173
E-mail: arch@crt.state.la.us
WWW: http://www.crt.state.la.us

Dr. Thomas H. Eubanks, SA
Address and FAX same as above.
(504) 342-8170
E-mail: teubanks@crt.state.la.us

MAINE
Earle G. Shettleworth, Jr., SHPO
Historic Preservation Commission
55 Capitol Street, Station #65

Augusta, ME 04333-0065
(207) 287-2132, FAX: (207) 287-2335
E-mail: sheshet@state.me.us

Arthur E. Spiess, SA
Address, telephone, and FAX same as above.
E-mail: arthur.spiess@state.me.us

MARSHALL ISLANDS
Carmen Bigler, SHPO
Interior & Outer Islands Affairs
PO Box 1454
Majuro Atoll, RMI 96960
(692) 625-4642, FAX: (692) 625-5353
E-mail: cnmihpo@itecnmi.com

MARYLAND
J. Rodney Little, SHPO
Director, Historical & Cultural Programs
Maryland Historical Trust
100 Community Place
Crownsville, MD 21032-2023
(410) 514-7600, FAX: (410) 514-7678
E-mail: mdshpo@ari.net
WWW: http://www2.ari.net/mdshpo

Richard B. Hughes, SA
Chief, Office of Archaeology
Address, telephone, and FAX same as above.
E-mail: hughesr@dhcd.state.md.us

MASSACHUSETTS
Judith McDonough, SHPO
Massachusetts Historical Commission
Massachusetts Archives Facility
220 Morrissey Boulevard
Boston, MA 02125
(617) 727-8470, FAX: (617) 727-5128
E-mail: JMcDonough@mhc.sec.state.ma.us

Brona Simon, SA
Address, telephone, and FAX same as above.
E-mail: bsimon@mhc.sec.state.ma.us

MICHIGAN
John R. Halsey, Acting SHPO, SA
State Historic Preservation Office
Michigan Historical Center
717 W. Allegan Street
Lansing, MI 48918
(517) 373-6358, FAX: (517) 373-0851
E-mail: johnh@sosmail.state.mi.us
WWW: http://www.sos.state.mi.us/history/
preserve/preserve.html

MICRONESIA, FEDERATED STATES OF
Rufino Mauricio, FSM SHPO
Office of Administrative Services
Div. of Archives & Historic Preservation
PO Box PS 52, Palikir, Pohnpei
E. Caroline Islands, FSM 96941
(691) 320-2343, FAX: (691) 320-5634

MINNESOTA
Nina Archabal, SHPO
Minnesota Historical Society
345 Kellogg Blvd., West
St. Paul, MN 55102-1906
(612) 296-2747, FAX: (612) 296-1004
E-mail: mnshpo@gold.tc.umn.edu
WWW: http://www.tc.umn.edu/nlhome/g075.mnshpo

Mark J. Dudzik, SA
Office of the State Archaeologist
Fort Snelling History Center
St. Paul, MN 55111
(612) 725-2411, FAX: (612) 725-2427

MISSISSIPPI
Elbert R. Hilliard, SHPO
Director, Dept. of Archives & History
PO Box 571
Jackson, MS 39205-0571
(601) 359-6850, FAX: (601) 359-6975
E-mail: msshpo@mdah.ms.us

Samuel McGahey, SA
Address same as above.
(601) 359-6940, FAX: (601) 359-6955

MISSOURI
Claire F. Blackwell, Deputy SHPO
Director, Historic Preservation Program
Dept. of Natural Resources
205 Jefferson, PO Box 176
Jefferson City, MO 65102
(573) 751-7858, FAX: (573) 526-2852

MONTANA
Paul Putz, SHPO
Montana Historical Society
Historic Preservation Office
1410 8th Avenue, PO Box 201202
Helena, MT 59620-1202
(406) 444-7715, FAX: (406) 444-6575
E-mail: anshp@selway.umt.edu

Mark F. Baumler, SA
Address and FAX same as above.
(406) 444-7721
E-mail: mbaumler@mt.gov

NEBRASKA
Lawrence Sommer, SHPO
Director, Nebraska Historical Society
1500 R Street, PO Box 82554
Lincoln, NE 68501
(402) 471-4787, FAX: (402) 471-3100
E-mail: nshs@inetnebr.com

Gayle Carlson, SA
Curator of Anthropology
Address, telephone, and FAX same as above.

NEVADA
Ronald M. James, SHPO
Dept. of Museums, Library & Arts
100 South Stewart Street
Capitol Complex/Upper Level South
Carson City, NV 89710
(702) 687-6360
E-mail: rmjames@lahontan.clan.lib.nv.us

Gene Hattori, SA
Historic Preservation & Archeology
Address same as above.
(702) 687-6362

NEW HAMPSHIRE
Nancy C. Muller, SHPO
Director, Div. of Historic Resources
Dept. of Cultural Affairs
State Historic Preservation Office

19 Pillsbury St., PO Box 2043
Concord, NH 03302-2043
(603) 271-3483, FAX: (603) 271-3433

Gary W. Hume, SA
Address, telephone, and FAX same as above.

NEW JERSEY
Robert C. Shinn, SHPO
Dept. of Environmental Protection & Energy
Cultural & Historic Resources
CN-402, 401 East State Street
Trenton, NJ 08625-0402
(609) 292-2885, FAX: (609) 292-7695

Lorraine E. Williams, SA
New Jersey State Museum
205 West State Street, CN 530
Trenton, NJ 08625
(609) 292-8594

NEW MEXICO
Phillip H. Shelley, SHPO
Historic Preservation Div.
Office of Cultural Affairs
Villa Rivera Bldg., 3rd Floor
228 East Palace Avenue
Santa Fe, NM 87503
(505) 827-6320, FAX: (505) 827-6338
E-mail: nmshpo@arms.state.nm.us

Lynne Sebastian, SA
Address, telephone, and FAX same as above.
E-mail: sebastian@arms.state.nm.us

NEW YORK
Bernadette Castro, SHPO
Parks, Recreation & Historic Preservation
Empire State Plaza
Agency Bldg. 1, 20th Floor
Albany, NY 12238
(518) 474-0443, FAX: (518) 474-4492

NORTH CAROLINA
Jeffrey J. Crow, Jr., SHPO
Director, Div. of Archives & History
Dept. of Cultural Resources
109 East Jones Street
Raleigh, NC 27601-2807
(919) 733-7305, FAX: (919) 733-8807

Stephen R. Claggett, SA
Address same as above.
(919) 733-7342, FAX: (919) 715-2671
E-mail: sclaggett@ncsl.dcr.state.nc.us

NORTH DAKOTA
James E. Sperry, SHPO
State Historical Society of North Dakota
Archaeology & Historic Preservation Div.
North Dakota Heritage Center
612 E. Boulevard Avenue
Bismarck, ND 58505
(701) 328-2672, FAX: (701) 328-3710
E-mail: jsperry@ranch.state.nd.us

Fern Swenson, SA
Address, telephone, and FAX same as above.
E-mail: fswenson@ranch.state.nd.us

NORTHERN MARIANA ISLANDS
Joseph P. Deleon Guerrero, SHPO
Dept. of Community & Cultural Affairs
Commonwealth of the Northern Mariana Islands
Saipan, Mariana Islands 96950
(670) 664-2120, FAX: (670) 664-2139

OHIO
Amos J. Loveday, Jr., SHPO
Ohio Historic Preservation Office
Ohio Historical Society
567 E. Hudson Street
Columbus, OH 43211-1030
(614) 297-2470, FAX: (614) 297-2496

Franco Ruffini, SA
Address, telephone, and FAX same as above.
E-mail: fruffini@freenet.columbus.oh.u

OKLAHOMA
J. Blake Wade, SHPO
Oklahoma Historical Society
Wiley Post Historical Bldg.
2100 N. Lincoln Blvd.
Oklahoma City, OK 73105
(405) 521-2491, FAX: (405) 521-2492

Robert L. Brooks, SA
Oklahoma Archaeological Survey
111 E. Chesapeake
Norman, OK 73019-0575
(405) 325-7211, FAX: (405) 325-7604
E-mail: rbrooks@ou.edu
WWW: http://www.ou.edu/cas/archsur/

OREGON
Robert L. Meinen, SHPO
State Historic Preservation Office
Oregon Parks & Recreation Dept.
1115 Commercial Street NE
Salem, OR 97310-1001
(503) 378-5019, FAX: (503) 378-6447

Leland Gilsen, SA
Address and FAX same as above.
(503) 378-6508, ext. 232
E-mail: leland.gilsen@state.or.us
WWW: http://www.ncn.com/~gilsen

PALAU, REPUBLIC OF
Victoria N. Kanai, SHPO
Div. of Cultural Affairs, Ministry of Social Services
PO Box 100, Govt. of Palau
Koror, Palau 96940
(680) 488-2489, FAX: (680) 488-2657
E-mail: histpres@palaunet.com

PENNSYLVANIA
Brent D. Glass, SHPO
Pennsylvania Historical & Museum Commission
PO Box 1026
Harrisburg, PA 17108-1026
(717) 787-2891, FAX: (717) 783-1073

Stephen G. Warfel, SA
Senior Curator of Archaeology
The State Museum of Pennsylvania
PO Box 1026
Harrisburg, PA 17108-1026
(717) 783-2887, FAX: (717) 783-4558
E-mail: swarfel@state.pa.us

PUERTO RICO
Lilliane D. Lopez, SHPO
Office of Historic Preservation
Box 82, La Fortaleza
San Juan, PR 00901
(809) 721-3737, FAX: (809) 723-0957

Miguel Bonini, SA
Address, telephone, and FAX same as above.

RHODE ISLAND
Charlotte Taylor, Archaeological Education
Coordinator
Rhode Island Historical Preservation Commission
Old State House, 150 Benefit Street
Providence, RI 02903
(401) 277-2678, FAX: (401) 277-2968

Fredrick C. Williamson, SHPO
Address, telephone, and FAX same as above.

SOUTH CAROLINA
George L. Vogt, SHPO
Dept. of Archives & History
PO Box 11669, Capitol Station
Columbia, SC 29211-1669
(803) 734-8592, FAX: (803) 734-8820

Bruce E. Rippeteau, SA
SC Institute of Archaeology & Anthropology
1321 Pendleton Street
Columbia, SC 29208-0071
(803) 777-8170, FAX: (803) 254-1338
E-mail: rippeteau@sc.edu
WWW: http://www.cla.sc.edu/sciaa/sciaa.html

SOUTH DAKOTA
Jay D. Vogt, Acting SHPO
SD State Historical Society
Cultural Heritage Center
900 Governors Drive
Pierre, SD 57501-2217
(605) 773-3458, FAX: (605) 773-6041
E-mail: jayv@chc.state.sd.us

James K. Haug, SA
State Archaeological Research Center
2425 E. St. Charles Street, PO Box 1257
Rapid City, SD 57709-1257
(605) 394-1936, FAX: (605) 394-1941
E-mail: jhaug@silver.sdsmt.edu

TENNESSEE
Herbert L. Harper, Deputy SHPO
Tennessee Historical Commission
2941 Lebanon Road
Nashville, TN 37243-0442
(615) 532-1550, FAX: (615) 532-1549

George F. Fielder, Jr., SA
Tennessee Div. of Archaeology
5103 Edmonson Pike
Nashville, TN 37211
(615) 741-1588, FAX: (615) 741-7329
E-mail: nfielder@mail.state.tn.us

TEXAS
Curtis Tunnell, SHPO
Texas Historical Commission
PO Box 12276, Capitol Station
Austin, TX 78711-2276

(512) 463-6100, FAX: (512) 463-6095
E-mail: thc@nueces.thc.state.tx.us

Patricia Mercado-Allinger, SA
Address same as above.
(512) 463-6090, FAX: (512) 463-2530
E-mail: osa@nueces.thc.state.tx.us
WWW: http://www.thc.state.tx.us

UTAH
Max Evans, SHPO
Director, Utah State Historical Society
300 Rio Grande
Salt Lake City, UT 84101
(801) 533-3500, FAX: (801) 533-3503
E-mail: cehistry.ushs@email.state.ut.us

Kevin T. Jones, SA
Address and FAX same as above.
(801) 533-3524
E-mail: kjones@history.state.ut.us

VERMONT
Townsend Anderson, SHPO
Director, Agency of Commerce & Community
Development
Div. for Historic Preservation
135 State Street, Drawer 33
Montpelier, VT 05633-1201
(802) 828-3226, FAX: (802) 828-3206
E-mail: tanderson@gate.dca.state.vt.us
WWW: http://www.state.vt.us/dca/historic/tax-
sht.htm/html

Giovanna Peebles, SA
Address and FAX same as above.
(802) 828-3050
E-mail: gpeebles@gate.dca.state.vt.us

VIRGIN ISLANDS
Mrs. Beulah Dalmida-Smith, SHPO
Dept. of Planning & Natural Resources
Foster Plaza, 396-1 Anna's Retreat
St. Thomas, VI 00802
(809) 774-8605, FAX: (809) 774-5416

Elizabeth C. Righter, SA
Dept. of Planning & Natural Resources
Div. for Archaeology & Historic Preservation
Nisky Center, Suite 321
St. Thomas, VI 00802
(809) 774-3320, FAX: (809) 775-5706

VIRGINIA
H. Alexander Wise, Jr., SHPO
Director, Dept. of Historic Resources
221 Governor Street
Richmond, VA 23219
(804) 786-3143, FAX: (804) 225-4261

M. Catherine Slusser, SA
Address, telephone, and FAX same as above.

WASHINGTON
David M. Hansen, SHPO
Dept. of Community, Trade, & Economic
Development
Offict of Archaeology & Historic Preservation
111 West 21st Avenue, SW, KL-11
PO Box 48343
Olympia, WA 98504-8343

(206) 753-4011, FAX: (206) 586-0250
E-mail: davidII@acted.wa.gov

Robert Whitlam, SA
Address and FAX same as above.
(206) 753-4405
E-mail: robw@cted.wa.gov

WEST VIRGINIA
Renay Conlin, SHPO
Div. of Culture & History
1900 Kanawha Blvd. East
Charleston, WV 25305-0300
(304) 558-0220 ext. 112, FAX: (304) 558-2779

Patrick Trader, SA
Address and FAX same as above.
(304) 558-0220 ext. 179

WISCONSIN
Jeff Dean, SHPO
State Historical Society of Wisconsin
Div. of Historic Preservation
816 State Street
Madison, WI 53706
(608) 264-6500, FAX: (608) 624-6404
E-mail: jmdean@facstaff.wisc.edu

Robert A. Birmingham, SA
Address and FAX same as above.
(608) 264-6495
E-mail: bob.birmingham@mail.admin.wisc.edu

WYOMING
John Keck, SHPO
State Historic Preservation Office
Dept. of Commerce
6101 Yellowstone
Cheyenne, WY 82002
(307) 777-7697, FAX: (307) 777-6421
E-mail: jkeck@missc.state.wy.us

Mark E. Miller, SA
University of Wyoming
Box 3431, University Station
Laramie, WY 82070
(307) 766-5301, FAX: (307) 766-4052
E-mail: mmiller@uwyo.edu

AFFILIATED INSTITUTIONS & RELATED ORGANIZATIONS

Below is a list of affiliated institutions and related organizations which will inform you further about archaeology both nationally and internationally. This list is by no means complete for there are any number of other organizations which deal with archaeology. The list is arranged in the following geographical areas: 1) International/US National, 2) USA State, and 4) Canadian Province.

Advisory Council on Historic Preservation
The Old Post Office Building
1100 Pennsylvania Avenue, NW, Suite 809
Washington, DC 20004
(202) 606-8503, FAX: (202) 606-8647
E-mail: achp@achp.gov
WWW: http://www.achp.gov

Advisory Council on Underwater Archaeology
1900 North Chaparral Street
Corpus Christi, TX 78401
(512) 883-2863, FAX: (512) 884-7392

Albright Institute of Archaeological Research
656 Beacon Street, 5th Floor
Boston, MA 02215-2010
(617) 353-6570, FAX: (617) 353-6575
E-mail: asor@bu.edu
WWW: http://scholar.cc.emory.edu/scripts/ASOR/wfaiar.html

>   26 Salah ed-Din St.
>   PO Box 19096
>   91190 Jerusalem, ISRAEL
>   (972) 2 6282131, FAX: (972) 2 6264424
>   E-mail: foxi@vms.HUJI.ac.il

American Academy in Rome
7 East 60th Street
New York, NY 10022
(212) 751-7200, FAX: (212) 751-7220
E-mail: aainfo@aarome.org
WWW: http://aarome.org/

>   Via Angelo Masina, 5
>   00153 Rome, Italy
>   (39) 6 5846431, FAX: (39) 6 5810788

American Anthropological Association
4350 N. Fairfax Drive, Suite 640
Arlington, VA 22203
(703) 528-1902, FAX: (703) 528-3546
WWW: http://www.ameranthassn.org

American Antiquarian Society (AAS)
185 Salisbury Street
Worcester, MA 01609-1634
(508) 752-5813
WWW: gopher://mark.mwa.org/

American Association for State & Local History
530 Church Street, Suite 600
Nashville, TN 37219-2325
(615) 255-2971, FAX: (615) 255-2979

American Association for the Advancement of Science
1200 New York Avenue, NW
Washington, DC 20005-3920
(202) 326-6670, FAX: (202) 371-9849
WWW: http://www.aaas.org/

American Association of Museums
1575 Eye Street, N.W., Suite 400
Washington, DC 20005

(202) 289-1818, FAX: (202) 289-6578
WWW: http://www.aam-us.org

American Association of Physical Anthropologists
Attn: Dr. Mark L. Weiss
Wayne State University, Dept. of Anthropology
Detroit, MI 48202
(313) 577-2552
E-mail: mweiss@sun.science.wayne.edu

American Center for Oriental Research (ACOR)
656 Beacon Street, 5th Floor
Boston, MA 02215-2010
(617) 353-6570, FAX: (617) 353-6575
E-mail: acor@bu.edu
WWW: http://scholar.cc.emory.edu/scripts/ASOR/acor.html

>   PO Box 2470
>   Jebel Amman
>   Amman, Jordan
>   (962) 6 846117, FAX: (962) 6 844181
>   E-mail: ACOR@go.com.jo

American Council of Learned Societies
228 East 45th Street
New York, NY 10017-3398
FAX: (212) 949-8058
WWW: http://www.acls.org/

American Cultural Resources Association (ARCA)
c/o New South Associates
6150 East Ponce de Leon Avenue
Stone Mountain, GA 30083
(770) 498-5159, FAX: (770) 498-3809
E-mail: tomwheaton@aol.com
WWW: http://www.mindspring.com/~wheaton/ACRA.html

American Institute for Maghrib Studies (AIMS)
Brigham Young University, Dept. of Political Science
Provo, UT 84602
(801) 378-3409, FAX: (801) 378-5730
E-mail: Donna_Bowen@byu.edu

American Institute for the Conservation of Historic & Artistic Works
1717 K Street, NW, Suite 301
Washington, DC 20036
(202) 452-9545, FAX: (202) 452-9328
E-mail: vnyaic@aol.com
WWW: http://palimpsest.stanford.edu/aic/

American Institute for Yemeni Studies (AIYS)
PO Box 311
Ardmore, PA 19003-0311
(610) 896-5412, FAX: (610) 896-9049
E-mail: mellis@mail.sas.upenn.edu

American Institute of Bangladesh Studies (AIBS)
U.S. Contact: Craig Baxter
Dept. of Political Science, Juniata College
Huntington, PA 16652
(814) 641-3646, FAX: (814) 641-3695
E-mail: baxter@juniata.edu

American Institute of Indian Studies (AIIS)
U.S. Contact: Kaye Hill
University of Chicago
1130 East 59th Street, 412 Foster Hall
Chicago, IL 60637
(773) 702-2075, FAX: (312) 702-6636
E-mail: kayehill@midway.uchicago.edu

American Institute of Iranian Studies (AIIS)
U.S. Contact: William Hanaway
19 Farm Road
Wayne, PA 19087
(610) 687-4714, FAX: (610) 687-2181
E-mail: whanaway@mec.sas.upenn.edu

American Institute of Pakistan Studies (AIPS)
Wake Forest University
C-301 Tribble Hall, PO Box 7568
Winston-Salem, NC 27109
(910) 758-5453, FAX: (910) 758-6104
E-mail: ckennedy@wfu.edu

American Numismatic Society
Broadway at 155th Street
New York, NY 10032
(212) 234-3130, FAX: (212) 234-3381
E-mail: info@amnumsoc.org
WWW: http://www.amnumsoc2.org/

American Oriental Society
University of Michigan, Hatcher Graduate Library
Ann Arbor, MI 48109-1205
(313) 647-4760, FAX: (313) 763-6743
E-mail: jrodgers@umich.edu
WWW: http://www-personal.umich.edu/~jrodgers/

American Philological Association
19 University Place, Rm. 328
New York University
New York, NY 10003-4556
(212) 998-3575, FAX: FAX: (212) 995-4814
E-mail: american.philological@nyu.edu
WWW: http://scholar.cc.emory.edu/scripts/APA/APA-MENU.html

American Research Center in Egypt (ARCE)
30 East 20th Street, Suite 401
New York, NY 10003-1310
(212) 529-6661, FAX: (212) 529-6856
E-mail: arce.center@nyu.edu
WWW: http://www.arce.org/

    Cairo Director
    2 Midan Qasr el-Doubara
    Garden City, Cairo, Arab Republic of Egypt
    (20) 3548239 , FAX: (20) 3553052
    E-mail: arce@brainy1.ie-eg.com

American Research Institute in Syria
PO Box 1504A, Yale Station
New Haven, CT 06520-7425
E-mail: leilan@yalevm.cis.yale.edu

American Research Institute in Turkey
The University of Pennsylvania Museum
33rd & Spruce Streets
Philadelphia, PA 19104-6324
(215) 898-3474, FAX: (215) 898-0657
E-mail: leinwand@sas.upenn.edu

Üvez Sokak No. 5
Arnavutköy
Istanbul 80820, Turkey
(90) 212 257 8111, FAX: (90) 212 257 8369
E-mail: gwood@boun.edu.tr (not fully reliable)

Horasan Sokak 2/2
Gazi Osman Pasa
Ankara 06700, Turkey
(90) 312 447 1266, FAX: (90) 312 446 7652
E-mail: arit-o@tr-net.net.tr

American School of Classical Studies at Athens
6-8 Charlton Street
Princeton, NJ 08648
(609) 683-0800, FAX: (609) 924-0578
E-mail: ascsa@ascsa.org
WWW: http://www.ascsa.org/

    54 Souidias Street
    GR-106 76 Athens, Greece
    (30) 1 723 6313, FAX: (30) 1 725 0584

American Schools of Oriental Research (ASOR)
656 Beacon Street, 5th Floor
Boston, MA 02215-2010
(617) 353-6570, FAX: (617) 353-6575
E-mail: asor@bu.edu
WWW: http://scholar.cc.emory.edu/scripts/ASOR/ASOR-MENU.html

Amerind Foundation, Inc.
2100 N. Amerind Road, PO Box 400
Dragoon, AZ 85609
(520) 586-3666, FAX: (520) 586-4679
E-mail: amerind@theriver.com

Anasazi Heritage Center
27501 Highway 184
Dolores, CO 81323
(970) 881-4811, FAX: (970) 882-7035
WWW: http://www.co.blm.gov/ahc/hmepge.htm

Ancient Near Eastern Society
Jewish Theological Seminary of America
3080 Broadway
New York, NY 10027
(212) 678-8856, FAX: (212) 678-8961

Andover Foundation for Archaeological Research
3 Longwood Drive
Andover, MA 01810
(508) 470-0840

Anglo-Israel Archaeological Society
3 St. John's Wood Road
London NW8 8RB, United Kingdom
(44) 171 286 1176

Archaeological Communications
Public Outreach & Education
5267 Guilford Avenue
Indianapolis, IN 46220
(317) 925-6986

Archaeological Conservancy
5301 Central Ave., NE, Suite 1218
Albuquerque, NM 87108-1517
(505) 266-1540
E-mail: archcons@nm.net
WWW: http://www.gorp.com/archcons/

Archaeology Abroad
31-34 Gordon Square
London WC1H 0PY, United Kingdom
(44) 0171 387 7050, ext. 4750, FAX: (44) 0171 383-2572
E-mail: arch.abroad@ucl.ac.uk
WWW: http://britac3.britac.ac.uk/cba/archabroad/facts.html

Association for Gravestone Studies
278 Main Street, Suite 207
Greenfield, MA 01301-3230

Association for Preservation Technology
PO Box 3511
Williamsburg, VA 23187-3511

Australasian Society for Historical Archaeology
University of Sydney
Box 220, Holme Building
Sydney, 2006 NSW, Australia
(61) 02 692 2763, FAX: (61) 02 692 4889

Australian Archaeology Association
c/o Dept. of Anthropology
University of Queensland
Brisbane, Queensland 4072, Australia

Australian Institute of Maritime Archaeology
c/o Dept. of Maritime Archaeology
W.A. Maritime Museum
Cliff Street
Freemantle, Western Australia, Australia

Biblical Archaeology Society
4710 41st Street, NW
Washington, DC 20016
(202) 364-3300, FAX: (202) 364-2636
E-mail: basedit@clark.net

British Archaeological Association
19 Shaston Crescent
Dorchester, Dorset DT1 2EB, United Kingdom

British Archaeological Mission in Yemen
c/o The British Academy
20-21 Cornwall Terrace
London NW1 4QP, England, United Kingdom

British Institute at Amman for Archaeology & History
29 The Walk, Southport
Lancs PR8 4BG, United Kingdom
(44) 1704 569664, FAX: same
E-mail: cm@biaah.demon.co.uk

British Institute in Eastern Africa
Box 30710
Nairobi, Kenya
254-2-43330/43721, FAX: 254-2-43365
E-mail: britinst@arcc.or.ke

British Institute of Archaeology at Ankara
Senate House, Malet Street
London WC1E 7HU, England, United Kingdom
(44) 0171 436 8649, FAX: same

British Institute of Persian Studies
c/o Institute of Archaeology
University College London
31-34 Gordon Square
London WC1H 0PY, United Kingdom
(44) 1223 249700

British School at Athens
Senate House, 3rd Floor
Malet Street
London WC1E 7HU, United Kingdom
(44) 171 3239597, FAX: (44) 171 3239598

British School at Rome
Via Gramsci 61
00197 Rome, Italy
(39) 6 3230743, FAX: (39) 6 3221201
WWW: http://britac3.britac.ac.uk/institutes/rome

British School of Archaeology in Iraq
31–34 Gordon Square
London WC1H 0PY, United Kingdom
(44) 171 733 8912

Canadian Archaeological Association/
Association Canadienne d'Archéologie
Space 162, Box 127
3170 Tillicum Road
Victoria, British Columbia V9A 7H7, Canada
(604) 388-5844, FAX: (604) 388-4490
WWW: http://www.pictographics.com/caa.homepage

Center for American Archaeology (CAA)
Kampsville Archaeological Center
PO Box 366
Kampsville, IL 62053
(618) 653-4316, FAX: (618) 653-4232

Center for Anthropological Studies
PO Box 14576
Albuquerque, NM 87191
(505) 296-6336

Center for Archaeoastronomy
PO Box X
College Park, MD 20741-3022
(301) 864-6637, FAX: (301) 699-5337
E-mail: jcarlson@deans.umd.edu
WWW: http://www.wam.umd.edu/~tlaloc/archastro/

Center for Archaeological Investigations
Southern Illinois University
Carbondale, IL 62901
(618) 453-5031, FAX: (618) 453-3253
E-mail: bbutler@siu.edu
WWW: http://www.siu.edu/~cai/index.html

Center for Archaeological Sciences
c/o Dr. George Brook
Geography Dept., University of Georgia
Athens, GA 30602
(706) 542-2856, FAX: (706) 542-2425
E-mail: gabrook@uga.cc.uga.edu

Center for Archaeological Studies
Boston University
675 Commonwealth Avenue
Boston, MA 02215
(617) 353-3415, FAX: (617) 353-6800
WWW: http://web.bu.edu/ARCHAEOLOGY/

Center for Archaeology in the Public Interest
Indiana University-Purdue University
Dept. of Anthropology
425 University Blvd., Cavanaugh Hall 433
Indianapolis, IN 46202-5140
(317) 274-1406, FAX: (317) 274-2347

Center for Materials Research in Archaeology & Ethnology
Massachusetts Institute of Technology, Rm. 8-138
Cambridge, MA 02139
(617) 253-1375

Center for Prehistoric Archaeology
P.D. #1, Box 414
Spring City, PA 19475
(215) 495-7459

Center for Remote Sensing
Boston University
675 Commonwealth Avenue
Boston, MA 02215
(617) 353-9709, FAX: (617) 353-3200
WWW: http://crs-www.bu.edu/crs.home.html

Center for Spanish Colonial Archaeology
4060 Morena Blvd., Suite G-250
San Diego, CA 92117
E-mail: acohen@simdiego.com

Center for the Study of Architecture (CSA)
PO Box 60
Bryn Mawr, PA 19010
(215) 526-7925, FAX: (215) 526-7926
E-mail: neiteljo@brynmawr.edu
WWW: http://csaws.brynmawr.edu:443/web1/csa.html

Center for the Study of Eurasian Nomads
Kazakh/American Research Project
1607 Walnut Street
Berkeley, CA 94709
(510) 549-3708, FAX: (510) 849-3137
E-mail: jkimball@garnet.berkeley.edu
WWW: WWW: http://garnet.berkeley.edu/~jkimball

Central States Archaeological Societies, Inc.
646 Knierim Place
Kirkwood, Missouri 63122

Centre d'Etudes Maghrébines à Tunis (CEMAT)
B.P. 404
1049 Tunis-Hached, Tunisia
(216) 1 246 219, FAX: (216) 1 348 378

Centro Camuno di Studi Preistorici
Attn: Dr. Emmanuel Anati
25044 Capo di Ponte
Val Camonica, Brescia, Italy
(39) 364 42091, FAX: (39) 364 42572
E-mail: ccsp@globalnet.it
WWW: http://www.globalnet.it/ccsp/ccsp.htm

Channel Islands Marine Archaeology Resources (CMAR)
16902 Cod Circle, #C
Huntington Beach, CA 92647
E-mail: mnorder@aol.com
WWW: http://weber.u.washington.edu/~nailgun/cmar/

Chicora Foundation, Inc.
PO Box 8664
Columbia, SC 29202-8664
(803) 787-6910

Colonial Williamsburg Foundation
Dept. of Archaeological Research
PO Box 1776
Williamsburg, VA 23187-1776
(804) 220-7330

Conference on New England Archaeology
c/o Paul Robinson
Rhode Island Historic Preservation Commission
150 Benefit Street
Providence, RI 02903
(401) 277-2678

Conservation, Environment & Historic Preservation (CEHP)
1627 K Street, NW, Suite 300
Washington, DC 20006
(202) 293-1774, FAX: (202) 293-1782
E-mail: cehp@mci.mail.com

Consortium of Social Science Associations
1522 K Street, NW, Suite 836
Washington, DC 20005
(202) 842-3525, FAX: (202) 842-2788
E-mail: socsciassn.@aol.com

Council for British Archaeology
Bowes Morrell House
111 Walmgate
York Y01 2UA, United Kingdom
(44) 1904 671417, FAX: (44) 1904 671384
E-mail: archaeology@compuserve.com
WWW: http://britac3.britac.ac.uk/cba/

Council for Northeast Historical Archaeology
Boston University, Dept. of Archaeology
675 Commonwealth Avenue
Boston, MA 02215
(617) 353-3415, FAX: (617) 353-6800

Council of American Overseas Research Centers
Smithsonian Institution, IC 3123 MRC 705
Washington, DC 20560
(202) 842-8636, FAX: (202) 786-2430
E-mail: caorc102@sivm.si.edu

Council on America's Military Past
518 West Why Worry Lane
Phoenix, AZ 85021

Council on International Educational Exchange (CIEE)
205 East 42nd Street
New York, NY 10017-5706
(800) 641-CIEE
E-mail: univprogs@ciee.org or
WWW: http://www.ciee.org/

Council on New England Archaeology
University of Massachusetts, Archaeological Services
T.E.I. Blaisdell House, PO Box 0820
Amherst, MA 01003-0820
(413) 545-1552, FAX: (413) 545-2304

Crow Canyon Center for Southwestern Archaeology
23390 Country Road K
Cortez, CO 81321
(800) 422-8975, (970) 565-8975, FAX: (970) 565-4859
E-mail: sgallagher@crowcanyon.org
WWW: http://www.crowcanyon.org

Current Archaeology
9, Nassington Road
London, NW3 2TX, United Kingdom
& FAX: (44) 171 4357517
E-mail: selkirk@cix.compulink.co.uk
WWW: http://www.compulink.co.uk/~archaeology/

Cyprus-American Archaeological Research Institute (CAARI)
656 Beacon Street, 5th Floor
Boston, MA 02215-2010
(617) 343-6570, FAX: (617) 353-6575
E-mail: asor@bu.edu
WWW: http://www.caari.org/

11 Andreas Demetriou Street
Nicosia 1066, CYPRUS
(357) 245 1832, FAX: (357) 246 1147
E-mail: caaridir@spidernet.com.cy

Deer Valley Rock Art Center
Arizona State University
PO Box 872402
Tempe, AZ 85287-2402

Desert Research Institute
University of Nevada System
PO Box 60220
Reno, NV 89506
(702) 673-7303

Earthwatch
680 Mount Auburn Street, PO Box 403
Watertown, MA 02272
(800) 776-0188
(617) 926-8200, FAX: (617) 926-8532
E-mail: info@earthwatch.org
WWW: http://www.earthwatch.org

Eastern Sites Research Society
Long Hill
Rowley, MA 01969
(617) 948-2410

Egypt Exploration Society
3, Doughty Mews
London WC1N 2PG, United Kingdom
(44) 0171 2421880, FAX: (44) 0171 4046118
E-mail: eeslondon@compuserve.com.uk

Epigraphic Society
6625 Bamburgh Drive
San Diego, CA 92117
(619) 571-1344

Etruscan Foundation
Fisher Mews, Suite D-2
377 Fisher Road
Grosse Point, MI 48230
(313) 882-2462, FAX: (313) 882-2462

Europa Student Travel Centre
The Director
Dept. of Archaeology
via Mezzo-Cannone,119
80134 Naples, Italy

Expedition Advisory Centre
Royal Geographical Society
1 Kensington Gore
London SW7 2AR, England, United Kingdom
(44) 171 5913030, FAX: (44) 171 5913031
E-mail: eac@rgs.org

Foundation for the Advancement of Mesoamerican Studies
268 South Suncoast Blvd.
Crystal River, FL 34429
(352) 795-5990/7721, FAX: (352) 795-1970
E-mail: FAMSIFL@aol.com

Four Corners School of Outdoor Education
PO Box 1029
Monticello, UT 84535
(800) 525-4456, FAX: (801) 587-2193
E-mail: fcs@igc.apc.org
WWW: http://olmkt.com/fourcorners/

Friends of Archaeology
Center for Archaeological Research
University of Texas at San Antonio
San Antonio, TX 78249-0658
(210) 458-4378, FAX: (210) 458-4397
E-mail: car@lonestar.edu
WWW: http://www.csbs.utsa.edu/research/car/index.htm

Getty Conservation Institute
1200 Getty Center Drive, Suite 700
Los Angeles, CA 90049-1684
(310) 440-7325, FAX: (310) 440-7702
WWW: http://www.getty.edu/gci/

Getty Research Institute for the History of Art & the Humanities
1200 Getty Center Drive, Suite 1100
Los Angeles, CA 90049-1688
(310) 440-9335, FAX: (310) 440-7779
WWW: http://www.getty.edu/gri

Historical Archaeology Conference of the Upper Midwest
c/o John P. McCarthy
Institute for Minnesota Archaeology
2635 4th Street, SE
Minneapolis, MN 55414
(612) 379-8364, FAX: (612) 379-8439
E-mail: JPMcc@@MTN.ORG

Institute for American Indian Studies
38 Curtis Road, PO Box 1260
Washington, CT 06793-0260
(203) 868-0518

Institute for Mediterranean Studies
7086 East Aracoma Drive
Cincinnati, OH 45237
(513) 631-4749, FAX: (513) 631-1715

Institute for Mesoamerican Studies
University at Albany, SUNY
Social Science 263, 1400 Washington Avenue
Albany, NY 12222
(518) 442-4722, FAX: (518) 442-5710

Institute of Archaeology
University of California
A210 Fowler, Box 951510
Los Angeles, CA 90024-1510
(310) 206-8934, FAX: (310) 206-4723
E-mail: ndavis@ioa.sscnet.ucla.edu
WWW: http://www.ioa.ucla.edu

Institute of Egyptian Art & Archaeology
3750 Norriswood Avenue
Communication & Fine Arts Bldg, Rm. 142
Memphis, TN 38152
(901) 678-2555, FAX: (901) 678-5118
WWW: http://www.memphis.edu/egypt/main.html

Institute of Field Archaeologists
The University of Manchester
Oxford Road
Manchester M13 9PL, United Kingdom
(44) 161 2752304

Institute of Museum Services
1100 Pennsylvania Avenue, NW
Program Office, Rm. 609
Washington, DC 20506
(202) 606-8539, FAX: (202) 606-8591
E-mail: imsinfo@ims.fed.us
WWW: http://www.ims.fed.us/

Institute of Nautical Archaeology
PO Drawer HG
College Station, TX 77841-5137
(409) 845-6694, FAX: (409) 847-9260
WWW: http://nautarch.tamu.edu/napina.htm

International Association for Obsidian Studies
San Jose State University, Dept. of Anthropology
San Jose, CA 95192-0113
(408) 997-9183, FAX: (408) 924-5348
E-mail: skinncr@csos.orst.edu

International Association of Egyptologists
c/o Dr. R. Freed
Dept. of Ancient Egyptian, Nubian, & Near Eastern Art
Museum of Fine Arts
465 Huntington Avenue
Boston, MA 02115
WWW: http://www.ashmol.ox.ac.uk/IAEPage.html

International Catacomb Society
61 Beacon Street
Boston, MA 02108
(617) 742-1285

International Centre for the Study of Preservation & Restoration of Cultural Property
13 Via di San Michele
I-00153 Rome, RM, Italy
(39) 6 585 531, FAX: (39) 6 5855 3349
E-mail: iccrom@iccrom.org
WWW: http://www.icomos.org/iccrom/

International Committee for the Conservation of Mosaics
Consorzio ARKE'
Via Valdieri 23
00135 Rome, Italy

International Council for Archeozoology
National Museum for Natural History
Smithsonian Institution
Washington, DC 20560
(202) 786-2503

International Council on Monuments & Sites (ICOMOS)
United States Committee
401 F Street, NW, #331
Washington, DC 20001-2728
(202) 842-1862, FAX: (202) 842-1861
WWW: http://www.icomos.org/

International Union of Prehistoric & Protohistoric Sciences
University Museum
33rd & Spruce Streets
Philadelphia, PA 19104-6324
(215) 898-4050, FAX: (215) 898-0657

Israel Antiquities Authority
Rockefeller Museum Bldg., PO Box 586
91004 Jerusalem
ISRAEL, , FAX: (972) 2 5602628
E-mail: harriet@israntique.org.il
WWW: http://www.israel-mfa.gov.il/archdigs.html

Israel Society for Assyriology & Ancient Near Eastern Studies
S.N. Kramer Institute of Assyriology, Bar-Ilan University
Ramat-Gan 52900, Israel
(972) 6 6927704, FAX: (972) 6 6927737
E-mail: amitzh@ashur.cc.biu.ac.il
WWW: http://www.biu.ac.il/~amitzh/research/index.htm

Maritime Archaeological & Historical Research Institute
PO Box 275
Bristol, ME 04539
(207) 677-2534

Maritime Archaeological & Historical Society
L'Enfant Plaza, PO Box 44382
Washington, DC 20028-4382

Midwest Bioarcheology & Forensic Anthropology Association
University of Indianapolis, Archeology & Forensics Laboratory
1400 East Hanna Avenue
Indianapolis, IN 46227-3697
(317) 788-3486 / 788-3565, FAX: (317) 788-3569
E-mail: narocki@gandlf.uindy.edu

Midwestern Archaeological Research Center
Illinois State University, Dept. 4641
Normal, IL 61761
(309) 438-2271

Ministère de la Culture, Direction du Patrimoine
Sous-Direction de l'Archéologie
4, rue d'Aboukir
75002 Paris, France
(33) 40 15 77 17
WWW: http://www.culture.fr/

National Association of State Archaeologists
WWW: http://www.lib.uconn.edu/NASA/

National Conference of State Historic Preservation Officers
444 North Capitol Street, NW
Hall of States, Suite 342
Washington, DC 20001
(202) 624-5465, FAX: (202) 624-5419
WWW: http://www2.cr.nps.gov/tps/shpolist.html

National Endowment for the Humanities
1100 Pennsylvania Ave., N.W.
Washington, DC 20506
(202) 606-8400
E-mail: info@neh.fed.us
WWW: http://www.neh.fed.us

National Geographic Society
Committee for Research & Exploration
1145 17th Street NW
Washington, DC 20036
(202) 828-5480, FAX: (202) 429-5729

National Institute for the Conservation of Cultural Property
3299 K Street, NW, Suite 602
Washington, DC 20037
(202) 625-1495, FAX: (202) 624-1485
E-mail: info@nic.org
WWW: http://www.nic.org

National Maritime Historical Society
5 John Walsh Blvd., PO Box 68
Peekskill, NY (914) 737-7878
(914) 737-7878
E-mail: seahistory@aol.com
WWW: http://www.marineart.com/nmhs/index.shtml

National Parks & Conservation Association
1776 Massachusetts Avenue, NW
Washington, DC 20036
(202) 223-6722, FAX: (202) 659-0650

National Preservation Institute
PO Box 1702
Alexandria, VA 22313
(202) 393-0038

National Science Foundation
4201 Wilson Boulevard
Arlington, VA 22230

National Trust for Historic Preservation
1785 Massachusetts Avenue, NW
Washington, DC 20036
(202) 673-4000, FAX: (202) 673-4038
WWW: http://www.nthp.org/

Nautical Archaeology Society
Membership Secretary
206 Mooreview Way, Skipton
N Yorks BD23 2TN, United Kingdom

 USA Administrator
 303 Brantley Drive
 Longwood, Florida 32779
 (407) 788-9006, FAX: (407) 788-4503

Netherlands Institute for Archaeology &
Arabic Studies in Cairo
PO Box 50
11211 Zamalek, Cairo, Egypt
20-2-3400076, FAX: 20-2-3404376
E-mail: niaasc@frcu.eun.eg.

New England Antiquities Research Association
305 Academy Road
Pembroke, NH 03275
(603) 485-5665, FAX: (508) 485-2395

Northeastern Anthropological Association
University of Massachusetts
Dept. of Anthropology, Machmer Hall
Amherst, MA 01003
E-mail: neaa@maple.lemoyne.edu
WWW: http://web.lemoyne.edu/~bucko/neaa.html

Organization of Irish Archaeologists
71 Carmel Street
Belfast BT7 1QE, Ireland

The Oriental Institute
1155 East 58th Street
Chicago, IL 60637
(312) 702-9514
WWW: http://www-oi.uchicago.edu/OI/default.html

Paleoanthropology Society
National Science Foundation
Archaeology Program
4201 Wilson Boulevard
Arlington, VA 22230
(703) 306-1751, FAX: (703) 306-0486

Palestine Exploration Fund
2 Hinde Mews
Marylebone Lane
London W1M 5RR, United Kingdom
(44) 0171 935 5379

Pan-American Institute of Maritime Archaeology
43 Melrose Street
San Francisco, CA 94131
(415) 334-3825
E-mail: jbeshears@aol.com
WWW: http://www.wbm.ca/users/nfisher/index.html

Passport in Time (PIT)
Attn: Carol Ellick
PO Box 31315
Tucson, AZ 85751-1315 20036
(800) 281-9176 or (520) 722-2716, FAX: (520) 298-7044
E-mail: SRIArc@aol.com

Prehistoric Society
University College London, Institute of Archaeology
31-34 Gordon Square
London WC1H OPY, United Kingdom

Preservation Action
1350 Connecticut Avenue, NW
Washington, DC 20037
(202) 659-0915, FAX: (202) 659-0189
E-mail: preservationaction@worldnet.att.net
WWW: http://www.preservenet.cornell.edu/presaction/home.htm

Russian Academy of Science, Institute of Archaeology
Dm. Ulyanov St. 19
117036 Moscow V-36, Russia
FAX: (095) 1260630

Safad & Galilee Reseach Center
Safad Branch, Bar Ilan University
Ramat-Gan 52900, Israel
(972) 6 6927704, FAX: (972) 6 6927737
E-mail: amitzh@ashur.cc.biu.ac.il
WWW: http://www.biu.ac.il/~amitzh/research/index.htm

School of American Research
Box 2188
Santa Fe, NM 87504-2188
(505) 982-3583

Shaker Heritage Society
Shaker Meeting House
Albany Shaker Road
Albany, NY 12211

Society for American Archaeology
900 Second Street, NE, Suite 12
Washington, DC 20002-3557
(202) 789-8200, FAX: (202) 789-0284
E-mail: headquarters@saa.org
WWW: http://www.saa.org/

Society for Arabian Studies
c/o The British Academy
20-21 Cornwall Terrace
London NW1 4QP, England, United Kingdom

Society for Archaeological Sciences, Radiocarbon Lab
University of California, Dept. of Anthropology
Riverside, CA 92521
(909) 787-5521, FAX: (909) 787-5409
E-mail: beards@citrus.ucr.edu
WWW: http://www.wisc.edu/anthropology/sas/sas.htm

Society for Clay Pipe Research
13 Sommerville Road
Bishopston, Bristol BS7 9AD, United Kingdom
(44) 0117 924 7662

Society for Historical Archaeology
PO Box 30446
Tucson, AZ 85751-0446
(602) 886-8006, FAX: (602) 886-0182
E-mail: sha@azstarnet.com
WWW: http://www.azstarnet.com/~sha/

Society for Industrial Archaeology
Michigan Technological University, Dept. of Social Sciences
Houghton, MI 49931-1295
(906) 487-2113, FAX: (906)487-2468
E-mail: pem-194@mtu.edu

Society for Libyan Studies
31-34 Gordon Square
London WC1H OPY, England, United Kingdom
WWW: http://britac3.britac.ac.uk/institutes/libya/index.html

Society for Post-Medieval Archaeology
20 Lytton Road
Clarendon Park, Leicester LE2 1WJ, United Kingdom
(44) 0116 270 7999

Society for South Asian Studies
The Main Wing, Elsworth Manor
Elsworth, Cambs CB3 8HY, United Kingdom
0171 636 1555, FAX: 0171 323 8999

Society for the Preservation of New England Antiquities Harrison
Gray Otis House, 141 Cambridge Street
Boston, MA 02114
(617) 227-3956

Society of Africanist Archaeologists
Bowdoin College, Dept. of Sociology & Anthropology
Brunswick, ME 04011
207-725-3924, FAX: 207-725-3023
E-mail: smaceach@pdar.bowdoin.edu
WWW: http://www.clas.ufl.eda/users/sbrandt

Society of Architectural Historians
1365 Astor Street
Chicago, IL 60610-2144
(312) 573-1365, FAX: (312) 573-1141
WWW: http://www.SAH.org

Society of Bead Researchers
PO Box 7304
Eugene, OR 97401
WWW: http://www.spiretech.com/~lester/sbr/index.htm

Society of Professional Archaeologists (SOPA)
Southern Methodist University, Dept. of Anthropology
3225 Daniel Avenue
Dallas, TX 75275-0336
(214) 768-2924, FAX: (214) 768-2906
E-mail: fwendorf@mail.smu.edu
WWW: http://www.smu.edu/~anthrop/sopa.html

South Carolina Institute of Archaeology & Anthropology
University of South Carolina
1321 Pendleton St.
Columbia, SC 29208-0071
(803) 777-8170, 734-0567, 799-1963, FAX: (803) 254-1338
WWW: http://www.cla.sc.edu/sciaa/sciaa.html

Southeastern Archaeological Conference
University of Mississippi, Dept. of Sociology & Anthropology
University, MS 38677
(601) 232-7339, FAX: (601) 232-7129
E-mail: sayjay@umsvm

Student Conservation Association
PO Box 550
Charlestown, NH 03603
(603) 543-1700, FAX: (603) 543-1828
WWW: http://www.sca-inc.org

Transitions Abroad
18 Hulst Road, PO Box 1300
Amherst, MA 01004-1300
(413) 256-3414, FAX: (413) 256-0373
E-mail: trabroad@aol.com
WWW: transabroad.com

UNESCO
7, place de Fontenoy
75352 PARIS 07 SP, France
(33) 1 45 68 10 00, FAX: (33) 1 45 67 16 90
WWW: http://www.unesco.org/

United Archaeological Field Technicians
PO Box 2356
Weirton, WV 26062
(304) 797-0207

United States Department of Agriculture
Forest Service
Box 96090, 12th & Independence, SW
Washington, DC 20090-6090
(202) 205-1687, FAX: (202) 205-1145

United States Department of Defense
US Army Corps of Engineers
CECW-PP, Casimir Pulaski Bldg.
20 Massachusetts Ave., NW
Washington, DC 20314-1000
(202) 272-8731

United States Department of the Interior
Bureau of Land Management
18th & C Streets, NW
Washington, DC 20240
(202) 452-0330, FAX: (202) 452-7701
E-mail: jdouglas@wo.blm.gov
WWW: www.blm.gov/education/education.html

United States Department of the Interior
National Park Service, Archeology & Ethnography Program
PO Box 37127
Washington, DC 20013-7127
(202) 343-4101, FAX: (202) 523-1547
WWW: http://www.cr.nps.gov

United States Department of the Interior
National Park Service, Cultural Resource Management
PO Box 37127
Washington, DC 20013-7127
WWW: http://www.cr.nps.gov

United States Department of the Interior
National Park Service, Preservation Assistance Division
PO Box 37127
Washington, DC 20013-7127
(202) 343-9583, FAX: (202) 343-3803
WWW: http://www.cr.nps.gov

University Research Expeditions Program
University of California
Berkeley, CA 94720-7050
(510) 642-6586, FAX: (510) 642-6791
E-mail: urep@uclink.berkeley.edu
WWW: http://shanana.berkeley.edu/urep/

Vacation Work Publications
9 Park End Street
Oxford OX1 1HJ, United Kingdom
(44) 1865 241978, FAX: (44) 1865 790885

Vergilian Society
PO Box 817
Oxford, OH 45056
(513) 529-1482, FAX: (513) 529-1516
E-mail: dutra_jack@msmail.muohio.edu

West African Research Association (WARA)
U.S. Contact: Edris Makward
Dept. of African Languages & Literature
1454 Van Hise Hall
University of Wisconsin - Madison
Madison, WI 53706
(608) 262-2380, FAX: (608) 262-6998
E-mail: emakward@macc.wisc.edu

    B.P. 6228
    Dakar Etoile, Senegal
    (221) 214770, FAX: (221) 222345

Wickliffe Mounds Research Center
PO Box 155
Wickliffe, KY 42087
(502) 335-3681

World Archaeological Society
120 Lakewood Drive
Hollister, MO 65672
(417) 334-2377

Zuni Cultural Resource Enterprise
Pueblo of Zuni, PO Box 1149
Zuni, NM 87327
(505) 782-4814, FAX: (505) 782-2393
E-mail: zcre@nm.net

USA STATE ORGANIZATIONS

ALABAMA
Alabama Archaeological Society
13075 Moundville Archaeological Park
Moundville, AL 35474
(205) 371-6369

Alabama Preservation Alliance
PO Box 2228
Montgomery, AL 36102
(334) 438-7281, FAX: (205) 438-7056

ALASKA
Alaska Anthropological Association
PO Box 230032
Anchorage, AK 99523-0032
(907) 762-2630

Alaska Association for Historic Preservation
645 West 3rd Avenue
Anchorage, AK 99501-2124
(907) 333-4746, FAX: (907) 762-2628

ARIZONA
Arizona Archaeological Council
c/o SWAC, Inc.
114 North San Francisco Street, Suite 100
Flagstaff, AZ 86001

Arizona Archaeological & Historical Society
Arizona State Museum
University of Arizona
Tucson, AZ 85721
(602) 326-4544

ARKANSAS
Arkansas Archeological Society
PO Box 1222
Fayetteville, AR 72701-1222
(502) 575-3556, FAX: (501) 575-5453
E-mail: hadavis@comp.uark.edu
WWW: http://www.vark.edu/depts/4society/index.html

Arkansas Archeological Survey
PO Box 1249
Fayetteville, AR 72702-1249
(501) 575-3556

Historic Preservation Alliance of Arkansas
PO Box 305
Little Rock, AR 72203
(501) 372-4757

CALIFORNIA
Central Sierra Archaeological Society
PO Box 1147
Columbia, CA 95310

Coachella Valley Archaeological Society
PO Box 2344
Palm Springs, CA 92263
(619) 327-4801

Pacific Coast Archaeological Society
PO Box 10926
Costa Mesa, CA 92627

Sacramento Archaeological Society
PO Box 163287
Sacramento, CA 95816

San Diego County Archaeological Society
PO Box 81106
San Diego, CA 92138
(619) 538-0935

San Luis Obispo County Archaeological Society
PO Box 109
San Luis Obispo, CA 93406
(805) 544-0176

Society for California Archaeology
California State University
Department of Anthropology
Fullerton, CA 93634
(714) 256-0332

COLORADO
Colorado Archaeological Society
920 Balsam
Cortez, CO 81321
(303) 565-6454

Colorado Historical Society
Office of Archaeology and Historic Preservation
1300 Broadway
Denver, CO 80203-2137
(303) 866-3395, FAX: (303) 866-4464
E-mail: daleh@lynx.sni.net
WWW: http://www.aclin.org/other/historic/chs/index.html

CONNECTICUT
Archaeological Society of Connecticut
Archaeological Services, PO Box 386
Bethlehem, CT 06751
(203) 266-7741

Connecticut Trust for Historic Preservation
940 Whitney Avenue
Hamden, CT 06517-4002
(203) 562-6312, FAX: (203) 777-2203

DELAWARE
Archaeological Society of Delaware
PO Box 12483
Wilmington, DE 19850-2483

Preservation Delaware, Inc.
Goodstay Center
2600 Pennsylvania Avenue
Wilmington, DE 19806
(302) 651-9617, FAX: (302) 651-9603

DISTRICT OF COLUMBIA
Potomac River Archeology Survey
American University, Dept. of Anthropology
Washington, DC 20016-8003
(202) 885-1848, FAX: (202) 885-2182

FLORIDA
**Black Archives History & Research Foundation
of South Florida, Inc.**
Joseph Caleb Community Center
5400 NW 22nd Ave., Bldg. B, Suite 101
Miami, FL 33142

Florida Anthropological Society, Inc.
PO Box 82255
Tampa, FL 33682
(813) 991-4643
E-mail: tsimpson@luna.cas.usf.edu

Florida Archaeological Council
PO Box 5103
Sarasota, FL 34277-5103
(813) 925-9906, FAX: (813) 925-9767
E-mail: acimain@compuserve.com
WWW: http://www.aci.crmsvcs.com

Florida Trust for Historic Preservation
PO Box 11206
Tallahassee, FL 32302
(850) 224-8128, FAX: (850) 921-0150
E-mail: JCARPENTER@MAILdos.state.fl.us

GEORGIA
Georgia Trust for Historic Preservation, Inc.
1516 Peachtree Street, NW
Atlanta, GA 30309

Society for Georgia Archaeology
University of Georgia
Dept. of Anthropology
Athens, GA 30602
(404) 542-3922

HAWAII
Historic Hawaii Foundation
PO Box 1658
Honolulu, HI 96806
(808) 523-2900, FAX: (808) 523-0800
E-mail: hhfd@lava.net

IDAHO
Idaho Archaeological Society
PO Box 1888
Boise, Idaho 83707
(208) 345-0550

ILLINOIS
Illinois Association for Advancement of Archaeology
c/o Dickson Mounds Museum
10956 N. Dickson Mounds Road
Lewistown, IL 61542-9733

Cahokia Archaeological Society
c/o Cahokia Mounds State Historic Site, PO Box 681
Collinsville, Illinois 62234

Mississippi Valley Archaeological Society
RR #1, Box 63
Huntsville, Illinois 62344
(217) 667-2285

South Suburban Archaeological Society
18442 Gottschalk St.
Homewood, Illinois 60430

Two Rivers Archaeological Society
RR #1, Box 63
Huntsville, Illinois 62344
(217) 667-2285

INDIANA
Indiana Archaeological Society
Attn: Mark Clapp, Route 1, Box 74
New Richmond, IN 47967

Little Turtle Archaeological Research Society
Attn: Kris Richey, 871 West Ryan Road
Columbia City, IN 46725

Northwest Indiana Archaeological Assoc.
Attn: Shirley Anderson, 164 East 550S
Kouts, IN 46347
219-462-6039

Southern Indiana Archaeological Society
Attn: Steven Preflatish, PO Box 332
English, IN 47118

Upper White River Archaeological Society
Attn: Bill Deilkes, 2004 South Pershing
Muncie, IN 47302
765-286-5174

White River Valley Archaeological Association
Attn: Curtis Tomak, 50 Lewis Place
Martinsville, IN 46151
765-342-9794

IOWA
Iowa Archaeological Society
The University of Iowa, Eastlawn Bldg.
Iowa City, IA 52242
(319) 335-2389

Iowa Historic Preservation Alliance
PO Box 814
Mount Pleasant, IA 52641
(319) 337-3514, FAX: (319) 337-3514
E-mail: JJSMTBARR@aol.com
WWW: http://Kcd.com/ihpa

KANSAS

Kansas Anthropological Association
Kansas State Historical Society, Archaeology Office
Attn: Virginia Wulfkuhle
6425 SW 6th Avenue
Topeka, Kansas 66615-1099
(913) 272-8681, ext. 268, FAX: (913)272-8682
E-mail: vwulf@hspo.wps.state.ks.us

Kansas City Archaeological Society
Attn: John Romine, President
37180 W. 303 Street
Paola, Kansas 66071
(913) 294-2916

Kansas Preservation Alliance
801 East 4th
Newton, KS 67114

KENTUCKY

Licking Valley Archaeological Society
c/o Bet Ison
65 Trent Ridge
Morehead, Kentucky 40351

W.S. Webb Archaeological Society
211 Lafferty Hall
University of Kentucky
Lexington, KY 40506

LOUISIANA

Louisiana Archaeological Society
c/o Coastal Environments, Inc.
1260 Main Street
Baton Rouge, Louisiana 70802

Louisiana Preservation Alliance
PO Box 1587
Baton Rouge, LA 70821
(504) 928-9304, FAX: (504) 926-2434

MAINE

Maine Archaeological Society, Inc.
PO Box 982
Augusta, ME 04332
(207) 246-2880

Maine Preservation
PO Box 1198
Portland, ME 04104
(207) 775-3652, FAX: (207) 775-7737
E-mail: presplan@aol.com

MARYLAND

Center for Urban Archaeology
33 S. Front Street
Baltimore, MD 21202
(410) 396-3156, FAX: (410) 396-1806

Archeological Society of Maryland, Inc.
c/o Myron Beckstein
6281 Tufted Moss
Columbia, Maryland 21045
(410) 381-1377

MASSACHUSETTS

Massachusetts Archaeological Society
Robbins Museum of Archaeology
PO Box 700
Middleboro, MA 02346
(508) 947-9005

Massachusetts Historical Commission
Massachusetts Archives Building
220 Morrissey Boulevard
Boston, MA 02125
(617) 727-8470, FAX: (617) 727-5128

MICHIGAN

Michigan Archaeological Society
PO Box 359
Saginaw, Michigan 48606

MINNESOTA

Council For Minnesota Archeology
DNR-Division of Parks, 500 Lafayette Road
St. Paul, MN 55104
(612) 297-5645

Minnesota Archaeological Society
Fort Snelling History Center
St. Paul, MN 55111

MISSISSIPPI

Mississippi Archaeological Association
PO Box 571
Jackson, MS 39205-0571
(601) 359-6863

Mississippi Heritage Trust
PO Box 577
Jackson, MS 39205-0577

MISSOURI

Missouri Alliance for Historic Preservation
2505 Plymouth Rock Drive
Jefferson City, MO 65109

Missouri Archaeological Society
PO Box 958
Columbia, MO 65205
(573) 882-3544, FAX: (573) 882-9410
E-mail: archms@showme.missouri.edu

MONTANA

Montana Archaeological Society
PO Box 2123
Billings, MT 59103

Montana Preservation Alliance
PO Box 1872
Bozeman, MT 59771-1872

NEBRASKA

Nebraska Archeological Society
6822 Platt Avenue
Lincoln, NE 68507

Nebraska Association of Professional Archaeologists, Inc.
c/o Nebraska State Historical Society, PO Box 82554
Lincoln, NE 68501
(402) 471-4760, FAX: (402) 471-3314

NEVADA

Nevada Archaeological Association
c/o Susan Murphy, Executive Secretary
9785 Tropical Parkway
Las Vegas, Nevada 89129
(702) 895-1411

Nevada Heritage
1405 Joshua Drive
Reno, NV 89509

NEW HAMPSHIRE
Inherit New Hampshire, Inc.
PO Box 268
Concord, NH 03301

New Hampshire Archaeological Society
PO Box 406
Concord, NH 03302
(603) 964-5750

NEW JERSEY
Archaeological Society of New Jersey
Seton Hall University
South Orange, NJ 07079
(201) 761-9543 or (609) 695-2205

New Jersey Historic Trust
CN 404
Trenton, NJ 08625
(609) 984-0473, FAX: (609) 984-7590

NEW MEXICO
Albuquerque Archaeological Society
PO Box 4029
Albuquerque, NM 87196

Archaeological Society of New Mexico
PO Box 3485
Albuquerque, NM 87110

Dona Ana Archaeological Society
PO Box 15132
Las Cruces, NM 88004

Grant County Archaeological Society
PO Box 1602
Silver City, NM 88602

New Mexico Archaeological Council
PO Box 1023
Albuquerque, NM 87103
(505) 820-7785

San Juan Archaeological Society
PO Box 118
Flora Vista, NM 87415

Taos Archaeological Society
PO Box 143
Taos, NM 87571

Torrance County Archaeological Society
PO Box 351
Estancia, NM 87016
(505) 384-2349

NEW YORK
Historic Hudson Valley
150 White Plains Road
Tarrytown, NY 10591
(914) 631-8200, FAX: (914) 631-0089
E-mail: mail@hudsonvalley.org
WWW: http://www.hudsonvalley.org

New York State Archaeological Association
c/o Annette W. Nohe, Secretary
7267 High View Trail
Victor, NY 14564-9716
(716) 924-3535

Suffolk County Archaeological Association
PO Box 1542
Stony Brook, NY 11790
(516) 929-8725, FAX: (516) 929-6967

NORTH CAROLINA
North Carolina Archaeological Society
109 East Jones Street
Raleigh, NC 27601-2807
(919) 733-7342, FAX: (919) 715-2671
E-mail: archaeology@ncsl.dcr.state.nc.us
WWW: http://www.ah.dcr.state.nc.us/~arch/ncas.htm

Preservation North Carolina
PO Box 27644
Raleigh, NC 27611

NORTH DAKOTA
North Dakota Archaeological Association
203 8th Avenue, NW
Mandan, ND 58554
(701) 777-3009

OHIO
Archaeological Society of Ohio
c/o Paul Wildemuth
2505 Logan-Thornville Road
Rushville, OH 43150
(800) 736-7815

Ohio Preservation Alliance, Inc.
65 Jefferson Avenue
Columbus, OH 43215

OKLAHOMA
Oklahoma Anthropological Society
Route 1, Box 62 B
Cheyenne, OK 73628
(405) 497-2662

Oklahoma Archaeological Survey
111 E. Chesapeake
Norman, OK 73019-0575
(405) 325-7211, FAX: (405) 325-7604

OREGON
Archaeological Society of Central Oregon
c/o Central Oregon Environmental Center
16 NW Kansas
Bend, OR 97701
(503) 548-5716

Association of Oregon Archaeologists
c/o State Museum of Anthropology
1224 University of Oregon
Eugene, OR 97403-1224

Oregon Archaeological Society
PO Box 13293
Portland, OR 97213
(503) 357-8322, 645-4050, 292-3029

Southern Oregon Historical Society
Attn: Carol Bruce-Fitz, 106 North Central Avenue
Medford, OR 97501-5926

PENNSYLVANIA
Society for Pennsylvania Archaeology, Inc.
State Museum of Pennsylvania, Box 1026
Harrisburg, PA 17108-1026
(717) 783-2887, FAX: (717) 783-4558

RHODE ISLAND
Narragansett Archaeological Society
220 Foote Street
Barrington, RI 02806

SOUTH CAROLINA
Archaeological Society of South Carolina, Inc.
Institute of Archaeology & Anthropology
University of South Carolina
1321 Pendleton St.
Columbia, SC 29208-0071
(803) 777-8170, 734-0567, 799-1963, FAX: (803) 254-1338

SOUTH DAKOTA
Historic South Dakota Foundation, Inc.
PO Box 2998
Rapid City, SD 57709

South Dakota Archaeological Society
c/o Archaeology Laboratory
2032 South Grange Avenue
Sioux Falls, SD 57105
(605) 336-5493, FAX: (605) 336-4368
E-mail: rossum@inst.augie.edu

TENNESSEE
Association for the Preservation of Tennessee Antiquities, Inc.
110 Leake Avenue
Nashville, TN 37205
(615) 352-8247, FAX: (615) 352-8247

Middle Cumberland Archaeological Society
240 Sterling Road
Hendersonville, TN 37076
(615) 898-5958
E-mail: kesmith@frank.mtsu.edu

Tennesse Council For Professional Archaeology, Inc.
c/o Garrow & Associates, Inc.
510 South Main Street
Memphis, TN 38104

Tennessee Anthropological Association
University of Tennessee, Dept. of Anthropology
Knoxville, TN 37996-0720
(615) 974-4408

TEXAS
Big Bend Archaeological Society
PO Box 1
Big Bend National Park, TX 79834

Clarendon Archaeological Society
HCR 5, Box 10
Clarendon, TX 79226

Coastal Bend Archeological Society
c/o Marion Craft, 907 Huisache
Refugio, TX 78377

Concho Valley Archaeological Society
Fort Concho, 630 S. Oakes Street
San Angelo, TX 76903-7013

Dallas Archeological Society
PO Box 8077
Dallas, TX 75205

East Texas Archeological Society
PO Box 630128
Nacogdoches, TX 75963

El Paso Archaeological Society, Inc.
PO Box 4345
El Paso, TX 79914
(915) 751-3295

Friends of Northeast Texas Archeology
10101 Woodhaven Drive
Austin, TX 78753-4346
(512) 873-8131
E-mail: TMdlbrk@aol.com

Houston Archaeological Society
PO Box 6751
Houston, TX 77265-6751
(713) 880-3369

IAS (Iraan Archaeological Society)
PO Box 183
Iraan, TX 79744

Lea County Archaeological Society
100 Cactus Lane
Andrews, TX 79714

Midland Archaeological Society
PO Box 4224
Midland, TX 79704

Panhandle Archeological Society
PO Box 814
Amarillo, TX 79105

Southern Texas Archaeological Association
PO Box 791032
San Antonio, TX 78279
(512) 494-0852

Southwest Federation of Archaeological Societies
c/o Francis Strickney (Secretary-Treasurer)
201 West Solomon Street
Midland, TX 79705

Texas Archaeological Society
c/o Center for Archaeological Research, University of Texas
6900 North Loop 1604 West
San Antonio, TX 78249
(210) 458-4393, FAX: (210) 458-4870
E-mail: txarch@onr.com
WWW: http://www.txarch.org

Texas Historical Commission
PO Box 12276
Austin, TX 78711-2276
(512) 463-6100, FAX: (512) 475-4872

Travis County Archaeological Society
c/o Texas Archeological Research Lab
Balcones Research Center, PO Box 9464
Austin, TX 78766-9464
(512) 691-4393

U.S. VIRGIN ISLANDS
St. Thomas Historical Trust
PO Box 11849
Charlotte Amalie, St. Thomas, VI 00801

UTAH
Utah Statewide Archaeological Society
College of Eastern Utah Prehistoric Museum
451 East 400 North
Price, UT 84501

VERMONT
Vermont Archaeological Society
PO Box 663
Burlington, VT 05401
(518) 747-2926

VIRGINIA
Alexandria Archaeology
105 N. Union Street, #327
Alexandria, VA 22314
(703) 838-4399, FAX: (703) 838-6491
WWW: http://ci.alexandria.va.us/

Archaeological Society of Virginia
PO Box 70395
Richmond, VA 23255-0395
(804) 273-9291, FAX: (804) 273-0885
WWW: www//2.dgsys.com/~asv

Association for the Preservation of Virginia Antiquities
204 West Franklin Street
Richmond, VA 2322o
(804) 648-1889
E-mail: apva@widomaker.com
WWW: www.widomaker.com/~apva/apva/apvahp.html

WASHINGTON
Washington Trust for Historic Preservation
204 First Avenue South
Seattle, WA 98104

WEST VIRGINIA
West Virginia Archeological Society, Inc.
PO Box 5323
Charleston, WV 25314-0323
(304) 562-7233, FAX: (304) 562-7235
E-mail: msling@aol.com

WISCONSIN
Wisconsin Archaeological Society
PO Box 1292
Milwaukee, WI 53201
(414) 229-4273

WYOMING
Wyoming Archaeological Society
1617 Westridge Terrace
Casper, WY 82604
(307) 268-2212, FAX: (307) 268-2224
E-mail: cbuff@acad.cc.whecn.edu

Wyoming Association of Professional Archaeologists
University of Wyoming
Box 3431, University Station
Laramie, WY 82071
(307) 766-5301

CANADIAN ORGANIZATIONS

ALBERTA
Alberta Underwater Archaeological Society
4323 115th Street
Edmonton, Alberta T6J 1PS, Canada

Archaeological Society of Alberta
314 Valiant Drive, NW
Calgary, Alberta T3A 0Y1, Canada
(403) 243-4340

Provincial Museum of Alberta, Archaeological Survey
12845-102 Avenue
Edmonton, Alberta T5N 0M6, Canada
(403) 427-2355

BRITISH COLUMBIA
Archaeological Society of British Columbia
PO Box 520, Bentall Station
Vancouver, British Columbia V6C 2N3, Canada

British Columbia Museums Association
514 Government Street
Victoria, British Columbia V8V 4X4, Canada
(604) 387-3315, FAX: (604) 387-1251
E-mail: bcma@MuseumsAssn.bc.ca
WWW: http://www.MuseumsAssn.bc.ca/~bcma/

Heritage Society of British Columbia
411 Dunsmuir Street
Vancouver, British Columbia V6B 1X4, Canada

Underwater Archaeological Society of British Columbia
c/o Vancouver Maritime Museum
1905 Ogden Avenue
Vancouver, BC V6J 1A3, Canada
(604) 980-0354, FAX: (604) 980-0358

MANITOBA
Manitoba Archaeological Society
Box 1171
Winnipeg, Manitoba R3C 2Y4, Canada
(204) 942-7243

NOVA SCOTIA
Nova Scotia Archaeological Society
PO Box 36090
Halifax, Nova Scotia R3J 3S9, Canada
(902) 426-9509

ONTARIO
Ontario Archaeological Society
126 Willowdale Avenue
North York, Ontario M2N 4Y2, Canada
(416) 730-0797, FAX: same

PRINCE EDWARD ISLAND
Prince Edward Island Museum & Heritage Foundation
Beaconsfield Historic House
2 Kent Street
Charlottetown, PEI C1A 1M6, Canada
(902) 368-6600, FAX: (902) 368-6608
E-mail: peimuse@bud.peinet.pe.ca

QUEBEC
Récherches Amerindiennes au Québec
6742 rue de Saint-Denis
Montreal, Province of Québec H2S 2S2, Canada

SASKATCHEWAN
Archaeological & Historical Society of West Central Saskatchewan
c/o Doug de Conick-Smith
PO Box 8
D'Arcy, Saskatchewan S0L 0N0, Canada
(306) 379-4318

Saskatchewan Archaeological Society
#5 - 816 1st Avenue North
Saskatoon, Saskatchewan S7K 1Y3, Canada
(306) 664-4124, FAX: (306) 665-1928

AIA LOCAL SOCIETY CONTACTS

Each member of the AIA is encouraged to belong to one of the 96 Local Societies in the United States and AIA-Canada, through which the world of archaeology is brought to life by lectures, field trips, films, museum visits, and other activities. For more information on programs in your area, please call the Local Society Contact listed below.

ARIZONA
Tucson
Call: Mary Voyatzis: (520) 621-3446

CALIFORNIA
Los Angeles County
Call: Shelby Brown: (310) 312-0339
North Coast
Call: Stelios Vasilakis: (916) 631-9099
Orange County
Call: Norma Kershaw: (714) 951-5586
San Diego
Call: Ron Fellows: (619) 465-3841
http://dot-net./~dyan/open.html
San Francisco
Call: Barbara McLauchlin: (415) 338-1537
http://userwww.sfsu.edu/~barbaram/AIASF.htm
San Joaquin Valley
Call: Claudia Mader-Kus: (209) 298-5544
Santa Barbara
Call: Glenn Mangold: (805) 893-3556
Stanford
Call: Nancy Delia Palmer: (415) 323-6517

COLORADO
Boulder
Call: Randall T. Nishiyama: (303) 497-6454
http://www.colorado.edu/CUMUSEUM/
Denver
Call: Marie T. Gingras: (303) 985-3054

CONNECTICUT
Hartford
Call: James R. Bradley: (860) 297-2392
New Haven
Call: Madeline Fitzgerald: (203) 436-2831
http://www.yale.edu/aia/

DISTRICT OF COLUMBIA
Washington, D.C.
Call: Ellen Herscher: (202) 338-6536
http://www.inform.umd.edu/WashSocAIA/

FLORIDA
Gainesville
Call: Robert Wagman: (352) 392-2075, ext. 273
Orlando
Call: Jim Bullard: (407) 896-9939
Southern Florida
Call: Shelia Soltis: (954) 720-2774
http://www.954.com
Tallahassee
Call: Christopher Pfaff: (904) 644-0306
Tampa Bay
Call: Suzanne P. Murray: (813) 985-9019
Athens
Call: Margretta Eagon: (706) 543-8187
Atlanta
Call: Ann Rhea: (404) 237-6546

HAWAII
Hawaii
Call: Robert J. Littman: (808) 226-8518

ILLINOIS
Central Illinois (Urbana)
Call: Jane A. Goldberg: (217) 333-3292
Chicago
Call: Peter J.J. Kosiba: (815) 838-0500 x5241
Rockford
Call: Sherrilyn Martin: (815) 397-9319
http://www.rockford.edu/AIA/AIA.htm
Western Illinois (Monmouth)
Call: William Urban: (309) 457-2388
http://www.monm.edu/academic/classics/aia/

INDIANA
Central Indiana
Call: Robert F. Sutton: (317) 257-6198
Call: Kevin Glowacki: (812) 855-6651
http://www.indiana.edu/~classics/AIA/AIA.html
Valparaiso
Call: Michael Kumpf: (219) 464-5174

IOWA
Iowa City
Call: Sandra Eskin: (319) 337-3019

KANSAS
Kansas City/Lawrence
Call: James S. Falls: (816) 235-2545

KENTUCKY
Kentucky
Call: Mary Lucas Powell: (606) 257-8208

LOUISIANA
New Orleans
Call: Thomas Jacobsen: (504) 529-1703

MARYLAND
Baltimore
Call: Gladys J. Callahan-Vocci: (410) 661-3424

MASSACHUSETTS
Boston
Call: Murray McClellan: (617) 353-3415
http://www.perseus.tufts.edu/classicsDept/aia.html
Western MA
Call: Diana Wolfe Larkin: (413) 586-6799
http://www.umass.edu/aia/
Worcester
Call: Mary Jane Rein: (508) 753-4395

MICHIGAN
Ann Arbor
Call: John Cherry: (313) 764-0112
Central MI (East Lansing)
Call: Dean John Eadie: (517) 355-4597

Detroit
Call: William H. Peck: (313) 833-7876

MINNESOTA
Minnesota/Minneapolis
Call: Kevin Callahan: (612) 625-3400
http://www.geocities.com/Athens/Acropolis/5579/mnaia.html

MISSOURI
Central MO (Columbia)
Call: Gene Lane: (573) 882-0679
St. Louis
Call: Judith Feinberg Brilliant: (314) 721-1889
http://www.stlcc.cc.mo.us/fv/users/mfuller/aia

NEBRASKA
Lincoln-Omaha
Call: Michael Hoff: (402) 472-5342

NEW JERSEY
Northern NJ (Madison)
Call: Timothy Renner: (201) 655-7420
Princeton
Call: Brooks Levy: (609) 258-3184

NEW MEXICO
Santa Fe
Call: John B. Ramsay: (505) 672-9201

NEW YORK
Albany
Call: John C. Overbeck: (518) 442-4048
Finger Lakes (Ithaca)
Call: Peter Ian Kuniholm: (607) 255-9732
http://www.arts.cornell.edu/dendro/AIA/
Long Island
Call: Beatrice Holland: (516) 796-7261
http://members.aol.com/ddetr/lis.html
New York City
Call: Lucille Roussin: (212) 501-9372
http://www.scils.rutgers.edu/~roccos/nysaia.htm
Rochester
Call: Hélène Vernou Case: (716) 381-9034
Staten Island
Call: Peter Russo: (718) 444-7865
Westchester
Call: Jane Bedichek: (914) 723-7021
Western New York
Call: Samuel M. Paley: (716) 645-2154

NORTH CAROLINA
Greensboro
Call: Prof. Jeffrey S. Soles: (910) 334-5214

NORTH CAROLINA
North Carolina
Call: Paul Rehak: (919) 684-6214

OHIO
Cincinnati
Call: George W. M. Harrison: (513) 745-1930
Cleveland
Call: Dr. Donald R. Laing: (216) 368-2251
Columbus
Call: Ms. Monica Fullerton: (614) 292-7481
http://kaladarshan.arts.ohio-state.edu/dept/LSS/
LocSocSa.html
Kent-Akron
Call: Gary Oller: (330) 972-8068
Oberlin-Ashland-Wooster
Call: Susan Kane: (216) 774-3681
Oxford
Call: Judith de Luce: (513) 529-1487/80
Springfield
Call: Vernon Dunlap: (937) 325-1335
Toledo
Call: E. Marianne Stern: (419) 255-8904

OKLAHOMA
Oklahoma City
Call: Farland Stanley, Jr.: (405) 364-5633
Tulsa
Call: Robert H. Patterson: (918) 631-2871

OREGON
Eugene
Call: Christina Calhoon: (541) 607-0569
Portland
Call: George Eigo: (503) 725-4954
Salem
Call: Ann M. Nicgorski: (503) 370-6250
http://www.willamette.edu/~anicgors/salemaia/
index.html

PENNSYLVANIA
Central PA (University Park)
Call: Dr. Wilma Stern: (814) 865-1506
http://squash.la.psu.edu/cams/aia/LocSoc.htm
Philadelphia
Call: Karen Vellucci: (215) 898-5723
Pittsburgh
Call: Prof. Edwin D. Floyd: (412) 624-4483
Southern PA (Chambersburg)
Call: Virginia Anderson-Stojanovic:
    (717) 264-4141

RHODE ISLAND
Narragansett (Providence)
Call: Mr. Derek B. Counts: (401) 863-2742

TENNESSEE
East Tennessee
Call: Mrs. Elaine A. Evans: (423) 974-2144
Mississippi-Memphis
Call: Prof. Fred C. Albertson: (901) 678-2941
http://sunset.backbone.olemiss.edu/depts/
classics/aia.html
Nashville
Call: Barbara Tsakirgis: (615) 322-2516

TEXAS
Brazos Valley
Call: Thomas F. Lynch: (409) 776-2195

Central Texas (Austin)
Call: Dr. Gretchen Meyers: (512) 471-5742
WWW: http://www.dla.utexas.edu/depts/
classics/AIA/index.html
Dallas-Fort Worth
Call: Mrs. Rivka Rago: (972) 625-4226
Houston
Call: Ms. Lyn Eade: (713) 869-3545*
Lubbock
Call: Dr. Nancy B. Reed: (806) 742-3096
Southwest TX (San Antonio)
Call: Ms. Polly Price: (210) 828-4722

VIRGINIA
Charlottesville
Call: John J. Dobbins: (804) 924-6128
Lynchburg
Call: Susan Stevens: (804) 947-8000, ext. 8533
Richmond
Call: Mrs. Getrude Howland: (804) 282-1141
Williamsburg
Call: Prof. Linda Collins Reilly: (757) 221-2164

WASHINGTON
Seattle
Call: Catherine Chatalas: (206) 527-4365
Spokane
Call: Vera Morgan: (509) 359-4221
Walla Walla
Call: Suzanne Martin: (509) 527-5718

WEST VIRGINIA
Ohio Valley
Call: Anita Hussey: (304) 863-8385

WISCONSIN
Appleton
Call: Elizabeth T. Forter: (920) 734-6798
Madison
Call: Loretta Freiling: (608) 262-3855
http://polyglot.lss.wisc.edu/classics/
Madisonaia.html
Milwaukee
Call: Jane C. Waldbaum: (414) 229-5014
http://www.execpc.com/~asellers/artifact3.html

CANADA
Edmonton
Call: Jeremy J. Rossiter: (403) 492-3539
Hamilton
Call: Michele George: (416) 525-9140
Montréal
Call: Kathleen Donahue Sherwood:
    (514) 481-3776
Niagara Peninsula
Call: Meg Morden: (905) 688-5550 x3575
Ottawa-Hull
Call: Gia Spina: (613) 729-4957
Toronto
Call: Maria C. Shaw: (416) 978-3290
Vancouver
Call: Eric De Bruijn: (604) 822-4555
Winnipeg
Call: Lea Stirling: (204) 474-7357/9502
http://www.umanitoba.ca/faculties/arts/classics/
aia.html

AIA PUBLICATIONS

*AVAILABLE FROM KENDALL/HUNT
PUBLISHING COMPANY*

ARCHAEOLOGY IN THE CLASSROOM:
A Resource Guide for Teachers and Parents
Contains information about educational materials:
books, magazines, curriculum and resource packets,
films, videos, kits, computer programs, and games.
The scope of materials covered is worldwide.
ISBN 0-7872-1875-8
Price: AIA members: $9.00, Non-members: $10.00

Shipping and Handling:
Add $4.00 for first copy and 50¢ for each additional copy.
Orders must be prepaid and made in US dollars or by an
international money order.

**To order by Visa, MasterCard, or American Express,
call AIA Order Dept.:**
(800) 228-0810 or (319) 589-1000

Or send orders and make checks payable to:
Kendall/Hunt Publishing Company, 4050 Westmark
Drive, Dubuque, IA 52002

AVAILABLE FROM AIA HEADQUARTERS

ARCHAEOLOGY ON FILM
Indispensable guide to films about archaeology.
Over 750 films listed, each with film synopsis,
distributors, purchase and rental prices.
ISBN 0-8403-9016-5
Price: AIA Members: $12.00, Non-members: $13.50

**THE AEGEAN AND THE ORIENT IN THE
SECOND MILLENNIUM B.C.**
by Helene J. Kantor
Reprint to mark the 50th anniversary of the AIA
Monographs Series. Features a new preface by Eric
H. Cline and James D. Muhly.
ISBN 0-9609042-3-9
Price: AIA members: $10.25, Non-members: $12.95

**THE ENTRANCE TO THE ATHENIAN
ACROPOLIS BEFORE MNESICLES**
AIA Monograph New Series 1
by Harrison Eiteljorg, II
A record of Eiteljorg's excavation of the remains of
the pre-Mnesiclean entrance. 146 pages with 18
plates and 39 figures. **ISBN 0-8403-9391-1**
Price: AIA members: $36.00, Non-members: $40.00

**RECENT EXCAVATIONS IN ISRAEL:
A VIEW TO THE WEST**
Colloquia and Conference Papers No. 1
Edited by Seymour Gitin
Contributions by Michal Artzy, William G. Dever,
Trude Dothan, Seymour Gitin, Barbara L. Johnson,
Lawrence E. Stager, Wolf-Dietrich Niemeier,
Ephraim Stern. **ISBN 0-7872-0486-2**
Price: AIA members: $27.00, Non-members: $30.00

Shipping and Handling:
Add $4.00 for first copy and 50¢ for each additional copy.
Orders must be prepaid and made in US dollars or by an
international money order.

Send orders and make checks payable to:
Archaeological Institute of America,
656 Beacon Street, Boston, MA 02215-2010,
(617) 353-9361, FAX: (617) 353-6550, E-mail: aia@bu.edu
(Visa, MasterCard, and American Express accepted.)